BLACK COSMOPOLITANS

BLACK COSMOPOLITANS

RACE, RELIGION, AND REPUBLICANISM
IN AN AGE OF REVOLUTION

Christine Levecq

UNIVERSITY OF VIRGINIA PRESS
Charlottesville and London

University of Virginia Press
© 2019 by the Rector and Visitors of the University of Virginia
All rights reserved
Printed in the United States of America on acid-free paper

First published 2019

ISBN 978-0-8139-4218-6 (cloth)
ISBN 978-0-8139-4219-3 (e-book)

1 3 5 7 9 8 6 4 2

Library of Congress Cataloging-in-Publication Data is available for this title.

Cover art: Jean-Baptiste Belley. Portrait by Anne Louis Girodet de Roussy-Trioson, 1797, oil on canvas. (Château de Versailles, France)

To Steve and Angie

CONTENTS

Acknowledgments ix

Introduction 1

1. Jacobus Capitein and the Radical Possibilities of Calvinism 19

2. Jean-Baptiste Belley and French Republicanism 75

3. John Marrant: From Methodism to Freemasonry 160

Notes 237

Works Cited 263

Index 281

ACKNOWLEDGMENTS

This book has been ten years in the making. One reason is that I wanted to explore the African diaspora more broadly than I had before, and my knowledge of English, French, and Dutch naturally led me to expand my research to several national contexts. Another is that I wanted this project to be interdisciplinary, combining history and biography with textual criticism. It has been an amazing journey, which was made possible by the many excellent scholars this book relies on.

Part of the pleasure in writing this book came from the people and institutions that provided access to both the primary and the secondary material. All the libraries and archives I visited impressed me with the quality of their holdings and with the friendliness and dedication of their staff. My thanks go to the Michigan State University Library, the Archives of Michigan; in Paris and Vincennes, the Bibliothèque Nationale, the CARAN (Centre d'Accueil et de Recherche des Archives Nationales), the Service Historique de la Défense; the Royal Archives in The Hague, Regionaal Archief Leiden, the University of Leiden library, and the University of Amsterdam library. The fast pace with which eighteenth-century documents are being digitalized has also been a source of delight.

I am immensely grateful to Kettering University for a sabbatical leave that allowed me to make great progress on the manuscript, and to—now retired—head of the Department of Liberal Studies, Karen Wilkinson, for her continuous support of my travel and research. To my reading group friends—Joy Arbor, Dave Golz, Whitney Hardin, David Marshall, Ben Pauli, Laura Mebert, Laura Miller-Purrenhage, Greg Schneider-Bateman, Denise Stodola, Pavitra Sundar—I owe both the benefit of sharp criticism and the memory of warm, collegial evenings around Denise's table.

Tremendous generosity from fellow scholars has helped transform the manuscript. While all of its weaknesses are my own, I warmly thank the following persons for giving of their precious time and expertise, in writing or in conversations, to help make it better: Daan Bronkhorst,

Vincent Carretta, Jeroen Dewulf, Kirsten Fermaglich, Eugene Hynes, Elisabeth Leijnse, Barbara McCaskill, John Saillant, Alyssa Goldstein Sepinwall, Michiel van Kempen. I am also deeply grateful to the two anonymous readers at the press, as well as to my editor, Angie Hogan.

For their friendship and support during the years I was writing this book—and talked about it every chance I got—I thank Brigitte Asselman, Cécile Blase, Ulric Chung, Yves Clemmen, Elisabeth Leijnse, Jean Mainil, Carine Mardorossian, Andrew Norris, and Hélène Varsamidou. Many thanks also to both my Levecq and my Manderfield families, for their love and encouragements.

Two persons have dramatically changed my writing—and my life. One is Hazel Rowley, who still daily inspires me. The other is Rich Manderfield, who constantly pushes me to think harder and look deeper, and who always makes it feel like an incredible adventure.

The book is dedicated to my dear friends Steve and Angie Elliston, whom I remember toasting on their sixtieth wedding anniversary as "the most inspiring couple I know." They are deeply missed.

Parts of chapter 1 were originally published as "Jacobus Capitein, Dutch Calvinist and Black Cosmopolitan" in *Research in African Literatures* 44.4 (Winter 2013): 145–66. They are reprinted with permission from Indiana University Press.

BLACK COSMOPOLITANS

Introduction

This book examines the life and thought of three extraordinary black men. Part of what makes them extraordinary is that they traveled extensively throughout the eighteenth-century Atlantic world. Unlike millions of uprooted Africans and their descendants at the time, these men did not have lives of toil and sweat in the plantations of the New World. One of them was born free, the other two became free in their youths, and it is this freedom that gave them mobility. What makes them especially extraordinary is the way they used this mobility and the nature of their physical and intellectual interventions in the world around them. These men share a consciousness of the violence and destruction directed toward people of African descent and a willingness to set themselves in motion in order to bring about change. And because they were literate and eager to express themselves, they gave a voice to their progressive perspectives. They were exceptional men, and their experiences and writings helped shape not only racial but also social and political thought in the eighteenth century.

If one judges from their biographies, they had little in common. These men lived in different national and ideological contexts, and to a great extent, they absorbed the ideas and beliefs that surrounded them. Jacobus Capitein was taken to the Netherlands from Africa as a child, and he took in the unique mixture of Calvinism, ethnocentrism, and tolerance that prevailed in the Dutch republic. Jean-Baptiste Belley lived in Saint-Domingue, a French colony, and emerged as a proponent of the ideals of the French Revolution. John Marrant grew up in Charleston, South Carolina, and was exposed to the influences of Methodism, the American Revolution, and later, Freemasonry. In many ways, these men had more in common with the people around them than with each other: their thought was anchored in its own, unique cultural background.

But they share something important: an intellectual strategy made possible by their cosmopolitanism and by the critical stance that it enabled. Through their travels and their exposure to various social and cultural contexts, these men developed a universalizing, multiracial view of human life that, in each case, radicalized surrounding ideologies. Even after inheriting the liberationist and revolutionary ideas that made the eighteenth century such a groundbreaking time, they pushed those ideas further in their own distinctive ways. They were cosmopolitans, not just physically but philosophically and politically. And as such, they made an important contribution to the ideological renewal that was the Enlightenment.

Because each of these men also had connections to the black communities around him, the picture that emerges is that of an eighteenth-century Atlantic world that fostered an elite of black thinkers who took advantage of existing ideologies in order to spread a message of universal inclusion and egalitarianism. Their contributions were the result of their own reflection, but also of an environment that made their physical and intellectual independence possible. Indeed, while they had different racial histories, Holland, France, England, and the American colonies all still carried a certain racial openness inherited from previous centuries. Black cosmopolitans exploited this openness before the nineteenth century, in a new racial turn, closed its doors on them.

Cosmopolitans

Though they never referred to themselves as such, in the most basic meaning of the term, all three men were cosmopolitans in that, to varying degrees, they had the freedom to travel, and they were exposed to different cultures. Capitein grew up on the West African coast and in the Netherlands, first in The Hague and then in Leiden, and he went back to Africa, where he served as a mediator between the whites on a Dutch trading post and the local population. Belley grew up in Saint-Domingue, traveled to Paris at the height of the French Revolution, went back to Saint-Domingue twice, and died in France. Marrant went from New York to Charleston, from there to London, from London to Nova Scotia in Canada, from there to Boston, and then back to London. Aside from Capitein's and Belley's original voyages from Africa, they were among the few blacks who traveled the Atlantic world for reasons other than the slave trade. Their exposure and openness to new cultures gave them a sense of multiculturalism one often associates with the cosmopolitan life.[1]

They were also cosmopolitan in the sense that they were familiar with, and actors in, spaces that were not determined by national identities or boundaries. Capitein had no clear national identity, and the marginal zone he occupied on the African coast after he returned forced him to think in terms of mixed communities. Belley was passionately French, but the troubles in Saint-Domingue throughout the 1790s kept its identity in a state of uncertainty. Marrant's life seems a moveable feast without any strong national connection or feeling.

More important, these men were cosmopolitans because they developed a particular sensibility reflected in the original meaning of the term: to varying degrees, they became citizens of the world. Their cosmopolitanism was more political than that of Ira Berlin's "Atlantic creoles," people of mixed ancestry and heritage who emerged on African and American shores during the early phases of the slave trade, and more philosophical than that of many free blacks who just tried to make a life for themselves in a racially fraught Atlantic world.[2] Their commitment to the world was not just about knowing and partly integrating other cultures. It was about developing an ethical vision of the world in which everyone had access to justice, the good society, and the good life as they conceived them.[3]

And it was about making this vision public. All three men actively participated in eighteenth-century print culture and addressed their ideas both to an undefined reading public and to the powers that be—whether Dutch intellectual and commercial institutions, French organs of revolution, or British movers of empire. Indeed, they were cosmopolitans who did not reject the power of the state to bring about change.[4] Driven by their desire to participate in print culture, they developed relationships with persons and networks that made the publication of their writings possible. Their variations on established genres, such as the slave narrative and the political pamphlet, made their contributions distinctive.

While cosmopolitanism is certainly no guarantee of an ethical or progressive vision, in these particular cases, it is these men's cosmopolitanism that helped radicalize their thought. The old republican ideals of civic virtue and communal life were still very much alive in the eighteenth century, and while the liberal desire for individual freedom was emerging with great force, the republican view continued to form an inspiration for those who did not think in those terms yet, or who were already envisioning the downsides of radical individualism. This book shows that the three men under study not only were inspired by these republican ideals but enlarged them into visions of interracial community and egalitarianism. Capitein's stoic Calvinist faith guided his decisions in Africa, and while he used it partly for purposes of indoctrination, it also fed his vision of a multiracial, multicultural community as the realization of God's new covenant. Belley's republicanism, or his devotion to the combined values of freedom, equality, and the common good, had both national and international dimensions. Marrant's ministry, as well as his chaplaincy for the black Freemasons in Boston, combined a concern for black communities with visions of universal egalitarianism. Taken together, their ideas show that among blacks were some of the most radical thinkers of the eighteenth century.[5]

REPUBLICANS

The fundamental value associated with black writers in the slavery era is the search for freedom. It is at the heart of the genre of the slave narrative, and it informs many black expressions of religious faith. American blacks throughout history have been able to resort to the ideas of the American Revolution in the most convincing ways, precisely because they saw their own aspirations as fully embodied by the founding ideals of the nation. This interpretation of American identity as anchored in notions of individual freedom and natural human rights reflects traditional views of the founding as an expression of a liberal political philosophy. In this view, the American Revolution was the concrete realization of John Locke's *Second Treatise on Civil Government*. In the treatise, Locke posits a natural state that existed before the institution of government, in which humans enjoyed freedom and equality within the bounds of the law of nature, which prescribes that "no one ought to harm another in his life, health, liberty or possessions" (9). In order to avoid disorder and rule by passion, and to ensure the preservation of property, men agreed "together mutually to enter into one community, and make one body politic" (14), a contract they were then free to dissolve if it became tyrannical. Locke's fundamental statement of individual freedom and natural rights has long been seen as one major source of inspiration for revolutionary and abolitionist thought in the Atlantic world.

In the past few decades, though, historians have highlighted another important strand of eighteenth-century Atlantic political thought, usually referred to as civic humanism or classical republicanism. Its importance resurfaced thanks to J. G. A. Pocock's groundbreaking book, *The Machiavellian Moment,* published in 1975. Pocock argued that eighteenth-century political thought was informed by theories of republicanism developed in early modern Italian city-states, themselves inspired by Greek and Roman philosophy. These theories, Pocock said, present republics as perpetually caught in a fight against *fortuna,* or the vagaries of time, and they seek to describe—or prescribe—ways in which republics can maintain their stability in the face of it. Partly relying on Aristotle, Polybius, and Cicero, they emphasize the importance for citizens of remaining free and independent so that they can devote themselves to the common good of the republic through the display of civic virtue. Pocock then highlighted the role played by republicanism in the English Civil War, as well as in the American Revolution. The book led to a paradigm shift in European and American historiography. Indeed, historians in the past few decades have emphasized how, among others, English, American, French, and Dutch political thought has been shaped as much by republican values as by the Lockean contractarianism that is usually associated with the Enlightenment.

This thesis led to heated debates among historians and political scientists about the actual differences between the two theories, the ways in which they overlap, the role of the concept of freedom in each of them, and the degree of their presence in particular national histories. In a 1992 article, Daniel T. Rodgers traced the course of these developments and quarrels among American historians, highlighting how a focus on republicanism swept through the historiography of the late eighteenth and early nineteenth centuries like an intellectual tsunami. The American Revolution was reinterpreted as a fundamentally republican reaction against British corruption, a fight for a public good, or the expression of a desire for civic participation. Social historians of the nineteenth century revisited class strife through the lens of labor republicanism. The concept came to be applied to women's history, and even to the history of the American South. Ultimately, it became "distended" and "harder to define." In legal philosophy, it came to mean "everything liberalism was not" (33)—the focus on civic life rather than on rights, the commitment to specific values and purposes rather than a neutral or pluralist position. Recently, similar discussions have been taking place about the role and the meaning of republicanism in Dutch and French history. One may wonder if the concept can still perform any interpretive work at all.

I believe it can. It is certainly the case that, by the end of the eighteenth century, ideas such as representative government and the balance of powers had complex and entangled roots and cannot simply be labeled liberal or republican. In fact, the word "liberal" did not yet have a political meaning, and people usually labeled "republican" any political system involving some degree of representation, sometimes even monarchies. But the notion of civic humanism has a specific history, which goes back to humanists of the Italian Renaissance. These humanists were certainly concerned about political liberty, which meant "both independence and self-government" (Skinner, 1:77). But they also emphasized that freedom's role is to build the commonwealth by spurring citizens to exercise their talents and display their public spirit. While the notion of civic virtue was not new, it was expanded and became a staple of humanist political thought, especially thanks to their rediscovery of ancient texts. Cicero's concept of *vir virtutis*, the man of virtue, led to the idea that men had to aspire to excellence in all things, devote their virtues and talents to the defense of their community, and achieve honor and glory in the process. In fifteenth-century Florence, Leonardo Bruni, a humanist, praised the excellence of Florence's constitution in that "it makes it equally possible for everyone to take part in the affairs of the Republic" (Skinner, 1:78). It was this freedom that led to the greatness of the commonwealth, by allowing men to exercise their talents and to display their virtue on its behalf. Sixteenth-century humanists such as Machiavelli emphasized political freedom, government by the people, public virtue, the dangers of luxury and of private wealth.[6] While notions of self-interest and self-preservation would emerge in the following centuries, the humanists' ideas remained influential.[7]

Particularly because of the predominance of liberalism in black intellectual historiography, I think it is urgent to show the extent to which black writers and thinkers were drawn to other conceptualizations of individuals and society, particularly to the concepts of republicanism and civic humanism. While these theories are sometimes still dismissed as "old" or "traditional" because they don't focus on the individual or on democracy, or because of their obvious gender bias, they actually provided black intellectuals a theoretical wherewithal that allowed them to imagine a radical transformation of society. This book argues that Capitein, Belley, and Marrant were profoundly influenced by what can be called republican values and that it is their cosmopolitan republicanism that drove their progressivism. Belley drew his sense of civic and military devotion to the common good from the revolutionary culture that surrounded him, both in Saint-Domingue and in Paris. Marrant slowly evolved from an evangelical outlook grounded in an individual relationship to the deity, to a vision of universal, republican brotherhood. And while he accepted and even promoted conservative ideas, Capitein absorbed the more radical and civic aspects of Calvinism and allowed them to shape his responses to his experiences after he left Europe. Through the lens of these three lives, and of those of many blacks around them, this book shows that black republicanism had a significant presence in the eighteenth-century Atlantic world.

Calvinists

The association of Calvinism with republicanism may be surprising. In "On Civil Government," the last chapter of *Institutes of the Christian Religion,* John Calvin seemed to recommend the political status quo. After criticizing "fanatics" (772) who argue that Christians should not be bound by civil laws because they are obeying a higher law, he argues that, because magistrates and kings are representatives of God, and they receive their power from God, they should be obeyed. He quotes Paul admonishing Timothy that all prayers and thanks be made to kings, "that we may lead a quiet and peaceable life in all godliness and honesty" (775). Indeed, peace and tranquility seem to be a priority for him. Even if a leader or a magistrate is not fulfilling his duty, private persons should not intervene in public affairs, "as it is impossible to resist the magistrate without, at the same time, resisting God himself" (797). Even tyrants should be obeyed, since they too are agents of God, who put them in place "to punish the iniquity of the people" (798). This argument fits well in a chapter that starts by stating that "it is of no importance, what is our condition among men, or under the laws of what nation we live" (771), compared to, says Calvin, the eternal freedom offered by the kingdom of Christ.

But the last few pages of the chapter offer a different view. Calvin suddenly argues that, sometimes, God sends "public avengers" (803) to deliver the people from tyrannical domination. The role of magistrates is to act as a rein on power, in a way similar to "the Ephori, who were a check upon the kings among the Lacedæmonians, or the popular tribunes upon the consuls among the Romans" (804). Not only do these ephors or tribunes act as a limit on the power of leaders, but it is their God-imposed duty to do so and to take action if the leader does not fulfill his divinely delegated function. While the first part of the chapter had seemed to encourage submissiveness, the last section condemns it.

As fleeting as the latter discussion is, it introduces a "constitutionalist element into the discussion of political authority." While constitutionalism was certainly not an exclusively Calvinist concept, since it had been theorized by scholastics and humanists, Calvinists made "an important contribution to the stock of radical political ideas available to his followers" (Skinner, 2:233) at the time.

Indeed, something about Calvinism inclined it toward revolutionary political theory. As Michael Walzer puts it, "What Calvinists said of the saint, other men would later say of the citizen: the same sense of civic virtue, of discipline and duty, lies behind the two names" (2). Walzer shows how Calvinists in the sixteenth and seventeenth centuries sought to destroy the traditional social order and rebuild a holy commonwealth. They abandoned notions of affectionate or family ties to envision a society bound by its obedience to God. God made agreements or covenants with men, and as a consequence, they had to honor the contract through renovation, discipline, and order. Calvinists were originally not interested in personal religious ecstasy; individual regeneration was inextricably bound to national regeneration. These ideas underlay the thought of the Marian exiles, who fled England when Queen Mary, a Catholic, started persecuting Protestants, and of the Puritans behind the English Civil War and the creation of a commonwealth in the middle of the seventeenth century. So from its beginnings, Calvinism had a civic, even a radical, dimension.[8]

Blacks around the eighteenth-century Atlantic world certainly felt that Calvinism had an egalitarian appeal. In spite of the seeming correlation between Calvinism and an acceptance of the status quo, many blacks who lived in Europe and North America in the eighteenth century embraced one form or another of Calvinist thought. Precisely because it emphasized God's all-knowingness, omnipotence, and providential guidance, it offered some solace against the cruelties and injustice that people of African descent were ceaselessly subjected to. In the choice between faith and good works, faith also seemed more easily achievable to people who were struggling for survival. To some, Calvinism may have implied a less than critical attitude toward the institution of slavery. But as it grew and developed, some people critical of the institution drew from Calvinism the very philosophical foundation that underpinned their abolitionism. It is this potential richness and complexity of Calvinism that sustained their views.

Many blacks who embraced Calvinism in the eighteenth-century English-speaking world came to it through the influence of George

Whitefield and his fiery brand of evangelicalism. The movement had emerged from the Church of England in the 1730s, and unlike John Wesley, another famous Methodist, Whitefield held to the doctrine of predestination, or the idea that God is the ultimate decider of human beings' individual salvation. His charisma and his appeal to emotion and personal transformation turned him into a major participant in the First Great Awakening, a revival of religious feeling that took place in the American colonies in the first half of the eighteenth century. As he traveled widely along the Atlantic seaboard, he often preached to crowds of thousands. Even though he was perceived as an egalitarian because he preached to all levels of society, he was not in principle opposed to slavery, and he even proposed its introduction in Georgia, where he ended up using slaves at his orphanage in Bethesda, ten miles from Savannah.

In spite of his stance on slavery, many blacks owed him their conversion, and several black writers paid tribute to him. Phillis Wheatley, a poet and a slave who lived in Boston and became famous as the first black author to publish a book, wrote an elegy to him. James Albert Ukawsaw Gronniosaw tells us in his narrative that he knew Whitefield very well and heard him preach in New York many times and that when he arrived in England, Whitefield helped him with expenses and lodging. Both Wheatley and Gronniosaw dedicated their works to Selina Hastings, Countess of Huntingdon, whose religious movement was strongly associated with Whitefield, who was one of her chaplains. In his autobiography, Olaudah Equiano describes hearing Whitefield speak at a revival meeting in Savannah in February 1765; Whitefield preached with "the greatest fervour and earnestness," and Equiano was "very much struck and impressed with this" (132). In his narrative, as we will see, John Marrant, who would later become associated with the Huntingdon Connexion, describes how he once entered a large meeting house in Charleston, South Carolina, and was overwhelmed when he heard Whitefield preach, and became convinced the minister was addressing him directly.

For many of these writers, and especially for those born in Africa, the moment of conversion represented an entry into a realm of spiritual freedom and a delivery from the darkness of paganism. As a consequence, slavery came across as a sort of "fortunate fall," a phrase used by historian Vincent Carretta to refer to various black writers' thankfulness for their introduction to Western values, even though this introduction happened through enslavement.[9] In "On Being Brought from

AFRICA TO AMERICA," Wheatley declares: "'TWAS mercy brought me from my *Pagan* land,/Taught my benighted soul to understand/That there's a God, that there's a *Saviour* too:/Once I redemption neither sought nor knew" (13). Even Equiano, an outspoken abolitionist, identifies his moment of conversion as a recognition of God's providential plan: "Now every leading providential circumstance that happened to me, from the day I was taken from my parents to that hour, was then, in my view, as if it had but just then occurred. I was sensible of the invisible hand of God which guided and protected me, when in truth I knew it not: still the Lord pursued me although I slighted and disregarded it; this mercy melted me down" (190). After this insight, he rushed back to the chapel in Westminster where he had heard a Calvinist preach, and was finally accepted as a member. For both writers, accepting God's providence meant that enslavement had been the price to pay for spiritual liberation.

Some of the black writers in this individualistic, new-birth strand of Calvinism embedded no explicit abolitionist statements in their narratives, instead focusing on the liberationist dimension of conversion. Gronniosaw is a case in point. Brought to the Raritan valley of New Jersey after he disembarked from Africa, he was raised by Theodorus Jacobus Frelinghuysen, a Dutch Reformed minister who had received a pietist education in the Netherlands and who, once in the colonies, developed a strict theology with an emphasis on inner spirituality, rebirth, and puritan practices. Whitefield himself visited his church and acknowledged his role in the revival that was then turning into the First Great Awakening. Recognizing a soul mate in theology and preaching style, he wrote in his journal that Frelinghuysen had been "the beginner of the great work . . . in these parts" (Tanis, 82). Gronniosaw's story is infused with Frelinghuysen's theology and is less a slave narrative than a spiritual autobiography. He seems proud to recount that, when he visited the Netherlands, he was interrogated by "38 ministers every Thursday for seven weeks together" (48), and they were satisfied. Clearly, Gronniosaw's theology was close enough to that of his interrogators in Amsterdam. He did not develop a major abolitionist voice.[10]

Other black writers who subscribed to the Whitefield school of Calvinism spoke against slavery, but their opposition does not really seem to have been inspired by it. In a February 1774 letter to Native American minister Samson Occom, Wheatley asserts that "in every human Breast, God has implanted a Principle, which we call Love of Freedom; it is impatient of Oppression, and pants for Deliverance" (153). Her vocabulary echoes that of the American Revolution more than that of her religious upbringing. In London, Equiano actively took up the cause of abolitionism in the late 1780s, first by publishing essays in various British magazines, and then finally by offering the story of his life as an example of the vicissitudes and wrongness of the system. Interestingly, though, in his essays, he refers to Christian compassion and its duty of "benevolence to all." In his first essay, moreover, he sounds like a fire-and-brimstone preacher, as he points out that "the oppressor and the oppressed are in the hands of the just and awful God, who says, Vengeance is mine and I will repay" (258). He seems to relish the fate reserved to the oppressor: "The studied and torturing punishments, inhuman, as they are, of a barbarous planter, or a more barbarous overseer, will be tenderness compared to the provoked wrath of an angry but righteous God! who will raise, I have the fullest confidence, many of the sable race to the joys of Heaven, and cast the oppressive white to that doleful place, where he will cry, but will cry in vain, for a drop of water!" (258–59). In an image that could have come from Jonathan Edwards, the famous Calvinist preacher, Equiano turns the concept of a wrathful god to the service of his fight against slavery. Surrounded by white abolitionists who were mostly Quakers or Anglicans, he decided to assert the liberatory potential of a Calvinist worldview, but more specifically of a millennialist one, looking toward the future installment of a virtuous world. It is this Edwardsian bent that motivates him here.[11]

And it is this particular strand of Calvinism that became the most overtly abolitionist. Its most outspoken black representative was the minister Lemuel Haynes. In his writings and sermons, we can see how Calvinism could be turned into a theological underpinning for abolitionism. In his groundbreaking book *Black Puritan, Black Republican: The Life and Thought of Lemuel Haynes, 1753–1833,* John Saillant points out that Haynes examined the slave trade and slavery "in a systematic, historicist way" (19). On the one hand, Haynes found much inspiration in images from the Old Testament. For example, in "Liberty Further Extended," an essay he composed in the 1770s, he expands on humanitarian arguments used by Anthony Benezet in *Some Historical Account of Guinea,* published in 1771, by highlighting how the blood of the innocent needs to be avenged. But while acknowledging that slavery was once legitimate under Israelite and Mosaic law, Haynes argues that it is forbidden in the New Testament because of "the new dispensation inaugurated by Christ" (Saillant, *Black Puritan,* 30). Indeed, the New Testament "undid the authorization of slavery in the Old Testament" (31). The new dispensation, in which spirit and love were essential, was universal, and so removed the old one by proving that it had not been interpreted properly. It is this historicist view that inspires Haynes's abolitionism.

By insisting on the superiority of the new dispensation, Haynes occupied a specific spiritual and political realm. His dispensationalism drew on the theories of Samuel Hopkins, the major representative of a New England theological movement called New Divinity. Hopkins wanted to reassert God's absolute sovereignty, and he argued that God not only permits sin but causes it, according to a master plan that will ultimately lead to the establishment of the good and the arrival of the millennium. As he put it in the title of one of his essays, sin is "an advantage to the universe."[12] The only way for human beings to promote the moral progress of the universe is to renounce love of the self and to practice "disinterested benevolence." So, unlike Whitefield's, Hopkins's strict Calvinism led to an ethics of communalism and social reform. To him, slavery had to be abolished so that the colonies could achieve moral regeneration. Building on Hopkins, Haynes applied the ideas of New Divinity to "the cause of interracial equality in the new nation" (Saillant, *Black Puritan,* 86). The slave trade and slavery had been providentially designed by God ultimately to create a racially harmonious society, and true virtue entailed working to help bring it about. Interracial brotherhood was the outcome of these Calvinists' dispensationalism. Hopkins and Haynes were proof that communitarian, egalitarian conclusions could be drawn from a historicist, Calvinist worldview. As we will see, both Capitein and Marrant, each in his own way, drew on this particular approach.

Racial Context

Capitein's, Belley's, and Marrant's ideological and political interventions were partly made possible by their surrounding culture. In keeping with recent trends in the historiography of racism, this book, by describing the racial context for each of these three lives, shows that racial thought in Europe was in flux throughout the eighteenth century. Shaped by several centuries of writings, art, and the physical presence of blacks on the European continent, racial thinking at the beginning of the eighteenth century was first and foremost monogenic: all humans were seen as belonging to one big human family, and if it was investigated at all, racial difference was usually ascribed to climate. In previous centuries, African culture had often been assessed in positive ways, though ethnocentrism had also assured Europeans of their own cultural superiority. In the course of the century, a new fad for scientific classification planted the germ of polygenism, or the idea of human groups as having separate origins. Moreover, the magnitude of economic interests tied to the slave trade and slavery contributed to more negative images of people of African descent. On the other hand, the spread of the Enlightenment promoted humanist and liberal ideas such as tolerance and individual dignity. As a result, by the end of the century, European racial thought was profoundly unstable, ready to tilt in different directions depending on the context.

The movement toward the kind of engrained racism that would become predominant in the nineteenth century does not seem to have been inevitable. The Greeks and the Romans, with few exceptions, had no clear racial prejudice, and Christianity carried the idea of the unity of humankind. Representations of blacks in medieval and early modern European art and literature were overwhelmingly positive. Even travel accounts about Africa before the eighteenth century were surprisingly evenhanded, full of instances in which a European observer admires Africans' cultural or physical features, even as, overall, the belief in European superiority was a given.

But by the eighteenth century, most of the blacks Europeans came in contact with on the European continent, in real life or in representations, were either slaves or people of lower status. Most major cities in Holland, France, and England, and especially ports, had a black underclass consisting of slaves temporarily in the country to learn a trade or free blacks working in the trades or as domestics. An African origin was usually associated with a lack of cultural sophistication or even with savagery, and reactions ranged from paternalism to contempt. There was also a trend of bringing African children to Europe. Sometimes they were sent by African rulers, in a conscious strategy to increase their power and access in the Atlantic commercial and cultural network. At other times, they were brought by European traders or administrators and ended up members of rich households, often functioning as symbols of wealth or as mere playthings.

While all three parts of this book show ways in which race was the defining element in encounters between blacks and whites in the eighteenth century, they also highlight the rise of Enlightenment liberalism, or a desire to move beyond race and to assess people on the basis of a common human core. Blackness was not systematically considered a sign of inferiority. In all three countries, to varying degrees, there are examples of blacks having illustrious careers. Mixed-race marriages were not uncommon. The growth of the abolitionist movement in the second half of the eighteenth century promoted a discourse of common humanity and egalitarianism. Some artistic and literary representations featured black characters with realism and complexity. Overall, then, this book shows that one cannot just dismiss the eighteenth century as a racist monolith, and one should particularly avoid projecting later attitudes back into it.[13]

By the eighteenth century, the racial atmosphere also varied subtly from Amsterdam to Paris to London. The Dutch seemed happy with what can be seen as an early version of multiculturalism, a relaxed if ethnocentric acceptance of difference in their midst, and a determination to live and let live, as long as a person was economically productive. The French tended to subsume all under the banner of their national identity; while blackness could be experienced as foreign, they also seemed quite ready to let it be trumped by national identity, and even to express admiration for it—to celebrate it. Like the Dutch, the British were phlegmatic about racial difference, which often mattered less than the idea of being a subject of the king. While ethnocentrism dominated Europe, each country integrated blacks into its social fabric in its own way.

The American colonies stand separate, marked as they were by slavery in the South or by a recent history of slavery in the North. While some free blacks managed to carve a space for themselves in these societies, the section about John Marrant shows that their relationship to the social and racial context was much more self-conscious and adversarial than in Europe. The notion of black inferiority was more deeply engrained in mentalities as well as in the social and economic life, and as with European countries, this racism would only deepen in the following century.

Each of the three men under study in this book found ways to negotiate the particular racial atmosphere that surrounded him and to carve out a particular place for himself. Interestingly, to them, race was not necessarily a dimension to be negated or erased. In this respect also, each in his own way tried philosophically to move beyond liberalism, to a place where blackness was not negative but somehow still mattered. Capitein perceived the combination of ethnocentrism and relaxed multiculturalism around him, but there are hints that he enjoyed maintaining the complexity of his identity rather than blending in. Belley was fully devoted to France, but his fiery nationalism did not prevent a certain degree of racial pride. Marrant defended the idea of Christian unity but also looked for ways to create black community. In their desire to blend humanism and racial consciousness, these men often sound quite modern.

The African Diaspora in an Age of Revolution

All three men, each in his own way, were touched by the revolutions that took place in the eighteenth century, whether ideological or material. While Belley's thought reflects the secular grounding of the French Enlightenment, Capitein and Marrant were both profoundly shaped by dramatic changes in Christianity. Belley actually participated in the military and political upheavals of the French Revolution, fighting to protect abolition, and speaking up as a representative at the Paris Convention. Capitein inherited a version of Calvinism shaped by the ideological revolution of the Dutch Enlightenment, and while it did not at first turn him into an abolitionist, it later motivated his vision of a broader community. Marrant's thought evolved from Methodism's focus on individual salvation and the liberal ideas of the American Revolution to a more communitarian consciousness and a more radical form of Christianity in black Freemasonry. All three were influenced by and participated in the age of revolutions.

This book contributes to the study of the African diaspora in a number of new ways. With its focus on biography and individual intellectual development, it offers a focused perspective in the study of the vast networks of transportation and exploitation that affected people of African descent in the eighteenth-century Atlantic world. By digging into three individual lives, it shows the multiple ways in which blacks were affected by and contributed to their environment and provides some thickness of description to lives that often remain sketchy in larger projects. The focus on free men also throws light on a dimension of the African diaspora that has only begun to be investigated. I chose these particular three precisely because they left us documents that make this kind of investigation possible.

More broadly, this book begins to sketch an international intellectual history of blacks in the eighteenth-century Atlantic world. By placing each of these men within his national context, it shows the multifaceted ideologies they were exposed to, as well as the ways in which they both absorbed and resisted their ideological environment. The mixture of Dutch, French, British, and American stories makes comparisons possible, whether they be about race, religion, or political thought. It is my hope that this combination of micro- and macrohistory adds a new facet to the ever-fascinating story of blacks in the eighteenth century.

The subject of chapter 1, Jacobus Capitein, was taken from Africa to Holland as a child. He proved a good student, studied theology at the University of Leiden, was ordained, and returned to the Gold Coast, where he worked as a minister at a Dutch trading post. This chapter traces his intellectual growth and argues that, once back in Africa, he tried to push the progressive potential of a Calvinism that had already been transformed by the Dutch Enlightenment. Specifically, it focuses on the way his notion of a new covenant gradually seems to have taken him from an acceptance of slavery to a multicultural, multiracial vision of human community. It is his diasporic, cosmopolitan identity, I argue, that allowed this rethinking of racial relations and hierarchies. This development, when placed alongside the ideas of men like Lemuel Haynes, a New England black minister, shows how blacks in the eighteenth century could take advantage of the complexities and possibilities of Calvinism, which is often associated with proslavery stances and the social status quo, and make it serve a different agenda.

Chapter 2 focuses on Jean-Baptiste Belley, who was taken from Africa to Saint-Domingue when he was still a baby and remained a slave until young adulthood. Once free, he played a role in the Haitian and French Revolutions. This chapter traces his life as a military man and political actor in Saint-Domingue and in France and argues that he went through a gradual ideological development toward egalitarian and republican thought. Because his life and ideas were at the heart of contemporary events, this chapter places him within various contexts, including the community of free blacks in Saint-Domingue, the beginnings of the Haitian Revolution, the role of republicanism in the rise of French abolitionism, and the growth of French racial thought until the eighteenth century. It shows that, through his presence and his commitment, Belley, like a number of other black cosmopolitans such as Etienne Mentor and Pierre Thomany, was one of the rare true spokespersons for the universal ideals that drove the French Revolution.

The third chapter traces John Marrant's numerous travels between the American continent and Europe and his intellectual evolution as he moved from one context to another. It first explores his individualistic outlook and how it was anchored both in the evangelical focus on new-birth conversion and a personal relationship to God and in the American Revolutionary context. It then shows his development of a more communal vision, as a preacher in Nova Scotia and a chaplain for the black Freemasons in Boston. Here the chapter identifies a more supple cosmopolitanism, as Marrant alternates universal ideals with black-identified solidarity. It is under the influence of Prince Hall and other black Freemasons that his international vision finds its most subtle expression.

1

Jacobus Capitein and the Radical Possibilities of Calvinism

On 10 March 1742, the audience seated in an auditorium at the University of Leiden listened to a lecture delivered in Latin by one of its students in theology. The event was quite special. Not that the lecture was groundbreaking, since many in the audience probably agreed with its central tenet. The student was arguing that Christianity made one free spiritually and as a consequence was perfectly compatible with slavery. The fascination lay in that the young man making the argument, Jacobus Elisa Johannes Capitein, was an African.

Even though Capitein has long been a source of interest as one of several famous Africans educated in Europe in the eighteenth century, critics have not been able to shake off the image he created with this lecture. There's no denying that, as celebrated as he was during his lifetime, today he makes us uncomfortable. Whatever his achievements and his unique life path, one may wonder, wasn't he a traitor to his race, a sellout, an Uncle Tom, a selfish opportunist? This sort of accusations, while rarely spelled out, haunts much contemporary commentary on Capitein.[1]

Some critics highlight what they think makes Capitein sympathetic or even admirable. After all, they point out, he was not the only person at the time indoctrinated with Christianity and with the idea that religious conversion and spiritual salvation matter more than any bodily ideal of freedom. His decision to return to the west coast of Africa in order to minister to Europeans and convert Africans deserves praise. His tragic, mysterious death five years after he arrived there even has a touch of martyrdom.

But the story gets even more complicated. It seems that Capitein did not make himself too popular with either the Africans or the Europeans during the last years of his life. At one point his morale was so

Jacobus Elisa Johannes Capitein. Engraving by François van Bleyswijck, 1742. (Rijksmuseum, Netherlands)

low that he considered resigning from his post. Finally, when news of his death reached Holland, it transpired that he had accumulated substantial debts. Is this man's reputation at all redeemable?

I would like to argue that, to some extent, it is. It is certainly the case that, in many ways, Capitein adhered to the imperialistic mind-set of his time and that his lecture no doubt helped solidify a generally uncritical stance toward slavery and the slave trade in eighteenth-century Holland. But the letters he sent to Holland during those five years in Africa show a man quite different from the one portrayed in the thumbnail sketch. They can help, if not dispel, at least modify his image as a mouthpiece for Western colonialism. They tell the story of a man unprepared by his scholarly upbringing to deal with the hardships of life on a colonial outpost, but they also reveal a determination to understand his new social and cultural context, as well as, ultimately, a cosmopolitan flexibility at odds with the intellectual stiffness evinced in the Leiden lecture. Capitein was as much an African as a European, and in the end, this multiple, diasporic identity allowed him, if only fleetingly, to rise above the strictures of his upbringing and to acquire his own unique cosmopolitan voice.

In this voice, we hear him struggling to expand the Calvinist perspective he had acquired through his education and trying to adapt it to his new circumstances and surroundings. In his own way, Capitein tried to broaden the notion of tolerance he had been exposed to while growing up. Indeed, while Holland's revolution against Spain had long been over, its unique climate of tolerance, as well as its increasingly enlightened brand of Calvinism, were parts of its continuing social and intellectual revolution. That Capitein tried to build on that movement while in Africa is clear in something that resonates from his writings—a desire to understand the perspective of others and an ability to think in terms of multicultural, multiracial communities. Capitein did not suddenly turn into a different man, of course, and the damage done by his lecture would never be undone. But he was a black Atlantic cosmopolitan who tried to use both his European and African diasporic experiences to, in his own special and limited way, expand the meanings of cosmopolitanism.

Dutch Republican and Diasporic African

On that day in Leiden, Capitein started his lecture with a short autobiographical account.[2] It is fairly straightforward and often sounds like a tribute to Dutch civilization and to the people who introduced him to it. The story Capitein told his audience that day makes clear that he received important values from his Dutch education, and it suggests that, in many ways, he became Dutch. He had grown up in educated, middle-class circles in two major Dutch cities. He had been trained in the teachings of the Dutch Reformed Church, the Dutch denomination of the Protestant church, at both the secondary and the university levels. He was well read and had been open to the influence of the adults who surrounded him. Overall, he implies, he had benefited from the generosity of an enlightened republic. His life had been a sort of "fortunate fall."[3] At the same time, though, the autobiography hints at hidden desires or a complex personality under the surface. Capitein remained conscious of his difference. One hears in his story a love for Holland and its people, but it is subtly combined with an awareness of and appreciation for his own multifaceted and mobile identity. In this youthful lecture, the impression is only fleeting, but it points at things to come.

•

That Capitein should feel thankful for his Dutch culture is not that surprising considering that he came under its influence as a young child. Born in West Africa, he was sold as an orphan of about seven or eight to Admiral Aarnout Steenhart at a place called St. Andrews River, currently Sassandra in Ivory Coast. Steenhart then took him to Shama, one of a dozen Dutch trading settlements on the coast, where he gave him as a present to his friend Jacob van Goch. Van Goch was a merchant for the *West Indische Compagnie* (WIC), the only Dutch company officially allowed to trade with Africa, and he had been working on the coast since 1712. He stayed there a few more years, and when he left for Holland in 1728, he decided to take the boy along with him.[4] They settled in The Hague, where Capitein soon started attending catechism school and then Latin school.[5] A few years later, he was off to Leiden.

Capitein quickly acquired a Dutch identity. In his lecture, he expresses his gratefulness for what he clearly considers good treatment by his Dutch family and for a privileged upbringing. He is thankful that to some extent, he was allowed to become Dutch. In fact, he uses this public moment as an opportunity to, as we would say today, thank all the people and organizations that made the event possible. He calls Van Goch "my greatly revered patron and Maecenas," and he praises him for taking him back to Holland with the goal that he would be "duly instructed in Christianity" and that he might "practice some trade which was not demeaning and thereby earn a living" (*Agony*, 86–90).[6] He also reads a long elegy to the memory of his catechism teacher, Johann Philipp Manger, and lists the various tutors and patrons who paid for and encouraged his academic development. A dutiful student in an eminently commercial culture, he presents himself as the hopefully satisfying return on all these people's investment.

The culture Capitein grew up in was not just commercial; it also liked to think of itself as tolerant and enlightened. The early modern period in the Low Countries had seen a tremendous explosion of humanist thought, characterized by a return to the classics in search of human wisdom and appeals to the use of reason and the display of tolerance.[7] Erasmus of Rotterdam has become the symbol of Dutch humanism, through his defense of human dignity, his social and moral engagement, and his rational, moderate approach to matters of faith. The role of education in shaping rational thought also led to a celebration of books and learning. In the course of the seventeenth century, these humanist tendencies morphed into what can be called an early Enlightenment. While the Dutch Reformed Church had become quasi-official, there was widespread freedom of the press that left room for rational critiques, not just of the Bible but of religious belief itself. Baruch Spinoza pushed faith as close to atheism as it had ever been; Adriaan Koerbagh—who was arrested for his views—subjected all things to the test of reason; Balthasar Bekker became famous for his writings against superstition; Franciscus van den Enden, a Jesuit from Antwerp, left the order and moved to Amsterdam, where he opened a Latin school that exposed students to religious doubt.[8] Many foreign writers published in Holland what they were not allowed to publish at home. French philosopher René Descartes lived in the Netherlands for twenty years, and his emphasis on reason and systematic doubt, as well as on the separation of body and mind, was influential. It was while living in Holland that John Locke composed his *Letter Concerning Toleration,* and it was well received.[9] While some of these books did not find a wide audience in Holland, and sharp attacks on religious faith—such as La Mettrie's or d'Holbach's materialism—were not popular, there was the sense of a mainstream, middle-class culture that valued tolerance and reason.

Most of the people in Capitein's social world belonged to this comfortable, enlightened middle class. Van Goch was a merchant; his sister, Elisabeth, "has been like a second mother to me"; their cousin, who was present at his baptism, was married to Peter Nesker, a successful notary;[10] his private language teacher was "a noblewoman" (*Agony,* 92); Manger's wife, Sara Elizabeth Meinertzhagen, to whom Capitein dedicated the Dutch edition of his lecture, was the daughter of a German merchant.[11] Even though theology students on a fellowship at the University of Leiden usually resided at the *Statencollege,* a sort of boarding school, for some unknown reason Capitein boarded in the city, like regular students. He stayed in three different households in the course of his studies: those of widow De Bruyn, Casper van Condet, and Pieter de Vogel.[12] The students he came in contact with, moreover, were predominantly from the upper middle class.[13] Overall, then, his social and affective connections were bound to make Capitein identify with the urban middle class and its values, including its sense of itself as ideologically balanced.

He was also exposed to a humanist, rationalist, and increasingly scientific culture through his studies, both in The Hague and in Leiden. At the Latin school, he received a thorough grounding in Latin and Greek texts.[14] In his lecture, he remembered the rector of the school, Isaac Valkenaar, as "someone widely known for his scholarly intellect." He also received private instruction in Latin, Greek, Hebrew, and Chaldean, from a woman "of immense endowments" (*Agony,* 92), who transmitted to him "a desire for learning."[15] Moving to Leiden in 1737 could only broaden his exposure. Ever since its inauguration with great fanfare in 1575, the University of Leiden had tried to be a beacon of humanist and enlightened thought. After a religious oath was abolished in 1578 "in order that everybody may be spiritually free" (Jurriaanse, 15), the number of students, Dutch and foreign, multiplied. The university quickly attracted the most distinguished scholars, such as French classicists Joseph Scalinger and Claude Saumaise. Daniel Heinsius, a famous scholar, taught the classics; his son, Nicolaas, a poet and scholar who visited all the major libraries of Europe and accumulated thousands of classical texts in his private library, studied in Leiden. The books and manuscripts of Isaac Vossius, deist and scholar, were sold to the school after his death. By the early eighteenth century, as Cartesianism made way for the Newtonian revolution, the university had become famous for its botanical garden, its anatomy room, and its laboratories. By the time Capitein attended, empiricism ruled, with such famous faculty as Willem 's Gravesande, mathematician; Pieter van Musschenbroek, specialist in mathematics and medicine; and Herman Boerhaave, botanist, chemist, and physician. It was a vibrant culture, and we will see below that Capitein's lecture reflected both his humanist studies and this broader Enlightenment climate.

There was another major strand of Dutch culture that was hard to miss—its religiosity. Historians have pointed out that the Dutch Enlightenment remained moderate and have found explanations in factors such as history, economics, and political structure. To others, Dutch middle-class rationalism was simply "wary of extremes."[16] But there is no question that religious faith remained a strong component of Dutch culture and that sustained religious attacks on enlightened thinking somehow paid off. In the course of the eighteenth century, the new spirit was shaped by what a critic has called "reforming lights"—philosophers and theologians who drew a sharp division between the realm of reason and the realm of faith, but who still ultimately took great sustenance from their Christianity.[17] As Margaret C. Jacob and Wijnand W. Mijnhardt put it, here was a country that "acted as a Calvinist bulwark while at the same time publishing some of the most impious books of the Enlightenment" (11). As a student in theology, Capitein was naturally part of this "Calvinist bulwark," and when we analyze his religious argument about slavery, we will see how his particular brand of Calvinism shaped his views.

•

Capitein's ideological outlook integrated another important element of Dutch culture: its political philosophy, and more particularly, its republicanism. Politically, the Netherlands had always been a bit of an outlier among European countries. It had been a republic ever since its separation from Spain at the end of the sixteenth century. In 1581, a number of provinces in the Low Countries signed the *Plakkaat van Verlatinghe,* or Act of Abjuration, which declared that they considered themselves no longer bound to Philip II, the Spanish king. In this exceptional document, which provided a lengthy explanation for their decision, they declared that, through his tyrannical rule and religious intolerance, the king had broken the contract that he, as a king, was supposed to uphold with his subjects. He had therefore lost his right to rule them, and they had decided to release him of this contract. This decision was a major step in the political history of western Europe. It acted on the idea that a king did not rule by divine right and his authority was dependent on the collective will of his subjects.[18] By the time Capitein came to the Netherlands, a fear of tyranny was still very much part of the political culture and gave it a republican foundation.

This did not mean, however, that there was harmony or agreement in political matters. In fact, the country had had a turbulent political history since its independence. After its separation from the Southern Netherlands, which was retaken by Spain, the Republic of the Northern Netherlands set about creating its political identity. Building on previous institutions, it became a federation of seven provinces. Each province sent representatives to the States-General, which met every day in the imposing gothic *ridderzaal* at the Binnenhof in The Hague. Each province also had its own assembly. Most of the representatives were nobles or regents—urban patriciates. Two functionaries were above this structure: the *stadhouder,* who held military as well as some political power and who, in recognition of the leader of the rebellion, had to belong to the House of Orange, and the pensionary of Holland, who led the delegation of the most powerful province.[19] The republic was sensitive to any hint of hankering for more power. Two pensionaries suffered a sad fate: Johan van Oldenbarnevelt was executed in 1619 after a series of religious quarrels; Johan de Witt was lynched by a crowd in 1672 after France invaded. After Willem II marched on Amsterdam in 1650 but died shortly thereafter, the position of *stadhouder* remained vacant for more than twenty years. Similarly, after Willem III died in 1702, most of the country was without a *stadhouder* until 1747, when Willem IV acceded to the position. Overall, the preference was for a mixed form of government, but clearly these swings were the expression of a country in search of a political identity.

As a consequence, by the time Capitein lived there, it had brought forth a variety of political theories, some of which would find echoes in his lecture. Even though the Dutch republic was fundamentally commercial and wealth oriented, most of these theories can be characterized as republican, in that they predate the focus on individual rights that would come to fruition in the course of the eighteenth century, and are concerned with the survival of the republic thanks to a free and virtuous citizenry. Indeed, throughout the seventeenth century, the Dutch had faced a dilemma that had been familiar to Italian humanists two centuries before. A variety of external and internal forces regularly threatened the existence of the republic, and the question was how to preserve its peace and stability without also undermining its citizens' freedom. Over against the accidents of *fortuna*, particular virtues and institutions had to be deployed. Faced with possible political instability, the Dutch found comfort and ideas either in Italian humanist and Greco-Roman literature or in a Calvinist providential design. In *Verhandeling van de vrijheid in de burgerstaat,* for example, published in 1737, Lieven de Beaufort defended the Machiavellian notion of civic virtue, though in this case, the ideal political system turned out to be an oligarchy—a reminder that republican thought did not necessarily entail the promotion of democracy. The result of a lack of paradigm was a Dutch political thought that was "eclectic" (Kossmann, 11) but for the most part relied less on emerging liberal ideas than on the possibilities of classic republicanism. Capitein certainly picked up on it.

•

The text of Capitein's lecture is a window into his ideological makeup. After his autobiographical account, he starts his scholarly discussion with a short chapter that defines slavery and states his overall argument. The second chapter, also fairly short, "explores the ancient origin of slavery and shows that nearly all societies made use of it" (*Agony,* 97). Chapter 3, the most substantial, then argues "that slavery and Christianity are not antithetical" (103). The whole text is peppered with quotes from classical, humanist, and biblical sources. While they are undoubtedly only a partial reflection of his learning and interests, these sources give us a peek into Capitein's ideological and political vision: they show that he was definitely drawn to a body of work with strong ties to civic humanism and classic republicanism. While he does not draw abolitionist implications from this outlook, it is important to understand his republican leanings because they create a foundation for the kind of thinking he would develop later, when he was confronted with a mixed-race community on the west coast of Africa.

The influence of civic humanism on Capitein comes across early on. In his explanation of the origin of slavery, he seems particularly drawn to the notion of fortune and to how it engenders particular social conditions, an emphasis that mirrors republican concerns with stability and peace over against the accidents of *fortuna*. He quotes Bisetus, a seventeenth-century writer who, in his comment on Aristophanes's comedy *Plutus,* writes that slavery was introduced by "Fortune, certainly not nature," as "the law of the nations and fortune make persons slaves to others." "This is fortune," Capitein continues, "which the heathen convinced themselves rules over human affairs arbitrarily." He then quotes Horace, the Roman poet, who in his *Odes* famously says: "Greedy fortune takes pleasure in snatching the crown from one, amid loud noise, and giving it to another." Indeed, he concludes, "It is human law and accident which have made humans into slaves." While he takes pains to distance himself from what he sees as a pagan concept of fate, the focus on fortune conveys a political vision that sees institutions as a bulwark against the vagaries of historical events. He certainly emphasizes that "nature has made all people free," and his repetition of a passage from Harmenopoulos, a fourteenth-century legal scholar who sees slavery as "something which is opposed to natural law" (*Agony,* 98), shows his acceptance of that principle. But the implication of his argument is that, once the practice had been introduced, an acceptance of the tradition became necessary for the sake of social and political stability.

This acceptance fits within what is probably the most striking philosophical strain in the lecture, though not explicitly mentioned: Stoicism. The very first book Capitein quotes from is Cicero's *On Duties.* As early as the fourteenth century, Italian political writers had turned to Cicero with renewed interest, as he was now recognized as a defender of civic virtue and of the Roman republic against the tyrannical tendencies that would soon break it apart.[20] Capitein only quotes from the book to justify his methodology—like Cicero, he starts with a definition—but with this reference, he is signaling an important part of his worldview. In *On Duties,* Cicero addresses his son Marcus, who is studying in Athens, and gives him ethical advice. Much of his argument is drawn from Panaetius, a famous Greek Stoic. Stoicism rested on the principle that the universe is a rational totality in which all elements have an equal role. Human beings can achieve happiness if they live in accordance with this rational universal order. This implies living rationally and virtuously, a goal that necessitates the control of one's emotions for the sake of virtue. If one succeeds, one becomes a true universal sage—a citizen of the world.[21] Capitein must have been aware of these philosophical implications when he quoted from *On Duties*.

Cicero's ethical advice clearly stems from his anxiety about the survival of the Roman republic. He makes a distinction between what is "honorable," or good for the whole community, and what is "beneficial," or good for the individual, and the thrust of his argument is that, ideally, the two should coincide, especially for men who take part in public life. By "honorable," he means the action is involved with four things: with truth, with preserving fellowship among men, with greatness of spirit, and with order and restraint.[22] Justice does not just mean an avoidance of harm to others; men who neglect to help others also "abandon the fellowship of life" (12). A great spirit disdains things that are external. Care and punishment should be allotted with the good of the whole republic in mind. Impulses should be controlled; men should not give in to rashness and carelessness but should display constancy and moderation.[23] With such principles, Cicero lays out a theory of social and political life that embraces a Stoic idea of orderliness, control, and stability.

There are other Stoic echoes in Capitein's lecture. He refers twice to Seneca, a famous Roman Stoic, once to quote his definition of a slave—one who serves unwillingly—and once to state Seneca's theory that "the Roman ranks of knight, freedman and slave were born out of ambition or injustice" (97). Though he does not mention him in the lecture, Capitein must have been familiar with the work of Justus Lipsius, a Southern Netherlands scholar who had been invited to Leiden shortly after its founding, and whose books became international best sellers. Besides Stoics, he also refers to philosophers who anchored their system of thought in reason, such as Henry More, an English theologian, and Christian Thomasius, a German philosopher.

The presence of Stoicism in Capitein's intellectual makeup partly accounts for his main argument about slavery. While some Stoics were critical of physical slavery, the major Stoic concern was "slavery of the soul" (Garnsey, 16). An individual was enslaved if he "cared about externals, including anything that happened to his body" (17), and physical slavery was seen as belonging to these "externals." As a consequence, the Stoics devoted little attention to ameliorationist or abolitionist thought. Just as in *On Duties* Cicero underlined how individuals' special talents necessarily assigned them a particular role in society, the Stoics tended to accept one's position in the cosmic order, as long as the highest form of virtue was attained.²⁴ From this perspective, Christianity partly echoed Stoicism. Paul even voiced the Old Testament idea that it is good to be a slave to God.²⁵

It is important to emphasize that Capitein does not reject the vital role of freedom in human happiness. He starts his argument by positing that "every human being is under his own authority according to natural law" and that "the common condition of early humankind permitted equal freedom to all humans" (97). While theories of natural law are as old as Aristotle, and while republicanism certainly advocated political liberty, associating natural law with freedom sounds much more modern. To Aristotle, the natural state is one of human association: "Man is by nature a political animal" (59). In the course of the sixteenth century, though, as constitutionalism took on a more specific shape in political writings, the theory of natural liberty emerged more fully, including the idea of a contract between ruler and people that underlay the Plakkaat van Verlatinghe through which the Dutch renounced their allegiance to the Spanish king. Interestingly, the Plakkaat was inspired by the *Apology*, written by the leader of the Dutch revolt, William of Orange, probably with the help of two French Huguenots who had been in the forefront of articulating constitutionalist theories.²⁶ Anchoring natural law in freedom then became commonplace in the seventeenth century. Its most famous promotor was Thomas Hobbes, who in *Leviathan* argued that humans in the state of nature are completely free. While he concluded that authoritarianism was the only possible source of order, other theorists such as Samuel von Pufendorf and John Locke drew more democratic implications from the view of nature as freedom.

A number of radical Dutch thinkers actually theorized the law of nature as freedom and promoted democracy as a result. Johan de La Court started from the assertion that men are naturally driven by their passions and by an urge for self-preservation and concluded that the only way to rein them in was through a form of democratic republicanism.²⁷ The more famous Spinoza was actually influenced by de La Court. To him, democracy was "the most absolute and the freest form of government" (Kossmann, 75). Similarly, Franciscus van den Enden, well known as Spinoza's teacher, wrote texts that were "militantly democratic" (Israel, "Intellectual," 9). The idea of democracy, or "rule by the mob," was still very much decried at the time Capitein was writing, so if he read these authors at all, he obviously did not endorse them. But he remained sensitive to what he obviously considered to be a natural right to freedom.

Overall, like many at the time, Capitein ignores what has been called a radical early Enlightenment, and his thought remains anchored in theories that give priority to notions of social unity and harmony rather than to individual freedom.[28] He even quotes from *Six Books of the Commonwealth* by French humanist Jean Bodin, for whom a harmonious society demanded a strong leader—a theory at odds with republican constitutionalism. As we will see, Capitein builds his case about the compatibility of slavery with Christian freedom on his Calvinist philosophy, and there are ways in which his republicanism and his Calvinism mirror each other. Overall, then, his intellectual grounding is the civic tradition of the common good. If bound to a tradition, though, it was not without progressive potential—and Capitein would realize that later on.

•

As amazing as Capitein's absorption of Western philosophical and political thought, he was still a young black foreigner in a white country. While he seems to have been enthralled by the cultural and political achievements of his adopted home, Capitein also makes it clear in his autobiography that he is conscious of his special status. He praises Holland for its glorious history and its strong, independent position on the world stage, but he also hints at his own marginality. One hears in his autobiography an appreciation for the complex ideological balance that the Dutch had managed to achieve by the beginning of the eighteenth century, but it is combined with an awareness of his own different, multifaceted identity. And it is an identity whose flexibility he seems to embrace.

While he expresses his love for the republic, for example, he also tries to keep it at a distance. In his description of growing up in The Hague, he pays tribute to Dutch national pride and its anchoring in republicanism, but he keeps his enthusiasm subdued. By 1728, the country had been without a *stadhouder* for many years, and the province of Holland, the most important one, was headed by Simon van Slingelandt, a staunch republican devoted to the strength and the independence of the republic. The Hague was not as cosmopolitan as Amsterdam, and the Binnenhof, the imposing complex of buildings where the States-General met, was a constant reminder of the ideals of the republic. Capitein says in a poem inserted into the lecture: "This is where Holland's forefathers came/and met to save the pact of nourishing peace" (87). Probably referring to the signing of the Treaty of Münster in 1648, through which Holland became officially independent from Spain, Capitein shows his awareness of Holland's history and his reverence for its founding fathers. Interestingly, though, he presents the signing as an act of peace rather than of independence, implying that it is the former rather than the latter that will "nourish" a young nation. He indirectly acknowledges that, just like the Dutch, he too has been "nourished" by the republic, but the soft praise keeps the nationalism understated.

He seems to have enjoyed most the quiet life and daily pleasures of living in The Hague. If, as his biographer Henri van der Zee speculates, "the coal-black boy must have made quite an impression in The Hague," Capitein chooses not to remember it.[29] He describes the city as "the place where our sequestered youth/was devoted to noble studies." "This place with a thousand roads and shady retreats," he continues, "fosters ease and lays cares aside." It is a "most delightful Dutch town," where he also "worked on the art of painting, in which I proved quite talented" (87). One imagines the boy walking through the middle-class neighborhoods of the city, enjoying the natural beauty of the huge city park, or standing by the windy seaside, and even though there's a hint of isolation, the image he creates is a positive one of quiet study and devotion to art in a haven far removed from the conflicts and the violence he may have witnessed as a child, when he was "orphaned by war or some other cause" (86). In his short life story, the episode in The Hague almost functions as the place of careless innocence that narratives of the Middle Passage locate in Africa. It is a peaceful, usually harmonious, neutral space the narrator occupies before the fall into national and racial consciousness. That Capitein situates it in Holland implies that for a while, what he appreciated about his new abode was less its Dutchness than the potential it offered for an open, unrestricted, unmarked form of identity.

Indeed, it is hard not to notice that he presents his decision to return to Africa as one that was more or less imposed on him. Two years after he arrived in the Netherlands, Van Goch sent him to the minister Johann Philipp Manger for catechism lessons, and Capitein remained his student for several years. Two boys he studied with then informed the son of Hendrik Velse, a famous proponent of evangelization, "that they thought I should steer my career-path toward the study of theology, so that, God willing, I might afterwards show my people the way to a better religion." "Now," he continues, "I admit that I do not clearly remember whether I disclosed to anyone that such an idea appealed to me," but when Velse broached the topic with him, "I replied that I certainly did not shrink from the proposal" (90). Would Capitein have gone back to Africa without the pressure he received? He seems to imply that life in Holland was pleasurable enough and that any marginalization he may have suffered was no serious impediment to his happiness. He sounds thankful for, rather than anxious about, his multiple identities as a Dutch-educated black Christian.

This relative comfort was maintained thanks to a few persons who played an important role in his life. One of those was Manger, who, after Van Goch, was the first male European adult to make a strong impression on him. Born in Germany in 1693, Manger studied in Utrecht and by 1725 settled down in The Hague as a minister for one of the Reformed churches. He was well known for his good character. He was also particularly concerned about poor foreign immigrants, so much so that one day in 1731, he prayed on his knees in an open field together with a number of German Christians who had just arrived in Dordrecht. In 1732, he celebrated the Lord's Supper for a group of people about to emigrate to Pennsylvania.[30] An immigrant and a defender of immigrants, Manger was the counterpart to Capitein's budding nationalism, providing him with a more universal awareness.

In a long elegy to Manger, also included in the lecture, Capitein presents him as a multifaceted man who retains all his dimensions even in death. He takes pains to praise both the public and the private man. Manger was a great man who taught him both "salvation" and "justice"; when he died, "noble Hague groaned balefully"; twice Capitein mentions an assembled "throng." But among the mourners is his wife, who first and foremost has lost a husband: "Death snatched you away from our marriage-bed./What day will renew our broken bonds?" In a mixture of classical and Christian images, Manger is seen both crossing the Styx and entering the house of Christ. His body is now lifeless, as his eyes "now stand stiff" and "a bloodless, pale look occupies his gentle face." But the poem ends with visions of the man on Mount Olympus, where "surrounded by soft linen among the denizens of heaven/you are now fed, as victor, with ambrosial food" and "drink from the glassy stream/water springing forth from the soil" (87–90). Manger appears both lifeless and as an enjoyer of food and drink, a classical god and a servant of Christ, a civic man and a passionate husband. Capitein praises him for this complexity, and in this, he may have been projecting his own sense of self.

But as he continues his account, the sense of an open, mobile identity does not remain. As if he is bemoaning a loss, the somewhat epicurean feel that predominated in his description of The Hague completely disappears in the last part of his autobiography, as he describes in quick succession the decision to study theology and go back to Africa, his secondary education both in public school and through a private tutor, his baptism, the financial help he received from Van Goch and various patrons, and his arrival at "this most distinguished of Holland's universities" (92–93). He does thank the superintendent of the Latin school where he studied for six years, Isaac Valkenaar, but does not say a word about the education he received there. One does hear a personal note when he explains the origin of his name, saying he was named "Jacob after my esteemed patron" and "Elisa after his sister, who has been like a second mother to me" (92). But he is now focusing on his duty, since "for the reasons stated above, the gospel must be spread" (93). He stoically accepts the challenge—as an African, as a Dutchman, as a Christian. It is not quite clear which part motivates him the most—it may even be a sense of saving virtue for a country that feels it is in a state of moral decline.[31] In any case, at this point, his variable identity has become less exploratory and more goal oriented. And if his audience had any doubts about his dedication, the main argument of his lecture would dispel them.

Being Black in Holland

While in his lecture Capitein expressed gratitude for his Dutch upbringing, one wonders what sort of reception Dutch society gave this young African. He remains silent on that count. Nowhere in the autobiography does he gesture toward his race as the source of anything other than an opportunity to develop a career. And even in that case, he says that people referred broadly to him teaching "my people the way to a better religion" (90), implying that the Dutch focused on cultural and religious difference rather than race. And indeed, Dutch racial attitudes in the eighteenth century were more nuanced than Holland's conduct on the world stage at the time might suggest. While there is no question that he was perceived as different, it looks like his environment welcomed him enough to make him feel accepted.

•

Even though he mentions that he was "sold" on the West African coast and that Steenhart, the man who bought him and gave him to Van Goch, was there "in order to buy slaves," Capitein makes no mention of the broader historical circumstances that account for his presence in Europe. Actually, he speaks of the two men in laudatory terms. He considers Van Goch "someone who will have my filial affection right up to the grave," someone who "doted on me with paternal love thanks to his good character which caused his fame to spread virtually throughout all Guinea." He calls Steenhart an "eminent man" and an "acclaimed admiral" (87).

Yet he knows that Steenhart was a slave trader. When he carried Capitein and Van Goch from Africa to Holland, Steenhart had just returned from a slave passage across the Atlantic. During the passage, 154 out of the 563 Africans on board had died. Capitein also knows that Van Goch had long worked for the WIC. The Dutchman had even twice applied for the position of director general on the coast but had been turned down. Finally, Capitein knows that, when he arrived in Middelburg, a major port in the southwestern province of Zeeland and a city he describes as "the door to the vale of Holland" (86), it was really more of a portal for the slave trade.[32]

Indeed, since his capture, Capitein had been caught in the tentacles of what was at the time a vast if declining Dutch empire. When the Dutch signed the Treaty of Münster in 1648, establishing peace with Spain after an eighty-year-long war of independence, they were at the zenith of their imperial power, and the greatest trading nation in the world. Besides their European trading network, they dominated the silk and spice trade in the East. Even though they would soon lose some of the Atlantic settlements they had taken from the Portuguese, such as the ones in Brazil and in Angola, their presence in the Caribbean and along the African coast had turned them into masters of the sugar and the slave trade. By the time of Capitein's lecture in 1742, this dominance had receded, but the Netherlands were still very much participants in the European colonialist exploitation of the Atlantic world, and they possessed several colonies, including six islands in the West Indies, and Surinam, a large area on the northern coast of South America.

This exploitation included slavery and the slave trade. When the Dutch first started trading in Africa at the end of the sixteenth century, they were also engaged in their independence fight against Spain, and they prided themselves on not indulging in the human traffic practiced by their papist enemies. Their focus was on gold, ivory, and pepper. Even though Isaac Duverne, a Dutch merchant, sold 470 Africans to Spanish settlers in Trinidad in 1606, the Dutch did not seriously start considering participating in the slave trade until they had established a presence in Brazil and the Caribbean and had taken the West African fort at Elmina from the Portuguese in 1637 and established themselves on the Angolan coast in 1642.[33]

The WIC had been founded in 1621 by a number of Dutch merchants, with an exclusive charter over West Africa and the Americas, and although they were hesitant at first, the slave trade picked up very quickly when they realized that not only their own but also Spanish, French, and English settlers in the Caribbean relied on them to meet their increasing demand for Africans. The island of Curaçao became a veritable international market in slaves. Even though Spaniards could officially buy only from merchants who had obtained the *asiento,* a contract provided by the Spanish government, smuggling was the rule of the day. In fact, many *asiento* holders commissioned the Dutch to provide them with the necessary merchandise. For example, when in 1662 the two Genoese merchants Domingo Grillo and Ambrosio Lomelino were awarded the *asiento,* they initially commissioned the WIC to bring two thousand slaves to Curaçao. Antonio Garcia, who received it in 1670, also contracted with the WIC. In 1684, it even went to a Dutchman, Balthasar Coymans, a sign that Dutch slave trading had reached a high point.[34] It is estimated that the Dutch transported a total of about 550,000 people from Africa to the Americas.[35]

One would expect such a powerful slave-trading nation to have developed a specific racial ideology, but when one examines the development of Dutch attitudes toward blacks until the eighteenth century, it is hard to uncover the kind of racism that would come to characterize later periods. Dutch views of Africans undeniably conveyed a belief in the superiority of Dutch culture and institutions. Many references to Africans diminished them in one way or another, often by presenting them as childish, uncouth, or exotic.[36] But these views were eminently flexible. In fact, throughout the Middle Ages, representations of blacks in northern European art and literature had been overwhelmingly positive. Even Dutch travel accounts about Africa contained evenhanded descriptions of Africans and their culture. And some blacks in Holland were well integrated. Overall, then, the status of blacks in Holland in the seventeenth and eighteenth centuries seems to have fluctuated between integration and stigmatization. While racial thought undoubtedly played a role in this movement, it appears that attitudes toward blacks mostly reflected the changing visions of a fairly new republic in search of an identity.

Early Dutch travel accounts about Africa reflect a mix of biased and egalitarian attitudes. While later accounts would become more openly imperialistic, these early texts illustrate how early Dutch attitudes toward the other combined a sense of superiority with a discourse of openness and fairness and thereby highlight the fuzziness of early European racial thinking. European views of Africans were anchored in culture and covered a wide span, from admiration to disgust. Critic Ernst van den Boogaart has shown that, in the case of the Dutch, Africans were usually evaluated in terms of "Dutch standards of proper living, of civility" ("Colour Prejudice," 40).[37] The Dutch were also eager to depict themselves as innocent compared to the cruel and exploitative Spaniards and to present their growing encroachment on the African coast as perfectly justified.[38] Two famous early Dutch travel accounts, for example, one by Pieter de Marees, entitled *Description and Historical Account of the Gold Kingdom of Guinea,* published in 1602, and the other by Pieter van den Broecke, *Journal of Voyages to Cape Verde, Guinea and Angola (1605-1612),* published in 1634, focus on describing complex commercial transactions between Europeans and Africans, and both authors are at pains to present themselves as objective observers of the cultures they are encountering. This seeming objectivity reinforces their self-image as respectful and noninterventionist partners in trade, and ultimately as good Christians. At the same time, though, they display a number of prejudices common at the time toward people who were not Christians and who were considered less civilized. Still, in the relationship between those two dimensions—the idea of the Africans being equal trading partners and the feeling of cultural superiority—the former does not necessarily appear as a cover-up for the latter. They exist side by side, mutually informing each other in order to create a complex web of ideas about the Africans and, more specifically, a Dutch concern with morality and respect for the other even as more colonialist visions were being shaped.[39]

In fact, the Dutch did not seem to adhere to any particular race theory. As in most of the Christian world, there were long-standing prejudices against the color black, which was usually associated with the devil. In the thirteenth-century epic poem *Karel ende Elegast,* Karel is frightened by a knight because of his black horse, his black shield, his black outfit, and he thinks the apparition is the devil.[40] But outlandish theories about blacks belonging to a different category of creation, or standing closer to animals than humans, were usually taken with a grain of salt.[41] The most famous homegrown theories came from Petrus Camper, a zoologist and anthropologist who received a degree from the University of Leiden just a few years after Capitein spoke there. As we saw, the University of Leiden had a high reputation in the fields of medicine, anatomy, and empirical methodology.[42] Camper is now often reviled for developing a facial angle theory, but he never intended this theory to be about the quality of the brain. He was in fact a monogenist and a proponent of physical equality between the races. A rigorous empiricist, he performed dozens of dissections of human bodies, black and white, and downplayed differences in skin color to emphasize similarities. In his 1764 lecture "On the Origin and Color of Blacks," given at the Anatomy Lecture Hall in Groningen, a major city in the north of the country, he tells of how in 1758, he conducted a public dissection of "a black Angolese boy" and how, counter to theories of links between blacks and apes, "I must confess that I found nothing that had more in common with this animal than with a white man; on the contrary, everything was the same as for a white man" (Meijer, 186). In this matter-of-fact statement of similarity, the scientist was giving scientific backing to what were probably general Dutch attitudes concerning race.

This egalitarian approach was quite distinctive compared to that of other European scientists who, while also monogenists, worked at identifying biological differences between races. Camper notably differed from the Count de Buffon, a French monogenist who nevertheless argued that original whites had "degenerated" into blacks under particular conditions. In the lecture, he argues that skin color depends on the color of the middle layer between actual skin and epidermis and ends up positing that, since whites have a middle layer that is less dark, "all of us are all black, only more or less" (Meijer, 184). Camper also criticizes Johann Friedrich Meckel, a German anatomist who argued in 1757 that the brains and blood of blacks are black, saying that "he probably would have thought in a friendlier and more reasonable way if he, as we do in our Country, had seen Blacks every day and had seen that whites, men and women, however superior they may feel to those colored people, do not judge them unworthy of their love" (185). He concludes that "it seems quite obvious that all Scholars, through their association of a very hateful image with the color black, acted as if a certain well-deserved curse, or wrath of the Divine Supreme Being, were the origin of the unfavorable color: and usually, if not always, this one-sided and absurd account worked in favor of the Whites, because they had devised it themselves and thus had accorded themselves superiority over others of a different color" (187). Again, it is not certain how representative his opinions were, but they were certainly heard, as he taught at several Dutch universities, gave many public lectures, and became an international celebrity.

By the eighteenth century, the issue of race was also inevitably tied to slavery, and the question of allowing the presence of slaves in the republic threw questions of economic and political stability against the idea of personal freedom. If the debate was not unique, in the Netherlands it started very early. In their attitudes toward blacks, the Dutch had always tended to make a distinction between a free Europe and the practice of slavery in the Americas.[43] Officially, there were no slaves in Holland. According to Paul Voet, a seventeenth-century lawyer whom Capitein quotes in his lecture, "Any slaves who might come over to us from elsewhere or enter the boundaries of our territories should by the very fact of their coming here obtain their freedom" (*Agony,* 128). In practice, though, the status of slaves who arrived in Holland varied widely.

The clash between commercial stability and individual freedom already took place at the end of the sixteenth century. When in 1596 a ship captured from the Portuguese arrived in Middelburg with about 130 Africans on board, city officials decided to set them back in "their natural liberty."[44] The stated reason was that the Africans were all baptized. The officials even encouraged citizens to employ them. But the shipowner decided to appeal to the States-General, requesting that he be allowed to take the Africans to the West Indies because they were his cargo. The States-General acceded to his request, and it is likely that the captain reembarked most of the Africans.[45] But they had first turned him down, and the wording of their permission is strikingly convoluted. It allows that the captain can do with the Africans "so as he sees fit," but they were not "prepared to take any further decision" (Hondius, *Blackness,* 141) in the matter. This refusal to positively intervene on behalf of the Africans' freedom shows the extent to which Dutch republicanism could be swayed by commercial interest.

Practice continued to vary until the end of the eighteenth century. Sometimes, tolerance was shown to slaveowners who found themselves having to stay in Holland for a short time. Of four Portuguese merchants who arrived in Holland in October 1625, one stayed in Amsterdam for a few months and was allowed to keep eight Africans and take them away with him when he left. Several court cases from the eighteenth century maintain the complainants' enslaved status. But others were liberated. Dienke Hondius mentions the 1656 case of Juliana, who belonged to the Portuguese merchant Eliau Burgos. Once in Amsterdam, Juliana refused to accompany him to Barbados because, a notary wrote, "the slaves here are free" ("Access," 381). In 1772, a court liberated an enslaved woman and her daughters.[46] A 1776 law finally decided that slaves who were not spoken for had to be freed after a presence of six months.[47]

Overall, the free blacks who lived in Holland in the sixteenth, seventeenth, and eighteenth centuries seem to have encountered paternalism and racial curiosity rather than racial hostility. Their number is hard to determine, but black men and women are mentioned frequently in notary archives.[48] Interracial marriages were accepted, and by the eighteenth century urban whites were used to seeing blacks living and working among them. A commentator writes that, when in 1801, a scene from the opera *Paul and Virginia* was performed in a *café chantant* in Amsterdam, alongside the usual audience the packed hall was "filled with a great number of blacks and moors, so that it looked as if all the black domestics from all Amsterdam were standing there to hold their fair that evening."[49] The story of Paul and Virginia, from the famous novel by Jacques Bernardin-Henri de Saint-Pierre, about two French children who grow up together on the island Isle de France, now known as Mauritius, in the Indian Ocean, features a number of black characters. The commentator notes that the performance that day was "the scene of the black," probably referring to the scene where the house slave Domingo sings an adagio.[50] "A very agreeable diversity was created by this occasion," he continues, "as one ended up pushed now against a pretty girl, now against a black."[51] It is hard to tell whether he finds both races equally attractive and is enjoying the multiracial character of the crowd or is contrasting a positive white and a negative black. In any case, race was an important marker, but one that did not seem to have well-defined connotations.

Possibly the clearest connotation had to do with social class, as most of the free blacks living in the Netherlands were poor or members of the working class. There are records of blacks being helped by the Jewish poor service, the Imposta, and of blacks forming a sometimes violent underclass.[52] Most were soldiers, servants, skilled laborers, or musicians. One of the earliest examples of such a free black in the Southern Netherlands is Antoon Rodrigues, who in 1566 was granted a testimonial for good behavior; he had been living in Antwerp for twenty-four years, working as a house painter.⁵³ In the seventeenth century, many of the black domestics in the Netherlands served Portuguese or Spanish merchants who came north to buy products they could sell on the African coast. In the eighteenth century, most of the blacks came from Surinam, which the Dutch had owned since 1667, and the Dutch Antilles, either with their masters or emancipated, and were thus associated with an inferior status.⁵⁴

On the other hand, one finds examples of blacks in the more comfortable working class, or even the wealthy middle class. Such is the case of Quaco, valet to John Gabriel Stedman, the author of a famous chronicle of eighteenth-century Surinam, who came to the Netherlands in 1777 and found employment as a butler to the Countess of Roosendaal.⁵⁵ Tabo Jansz, servant to Adriaan van Bredehoff, a Dutch politician, used the twelve thousand florins he inherited from him to open a tobacco shop. The fact that he stayed in Oosthuizen, the same small town in North Holland where he had long lived as a servant, indicates the possibility of social mobility for blacks. Soon afterward, he married a Dutch woman, Wolmetje Bakkers, and changed his name to Adriaan de Bruijn—which translates as "Adrian the Brown," a sign that race remained a marker.⁵⁶ Jacob Rühle, son of a German man and an African woman, was a manager of the WIC's warehouse in Amsterdam. He became wealthy from his participation in the slave trade and from his family's holdings in Surinam.⁵⁷ Johanna Emicke, daughter of a German plantation manager and a slave woman, moved from Surinam to the Netherlands and married a white Dutchman in 1829. According to the marriage contract, the estates were kept separate, and her wealth amounted to twenty thousand florins.⁵⁸

The image we get from the records, then, is of a variety of people who went about their daily lives, worked, fell in love, got baptized, got old, became respectable, or committed crimes. It is a variegated group, and nothing seems to suggest that their skin color was a fundamental badge of shame. In 1770, a black man from Berbice, currently British Guiana, was baptized in the Frisian village of Dongjum. He had been emancipated as a reward for his "loyalty and bravery" and had settled in Friesland, a province in the far north of the country. Christiaan Congo Loango was born in Central Africa and brought to Holland from Surinam as a valet. He lived in The Hague, got baptized, and married twice. Because he had no birth certificate, he provided authorities with seven character references, and they give us a hint of his connections to probably white workers, as they came from two potato venders, a painter, a shoemaker, a coachman, a fishmonger, and a tailor. Records also show that eleven of his children died in infancy, a cruel reminder of the sufferings commonly shared by many people at the time. In 1829, he received relief from the authorities after an official request from his wife, who described him as "a very good man, being a negro from the Congo." "Now he is blind," she continues, "in his 60s, and has been in this country since he was 16; he is also tormented with rheumatic pain."[59] In 1679, on the other hand, Louis the Moor was sentenced in Leeuwarden, a northern town, to a year in prison for "great wilfulness and godless actions." A group of blacks who had been living in Jodenbreestraat in Amsterdam since 1632 were said to engage in theft and prostitution. In 1768, a certain Christina was sentenced to two years' detention in the Spinhuis, a women's prison in Amsterdam, because she allegedly had an "exceedingly bad and indecent way of life." The Spinhuis owed its name to the women's forced activities within its walls, which included spinning and sewing while sitting together in a large hall. In her punishment, Christina was also a symbol of integration.[60]

Like other Europeans, the Dutch also welcomed a number of black children or young adults, from Africa or from the colonies, who came to the metropole to receive some degree of Western education. These children formed a small, varied group of elite black cosmopolitans that Capitein in many ways belonged to, even if he had been brought to Holland against his will. Jan Elias van Onna, born a slave in Surinam, was freed in 1773, and came to Holland in 1787, where he studied legal and notarial practices. Jan Weyne studied law at the University of Harderwijk, in a town in the center of the country. Philip Samuel Hanssen studied law at the University of Leiden.[61] His sister Susanna, born free in Surinam in 1750, also came to the Netherlands and received an education while living with her brother. Her son would be the artist Gerrit Schouten, renowned for his miniatures of Surinamese life.[62] In his account of his life as a mixed-race plantation overseer in Surinam, Egbert Jacobus Bartelink mentions an old slave woman who had a son with a plantation manager: "The father had bought the son from the plantation, had emancipated him, and had later sent him to study in Holland, where the boy did very well."[63] Of another manager, he says: "He was very attached to me, which I attributed to the fact that he had two mixed-race children—two boys—whom he loved very much. He gave them a good education, and they later found excellent positions in the East as well as in Holland."⁶⁴ Clearly, sending black children to Holland for an education had become commonplace by the second half of the eighteenth century.

Interestingly, the life stories of these travelers highlight the way in which many black cosmopolitans in the seventeenth and eighteenth century worked and thought within prevailing ideas and customs. Indeed, it is their cosmopolitanism that allowed them to accept the status quo and get up in life. After his return to Surinam, Van Onna became the owner of several plantations and more than a hundred slaves.⁶⁵ Elisabeth Samson, who stayed in the Netherlands from 1737 to 1739, went back to Surinam and ended up owning several plantations, including slaves.⁶⁶ In his postemancipation look back at his life as an overseer, Bartelink mentions that he sent his oldest son to Europe to get an education. If one may judge from his account, he was certainly hoping that this stay in Europe would provide his son with the necessary credentials to find a good position, as did the sons of the manager referred to earlier. His mind-set, already clear in the title of his memoir, *Hoe de tijden veranderen* (How the times change), comes across in how he presents former plantation life as the good old days, during which the slaves were not that badly treated. He keeps praising the Dutch men who treated him with respect, and his son's ability to travel seems to be part of a continued attachment to the work ethic and hierarchical values he inherited from his Dutch superiors.⁶⁷

At the same time, though, travel overseas could lead to more enlightened or critical views. After the highest court in Surinam denied her the right to marry a white man, Elisabeth Samson appealed to the States-General in Holland and won the case. According to a contemporary, a slave named Baron was taken to Holland by his master. There he was baptized, learned Dutch, French, and English, and practiced fencing and the use of weapons. When he went back to Surinam, he joined the *marrons,* escaped slaves who lived in the backcountry, and participated in the Boni rebellion in the second half of the eighteenth century.⁶⁸ In spite of his nostalgia for the good old days, Bartelink makes it clear that when emancipation came in 1863, he identified with the slaves: "On the various plantations where I worked with slaves, I had seen in the people that desire for freedom, and together with them I had longed for liberation."⁶⁹ If it hadn't been for the kindness of the Moravian Brothers, he continues, "the people would probably have revolted against the government."⁷⁰ Sending his son abroad may be a reflection of his understanding that times had to change after all, a bit as if the son represented a new generation, unlike himself who, when once asked if he wanted to go to Holland, had answered: "Are you kidding?"[71]

There was one special category of blacks whose job it was to come to Holland, and who were particularly well treated—African ambassadors. As early as the fifteenth century, Philippe Le Bon, Duke of Burgundy, who ended up ruling a major part of the Low Countries until his death in 1467, participated in growing contacts between Europe and Ethiopia. It was widely believed that the king of the Ethiopians was the direct descendant of Solomon and the queen of Sheba, who is mentioned in 1 Kings. These contacts were seen as beneficial to both sides, as Europeans wanted to enlist the help of Christians against Muslims, especially after the fall of Constantinople in 1453, and Ethiopians hoped that Europeans would help them too. The Portuguese used Ethiopians as interpreters in Africa, partly hoping they would help to find Prester John, a legendary Christian ruler. There were attempts to unify the Ethiopian church and the Catholic Church. A monastery for Ethiopian pilgrims was established in Rome. Many Ethiopian ambassadors made their way to Italy, Spain, and Portugal, and in 1452, an Ethiopian ambassador known as Jorge visited Philippe le Bon.[72]

In the next centuries, African ambassadors to the Netherlands received good treatment because, while they were enslaving Africans, like Portugal, England, and France, the Dutch had also been conducting trade with Africans for generations. Even though commercial relations were not always easy, they considered the Africans partners in trade. They devised diplomatic moves, signed or agreed on contracts, formed alliances, bought and sold merchandise. In many ways, Africans were equal partners in a global capitalist enterprise. The Dutch even got used to the presence of African ambassadors on their soil, with all the paraphernalia the position entailed. A painting from the middle of the seventeenth century entitled *Dom Miguel de Castro* shows an ambassador from the Congo come to Holland to ask for help in resolving an internal conflict. His imposing physique and richly decorated outfit seem meant to command admiration: he is portly, and he wears a wide-brimmed hat with a red feather, an ornate blouse covered with a beaded jacket, a big white collar over the shoulders, and a carved scabbard belt across the chest. Olfert Dapper, a famous author of geographical accounts, refers to him and his two servants in his book on Amsterdam, describing them as "strong and sprightly of body" and "highly quick of limb" (Kolfin, 81). It is probable that the Dutch government lent him a favorable ear, since the Dutch had recently taken Luanda, in current Angola, from the Portuguese. Obviously, some blacks in Holland were respectfully received. Capitein seems to have been one of them—or at least that is what he affirmed publicly.

Capitein, Calvinism, and Slavery

By the time he gave his lecture, Capitein had been studying theology at the University of Leiden for five years, and so had become fully immersed in the teachings of the Dutch Reformed Church. The lecture obviously offered him an opportunity to display his erudition and his powers of exegesis, since as we saw, it is a real compendium of ancient, humanist, and biblical quotations. But it also represented his official statement of allegiance to the Dutch Reformed Church, or at least to what the church had morphed into by the first half of the eighteenth century. Like all Calvinists, Capitein speaks from a sense of predestination and providential design, and he believes that God made several covenants with humankind. But he also specifically adheres to a historicist vision, arguing that God's plan has been gradually unfolding and has now been realized in the New Covenant, as expounded in the New Testament. These dimensions of Capitein's Calvinism serve a conservative purpose, as he uses them to argue that Christianity and slavery are perfectly compatible, since they are part of God's design. Ironically, though, this historicism also contains the seeds of more progressive views toward slavery that would develop among black Calvinists later in the century. As we will see, it underlies Capitein's turn toward a slightly more open social vision later in life.

When Capitein arrived in Leiden in 1737, the university was emerging from a long century of sometimes acrimonious theological debate. Though it had been founded as a Protestant institution, it originally had a "moderate, conciliatory, and essentially anti-extremist attitude" (Lunsingh Scheurleer and Posthumus Meyjes, 2). With the influx of refugees from the Southern Netherlands at the end of the sixteenth century, though, "precisians" got the upper hand. Justus Lipsius was one of several scholars who resigned, and in 1594, Franciscus Gomarus, a strict predestinarian, was appointed professor of theology. A decade later, voices started coming out against the strict predestinarian orthodoxy. These Arminians were followers of Jacobus Arminius, who had been appointed professor of theology, and came to be known as Remonstrants. The Synod of Dort, which met from 1618 to 1619 in the city of Dordrecht, in South Holland, reaffirmed the orthodoxy, and the university lay low for a while. Then in the middle of the century, tensions flared up again among theologians and philosophers, this time about the validity of Descartes's philosophy, and a major conflict broke out. Gisbertus Voetius, a professor of theology at the newly founded University of Utrecht, in the heart of the country, was strongly opposed to Descartes, whose rationalism threatened the Aristotelian view that substantial forms or essences inhabit matter.[73] He also had pietistic tendencies, which promoted, among others, a strict Sunday observance, austerity in dress and hairstyle, and the avoidance of diversions such as dancing and cardplaying. Johannes Coccicius, who taught theology in Leiden, encouraged his followers to think for themselves and to devote much time to exegesis and philology. Voetians saw Cocceians as too little focused on piety and too much on reason and learning. Cocceians found piety a superficial objective compared to a perspicacious reading of the Bible. At the time Capitein arrived, Cocceius's influence still predominated.

In his training, Capitein was exposed to the main ideas of the Cocceians, particularly their covenant theology. Anchored in historicism, this theology implied that the Bible contained prophecies of the Christian Church that gradually realized themselves through several "covenants" or special agreements between God and humankind. For example, Cocceius distinguished a "covenant of works," which was in place before Adam disobeyed God, and a "covenant of grace," which unfolded afterward. World history, then, was a gradual unfolding of the Kingdom of God in the course of time, until a new form of unity or harmony in the world was achieved. This approach meant that Cocceians devoted much biblical exegesis to an analysis of prophecies or the way certain elements of the Old Testament were "types" or symbols of elements in the New Testament. Based on detailed interpretations of the Bible, Cocceianism represented a blending of religion and rationalism that came to dominate Dutch religious consciousness in the eighteenth century.[74]

The theologians Capitein studied with were certainly representative of this trend. Taco Hajo Van den Honert, who taught theology at Leiden until his death in 1740, analyzed the Bible closely and systematically in order to prove the gradual revelation of God's plan. His son Johannes, who taught in Leiden from 1734 to 1758, was known as an excellent scholar and a moderate Cocceian. Although he published a complaint about the decline of religion, and some of his admonitions sounded pietistic, he was "deeply interested in the Christian's responsibility for public life" (Van den Berg, 224). Johannes Alberti, appointed professor in 1740, was famous for his rigorous linguistic study and exegesis of the Old Testament. When he signed up for the degree in theology on 22 June 1737, it was this particular philosophical and intellectual community that Capitein was entering. Books by both Cocceius and Van den Honert stand on a shelf behind him in one of the several portraits that were made of him.[75] Capitein's Calvinism, then, differed from the more emotional or pious form of Calvinism many blacks would be exposed to later in the century, whether in the person of George Whitefield, who emphasized the experience of the new birth, or of Theodorus Jacobus Frelinghuysen, Gronniosaw's mentor, who was a Voetian.

Capitein's lecture reflects his training as a Cocceian in that he organizes his argument rationally and historically. As we have seen, he starts chapter 1, in which he defines what he means by slavery, by quoting Cicero's dictum that "every argument about something which is rationally undertaken should proceed from a definition." He then defines slavery as "a status in which someone is unwillingly subjected to the authority of another" (95). In chapter 2, he aims to prove the "ancient origin of slavery" by showing that "nearly all societies made use of it" (97). And in chapter 3, he moves on to the meaning of the New Covenant, which has replaced the old Mosaic law, up until the present day. Under the New Covenant, he argues, slavery and freedom are spiritual rather than bodily concepts. So he builds his thesis by covering the whole biblical history of humankind, with "the New Dispensation superseding the Old" (107). It is this historical continuity in change following the divine will that buttresses his argument.

When trying to locate the origin of slavery, Capitein goes back to Genesis. Interestingly, he rejects Aristotle's argument in *Politics* that some people are naturally slaves and that slavery is anchored in natural law. He insists that, on the contrary, "it is not nature but human law and accident which have made humans into slaves" (98). The first such "accident" happened in Genesis 9:25, when Ham saw his father Noah lying drunk and naked in his tent, and as a consequence, his son Canaan was cursed to be "a slave of slaves to his brothers" (99). This, Capitein argues, is when the history of slavery began. Unlike a popular theory at the time, Capitein does not attach a racial meaning to Ham's episode, which functions purely as a historical marker and not as justification for the enslavement of Africans. The practice then spread quickly, either through commercial transactions or through the "law of nations." The law of nations became "established by popular vote," while Leviticus 25 established slavery among the Jews by "divine institution and mandate" (100). Even though Capitein adopts a common explanation for the origin of slavery, and he connects Ham's story to the act of a "sinner" (99), the thrust of his argument is clearly historical. Wanting to locate "when such a change in human relations took place" (98), he posits that it arose "soon after the flood" (99) and then became widely accepted among the people. The chapter sounds more like social and political science than like theology or philosophy.

When he turns to the New Covenant, Capitein uses a different kind of argument, but it is still fundamentally historicist. His main argument is that any reference to freedom in the New Testament needs to be interpreted metaphorically, as referring not to bodily but to spiritual freedom. More specifically, any mention of deliverance from slavery means a relinquishing of "the burden of ceremonial law" (104), that is, the law of Moses. He starts with an exegesis of 2 Corinthians 3:17, "where the spirit of the lord is, there is freedom." Freedom here, he posits, is opposed to "the yoke of slavery in the form of Mosaic law" (105). This "reign of prescribed law" led to the "servile fear of the Israelites." The New Dispensation relieves Christians of this slavish fear and brings them into grace, as implied by Capitein's reference to Romans 6:14, which promises deliverance from sin not through law but through grace. Paul is referring not to the "literal sense in Mosaic law" but to the "mystical sense . . . something that was not understood in its full sense until the time of the Gospel" (107). Similarly, Capitein notes that in Galatians 5:1 Paul says, *"For freedom Christ has set us free; stand fast therefore, and do not submit again to a yoke of slavery,"* and thus proposes "that slavery is the outer observance of Mosaic law, called the covenant of Sinai" and that "by freedom he means the Dispensation of the New Testament, freed from all those rituals" (108). Capitein's interpretation of slavery and freedom in the Bible is clearly guided by his historicist, New Covenant theology.

His eschatology buttresses this approach. Interpreting John 8:32, *"And you will know the truth, and the truth will make you free,"* he argues that, when they respond to Jesus that they have *"never been in bondage to anyone,"* the Jews misinterpret Jesus's message. Their minds were "bent more on carnal than on spiritual affairs" (111), things that "cannot show the way to everlasting life or extend Christ's kingdom on earth." Freedom here means freedom from sin, which "can lead us to justice" (112). He then quotes from John Calvin, who early in the chapter "On Civil Government" from the *Institutes,* argues that "Christ's spiritual kingdom and the civil order are entirely different matters." Calvin then refers to the same passages from Galatians 5 and 1 Corinthians 7 that Capitein himself has quoted before, commenting that "spiritual freedom can perfectly well coexist with civil bondage" (116). Indeed, says Calvin, it "makes no difference what one's status among humans is or under what nation's laws one lives, since Christ's kingdom does not consist in these things at all" (116–17). To Capitein, the human community needs to strive for justice and freedom from sin, but he projects those ideals into the distant future of Christ's kingdom on earth.

In the last part of the lecture, Capitein goes back to a purely historical argument, positing that, unlike what his "opponents" (117) say, slavery was an accepted practice among early Christians. He brings up laws issued by Constantine the Great, which promoted manumission. Against people who argue that the laws correspond to a wave of manumissions among Christians in the early fourth century, he asks "why this custom was eventually introduced after so long a stretch of time since the age of the Apostles and the first Christians" (120–21). He concludes that these manumissions had nothing to do with Christian doctrine but were meant to increase Christian authority "in human affairs" (121). Similarly, to those who argue that slavery disappeared from the Netherlands because of Christian principles, he answers that the disappearance "must be attributed to political considerations," as slavery existed "both before and after the Netherlands was enlightened by the health-giving glow of the Reformation" (126). With this argument, he reaffirms that slavery does not contradict Christian freedom.

With this lecture, Capitein proclaimed his allegiance to the Dutch Reformed Church of his time. His defense of slavery is anchored less in an essentialist or a racial view than in a historicist theory about the workings of God's providence in the world. He clearly rejects Aristotle and his argument from nature. He makes no mention of the enslavement of Africans; in his concluding reflections, he even mentions the possibility of reinstituting slavery in Holland in order to prevent an accumulation of "dishonest and lazy people" (131) who cannot handle freedom. His reasoning is that if God has allowed slavery to exist since the beginning of times, then it must be compatible with his current plans. He does acknowledge that "Christian charity does not permit Christians to brutalize their slaves and it offers, with the passage of time, the opportunity for slavery to be utterly removed" (127). But like Cocceius, who had a "dynamic, historicizing" approach to the issue, he doesn't yet draw abolitionist conclusions from it.[76]

•

It may seem that Capitein's Calvinist upbringing predisposed him to an acceptance of slavery, and many Calvinists before him had adopted a similar stance. As early as 1627, the merchant Willem Usselincx, who had hoped that the Netherlands would engage in colonization with the use of Dutch farmers because he found slavery inefficient, argued that bodily slavery did not preclude spiritual freedom through Christianization.[77] In 1638, Godfried Udemans, a puritan pastor, published a book of spiritual advice for merchants and mariners, *'t Geestelijck roer van 't coopmans-schip* (The spiritual helm of the merchant's ship), in which he also says that what matters is the distinction between spiritual and bodily freedom, though he does recommend that slaves who convert to Christianity be set free.[78] Like Capitein, commentators often justified their views on the basis of specific passages from the Bible, such as the curse of Ham or Paul's epistle to Philemon, in which he tells him he is sending his slave, Onesimus, back to him.[79] Johannes Crucius wrote a sermon based on Paul's letter arguing that physical slavery does not diminish Christian freedom.[80] These men, including Capitein, who mentions him, also knew that they had backing from Hugo Grotius, a famous seventeenth-century Dutch jurist, who considered the practice of slavery legitimate because it had long been part of the law of nations.[81] It seems that the Reformed Church had capitulated, influenced not just by its "internal logic," but also by "reality."[82]

A Reformed voice here and there did make itself heard against any form of slavery. In *Swart register van duysent sonden* (Black register of a thousand sins), published in 1679, Jacobus Hondius, a pastor from North Holland, counts the slave trade and the mistreatment of Indians and other heathens a sin. A generation later, the minister Bernardus Smytegelt, who was from Zeeland, the province of the slave-trading port Middelburg, was not afraid to speak out against slavery. Both Hondius and Smytegelt argued from the Eighth Commandment, "Thou shalt not steal." In their sermons, they drew from fundamental Christian texts, such as the Apostles' Creed, which consists of twelve basic articles of faith, and the Heidelberg Catechism, a specifically Calvinist catechism. They were also very much inspired by *Het Schat-boeck der Christelycke Leere,* a theological handbook that went through many editions. Following this handbook, Smytegelt made a distinction between serious stealing and less serious stealing, and, referring to Exodus 21:16, which condemns kidnappers to death, he ranked kidnapping among the former. He then added slave trading as a specific example, making it clear that the Old Testament could be a grounding for abolitionism.[83] Another catechism, by Cornelius Poudroyen, also referred specifically to the East and West Indies and linked the Fifth Commandment, "Honor thy father and thy mother," to a criticism of parents who sell their children; he also argued that if someone wants to sell himself, one should buy that person and free him or her.[84] Poudroyen, who had studied with Voetius, showed the possible radical consequences of the Voetian focus on literalism and piety. But these were lone voices, and they had little influence.

Moreover, a number of secular arguments contributed to a defense of slavery. In his overview, Hugo Grotius argued that, historically, there were a number of reasons why people had given up their freedom, such as escaping hunger, poverty, persecution, or execution. Usselincx also reasoned that some people were better off being enslaved because they could not handle freedom.[85] Pastor Heurnius wrote from the East that many people around him had "such a slavish mentality" that they preferred the protection provided by enslavement to the dangers of liberty. To him, slavery was a way of compensating for a society marked by social and economic inequality.[86]

It may not be surprising that Capitein seems to have been sensitive to these more political arguments. At the end of his lecture, he quotes Augier Ghislain de Busbecq, a Flemish diplomat: "Not everybody's nature can endure resourceless freedom and not everyone is born so that they can have control over themselves and know by their own judgment what is right. They need the leadership and rule of their betters" (130). From this perspective, slavery turns into part of the providential plan designed to ensure the development of a harmonious and virtuous society. As such, it trumps the Eighth Commandment, which was usually applied to cases such as beggars having children beg on the streets or people putting girls into prostitution, but not to slavery.[87] While Capitein had originally rejected Aristotle's notion of natural slaves, he was open to an argument that came very close to it for the sake of social and political harmony. By merging his republican grounding with a Cocceian covenant theory, he arrived at conservative conclusions.

But he did not have to. The idea of the covenant, and of a covenanted community, led to radical conclusions among some Calvinist thinkers. According to that interpretation, every single member of the community was bound to his or her promise to God and also had to expel anyone, even a magistrate, who did not contribute to the moral and social goals of the commonwealth.[88] In fact, early in the seventeenth century,

Johannes Althusius, a German political scientist who lived in Friesland for many years and published in Dutch, defended precisely this kind of theory. While, as famous Dutch historian E. H. Kossmann points out, he thought in terms of social order rather than of individual rights, it is still the case that the notion of a covenanted community realizing its promise could have radical implications.[89] Indeed, once in Africa, Capitein would put his theories to different uses. In his lecture, though, he made it clear that he was aligned with his conservative audience. He branded as "fanatics" all those who, "charged up with meaningless spirit," argued that "every magistrate in the Christian world should be removed." Being against those fanatics, "our adversaries" (103), was an important part of his image.

Shaping His Own Image

Shaping his image for the public was something that Capitein apparently knew quite well how to do—and something that contributed positively to enhancing black visibility in the Netherlands, even if his image was tied to a conservative argument. During the few months between his lecture and his departure for Africa, he enjoyed a moment of celebrity that must have comforted him in the choices he had made. Indeed, he became one of the best-known persons in the Netherlands in the eighteenth century, though this fame would quickly dwindle afterward. In their introduction to *Uitgewrogte predikatien,* a publication of some of his sermons, the editors mention that the lecture was received "with much praise and admiration."[90] The lecture was published in Latin, and soon afterward, a Dutch translation came out, and it went through four printings that year. For the rest of his short life, Capitein would remain conscious of the powers of the publishing world. Several portraits of him were also made and circulated widely throughout the republic. All his decisions in this time period indicate that he was aware of the potential rewards of the public's interest in a Dutch-educated African and that he completely embraced the culture that had raised him. Again, though, it seems he adhered to the ideas and methods of his contemporaries, but loosely enough that he retained some independence and flexibility.

•

Overall, Capitein was aware that he was a bit of a curiosity, and he seemed willing to capitalize on that fact. Except for Van Goch, his sister, and his cousin and her husband, we do not know how many people attended his baptism, which took place in the old gothic Kloosterkerk in The Hague on 8 July 1735, when he was about eighteen.[91] But it resonated enough that a Marten Smets wrote a poem about it:

> Who has ever heard such a thing?
> In days gone by, a Moor was baptised by Philip.
> Today, Capitein, another Moor, receives baptism from Philip
>   Manger, that he may live in the true Light. (Kpobi, 58)[92]

The poet refers to Acts 8:26–40, in which Philip the Evangelist converts and baptizes an Ethiopian eunuch. He conveys the Dutch sense of proud astonishment that often marked reactions to Capitein. The African was praised as an exceptional man, but the praise also indirectly confirmed the superiority of Christianity and Western civilization. This first public moment must have impressed upon Capitein how his good fortune depended on his adherence to Christianity.

Shortly after his lecture, several portraits of him started circulating, spreading the image of the scholarly African. They usually show him wearing an elaborate black gown with a white neckband, as well as a black wig. One portrait shows him holding a book, with a bookcase in the background displaying, among others, works by Johannes Cocceius and by Taco Hajo Van den Honert, the Coccean who had been a professor of theology in Leiden. Another portrait shows him wearing a similar outfit and seated behind a table, his right hand on his chest and his left hand resting on a Bible that lies open on the table. The portraits were featured in the Latin and several Dutch editions of his lecture. They became so popular that prints of him decorated the walls of Dutch homes until the end of the eighteenth century; many people professed they had heard him speak.[93] Whether or not the portraits were his idea, he obviously agreed to pose for them, and he even took one of them with him to Elmina.[94]

These portraits brought a new variation to a long history of Dutch portraits of blacks. Capitein must have been aware of the attraction these portraits had for a Dutch public that was not unfamiliar with images of blacks in Dutch settings. Just like the poems about him, the portraits show a mixture of pride about the superiority of Western culture, especially when it comes to its intellectual and religious traditions, and admiration toward an African who has been able to assimilate into it. Indeed, they can be placed within the history of northern European art, whose representations of blacks, while overall positive, show a wide arc over the centuries from the complex and dignified to the stereotypical.

Medieval art representing blacks often conveyed an awareness of racial and cultural difference but without the animus or racist baggage of later representations. The most striking illustration is nativity scenes, in which one of the Magi was almost systematically portrayed as an African. These scenes became particularly popular in the Low Countries and went into virtual mass production, possibly because the richness of the Magi's clothes and presents suggested contemporary luxuries acquired through international trade. The familiarity with black figures may explain why, in the thirteenth century, a magnificent statue of Saint Maurice portraying him as black was made for the Magdeburg Cathedral in Germany. It is possible that the statue was made under the influence of Holy Roman Emperor Frederick II, who had been brought up in Sicily, which had a significant black presence due to its Muslim past, and where artistic representations of Africans were common. He had two black personal assistants, Musca and Marzuch, and his chamberlain, Johannes Maurus, was a black Muslim. This black entourage shows his desire to expand his prestige around the Mediterranean, and portraying Maurice as black may have been part of this policy.[95] As the story goes, Saint Maurice was the leader of an Egyptian legion in the third century, and because he allegedly died for his Christian faith by refusing to honor Roman gods, he became an immensely popular saint. The artist's decision to carve him as a black man put the image of a black saintly warrior in the heart of western Europe. The face of the statue is very dark, has clearly African features, and is attractive and complex.

Positive images predominated in the fifteenth century, which marked a first encounter with real Africans in the northwest of Europe. In their famous illuminated manuscript, *Les très riches heures du Duc de Berry* (The very rich hours of the Duke of Berry), the Limbourg brothers depicted several scenes that included realistic depictions of blacks. In 1430, Philippe le Bon, a Duke of Burgundy who ruled a major part of the Low Countries, married Isabella of Portugal, ensuring a strong connection between northern Europe and a country that, since the beginning of the century, had been busy exploring the western coast of Africa and establishing trade connections there. Portugal needed trading goods such as fabrics and imported a lot of them from northern Europe, and as a consequence, blacks became a familiar sight in Flemish cities such as Ghent, Bruges, and Antwerp. Until the Treaty of Münster in 1648, which led to the closing of the Scheldt River, Antwerp was the biggest European colonial market and a hub for international merchants. According to Jan Denucé, the city counted the highest number of blacks after Lisbon, and city registers mention the birth of a good number of black children in the sixteenth century.[96] Philippe Le Bon commissioned the Flemish miniaturist Loyset Liedet to illuminate many manuscripts, and several of these feature black figures who are clearly presented as dignified allies.[97] It is in Antwerp that one of the earliest European model-based representations of a black person, *Portrait of Katherina*, by Albrecht Dürer, was drawn. The subject was the servant of a Portuguese trade representative in Antwerp.

In the next three centuries, images of blacks in the Low Countries were often positive while respectful, and even admirative, of racial difference, and some major painters produced arresting, complex, and beautiful renderings of black figures. In *The Four Rivers,* Pieter Paul Rubens, a famous seventeenth-century Flemish painter, places a bejeweled Ethiopian nymph in the center of the painting, as the source of the River Nile, and presumably the cause of its fertility. His *Four Studies of the Head of a Negro* remains a milestone in the sophisticated depiction of a black in Western art. The amazing *Moses and His Ethiopian Wife* by Jacob Jordaens, another Flemish painter, shows Moses and a black woman standing partly behind him, the two of them forming a tight couple looking directly at the viewer. Even though Moses appears the prominent figure, with one hand outstretched and the other holding the tablets of the law, his wife's intelligent gaze, wide-brimmed hat, and rich attire convey a sense of dignity and importance.[98] In *Solomon Welcoming the Queen of Sheba,* Jan Boeckhorst, also Flemish, shows the two rulers leaning forward toward each other in a movement of seemingly irresistible attraction. Artists in the Netherlands also produced sophisticated portraits of blacks. Jan Mostaert made a splendid painting of an African man as early as 1520, in which the man's posture, sword, and elegant attire clearly suggest taste, nobility, and high standing.[99] A century later, Rembrandt van Rijn painted *Two Africans,* a subtle depiction of two black men dressed as Roman soldiers. As Elizabeth McGrath points out, these artists "clearly took an artistic interest in the figuration of blackness, not only in terms of familiar devices of opposition and variety, but by visualising the possibility of physical attraction between blacks and whites" (277).

As time went on, however, especially over the course of the eighteenth century, more and more stereotypical black figures appeared in paintings. Many standard figures, such as young black pages and servants, are to be found in representations of the Dutch middle class in the seventeenth century.[100] According to Allison Blakely, "The Lowlands produced more of this type of art than any other area in the world," and "England was the only other country that even comes close in this regard to the Netherlands and Belgium" (105). One finds young black servants performing all sorts of tasks, whether it be presenting food or flowers to richly clad white ladies or holding a helmet for an admiral who is busy conquering the world as he stands by a telescope, a map, and a globe. Clearly, blacks became associated with a servile status, and while their presence commonly served to accentuate the white characters' beauty or sophistication, they more or less blended into the background and disappeared.[101]

The portraits of Capitein could be seen as belonging to that trend in Western art, in that they represent him as having completely absorbed Western influence in spite of his Africanness. One of the portraits features the following short poem by Capitein's friend Brandijn Ryser:

> Observer contemplate this African: his skin is black
> but his soul is white, since Jesus himself prays for him.
> He will teach the Africans faith, hope and charity;
> with him, the Africans, once whitened, will always honor the
>   Lamb. (*Agony*, 49)

Whiteness here can have the traditional meaning of salvation, but it also very much sounds like a racial attribute. Deep down, the poet says, Capitein is white like us. The Dutch public's adulation of this young African was thus based on a negation of its multiculturalism, on a whitening and erasing of his difference. Capitein seemed happy to go along with the suggestion.

It is hard to evaluate the role Capitein played in the building of this image. There are indications that he was uncomfortable with his popularity. During the few months before his departure, he gave several sermons throughout the country, two of which were immediately published because attendance had been so huge that many people had not been able to hear him. One of those sermons was in Ouderkerk aan den Amstel, and at the time, he stayed at the country house of Willem Backer, one of the directors of the WIC.[102] One might think that such royal treatment might have improved his confidence, but in their introduction, the editors of *Uitgewrogte predikatien* write that one reason they are publishing the sermons is that the big crowds made Capitein feel a bit indisposed and so affected his performance.[103] In his 1744 introduction to the publication of Capitein's inaugural sermon at Elmina, Hieronymus de Wilhelm, a former fellow student and probably a friend, alleges that the book of sermons was published without Capitein's knowledge or the advice or authorization of friends and that the sermons in the book differ significantly from the ones Capitein gave.[104] It is not hard to believe that some publishers tried to take advantage of Capitein's sudden fame.

He was clearly also not responsible for the various poems he inspired countless people to write in his honor. The fourth Dutch edition of his lecture contains, besides an introductory poem by Brandijn Ryser, seven more poems written by, among others, a widow, a medical student, a law student, and a painter. The collection of sermons starts off with five poems. Albert Eekhof, his biographer, found more published poems in a box at the provincial library of Zeeland in Middelburg. All these poems praise Capitein for his academic achievement, his friendliness, and his aptitude as a representative of God both in Holland and abroad. They wish him well in his endeavor to convert the Africans. In one of those poems, interestingly, Capitein is encouraged to spread the Gospel, even if he stands in the way of plunderers who "are buyers and sellers of their fellow men, O! shameful evil!"[105] In the end, whether he planned it or not, Capitein's reputation turned him into a famous emissary out to Christianize Africa and Westernize the Atlantic world. Still, this surge of creativity about the phenomenon of Capitein—and the mention of his possible antagonizing of slave traders—indicates that he helped promote an image of Africans as capable of cultural interventions.

He was certainly able to shape his image with the five sermons he gave while in the Netherlands: two about Ephesians 2:19, one about 2 Timothy 2:8, and two about Proverbs 8:18. Indeed, all of these biblical passages emphasize ideas that mattered to this young black Calvinist. In Ephesians, Paul stresses the importance of the unity of the church and warns against division and self-interest; the second chapter urges the reconciliation of Jews and Gentiles; verse 19 tells the converted Gentiles that "you are no longer foreigners and strangers, but fellow citizens with God's people and also members of his household." In the second chapter of 2 Timothy, Paul compares himself to a soldier of Christ, an athlete, and a hardworking farmer, all of whom persevere and stay focused on higher goals. The eighth chapter of Proverbs sings the praise of wisdom and rightfulness over against the lure of material wealth: "With me are riches and honor, enduring wealth and prosperity." Capitein's popularity may have been due to the fact that he was reminding his Dutch audience of their own deep stoic yearnings in an age of materialism. The sermon on Timothy, for example, emphasized "acceptance of suffering and oppression as an inevitable aspect of a Christian's life" (Kpobi, 125). His racial difference made his calls for unity and citizenship even more real.

•

One wonders if the Leiden lecture was really less an endorsement of surrounding ideology than a rite of passage he deemed necessary to achieve some independence. While his stance on slavery tallied with predominant Dutch views, the lecture can also be seen mostly as a way to sell his evangelization plans. His whole education had been pursued with that goal in mind. He starts the preface to the lecture by referring to a thesis he wrote at the end of his secondary studies, entitled *De vocatione ethnicorum* (On the calling of the heathen). According to his description of it, the thesis laid out the major reasons why evangelization is necessary, and it gave some specific advice on how to deal with heathens gently and persuasively. It is imperative to spread the Gospel, he argued in the thesis, because one of the features of the New Dispensation is that "worship of God must no longer be restricted to one place or one race" (*Agony*, 83). The Gospel has to be taken to "people across the seas, people who have until this day been enveloped in the darkest cloud of ignorance, and who have not been reached by God's word" (85). His whole lecture then comes across less as an intervention to promote slavery than as reassurance that evangelization will not threaten its existence. In its conclusion, he hopes to have shown that "slavery does not impede the spread of the Gospel in those Christian colonies where it prevails right up to the present day" (131–32). By the time he gave the lecture, he had already received an offer from the WIC, so the whole argument serves as a justification for the work he was about to undertake rather than a wholehearted embrace of the institution of slavery.

Even that undertaking, moreover, does not always seem to conjure up his deep enthusiasm. In the will he had drawn up in January 1734, Van Goch had already asked that his heirs, his two sisters Elisabeth and Catharina, make sure that Capitein be well taken care of and receive the planned religious education so he could go back to "the coast of Guinea to seek his fortune there."[106] So from very early on, a plan had been laid out for Capitein. Indeed, his defense of his mission in the lecture often sounds like an expression of a sense of duty. Certainly, he is thankful to be a Christian, and he feels that his life's work should be an expression of his gratitude to God. But he often emphasizes obligation rather than gratitude. For example, he is aware of "God's providential care for me" (86), and he understands that "those who by God's wondrous prudence and goodness converted from paganism to Christianity can be of use in spreading the Gospel." As if catching himself, he then adds that they "should in fact commit themselves to this endeavor." As a consequence, just as in Matthew 10:6 the apostles were told to take care of the Jews first, "hence I have always thought that the greatest obligation was placed upon me also to be useful to my people at some time." Again, there comes an addendum: "This, I would say, is the greatest obligation, and no injustice" (85). He is always careful to convey his adherence to the program of evangelization laid out for him, but one may wonder, as we did earlier, to what degree his desire to perform the work of evangelization away from the comforts of Holland was heartfelt and whether the evangelical zeal expected from him was not tempered by his interest in other things of this world.

Among his motivations was also clearly a desire to achieve a degree of financial independence. The number of people he thanks shows he benefited from numerous persons who invested in his education. The list is long, but he dutifully mentions them all: Van Goch raised him and paid for his studies; Hendrik Velse suggested he be sent to the Latin school and "set aside his own funds for me" (90); F. C. Roscam, an educated woman who taught him languages privately, "makes her house available to young students without charge"; "the influential and noble Peter Cunaeus" (92) became his patron; finally, in order that he be able to attend college, "the most honorable curators of the University of the Hague and the most eminent senators of Holland graciously bestowed their patronage on me" (93).[107] As one of the five *maecenaten,* or directors, Cunaeus made it possible for Capitein to receive funding from the Hallet scholarship fund. The conditions of the scholarship involved good moral behavior on the part of the student, as well as the delivery of one lecture every year that would be dedicated to the *maecenaten.* The title page of Capitein's published lecture is followed by a dedication that lists the names of the directors of the Hallet scholarship fund.[108] Finally, the minutes of the 3 July 1741 meeting of the Hallet fund managers reveal that Capitein did not want to leave as early as he did, but the WIC insisted, so he planned to leave in April but asked the *maecenaten* to still allow him the funds for a whole year so he could use them to purchase books and other necessities for the journey. The *maecenaten* readily agreed.[109]

All these financial acknowledgments and arrangements show that, as pointed out earlier, Capitein had absorbed an important dimension of Dutch culture. One wonders how many times his various patrons impressed upon him that, as an African, he could not take his good treatment for granted, how in fact, he owed them something in return for their largesse. He seems to have absorbed the lesson but also to have shaped the opportunities that came his way as well as he could. He was not just motivated by religious considerations, though he certainly maintained the image that he was.

Calvinist and Cosmopolitan

It does appear that, when he left for Africa in 1742, Capitein thought of himself as a representative of Dutch, and overall Western, interests. Of course, he conceived of his religion as a fountain of universal truth. But he was also aware of his position as intimately bound up with the interests of the WIC, and he may have seen an intricate connection between his own status and Holland's national glory. First of all, he was an employee paid by the company, and his not insubstantial salary—the second highest after that of the director general—was an indication of his rank. Moreover, he had left Holland a famous man. Throughout his career at Elmina, the major Dutch post on the West African coast, Capitein would regularly send pieces to Holland to be published, thus maintaining a public persona that, though it highlighted his difference, made him a part of the eighteenth-century Dutch discourse about Africa.

Yet Capitein's letters during the five years he stayed at Elmina show a gradual change, if not in ideology, at least in perspective. After spending fifteen formative years in Holland, Capitein now saw his life itinerary as an arc that had brought him back to "my kindred according to the flesh." These people did realize that "I differ from them in manner of life and in religion" (Kpobi, 235), but he conceived of this marginality as having potential. While his main objective was to convert Africans, he seems to have developed a sensitivity for others' points of view. His mission entailed the expansion of the Calvinist covenant, but within this particular ideological framework, there was a republican element that allowed him to adapt to his new environment and to make gestures toward new forms of community. His untimely death cut the process short, but it seems that Capitein was on his way to developing a more inclusive, multiracial form of cosmopolitanism.

•

From the moment he arrived at Elmina on 8 October 1742, Capitein became part of a strictly enforced social hierarchy inside the castle. The Dutch had occupied the place since 1637, and it had become the headquarters of WIC activities on the western coast of Africa. It was a little world all to itself, since the company was fairly independent, having been given broad powers by its charter to establish settlements and administer them, pass contracts, wage war. The year Capitein arrived, the castle housed 107 people, out of 241 employed by the WIC on the African coast.[110] At its head was the director general, Jacob de Petersen, who relied on a council made up of high-ranking officers, including the superintendent, the financial executive, the equipage master, the military commander, the chief administrator, and the chaplain. The chaplain was considered third in the hierarchy, after the director general and the superintendent.[111] As a chaplain, Capitein was an important representative of the moral and religious order inside the castle.

His initial correspondence with the company, though, seems more bent on secular concerns, as he presents himself as a—grateful—representative of its political and financial power. In his introduction to the edition of the first sermon he held at Elmina, barely two weeks after he arrived, he addresses the WIC as the rightful owner and "lawful masters" (Kpobi, 217) of the coastal area, which he later calls "this your country, Most Noble and Honourable Gentlemen." He then reminds his readers that he has now returned to the site of his early education, a place that his benefactor left after working "industriously and faithfully for a period of sixteen years." After establishing this historical continuity between himself and Van Goch, he points out that, by giving his first sermon, "I have obtained a closer and better relationship with you, Most Noble and Honourable Gentlemen." He then expresses the hope that in the future, "your sons" (218) will continue the work they have started. Religious objectives are of course very much present in the text, but what comes through more strongly is his preoccupation with his status as someone who displays "loyalty" and who plays his role among his "fellow-citizens" (217). In the closing paragraph, usually a moment of formulaic wishes for the addressee's well-being, he asks that the Lord extend their lives to old age, fill their houses with blessings, make those who lie under their roofs "receive blessings of breasts and of the womb, with income from the East and from the West, from the North and from the South," and make their lives "overflow with income" (219). This rather capitalist take on Genesis 28:14, which does not have the notion of income, reveals that he thinks of Africa as a site for both ideological and financial investment. In his first letter to the company, he describes his task as "spreading the gospel and promoting the interests of your Company" (234), putting the two objectives in an indissoluble bond.[112]

In this initial response to his new environment, Capitein was adopting a view that was fairly similar to that of the WIC. This attitude can best be described as a mixture of a sense of sovereignty with an awareness of how collaboration with the townspeople served the company's financial and commercial interests. In its relationship to the town over the past century, the WIC had managed to play an important role in the lives of the townspeople while at the same time maintaining its aura of independence, separateness, and occasional superiority. The Elminans had mostly acquiesced, since in many ways acquiescence gave them some protection and was also in their own economic interest. So the townspeople and the WIC employees were caught in a relation of "mutual advantage and self-interest" (Feinberg, 145), with the company possessing some authority, but both sides aware that they were dependent on the good will of the other. In 1722, the WIC had posted placards at all its trading posts that urged company personnel to "treat all natives with gentleness and friendly words and deeds, in order that they bring their commerce to the company factories . . . so that the WIC might benefit" (Postma, 70).

This combination of collaboration and authority manifested itself in commercial, judicial, and military matters. The contract between the fort and the town enforced a certain dependence on the Africans. The director general was also regularly asked to join the town's elders to sit in court and participate in judgments. There was a tribunal at the castle that heard cases on appeal, and Elminans often filed wills with the WIC. The Dutch also took advantage of the *asafo* system, in which the town was divided into several wards, each with its own military unit. Regularly they would pay the wards in exchange for military assistance. After the WIC purchased Fort Groß Friedrichsburg from the Brandenburg African Company and the occupier, John Conny, refused to leave it, the Dutch enlisted a number of *asafos* in order to oust him. The 1724 expedition resulted in a reorganization of the wards into a ranking system that profoundly transformed the relationship between the wards and gave the ward leaders increasing political power. In 1755, after several conflicts erupted between the wards, the Elminans and the Dutch signed a contract; one of its provisions entailed that "major problems between the wards were to be brought to the director general" (Feinberg, 108). The ward leaders were a force to be reckoned with, but the ultimate judge remained the director general.

This does not mean that the Elminans did not assert their independence when they felt it necessary. In 1738, Director General Martinus de Bordes ordered Elmina to attack Eguafo, as a follow-up on their victory over the Fante. The Elminans refused. De Bordes threatened to fire on the town and even started negotiating with the enemies. When he prevented the townspeople's boats from reaching the sea, they asked for an explanation and, not receiving any, they started crowding up in front of the castle. The Dutch then fired into the crowd. At this point, the townspeople blockaded the castle, seized WIC property, and imprisoned WIC employees and slaves. De Bordes, outraged by what he considered insolent and hostile behavior, bribed the Fante to attack the town. The townspeople successfully resisted. Only with the death of De Bordes was a truce finally reached between the castle and the townspeople.

The Elminans could also exert pressure when it came to sending Africans overseas. In 1732, Tekki, an assistant to the broker or middleman Abocan, was accused of trying to eliminate him. The attempted act was considered treasonous by the Elmina leaders because Tekki was associated with the Fante, who were enemies of Elmina. Tekki was charged and incarcerated in the castle at the request of the leaders, who then insisted that he be banished to America. Director General Jan Pranger acceded to their request and deported Tekki to Surinam. Once in Surinam, Tekki brought his case before the WIC authorities. In Amsterdam, the directors of the WIC reviewed the appeal and rejected it, but ten years later, he was finally allowed to return to Elmina. The Dutch immediately put him in prison, but this time, the leaders asked the director general to release him. De Petersen complied, and the case was settled.[113] In another episode that took place in 1746—when Capitein lived at the fort—a ship from Amsterdam captured seven Elmina men and took them to the West Indies to be sold as slaves. Faced with the Elminans' anger and demand that the men be returned, De Petersen notified the directors in Amsterdam and asked them to find the men and return them to Africa. He assured the townspeople that what had happened was "without the least legal basis and contrary to the right of the people on this coast" (Feinberg, 142). Five of the men were finally returned in 1750, and the relatives of the deceased were compensated. When Capitein arrived at Elmina, he must quickly have become aware of the complex jockeying that marked the relationship between castle and town. In any case, his first letters seem to reflect a heightened awareness of his position as a representative of Dutch power on the coast.

•

But life as a chaplain at Elmina was not easy. Most of the employees who worked there did not belong to the most reputable layers of European society. Many were prone to drinking and fighting and generally exhibited behavior typical of what was then called the "dregs" of the nation. Even among the upper echelons of the hierarchy, there was much friction and corruption. When Director General Abraham Houtman, shortly after he arrived in September 1722, tried to fight corruption, he received so much pushback that he tended his resignation in May 1723, stating that his colleagues were lazy, did not know anything about trade, and were most of the time drunk.[114] Lack of hygiene, boredom, excesses, and general distrust were a major part of life at the fort.[115] Capitein's duties as a chaplain involved delivering sermons, performing sacraments, holding catechism lessons, and tending to the sick and the dying. A few months after he arrived, he sent the WIC a general assessment, in which he noted that attendance at catechism was very low because most people living at the castle were either Catholic or Lutheran, and the Reformed were "thoroughly occupied with daily activities" (Kpobi, 237).[116] There were only seventeen Reformed Church members, most of whom did not have an attestation of their membership, and Capitein thought it best that they send for their attestation papers or make a new confession of faith before they were allowed the communion. Few seemed interested. His work as a minister did not promise to be rewarding.

The history of ministers at Elmina was certainly no good omen. There was no religious component in the company's original charter, but after the Amsterdam consistory sent a delegation to the directors in July 1623, ministers and *ziekentroosters,* or comforters of the sick, started being appointed.[117] Most ministers on the Gold Coast have stories of failure. Jan Hermansz, who arrived at Fort Nassau in 1617, left almost immediately, as heavy drinking, loudness, and mocking attitudes made him feel as if he were "casting pearls before swine" (Frijhoff, 312). Jonas Michaëlius arrived there in late 1625, after the fleet he was on, bound for Brazil, was redirected to the African coast; he left within the next two years.

During his short stay, he wrote to the Classis of Enkhuizen, in North Holland, asking if he could baptize two "mulaetkens"; the African mothers had made the request, counting either on financial advantage or on access to education; the children could then be sent to Holland for instruction in the Reformed religion. We do not know if the baptism took place.[118] Laurentius Benderius, who was at Fort Nassau from 1630 to 1633, tried to convert Africans, but to no avail; he even opened a school, but he gave up after a few months, partly because of a lack of books in the language of the native people.[119] Meynaert Hendricksen tried to start a school at Elmina in the 1640s, but the WIC never sent a teacher, and the project fell apart.[120] In 1667, Bartholomeus Ysebout complained of all the drinking and "whoring" that was going on at Elmina.[121] By "whoring," he meant the widespread practice of *calacharen*—a word derived from the Portuguese *casar*—or cohabitation between white men and African women. His constant moralizing turned him into a laughing stock, and in 1670, he asked to be relieved of his post. In 1731, J. C. Schies also sounded thoroughly discouraged. He was distraught about the sexual mores. He had also tried to learn the language of the local Africans, but without success. A few years before Capitein's arrival, Christian Jacob Protten, a mulatto who had been trained in Europe as a Moravian missionary—the Moravian denomination was well known for its missionary work—tried to set up a school, but because of conflicts with Director General De Bordes, he was imprisoned, and he left Elmina shortly after being freed.[122] Most of these attempts seem to have been hampered by problematic relationships ministers had with both Europeans and Africans.

Most Protestant ministers on the Gold Coast, black or white, had little luck with conversion or even school instruction. Philip Quaque, one of the most famous Africans to have trained in Europe and returned to the coast, had little to show for the forty-five years he spent at Cape Coast Castle as an Anglican minister. The many letters he sent to the Society for the Propagation of the Gospel are suffused with feelings of isolation and failure. In the end, he converted few people and rarely managed to foster sustained interest in his young scholars.[123] His predecessor, seasoned missionary Thomas Thompson, had had high hopes but equally little luck.[124] Christian and Rebecca Protten set up a school at Fort Christiansborg in Accra, specifically intended for mixed-race children, who were "to be educated to serve the interests of the Danish government and the fort" (Sensbach, 223), but the task proved difficult. Like Protestants all over the Atlantic world, these ministers found that cultural and linguistic differences, combined with an often unappealing religious practice—certainly compared to Roman Catholicism—enticed few native inhabitants. The Dutch Reformed Church had similarly little success with Indians in the New World, though not for lack of effort.[125] For more complex reasons, Protestant slave conversion was also hit and miss.[126] Not until the rise of more emotional forms of evangelicalism in the course of the eighteenth century did nonwhite Protestantism gain significant ground.

From the beginning, Capitein was aware that his work entailed building a strong relationship with the townspeople. The town was economically heavily dependent on the castle. It had about fifteen thousand inhabitants, many of whom survived by selling vegetables, fruit, and fish to the Europeans. The castle was also always in need of domestics, rowers, and skilled workers. All in all, the WIC gave the townspeople enough employment that they made about seventy thousand guilders a year.[127] Most inhabitants lived on the peninsula on which the castle was built, which was separated from the rest of the town by the Benya River.[128] Many houses were made of stone, and the houses stood very close together, so that the overall impression was "of a tightly packed settlement, with the majority of the town's more than 1000 stone buildings crowded close to the castle" (Feinberg, 80). By the time Capitein arrived, though, a good portion of these buildings had been destroyed by cannon shot and fire during the major conflict that had taken place between the Dutch and the Elminans a few years before. Overall, the main contacts between the Dutch and the Elminans outside the castle seem to have taken place at the market or in the sexual relationships between WIC employees and African women—though these relationships were officially condemned by the company's policy.[129]

Capitein quickly invested himself in his conversion work, and more particularly in the teaching of literacy, all the time being aware that the townspeople's collaboration was important. As soon as he arrived, he established a primary school. In the assessment, he is happy to announce that eighteen to twenty children have enrolled. They included black children and *Tapoejers,* the children of white fathers and black mothers, either enslaved or free, as well as a few white children.[130] He sounds genuinely thrilled when he reports on their academic progress. "As concerns the zeal, natural intelligence and progress of this small group of schoolchildren," he says, "to this point we are astonished and thoroughly satisfied." By "we," he is referring to himself and Elmina's teacher, Abraham Suurdeeg. "Their natural intelligence varies," he continues, "as it does among other peoples, with one person being more able than another." Overall, "their progress to this point exceeds what we had expected." He even hopes that he might send a few of those children to Holland for their education, provided the WIC approves, and "with the consent of the children themselves, their parents and teachers" (Kpobi, 239). A few months later, he is overjoyed to report an attendance of forty-five pupils as a result of a conversation he decided to have with the elders of the town. The school has now been moved to a bigger room, and Capitein sounds happy and more confident. The letter is dated 18 April 1743. In his November 1743 letter, he indicates that the number of students has yet increased. In his 29 October 1744 letter, he states that most of the schoolchildren are now able to read, most know the Lord's Prayer and the Ten Commandments, and the more advanced are learning the Heidelberg Catechism. He is now impatient to send a few of them to Holland for higher education. Indeed, fourteen of the additional children had been sent by the Ashanti king, Opoku Ware, who had heard of Capitein, and who originally wanted them sent to Holland for an education, as part of his strategy to promote a rapidly expanding Ashanti empire. As late as 23 May 1746, Capitein tells the WIC that he has "once again enlarged the school" (255). All of this indicates that Capitein was among the most successful literacy promotors on the Gold Coast; his group of students was exceptionally interracial.

The fact that Capitein expresses such strong enthusiasm about this part of his mission indicates a commitment to creating shared knowledge and shared moral goals in a situation that was racially, culturally, and politically unique. Eurocentrism and ethnocentrism were of course major ingredients here, but his identity as an African and a native of the Gold Coast added some subtlety to his position. Indeed, in his first sermon at Elmina, he states the well-known yet apparently still amazing fact that "yes, my early education actually took place in this your Main Castle (where I now find myself)" (Kpobi, 217). His caveat about seeking consent from parents and children shows an awareness of both the townspeople's and the whites' preoccupations and priorities. (By contrast, a century earlier, ministers in Brazil had devoted energy and money to a plan to educate Tupi children without consulting with the parents, and the plan foundered.)[131] Capitein was aware that some parents refused to send their daughters to school and catechism because it would "spoil" them for *calacharen*. The parents knew that, once Christian, their daughters would understand that this sort of relationship would "not be tolerated in the fatherland for religious reasons" (239).

Capitein also realizes that the reason very few white Reformed men would ever attend communion was that they did not want to relinquish the practice and so could not take communion with a good conscience. He also knew that the Thirteenth Article of the Instructions to Ministers required that such behavior "*be punished with appropriate exhortation and reprimand* as an *undisciplined and improper act.*" Still, he writes the WIC, "seeing that this practice is of such long standing here, and is so deep-rooted that it can be countered only by appeal to certain selected texts from Holy Scripture," he prefers to "await further orders" (238). While he duly presents the situation as morally reprehensible, Capitein's tone is rather impatient and pragmatic. He understands and evaluates the needs of all the parties involved and seems to realize that decisions by the book may not work. As he puts it in the April 1743 letter, "I remind myself constantly that the initial plans of all undertakings, and especially the work which I have to do here, are often subject to change" (241).

With this last statement, Capitein displays a pliability and a flexibility that sound new. Finding himself in a new community, he became quickly involved, made a substantial contribution to educating a multiracial group of children, developed regular contacts with the townspeople, and tried to be a minister to all around him. Even though he did not approve of it, he also understood the sexual dynamic of the community, and far from being appalled, he seemed to desire a solution that would not undermine the contacts that were being established between castle and town. He was equally aware of the economic motivations behind such behavior since, as he put it in a letter a few years after arriving, cohabitation was advantageous to the girls' families and as a consequence, "many of these concubines are to be found here, who are not only loved far more than the minister and the beadle but also earn more than both of them put together" (Kpobi, 252).[132] In the same letter, he points out that some white Christian men genuinely want to avoid cohabitation and wish to marry an African woman. But since the Great Statute Book instructed that a Christian was not allowed to marry a non-Christian, he asks his readers for advice. And one does feel some impatience—what makes Kwesi Kwaa Prah say that, "in his own flabby, inconsequent, and indecisive way," Capitein "seemed to express inarticulate and rather muted rebellion" (2). The best way he knew how, Capitein projected himself into the lives of blacks and whites around him as he searched for ways to foster a harmonious, integrated community.[133]

These actions were of course part of his missionary theology. In *On the Calling of the Heathen,* he had argued that it was important to establish "an intimate relationship" with the people one aims to convert, so that "while they learn of that delightful sweetness of Christian brotherhood, they are drawn into it" (*Agony,* 82). In this, he was obviously influenced by Hendrik Velse, one of his mentors, who had made similar recommendations in an essay about the work performed by Danish Moravian missionaries in Tranquebar, in the south of India. Velse particularly insisted on learning the language of the people, and Capitein would follow those recommendations closely.[134]

But while it is clear that Capitein was following all these formulas and recommendations during the first years of his stay at Elmina, his letters also reveal a deep emotional involvement in his work that suggests he may have developed a new vision of community, or that he drew from his republican foundation to respond to his new environment. His sympathy extends to the various people and communities around him. He may even have felt a certain elation at the thought that his cosmopolitan background was, for the first time in his life, allowing him to create new kinds of bonds and a sense of communal living. True, his notion of community was limited. Nowhere does he make mention of slaves, even though slaves were regularly held in the castle. The loss of the WIC monopoly in 1734 meant that free traders were now the only participants in the purchasing and transporting of Africans, but they regularly stopped at Elmina.[135] It is also the case that his work had to stand within the limits of a Christian evangelical ideology. But within that small sphere of influence, it seems that Capitein reconceptualized himself as the promoter of a community anchored in positive interracial exchange. And it is his republican outlook that made this growth possible, through his constant focus on the common good of the community.

His stake in the project was also personal. A few months after his arrival, he wrote to the company that he wished to marry "a young negress who was not only born here in Elmina, but has also shown herself to be fitter for and better capable of education than most." The major reason he mentions for wishing to marry her is "the happier advance and more rapid achievement of this my great objective" and the hope he would "win the affection and trust of the negroes here at Elmina." While these reasons did fit with his overall project, he also speaks from the Africans' point of view, saying he truly believes that his work is "in their best interests" (Kpobi, 235). But then he also points out that the marriage will help him to "preserve and arm myself against the temptations of Satan" (236). In other words, Capitein had found an attractive young woman, and he wanted her. Suddenly, he was building a new vision of his future: they would get married and start a family, and he would become a full and respected member of the local community. He had met the parents, and they had given their permission. His gradual rapprochement with Africa was about to get a boost, and the letter can barely hide his excitement.

But there was a glitch. The young woman had first to be educated and Christianized, but no one at the castle was available or proper for individual instruction, and the parents did not want to send her to Holland. Capitein urgently asked the company for advice. Then, two months later, in April 1743, he writes full of joy that he is particularly happy about the increase in school attendance because the young woman can now attend school with other children her age, and very soon nothing will stand in the way of their marriage. Still, the plan fell apart. In February 1745, the Classis—the official organ of the Reformed Church in Amsterdam—wrote him a stern letter reprimanding him for his plans to marry a "heathen." This they deemed "in many respects unbecoming." They reminded him that he had been "set apart as a leader in the congregation by the laying on of hands" (Kpobi, 250).[136] Finally, in a May 1746 letter, Capitein announces that he has "long since dispensed with this intention," and he has married a recently arrived "young European Christian girl" (252). Critics speculate that the young girl had been sent specifically for him from Holland. A scandal had been averted.

The racial and cultural politics of this conflict show the extent to which Capitein tried to take control, not just of his personal life, but of his ideological trajectory. In its 3 October 1746 letter, the Classis writes: "That you have abandoned the idea of marriage with a negress who has not yet become a Christian in the hope that she would become one, and have now bound yourself in marriage to a Christian girl is very pleasing to us" (Kpobi, 257). Interestingly, the Classis was more than ready to promote an interracial marriage over an intraracial one in order to enforce their religious ideology. This attitude is after all not that surprising considering the Dutch history of racial thought sketched out earlier. It is Capitein's move that is surprising. Natalie Everts has shown that a number of European men and African women developed meaningful relationships on the Gold Coast.[137] But as a representative of the Dutch Reformed Church on the African coast, Capitein knew that he symbolized a particular cultural order. Still, he was willing to tamper with this order and even showed enthusiasm about doing so. His new cultural vision, which was also subtly coming across in his numerous questions regarding sexual rules, was to him the logical political consequence of a diverse environment.

By the time the Classis answered, though, Capitein had developed a bleaker outlook, especially after a significant event undermined his progressive, historicist vision. On 1 July 1745, he writes the WIC that, after a "diligent enquiry," he has found the community's church and baptismal register. He is appalled to discover that the register is very incomplete and even suspects that some of it has been suppressed. He finds a list of baptized children for the years 1683 to 1735 and 1740, then about sixty pages of blank paper, then a complaint from the minister, Isaacus Ketelanus, that the Lord's Supper was not celebrated for forty-two years until 1733. The rest of the register alternates blank pages with a few lists of names. He draws several conclusions from this find, but the first reaction is horror at the loss of church records. Later in the letter, he asks to be "relieved of my duties" because "if the condition of our congregation and school must remain always as it is even now," then the lack of interest on the part of the people of Elmina and, what is more, "their hope that they and their descendants will be freed of even the least expense in this regard," will ensure that his work will come to naught, and both the Europeans and the Africans will ensconce themselves in what he considers a heathen state. While he points out that, as a result, the expectations of the people who "spared no costs to enable me to study" (Kpobi, 248) would be dashed, it is his religious vision of the spreading of the New Covenant to Africa that suddenly falls apart. With the past erased or blank, and the future an image of recession, a historical trajectory he does not want to be a part of, one that goes against his covenantal theology, Capitein prefers to leave.

And yet, in that same letter, he can't help making plans. He concludes from the register that both legitimate and illegitimate children were baptized and then sent back to their parents without receiving any further religious instruction. Ideally, he would baptize the children and place them in a sort of seminary or orphanage where they could be sheltered from heathen influences. He then asks the directors of the WIC to read particular sections from Velse's essay on the Danish missionaries and to give him moral and financial support in order to carry out that plan at Elmina. The text he refers to is actually about evangelization in the West Indies. In this text, Velse suggests establishing plantations where black children could be Christianized apart from the others. They would also learn a trade, so that they could later be returned to plantation work.

The plantation would then miraculously be transformed into a virtuous village, with the owner acting more as a paternalistic lord than as an authority figure.[138] It is not quite clear how Capitein envisioned bringing about this project in the context of Elmina, and the colonialist implications of this sort of social engineering are more than obvious. But within the frame of his ideological resources, Capitein was searching for a way to promote a harmonious, religious, and productive social unit. Interestingly, though, while the WIC had given him carte blanche when it came to the baptism of children, it responded rather coolly to the idea of "a nursery school or orphanage" (Kpobi, 256).[139] It seems that, in his vision of social harmony, he had diverged from the company's fundamentally commercial ideology.

No one knows how Capitein died, but we know that his last year at Elmina was rife with conflicts and disappointments that made him feel isolated and unsupported. It took two years for the WIC to answer his letters, and its first letter, which he received on 3 May 1745, although positive, was short and perfunctory. The first substantial correspondence he received from Holland came from the Classis, whose members felt they had many reasons to upbraid him: he had not written them; they had heard the rumor of a marriage with a heathen; his recently published translation of the Lord's Prayer, the Twelve Articles of Faith, and the Ten Commandments into Fante contained major errors. One year after arriving at Elmina, Capitein had already put into practice one of the principles he had advocated in *On the Calling of the Heathen,* learning the language of the people to be converted, and he had asked his friend Hieronymus de Wilhelm to shepherd his translation to publication.[140] The publisher, Jacobus de Beunje, took the liberty to add a preface, in which he pointed out various errors in the Dutch text. The Classis, thus informed, was particularly aggrieved by the fact that Capitein had translated the beginning of the Lord's Prayer as *"Father of us all, who is in heaven,"* since *"of us all"* was not to be found in the Greek text or in any European translation. They also objected to the fact that the translation of the Fourth Commandment, which is about resting on the Sabbath, did not include the servants. The publisher had noted that it did not include the sons and daughters either. The Classis suggested that any future translation "should always be undertaken through communication with the Classis and with its approbation" (Kpobi, 250).

With its narrow concerns, the Classis must have seemed awfully out of touch with the new realities of his life. According to John D. Kwamena Ekem, Capitein's translation of the Lord's Prayer reveals an awareness of his audience's culture and a willingness to adapt New Testament concepts to an Akan worldview. When he translates the beginning of the prayer as a dedication to the "Father of us all who is unquestionably in the exalted place above" (Kwamena Ekem, 75), Capitein blends the "Judeo-Christian theological concept regarding God's Majestic nature" with African myths about a more concrete divine abode after withdrawal "as a result of being hit by the old lady's *fufu* pounding pestle" (76). The injunction that God's name "be mentioned/handled with due reverence" (77) takes into account the importance of naming in many African cultures. The wish that God "not allow our heads to be pushed into evil" and "not allow others to harm us" (77) calls up surprisingly concrete images in a context of slavery and violence. Overall, Capitein's translation reinforces the idea of "God as the ontologically exalted One who exercises providential parental care towards creation and deserves our liturgical as well as ethical reverence." This reverence "has practical implications for interpersonal relations and is concretized in reciprocal forgiveness and peaceful coexistence" (75). It seems that Capitein's contact with the people at Elmina helped him bring out the more communal elements of the Calvinism he had been brought up with. The new situation, his new functions, and a new emotional outlook unlocked his more republican leanings.

His answer to the Classis, on 21 May 1746, confirms the impression that he has moved beyond petty theological disputes and is mostly concerned with the well-being of his community. He points out that he did write to the WIC and sent a thorough report, as he had been instructed to do, and he assumed that the company would share this information with the Classis. In regard to his marriage plans, he says: "I will indeed admit that it was a great undertaking, but must also say that it was not a rash notion. I could argue the merits of this with the venerable Classis, affording adequate reasons, but as I have long since dispensed with this intention . . . I shall pass over the reasons" (Kpobi, 252). His recent marriage to the young Dutch woman and his awareness of the Reformed Church's disapproval cannot prevent him from defending an idea that would have brought the two communities closer together. Immediately afterward, he broaches the subject of young Christian African men who wish to marry: what advice to give them? There are hardly any Dutch Christian women available, and as he has already pointed out to the WIC, parents in the community are reluctant to have their daughters converted. This is when he also brings up the issue of European soldiers who want to marry non-Christian African women: "What should one advise such a person?" Knowing full well that the members of the Classis are far removed from the complexities of his diverse community, he quickly concludes: "But enough of this" (253).

Apparently, both the WIC and the Classis were far removed from Capitein's financial realities too since, shortly after he died on 1 February 1747, they discovered that he was deeply in debt. In a letter to the WIC dated 1 April 1747, De Petersen belittles Capitein's complaints about his treatment at the castle, emphasizes that he has always been well treated, and actually accuses him of forgetting his duty as a minister and of being seduced by the pleasures of commerce. Capitein owed money to people as varied as a surgeon in Amsterdam, a clerk, and a wine seller. According to the surgeon, who came to Elmina expressly in order to pursue him, Capitein said: "I don't have it. Sell my bed; I don't care. Let those who want money do the worrying, not those who owe money."[141] He is also supposed to have said: "What does Van Buren want with me—that I should trim down my table and let my belly go empty just to please him. No, I won't—I won't!"[142] A different image suddenly emerges—a man out for his own gain, concerned with his earthly needs, definitely not a stoic.

But maybe the various images are not that contradictory. From his Dutch education, Capitein had inherited a vision of society based on various forms of exchange. He was so much aware of what he owed Van Goch, for example, that he asked the WIC to instruct a notary in The Hague, Peter Nesker—probably the same Nesker who attended his baptism—to take three hundred guilders out of his salary every year and give it to Van Goch, "[in token of] the everlasting obligation which I owe him" (Kpobi, 242). After arriving in Elmina, he apparently picked up or kept up an interest in commerce, but at the same time, he also developed an expansive vision of interracial collaboration. Of course, the project had to fit within the bounds of his Christian ideological framework, and it was also inevitably part of Holland's development as a colonialist nation. But it still displayed an inclusiveness that reflected his cosmopolitan experience. Indeed, it seems that, once in Africa, he actually did find slavery distasteful. He ends his first sermon by pointing out that, had he not been as lucky, he "would otherwise have wasted my tender years and age in bodily slavery" (231). All the signs before his death indicate that he wished the same kind of luck to all the young Africans growing up around him.

•

Capitein's life story is usually presented as the story of a failure and, consequently, as one that reinforced prejudices about Africans. It is striking that, in spite of his popularity when he left the Netherlands, little was made of his death, and nobody seems to have enquired into it. Even the WIC dealt with it cursorily: the notes of its 17 October 1747 meeting just mention the "announcement of the death of minister Capitein."[143] Rather than being completely forgotten, though, he became the stuff of legend—and of racial paranoia. In 1854, a "curious" writer inquired in a magazine what had become of him: all he had heard was that Capitein had been a Hottentot, had returned to South Africa, and had "forsaken the civilization he had received in this country, as well as all the knowledge one expects from a Doctor of Theology, and returned to live with his tribe, as if he had never lived among civilized people, but rather had lived among the Hottentos since his birth without any interruption."[144] Similar stories about Capitein "reverting" to heathenism and barbarism were seemingly plentiful and fit the racial mind-set of nineteenth-century Europe.

But if it is hard to measure the impact, negative or positive, he had on Dutch and African society, Capitein remains a representative of an eighteenth-century black intelligentsia that tried to push the boundaries of the ideas surrounding it. The hostile reactions he received from some people at Elmina castle may have been a sign that they found his insistence on real connections with the townspeople disturbing, or his focus on giving them the power of literacy dangerous. In a 9 May 1746 letter to the director general, the WIC complained about the employees "who speak with contempt of the minister's laudable attempts and God-fearing work, to teach the children of the natives, and to bring them to the knowledge of God." The letter further asks that Capitein be respected and sustained in his endeavors and that his critics be held in check.[145] Capitein's refusal to bend to the rules of the African outpost and his adherence to the ideas he had received through his cosmopolitan education indicate a perseverance and, possibly, a new ideological commitment. Rather than holding him back, moreover, his Calvinist upbringing gave him strength and the confidence that he was fulfilling a providential plan. If he did "go native," it is not in the racist sense implied by the "curious" writer. It is in his desire to extend and radicalize the republican and Calvinist grounding he had acquired in Europe. Maybe in that sense, then, he can be called a martyr.

2

Jean-Baptiste Belley and French Republicanism

On 3 February 1794, or 15 Pluviôse of Year II in the republican calendar, as the National Convention in Paris was going about its daily business, a delegate announced that three men were seeking admission as representatives for the northern province of Saint-Domingue, a French colony in the West Indies. Their election had been duly verified, and their credentials were in order. The decision to admit them was made quickly. This procedure may have been routine, but the three delegates who soon after walked into the hall were not: Louis-Pierre Dufaÿ was white, Jean-Baptiste Mills was biracial, and Jean-Baptiste Belley was black.

The assembly, which had been expecting them, was ecstatic. Just before the announced men came in, a jubilant representative had exclaimed that the old "aristocracy of the skin" had finally expired: "Liberty triumphs, equality is consecrated."[1] Georges Danton, the famous revolutionary, had expressed outrage at the treatment the three men had received from whites, who had tried to prevent them from reaching France. After the three deputies entered, another representative declared that the Convention had long desired to have men of color in their midst, and he asked that these men receive a "fraternal accolade" from the president (Ray, 19:387). The president proceeded to embrace the men, and all rejoiced. The next day, in an unprecedented move, and to loud clapping and shouts of celebration, the Convention abolished slavery in all of France's territories.

What brought Belley, a former slave, to be present at this historic moment? His life and his writings show that he became increasingly attached to France and that he was ready to serve what he considered his country, even to fight and die for it. It is this readiness to serve that, combined with the upheavals that took place in Saint-Domingue in the last decade of the eighteenth century, led to his election. But his attachment to France was also much more than the endorsement of a national identity. To him, France after the Revolution represented progressive

Jean-Baptiste Belley. Portrait by Anne Louis Girodet de Roussy-Trioson, 1797, oil on canvas. (Château de Versailles, France)

cosmopolitan ideals he adhered to, as the only nation in the world seemingly committed to multiracial democracy and republican citizenship. He saw in the French Republic the true promise of universal equality, over against the parochialism of racist, power-hungry white colons, as well as, later on in the decade, the racial nationalism of independentist black leaders. He was proud of his blackness, but his vision was inclusive and egalitarian. To some extent, the French Revolution contained, and acted on, this vision. Belley's formidable career, punctuated by crisscrossings of the Atlantic, reveals the mind of a patriot, a revolutionary, and a cosmopolitan all in one.

Being Black in Saint-Domingue

According to the declaration he signed as a deputy to the Convention, Belley was born in Gorée, a small island off the coast of Dakar, Senegal, in 1746.[2] Since he adds in a marginal notation that he has lived in Cap-Français, currently Le Cap, a town on the northern coast of

Saint-Domingue, for forty-six years, we know he was brought to the island as an infant. His rise to the status of representative means that, by the time he arrived in Paris, he had accumulated an exceptional knowledge of the various racial and social strata that defined the colony, and that he had made clear political choices. It also testifies to the complex and unique politics of race, class, and slavery that dominated life in the French colony in the second half of the eighteenth century.

•

At the time Belley disembarked on the island, Saint-Domingue was France's richest and most valuable colony, and most of this wealth was created by slaves. Unlike the other Caribbean islands that belonged to the French colonial empire, Saint-Domingue had become French a bit haphazardly. The other islands, which included Guadeloupe and Martinique and were part of the Lesser Antilles, extending from the north to southeast of the Caribbean Sea, had been the target of systematic settlement by the French government since 1635. Saint-Domingue, the western part of Spanish-occupied Hispaniola, had been officially granted to the French at the Treaty of Rijswijk in 1697, after years of incursions by pirates from the island of Tortuga just northwest of the island, and the subsequent increasing presence of French settlers. Half a century later, it was on its way to becoming the world's first producer of sugar and coffee. Toward the end of the century, it would be studded with roughly six hundred sugar plantations in the coastal plains and three thousand coffee plantations in the mountainous interior, the rest being taken up by indigo and cotton. When he arrived, Belley became one of roughly 150,000 enslaved blacks, most of whom provided the work on these plantations. By the end of the century, the slave population had grown to 500,000. Historians estimate that about 685,000 slaves were brought from Africa in the eighteenth century alone.[3]

How harshly the slaves were treated can be gathered from these statistics. Half the slaves died within a few years of their arrival. "They are always dying" (Dubois, 40), one woman complained. Slaves who worked on plantations had a harsh life, whether it be a sugar or a coffee or an indigo plantation. If they were field slaves, they did hard and often dangerous physical labor, especially when it came time to harvest and process the crops. Enslaved women often suffered sexual exploitation. In 1685, Louis XIV had issued the *Code noir,* or the black code, a compilation of sixty articles that regulated the lives of slaves in the colonies and of blacks in general. While it spelled out various deprivations and harsh punishments that slaves were subject to, it also clearly stated a number of duties incumbent on the masters, such as the allocation of food or of free days. By the second half of the eighteenth century, though, the protective sentiment underlying the *Code noir* had little to show for it. Some of the practices it had encouraged remained in place, such as free time on Saturdays and Sundays, which most slaves used to cultivate their own plots or to sell their wares at markets. But these were just pockets of independence in an otherwise ruthless and violent system.

Belley lived in Le Cap all his life, first as a slave and then free, and so unlike plantation slaves, he was part of a bustling, cosmopolitan environment. Le Cap was the largest city in the colony and an economic and cultural center. Situated in the large, fertile northern plain mostly dedicated to the cultivation of sugarcane, it functioned as a big marketplace surrounded by established plantations. It was also the major port of the island, much easier to reach from Europe than the other ports along the west coast, and the dock always bustled with hundreds of arriving or departing visitors, sailors, soldiers, stevedores. With most houses built from stone, and many of its fifty-six streets paved, a contemporary commentator called it "the Paris of our island" (Dubois, 24). It had a huge government compound covering a city block, a large hospital, a parish church with an impressive colonnaded façade, several squares with elaborate public fountains, and a large compound of army barracks. Though it was not the official capital—that was Port-au-Prince, in the western province—it was the seat of the governor, the intendant, and the navy commissioner, as well as of the *Conseil supérieur,* a very active upper court. There was a theater, which had three performances a week during the season, and a newspaper. There also seems to have been no strict policy of housing discrimination, even if whites and blacks were mostly concentrated in specific areas of the city.[4] In 1789, the population of Le Cap was about 5,450 whites, 3,400 free people of color, and 10,000 slaves.[5] Belley had plenty of opportunities to interact with members of all groups, in what was at the time a unique multiracial environment.[6]

As an urban slave, he was probably better treated than field slaves. He may also have benefited from positive prejudices about Africans from Senegal. Médéric Louis Elie Moreau de Saint-Méry, author of a major contemporary description of the colony, gives voice to those prejudices when he says: "The *Senegalese* . . . are tall and well made, slender, ebony black. . . . In his moral stance, the Senegalese also has the marks of a certain superiority. He is a cultivator, intelligent, good, faithful, even in love, grateful, an excellent domestic servant."[7] In a tight urban environment, moreover, slaves were more likely to be scrutinized as revealing of their masters' status. They were also more likely to learn skilled trades and become masons, carpenters, mechanics. Louis Mercier says of the urban slave: "He is everywhere: at market, in the stores, in the streets, on the quais; he drives the coaches, he fills the barrels of sugar and coffee, and rolls them; he is in the holds or on the wharfs; the canoes are driven by him; he is a coachman, excites the passion of the horses in the city and in the country; Le Cap brims with his words, often noisy and incomprehensible to the uninitiated."[8]

Since he was literate and well informed about revolutionary ideas, one can assume that Belley took advantage of various accesses to French culture available in the city or that he was at least aware of them. In 1784, the theater put on Pierre Beaumarchais's comedy *Le mariage de Figaro,* well known for its ridiculing of the aristocracy and its symbolic empowerment of the middle class. In its most famous line, Figaro asks Count Almaviva what he has done to earn all his privileges and answers the question himself: "You took the trouble to get born, and no more." Belley may have seen the play, since by that time, the spacious theater hall reserved ten boxes for free people of color—three for blacks, and the rest for people of mixed race, this division being the result of light-skinned daughters' demands, according to Moreau de Saint-Méry.[9] There was also a reading culture in Saint-Domingue; newspapers advertising sales of belongings mentioned sometimes considerable amounts of books.[10] Bookstore catalogues show that there was interest in classics, theater, history, contemporary literature, and scientific treatises. Specific authors mentioned in those ads include Jean de la Fontaine, author of didactic fables; Boileau, a sharp literary critic; Molière, a playwright famous for mocking human foibles; and Jean-Jacques Rousseau, a major theoretician of social equality. Bookstores at the time looked very much like drugstores with books in them, carrying items like creams, powder, vinegar, tobacco, toothpaste, and perfume, which made exposure to books for a young black man easier. Le Cap also had three *cabinets littéraires,* which functioned as libraries and offered access to the latest newspapers and magazines from France. While it is unlikely that Belley was able or allowed to patronize them, they contributed to the introduction of new ideas into the colony.

And these new ideas did spread. In 1787, a traveling wax show had likenesses of Voltaire and Rousseau in addition to those of Louis XVI and Marie-Antoinette, giving us a hint as to the popularity of those writers.[11] While they are both associated with the intellectual revolution of the Enlightenment, they actually embodied two slightly different branches of it. Voltaire used his sharp wit to advocate freedom and tolerance; his concern was with individual rights over against the stifling influence of tradition and religion. Rousseau, while also concerned with individual freedom, focused on the best ways for people to live socially and politically. In *The Social Contract,* published in 1762, he argued for the republic as a political model, which he saw as a unified, collective body kept in motion by the general will. Like many thinkers of his day, Rousseau was steeped in the study of Greek and Roman classics; he drew from his admiration for classic republicanism, which emphasizes a devotion to civic virtue and active citizenship. Even if Belley had not been exposed to those ideas before then, he would catch up quickly in the year before he left for France.

Living in Le Cap, Belley also had the opportunity to learn much about the lives of the slaves who lived on the neighboring plantations. These slaves regularly came to the city to sell their food or artifacts or to attend church. As many as fifteen hundred slaves converged on the *place de Clugny* on any given Sunday, selling their products to nonwhites.[12] Mass was mostly a social occasion, as Christian religious feeling in Saint-Domingue does not seem to have been very strong. Jean-Baptiste Labat, a French clergyman and travel writer who preached in Le Cap in 1701, was struck by how the assembly seemed to consider Mass a sort of spectacle: "They conversed, laughed, and had a good time."[13] Various visitors in the course of the eighteenth century commented on the lack of moral values in the colony and directly related it to poor religious practice and overall indifference about matters religious.[14] Still, slaves in the northern plains, less isolated than in the mountains, were more likely to attend church, partly because, during the first half of the century, they had been the focus of Jesuit attention. Father Boutin, for example, learned several African languages and started the practice of the *messe des nègres,* a Mass specifically designed for slaves. Because some Jesuits also showed concern for the way slaves were treated, and occasionally protested and took action, Christianity among slaves around Le Cap was not necessarily associated with acquiescence. In 1762 the *Conseil supérieur* criticized the Jesuits' work, arguing that it encouraged slaves to meet independently and develop their own form of religious leadership.[15] Being in contact with slaves from the surrounding plantations must have opened Belley to the ideas and aspirations of some of the most exploited people on the island.

In an essay published in Paris in 1795, Belley asserts that he has been free for about thirty years, having won his freedom "through hard work and sweat."[16] We do not know exactly how it happened, but it means that, by the end of his teen years, he joined the contingent of free people of color who lived in Saint-Domingue. As in all other slave colonies, blacks and whites had had sexual relationships since the beginning of the settlement. Still, Saint-Domingue was exceptional for the size and civic status of its free black population. In 1789, it had roughly 28,000 free people of color—of whom two-thirds were of mixed race—31,000 whites, and 465,000 slaves. Free people of color formed a significant contingent in the colony—numerically, socially, and economically. Becoming part of this group, especially in the major city of Le Cap, must have led to a dramatic transformation in Belley's outlook on his own life and possibilities. It also got him entangled in the politics of race and class associated with that group, just at a time when tensions were beginning to rise.[17]

Interestingly, for the greater part of the seventeenth century, laws regarding free people of color seem to have targeted social status rather than race. Until 1680, in fact, mixed-race children were declared automatically free, arguably as a form of punishment to white fathers. Only later did the rule of *partus sequitur ventrem* predominate. Borrowed from Roman civil law, it held that the slave status of the child should follow that of the mother. The reasons for this change were mostly of an economic or of a moral nature, as partisans bemoaned the loss of property or argued that the old system encouraged enslaved women to seduce white men. A number of other laws passed in the second half of the seventeenth century are similarly not racially based. A law about absolving whites from taxes was quickly reinterpreted as applying to all people who were born free, whatever their skin color. Another measure condemning people who harbored slaves to enslavement was similarly clarified as applying only to people who were not born free. In all these cases, the inspiration was Roman law, which focused on freedom status rather than any racial or ethnic consideration.[18] Throughout the seventeenth century, mixed-race people in the French colonies were considered "more like Europeans than Africans" (Elisabeth, 139), and their allegiance to whites rather than to slaves was assumed.

The *Code noir* confirmed this. Article 9 stated that any white man who had illegitimate children with an enslaved woman had to pay a heavy fine; if he was their owner, he would lose both the mother and the children; if he married his slave, however, she and the children would be free. While most free blacks were born out of wedlock, the law condoned—and possibly encouraged—interracial marriage. The *Code noir* also declared that any master at least twenty years of age was allowed to free his slaves without any justification, and it prescribed that any slave who was the sole legatee of his or her master, or executor of his will, or his children's guardian, be set free. All freedmen had the same "rights, privileges, and immunities" as persons who were born free. One article demanded that former slaves show "particular respect" to their former masters, and there was heavier punishment for theft or sheltering of a fugitive slave. Otherwise, there were no stated restrictions on their civic or political freedoms.[19]

This group, free blacks, grew in economic status. Unlike in any other colony of the New World, here was a group of free people of color who rivaled the whites in numbers and whose wealth seemed to be growing. Many of them were small landowners and lived in the countryside; others were urban business entrepreneurs; others were employees, artisans, tradesmen. Some of them were quite wealthy, and together they owned about 30 percent of the slaves in Saint-Domingue.[20] As shown by Dominique Rogers, they also benefited from major civil rights, such as the right to marry, the right to draw up contracts, and the right to bequeath and to inherit property, and they often won court cases to defend those rights. Over the course of the eighteenth century, as the colony's reputation grew, and especially after the end of the Seven Years' War in 1763 made travel safe again, more and more men came from the metropole to try their luck. Everywhere they went, they ran into competition from free people of color.

Over the course of the eighteenth century, then, royal and colonial administrators decided that the power of this group had to be curtailed, but it is hard to disentangle the motivations behind the various discriminatory decrees they promulgated. The decrees seem mostly aimed at depriving of economic power a group that the whites saw as threatening competition and that was feared to be sympathetic to slaves. To the extent that they aimed to associate whiteness with superiority and control, they did contribute to installing a racist order. Still, the nature of this racism is often hard to pinpoint. The 1724 version of the *Code noir*, which was specifically designed for Louisiana, suddenly proscribed all marriages between blacks and whites. This law was not followed in the islands, where such marriages had existed for a long time, but the notion of *mésalliance* meant that a white person marrying a black person lost his or her social standing. The *Code noir* was gradually reinterpreted.

For example, the article stating that a free black owed respect to his former master was gradually extended to the idea that all free people of color owed respect to all whites.[21] A 1764 royal decree forbade people of African descent from practicing medicine, surgery, or pharmacy. A 1773 law forbade free people of color from adopting the names of whites. A 1779 sumptuary law made it illegal for people of color to dress like whites. Some people, white and black, objected to these policies, arguing that they created racial division and undermined the interests of the colony, and some of them resisted them. Indeed, free blacks usually had connections to whites, either through direct blood ties or through common interests. Many children of white fathers received assistance from them. Many whites sensed that free blacks were attached to their social and economic status and that, in the face of an increasingly vocal abolitionism, they could be strong allies in the fight to maintain slavery. So it seems that in practice, ideas about and behaviors toward free people of color varied widely.[22]

Being from Senegal, Belley had deeply black skin, and while free full-blooded blacks were not unusual—there were about ten thousand of them in the colony, as we saw—one wonders about his status among free people of color and within Saint-Domingue's society as a whole. It is hard to determine what role shade of skin color played in social relations. Many multiracial families included both wholly African and mixed-race people, and people originally from Africa could have strong ties with whites. Some white colons even argued that, since they had pure blood, Africans were superior to people of mixed race.[23] Some Africans were quite wealthy, while some mixed-race people were poor.[24] For many years, the colonial census used the category "free mulattoes and negroes" to register all free blacks. In the 1782 census, this group was split into two categories, "free people of color" and "free negroes," but the primary motivation seems to have been a desire to count as "people of color" people who until then had been seen as white or whose racial origin had simply not been mentioned in official documents.[25] So to some extent, degrees of blackness did not influence relationships.

But in other ways, they did. Many mixed-race people considered their closeness to whiteness a positive attribute, and some of them would try to take advantage of it in the struggle for civil rights. So they often tried to keep their distance from full-blooded blacks, whose skin color symbolized enslavement and degradation. Nonmixed blacks, on the other hand, developed forms of in-group solidarity that contributed to the sense of a separate identity. They were called *nègres,* after all, as distinguished from *mulâtres*. A list of about fifty documents cosigned by Belley shows that blacks formed a sort of large family, with members attending each other's weddings, baptisms, and funerals. In a 1777 document, Belley is described as a *perruquier*—a wigmaker. It is probably through this popular line of work that he became financially independent. Also listed are people like Pierre Augustin, a wealthy landowner who had also started out as a *perruquier*.[26] The list also includes several instances of black slaveowners marrying their own slaves. Within this community, then, bonds were anchored in race rather than social status.

It is hard to know exactly what kind of relationships existed between a black slaveowner and his or her own slaves. They probably covered a range from the exploitative to the protective. In the declaration he signed in 1795, Belley wrote that he used to be "the owner in Saint-Domingue of thinking property" but that "thanks to the just and beneficial decree of 16 pluviôse," that was no longer the case.[27] So apparently Belley was able to exploit all the openings made available by a society in flux, including owning slaves. How many slaves, what kind of work they performed for him, to what extent they benefited from the urban context and from Belley's own personal history as a slave—all that remains unknown. What we know is that, when the time came to elect deputies who would represent the slaves' desire for freedom in Paris, he was among those chosen.

In many ways, Belley does not seem to have let his blackness stand in his way. While many free people of color benefited from inherited assets, he belonged to that rare category of men and women who managed to buy their freedom through hard work. Such people existed, but they often lived in poor conditions, unless they managed to become artisans or to establish a small commerce. His literacy also seems exceptional in a society that routinely denied free people of color access to schools and where hiring tutors was the best, but an expensive, solution.[28] It is quite possible that his owner provided him with instruction, fostering his self-esteem, and, if white, giving him an insight into the value of interracial collaboration. Indeed, Belley's African birth may have helped him make connections with whites, many of whom disliked members of the mixed-race caste for moral or economic reasons.

But his owner may have been a free person of color. It appears that free people of color were more likely to buy African-born slaves and to give them training in order to increase their value. In the city, white master tradesmen were often paid to train slaves. Domestic slaves also often helped in the master's business. Stewart R. King mentions the example of a man who rented the services of a washerwoman not to wash his clothes but to assist him in his business of hair care and wigmaking. Joseph, a free black living in Le Cap, identified himself as a journeyman goldsmith, indicating he belonged to a fraternity of French journeymen; he probably joined while studying his trade in France. Pierre Augustin, already mentioned, a free black probably born in Africa and brought to the colony very young, was trained by his master as a wigmaker in Le Cap and became quite wealthy. Clearly, the city offered Belley plenty of examples of how to become skilled and independent, even as a black man born in Africa.[29]

•

It may be no surprise that, in his attempt to navigate the increasingly suffocating racial terrain, Belley decided to become a member of the colony's armed forces. In the second half of the eighteenth century, most of the militiamen and police on the island were free men of color. This situation had developed for a number of reasons. It was hard to attract metropolitan soldiers to the colony, and if they came, they were often subject to diseases. If they stayed, they often tried to find more lucrative occupations in civilian life. Similarly, local whites rarely found the armed forces a good way to raise their social status, and many of them resisted enlistment. As a consequence, free men of color were relied on to fill the ranks of the *maréchaussée,* or rural mounted police, the militia, and the regular armed forces. For slaves, moreover, these occupations often meant manumission. The tasks of the *maréchaussée* consisted in policing and generally upholding the law, with a major focus on patrolling the countryside to search for runaway slaves, fugitive soldiers, and other lawbreakers. By the middle of the century, all members of the *maréchaussée* were free men of color, including the *brigadiers,* the noncommissioned officers at the head of each unit. Members of the militia were at first predominantly white, but after several white rebellions, the ratio changed: in 1789, black militia units numbered 104 out of 156. Their main functions in peacetime related to internal security and garrison duty. As for the armed forces, there were regular white regiments stationed on the island, but free men of color were enlisted for special conflicts such as the Seven Years' War and the American War of Independence. Some of them did serve in the regular army. As Stewart King points out, "The life of a professional soldier in the eighteenth century was hard, but it was not without its rewards in the form of a certain dignity, stability, and regular pay" (74). Belley would be one of them.[30]

As has been the case in many cultures throughout the centuries, participation in the military provided an opportunity to create a symbolism of citizenship. So blacks in the military could be a source of inspiration. One famous character, whom Belley probably knew, came to represent this. Captain Vincent Ollivier became famous for his military deeds. Originally a slave, he participated in the siege of Cartagena, a city on the northern coast of what is now Colombia, that took place in April 1697. This expedition was under the leadership of Bernard Desjean, Baron de Pointis, a French admiral who, in March, had made a layover in Saint-Domingue in order to request assistance from the governor. Ollivier became part of a fleet that included 2,300 sailors, 2,000 soldiers—including 110 free blacks—and 650 buccaneers who broke through Spanish defenses and looted the city. He was captured on his way back and ransomed by the Dutch to France, where he was presented to Louis XIV. He then fought in Germany with Louis-Hector, Marquis de Villars, during the War of Spanish Succession. Back in Saint-Domingue, he was named captain general of the black militias in the district of Le Cap. From then on known to all as "Captain Vincent," he was widely respected and received in all circles, including at the governor's table. According to Moreau de Saint-Méry, his wisdom and sharp memory made his conversation "always interesting." His striking appearance in his old age, black skin contrasting with white hair, made an effect that "commanded respect."[31]

Ironically, though, while the armed forces provided an avenue for enhanced status, they were also an area where racial segregation and subordination gradually solidified. It seems that originally, militias were simply made up of free men, black and white alike. Then gradually, as they realized that they had little chance for advancement, free men of color demanded their own militias. For a while, these militias provided opportunities for high positions, since the chain of command was made up of black officers. Captain Vincent is one example. Etienne Auba is another: after fighting in the siege of Cartagena, he too was freed, and he was named captain of the black militia of Fort-Dauphin, in the northeast of Saint-Domingue.[32] Many others served as captains of their companies. Militias were eliminated at the end of the Seven Years' War, but when a royal order put out in 1768 reestablished compulsory militia service, it seemed to take for granted that the militia units would be divided along racial lines. The royal order divided the colony into twelve areas, and each area was to form several militia units, made of either infantry or horse-riding dragoons. Each infantry militia unit was commanded by a captain, a lieutenant, and a second lieutenant; it was composed of at least two sergeants, eight corporals, forty fusiliers, and a drummer. Now, though, all officers of black companies had to be white; only officers of a lower rank could be black, "to promote emulation." The trend toward increased discrimination was thus alive and well in the military.[33]

But the armed forces kept their appeal, and for Belley, they were an opportunity to increase his social status and make connections. In 1768, he was twenty-two years old, and so he was enlisted in the militia. The fact that every member of the infantry militia received a shotgun and a bayonet, two pounds of powder, and six pounds of bullets must have given this athletic young man some satisfaction. By joining the militia—there were five black companies in Le Cap by 1777—he also became part of an active network that King calls the "military leadership group." It is clear that nonmixed blacks who were part of the military world—whether it be the militia, the *maréchaussée,* or the regular armed forces—developed relationships that were made even stronger by their racial connection. Like blacks in general, blacks associated with the military not only knew each other but formed a sort of pseudo-kin family that provided support and also participated in many of the other members' important life events. They acted as godfathers at baptisms, witnesses at marriage ceremonies, mourners at funerals, and cosigners of manumissions and other economic transactions. These practices, much more common in the military group than in the planter elite group, highlight a sense of solidarity that was separate from both the white and the mixed-race world.

As we saw, Belley participated in at least fifty of these family acts, often along with fellow military men such as Joseph *dit* Cezar, bandmaster in the Le Cap militia; Louis La Rondière, sergeant in the Le Cap militia; and Pierre Augustin, the wigmaker turned wealthy landowner. In 1781, he attended the funeral of Jean-Baptiste Magny *dit* Malic, a sergeant and the son of a free black couple in Le Cap, who had become wealthy and well respected. So Belley had plenty of opportunity to develop relationships with this world of proud black masculinity. As Jean-Louis Donnadieu puts it, Belley "knows a lot of people, is in high demand, elicits confidence"; he is "a man of influence, probably respected and listened to."[34]

The year before his death, another man of influence, Captain Vincent, could be seen telling his war stories to the young black men who were enlisting to go fight in the American War of Independence, and

Belley was most probably among them.[35] In the course of spring 1779, Vice Admiral Charles Hector, Count d'Estaing, who had been fighting the British in the Caribbean and in the American colonies with little luck, was recruiting as many forces as possible in the islands. He arrived in Le Cap at the end of July, just after retaking Grenada, and two weeks later, when he set sail toward Charleston, South Carolina, to help the American rebels, his force included 545 free blacks, who formed the Chasseurs Volontaires.[36] This light-infantry unit, which had been created for the first time during the Seven Years' War in order to defend the colony, had been re-formed by an order from the governor, the Comte d'Argout.[37] The order opened with the statement that the king had "complete confidence in the attachment and the faithfulness of his free subjects, people of color, in Saint-Domingue."[38] It went on to describe its composition and stated that pay, ration, and treatment would be the same as those of white companies. King surmises that the main motivation for free blacks to join the Chasseurs Volontaires must have been patriotism, as pay was low, and there was also little hope of making lasting connections with white officers who might have actual local influence.[39] So if he participated in the campaign, Belley may have found among his peers and his leaders a strengthening of the patriotism that would sustain him for the rest of his life.[40] And as we will see, this was a patriotism that was very much anchored in ideas of manly courage and civic virtue.[41]

Laurent-François Le Noir, Marquess de Rouvray, the commanding officer of the Chasseurs, clearly had a high opinion of the free black soldiers, and his confidence may have contributed to their sense of patriotic pride. He hoped that they would say to themselves: "I must make the whites blush for the scorn they have heaped on me in my civil status, and for the injustices and tyrannies they have continually exercised over me with impunity. I must prove to them that as a soldier I am capable of at least as much honor and courage and of even more loyalty" (Garrigus, "Catalyst or Catastrophe?," 117). Born about forty miles south of Paris, Rouvray would make his way up in the military hierarchy, being promoted to colonel in 1768 and to field marshal in 1788. He and his wife, who was from Martinique, had settled in Saint-Domingue, where they had bought a sugarcane plantation and a coffee plantation. In the next few years, Rouvray would stand out as a great believer in the rights of free blacks, or at least in the necessity of these rights for the good of the colony. As a delegate to the first revolutionary assembly in 1789, he would cosign a letter that, while alerting constituents about the dangers of the new craze for liberty in Paris, advised them to treat free blacks with justice and respect.[42]

Rouvray represented many of the social and racial contradictions that Belley must have observed in whites he came in contact with. While in Paris, as the Revolution had just broken out, he would write a pamphlet warning against how newfangled ideas of natural liberty spelled disaster and destruction for the colonies and for France. His argument in the piece is not fundamentally racial, though: some people like to defend the idea of natural rights, he says, "as if an empire, a government, a marine, and colonies were *states of pure nature*."[43] To him, abolitionists should not be allowed any influence, since they "have little knowledge of big questions concerning the administration, commerce, politics and balance of empires."[44] His concerns are primarily economic and geopolitical, as he is convinced that French abolitionists are part of a vast British conspiracy to destroy France and its empire. On the other hand, Rouvray would never give up on his belief in the decency and the patriotism of free blacks. Soon after a major slave uprising started in Saint-Domingue in August 1791, he stood up in the Assembly held in Le Cap and urged his audience to enlist them, praising their endurance and commitment to the colony. To Rouvray, those qualities made them deserving of equal rights. In the letters he wrote his daughter in the following years, while he fumes against the Revolution, abolition, and the ideas of republicanism and democracy, and while in her own letters his wife makes statements about free blacks that almost smack of genocide, he still defends them. In June 1792, he writes that he "cannot praise them too much," and that the recent law giving them political equality "will play an important role in saving us."[45] These ideas must have been felt by the men under him.

Besides their communication with Rouvray, the free blacks were also under the leadership of a man, d'Estaing, who seemed to value them as equals. His printed orders for this expedition promised that "'people of color' would 'be treated at all times like the whites,'" as they aspired "to the same honor" and would "exhibit the same bravery" (Lawrence, 65). This language hints at d'Estaing's admiration for the virtues of ancient Rome. Like many of his generation, d'Estaing found inspiration in the values of the Roman republic, with its focus on civic virtue, patriotism, and courage. A few years later, he would write a play called *Les Thermopyles: Tragédie de circonstance,* about the famous battle between the Greeks and the Persians. The play presents Leonidas, king of the Spartans, as the quintessential patriotic hero, ready to die in order to protect his people and his state. D'Estaing himself would be sympathetic to the Revolution, though like many, he would be guillotined on the suspicion that his commitment was only partial. In any case, during the battle of Savannah, he seemed to think of the free blacks as men whose bravery equaled that of Greek and Roman soldiers.

And these men did have a chance to prove their bravery. The battle of Savannah was a real bloodbath, in which about one thousand men were killed or wounded.[46] It started with a two-week siege, during which the allies dug trenches and the British efficiently reinforced the city. As soon as they noticed the trenches, the British made a sortie with six hundred strong, but the French troops, among whom were the Chasseurs Volontaires, pushed them back with bayonets; as a result, forty men were killed.[47] When the assault finally took place on 9 October, the Chasseurs Volontaires were part of the troops that created a diversion to the east of the main assault.[48] Finally, after the battle, they were charged with defending the retreating army from the enemy. The free men of color most definitely came out of the whole episode with a good reputation. In a letter to the minister of the marine, Rouvray made it clear that they had "distinguished themselves by their heroics in this fight" (S. King, 66).[49]

On the other hand, they had many reasons to be bitter about the whole enterprise. Like many others, they must have questioned the wisdom of some of the decisions made. Because the campaign lasted much longer than expected, living conditions for the force became extremely hard, as soldiers and sailors alike dealt with heat, cold, hunger, and illness. The assault through a swampy area, which some of the vice admiral's advisors had argued against, could not put a dent in the British defenses, which had benefited from the work of a highly qualified engineer, as well as from the arrival of Lieutenant Colonel John Maitland and his contingent from Beaufort, who had managed to trick the allies and reach the city through the eastern swamps. It may not be surprising that, by the time of the retreat, when d'Estaing refused to embark at Charleston for fear of more desertion by the many discontented troops, Rouvray was alerting him about "the 'spirit of insubordination' in the Negro corps he commanded" (Lawrence, 129).

The aftermath of the Savannah expedition also reminded the Chasseurs of their subordinate status and of the need to resist it. One unit escorted the wounded to Charleston and was still there during the British siege of the city in the spring of 1780.[50] Some units were taken to various Caribbean islands, such as Grenada and St Lucia, to reinforce local garrisons, while others were taken to France. While the latter appeared at the court and were "commended for their valor," it took an intervention from Rouvray to remind the government that these men were independent citizens who yearned to return to their civilian lives.[51]

And the authorities needed reminding. In March 1780, the governor put out orders to form a new unit called the Chasseurs Royaux. This time, though, the service was not voluntary; black men from each parish were being conscripted into regular service. Reactions came fast. Not only did very few men enlist, but white officers also complained. Jacques Mesnier, captain of a mixed-race militia at Le Cap, reminded the governor that "I command . . . only free men, who have the ability to choose the company in which they will do their service" (Garrigus, "Catalyst or Catastrophe?," 120–21). After the king made it clear that he didn't approve of the governor's measure, the project was tabled. The episode was a foretaste of the complex alliances that would be made and unmade during the Haitian and the French Revolutions.

The Savannah campaign must have contributed to Belley's ideological development. The values of freedom, patriotism, and civic virtue had now been placed in a context of international and interracial collaboration, even as he was constantly reminded that he served at the whims of white officials. As he came back to his tightly bound black community in Le Cap, the sense of racial and social fluidity had expanded. Alyssa Goldstein Sepinwall has shown that embracing the principle of universalism in France's late eighteenth century often entailed promoting homogeneity or homogenization at the same time.[52] If Belley was moving toward a universal vision, it could not so easily be contained.

An Age of Revolution

When the French Revolution rippled into the colony, Belley plunged into it. Already before 1789, he was probably exposed to abolitionist ideas, both homegrown and imported. His personal and professional contacts with the free community, including during the Savannah campaign, made him part of a group increasingly bent on vindicating its political rights. Once the events started, the general animation about what was going on in Paris must have added to his sense of impending change. Indeed, in many ways, his connections with the various strata of Saint-Domingue gave him the knowledge and the convictions he would exploit as a cosmopolitan. The fact that each social group had its own fractures and dissident voices shows that, to some extent, race and class remained fluid concepts in the French colonial world, and it is this fluidity that made Belley's new universalism possible. While every social group was bent on defending its own interests, he would develop a language of universalist inclusion.

•

When they heard that, in August 1788, Louis XVI, facing empty royal coffers, had decided to convene the Estates-General and called for the election of representatives, some white colons reacted almost immediately and in a predictable way. They organized and elected deputies, in a process that was far from orthodox, and barred free people of color from participating. The election process also entailed putting together so-called *cahiers de doléances,* lists of complaints to be addressed by the future political body. In their *cahiers de doléances,* the white colons of Saint-Domingue took care to exclude people of color from political life. When on 20 June 1789 the representatives famously assembled in a tennis court hall in the city of Versailles, about ten miles from Paris, swore that they would stick together as a national Assembly that represented the people, nine white Saint-Domingue delegates were present and took the oath.[53] And so the very moment that signaled the beginning of the French Revolution also saw an attempt by white colonial power to assert its own freedom to maintain an order based on discrimination and enslavement. This very peculiar notion of freedom augured the ways in which, in the coming years, the meaning of the Revolution would gradually split and multiply.

The white colons present in Paris were not necessarily unified, though. Several colons who had just arrived in Paris from Saint-Domingue and were unhappy about the voting process that had taken place in the colony started gathering in order to define their own priorities. They feared that the deputation—soon reduced to six in the Assembly—would undermine the colony's interests by making these too dependent on the will of the metropole; more particularly, they feared that the Assembly would constantly raise the issue of slavery.[54] They also wanted to be in control of lobbying for the main item on their agenda, the independent creation of three colonial assemblies in Saint-Domingue that would have policing and legislative powers. So they decided to form a club. The first official meeting of what would soon be known as the Club Massiac, which would defend the interests of white plantation owners big and small, took place on 20 August. In September, in collaboration with the deputies, they obtained the king's approval for an election process that would determine the formation of assemblies in the colonies. In their minds, the white planters had achieved considerable autonomy in the colony's legislative decisions.⁵⁵

The white colons' desire to become more independent from the metropole was certainly not lessened by the portentous events that took place in Paris in that summer of 1789. The process of electing representatives and putting together *cahiers de doléances* had given the French a taste for democracy. The king realized that his power was eroding when, against his wishes, the three separate orders of the Estates-General—the nobles, the clergy, and the Third Estate—finally met as one national Assembly on 27 June. In the next weeks, the people of Paris noticed that royal troops were increasing their presence in the city, and tension grew. When on 12 July the news spread that the king had just removed Jacques Necker, his finance minister, widely seen as someone who was working for the common people, huge crowds assembled in various parts of the city to express their discontent. Some invaded the opera, some started tearing apart the wall that circled the city and whose customs posts symbolized high prices, and others looted a commercial depot. The royal troops retreated, and the people started forming militias. The next day, they set about finding munitions. The day after, on 14 July, close to one thousand people found themselves in front of the Bastille, an old prison where 250 barrels of powder had been consigned. Negotiations with the governor of the prison quickly foundered, the fortress was taken, and the governor was beheaded. When the king visited the city a few days later, his status as a leader had dramatically changed, and for a fleeting moment, the people felt they were in control of their fate.

While these events looked like spontaneous democracy in the streets, the National Assembly soon worked on making it a political reality. On 4 August, it abolished all feudal rights. Throughout the night, aristocrats surpassed each other in proposing reforms, such as a universal income tax and the abolition of feudal dues and tasks. It was, as an observer put it, "a moment of patriotic drunkenness" (Schama, *Citizens*, 439). In the next month, the Assembly put together the Declaration of the Rights of Man and of the Citizen, one of the founding documents of liberal democracy. It was based on the idea that human beings have a certain number of inalienable, natural rights. They are born and remain free and equal. They are presumed innocent until declared guilty, have freedom of opinion and freedom of speech, and enjoy equality before the law. Over the course of a few months, France had fundamentally reshaped its identity.

If they seemed both a boon and a threat to the members of the Club Massiac, these events were encouraging to another group that was in Paris to defend its rights: the free people of color. On 29 August 1789, only nine days after the first meeting of the Club Massiac, about thirty of them met in the office of Etienne Louis Hector Dejoly, a white attorney, whom they had chosen as their spokesperson. The main goal was to prepare their own *cahier de doléances*. On 9 September, Dejoly and a few members paid a visit to the Club Massiac, during which he read a memorandum asking for more rights for free people of color. After it became clear that the club would not budge, the people of color decided to prepare a visit to the Assembly. They now called themselves Société des Colons Américains, a clear statement of equality with the white planters. On 22 October 1789, a delegation of these men stood in the National Assembly, as their spokesman read aloud their address. It starts with a dramatic statement: "There still exists in one of the lands of this empire a species of men scorned and degraded, a class of citizens doomed to rejection, to all the humiliations of slavery: in a word, Frenchmen who groan under the yoke of oppression." Throughout the address, the emphasis is on the fact that free blacks who were born "citizens and free" (Dubois and Garrigus, 68) are treated as second-class citizens, with no right of representation and many forms of social and economic exclusion. They evoke recent revolutionary events, including the Declaration of Rights, "those inalienable rights based on nature and the social contract" (69), to demand justice from the Assembly. While they used the metaphor of slavery, the free people of color did not touch on that issue. All their arguments were based on the idea that they were free French citizens, and as such, they deserved political rights and representation in the Assembly.

What was the relationship between mixed-race men and full-blooded blacks in Paris at this point? Interestingly, the *cahier* left with the president of the Assembly on 22 October included the names of nonmixed blacks. The presence of these names implied that the demands of these people were equally valid. In an underhanded way, the free people of color were also making a statement about racism.[56] Still, the address referred to people who were born free. Moreover, a complaint sent by nonmixed blacks to the Assembly and included in the minutes of 28 November hints that the two groups were at odds. "The negro comes from pure blood," it starts dramatically; "the mulatto, on the other hand, comes from mixed blood; it is a mixture of white and black, a bastardized species." Therefore, it continues, "it is as obvious that the negro is above the mulatto as that pure gold is above tainted gold." In the social order, then, blacks should be classed above mulattoes, and they should certainly be represented at the Assembly. They are even confident that the white deputies of Saint-Domingue, their "natural protectors," will not suffer "an exclusion that would be injurious to the purity of their origin."[57] It then becomes clear that the blacks are furious about a gift of six million *livres* that the mulattoes made to the nation without including them. "More generous than their children," they propose to give twelve million (Mavidal and Laurent, 10:329). This amazing document is one of the few clear statements of racial, social, and economic rivalry between the two groups.

From this moment on, any discussion of black rights in the Assembly was prevented by the white colons. Not all of them agreed with this strategy. In a letter dated 3 November, Fleuriau de Touchelongue, who speaks for the branch of the Club Massiac in La Rochelle, a major French port, states that whites cannot afford to refuse what they are being asked. To him, the request is "so perfectly right in the eyes of reason, of humanity, and of any creole not completely blinded by his own interests, that it cannot be questioned for even one minute."[58] Jean Barré de Saint-Venant, who had spent thirty years in Saint-Domingue, argued that "it is time to forget our prejudices; the survival of our colonies depends on it. . . . I think that the free people of color and even the blacks who have some property must be allowed to vote on taxes and on the law that rules them."[59] But these were lonely voices. When the Credentials Committee finally decided in favor of the free people of color, who like the whites had done some lobbying, both the white deputies and the club members put pressure on the committee's chair; twice he tried to present the report to the Assembly, and twice he was prevented.[60] The white colons were satisfied.[61]

This defeat for the people of color augured more than two years of legislative failures in the Assembly. In March 1790, the Assembly created a Comité des colonies, made up of twelve members, most of whom were in favor of slavery. On 8 March, the committee proposed a law that allowed the colonies to create their own assemblies, whose members would be elected by "citizens." When the Comte de Mirabeau, a man of principle and a famous orator, tried to raise the question of who these "citizens" were, he was shouted down, and the decree passed. .When the final text was proposed to the Assembly on 28 March, the term "citizens" had been replaced with property-owning "persons." The Abbé Grégoire, who would become known for his defense of the rights of blacks, abolition, and universal suffrage, asked that people of color be explicitly mentioned. But his proposal was turned down, and so the Assembly basically left the colonies—and hence the white colons—to their own devices. A 12 October consideration stated that "no laws on the state of persons will be decided for the colonies, except on the explicit and formal request of their colonial assemblies."[62] It seemed that, as far as the colonies were concerned, the revolution only applied to whites.

Meanwhile, in Saint-Domingue, the politics of race and class created shifting alliances. After poor whites made their grievances heard, elections for a general Assembly granted the vote to all whites who had been in the colony for at least a year. Free blacks also demanded inclusion in local assemblies; several times they were met with violence and destruction. When the recently formed General Assembly in Saint-Marc, in the western province of Saint-Domingue, received the 28 March instruction, it renewed itself without letting free blacks vote. It also asserted its independence from metropolitan regulations and opened all the ports to foreign trade. The governor marched on the Assembly, with the aid of white and black troops. Eighty-five representatives leapt on a ship, the *Léopard*, and headed to France to air their grievances. In the fall of 1790, Vincent Ogé, a free man of color and a wealthy merchant from Le Cap, and a number of free men of color organized a rebellion in Grande-Rivière, a town to the east of Le Cap. He and his fellow conspirators fled to Santo Domingo, the Spanish section of the island, were extradited, and were broken on the wheel on 6 February 1791, after which their heads were displayed on pikes. While Ogé had been fighting for his own class, his story resonated throughout the colony. It also resonated in Paris, where people aired an increasing dislike for the white colons. When on 15 May 1791 the Assembly finally passed a timid law granting political rights to people of color who had been born of free parents, whites in the colony were enraged and refused to apply the decree.[63]

In August 1791, a massive slave insurrection started in the northern province. Well-organized slaves went on a rampage, burning houses and fields, destroying machinery, and killing whites. They were unable to take Le Cap but managed to take control of much of the northern plain. By the end of September, all the plantations within fifty miles of Le Cap had been destroyed, and the number of rebels had reached at least twenty thousand.[64] They resisted many attacks by troops, which included free blacks. Meanwhile, in the western and southern provinces, clashes between whites and free blacks continued, with each side enrolling slaves in its fight. In order to put a stop to the fighting, some agreements were signed, but very soon the provinces reverted to chaos. In France, the National Assembly was dissolved after it put together a constitution, and a new round of voting led to a legislative Assembly, which now functioned within a constitutional monarchy. On 4 April 1792, the Assembly finally voted to extend citizenship to all free people of color. In June, it sent three commissioners to Saint-Domingue, as well as troops. The objective was to apply this latest decree, neutralize the slave revolt, and restore slavery.

•

How closely was Belley, and were free blacks in Le Cap, following all these events? News of what was happening in Paris reached the city, in spite of efforts to control the flow of information. By May 1788 copies of a French paper that included articles criticizing the slave trade and discussing the abolitionist movement in England had reached the colony. It created a "great sensation." Similarly, news arrived of the activities of the *Société des Amis des Noirs,* or Society of the Friends of the Blacks, an abolitionist society founded in 1788. The colons did try to prevent the spread of new ideas. The Club Massiac wrote to various port towns in France, asking them to prevent blacks from leaving the country. Letters for slaves or free blacks were checked on arrival. But overall, people could not be prevented from loudly discussing revolutionary events as they were happening. When the slave insurrection started, refugees started pouring into Le Cap. Very soon the city was in a panic. Slaves were publicly executed, wounded soldiers could be seen carried to the hospital, and the noise of gunshots and cannons was constantly in the background. Whether they wanted to or not, blacks and whites in Le Cap were caught up in what would become known as the Haitian Revolution.[65]

The situation must have been difficult for Belley and for free blacks in general. The argument of free people of color for political rights had been based on the fact that they were free. At this point, they had not officially been linking their situation to that of slaves—on the contrary, the argument had been that political freedom for free blacks would cement their relationship with whites. But the revolt made slaves' demands impossible to ignore. Little is certain about how the slaves organized and how they developed their ideals, and different historians have pointed to different origins. The possibilities range from long-brewing ideas of resistance to sudden inspiration from events in Paris.[66] François, who testified after being arrested, says that the insurrection "had been planned for a long time." He does add that, at a big gathering of slave delegates that took place on 14 August, papers were read "by a mulatto or quarteroon . . . who announced that the King and the National Assembly had accorded them three days of freedom per week; that the white planters were opposed to this and that they must await the arrival of troops who would come to enforce the execution of this decree" (Fick, 261). When a rebel was captured a few weeks after the insurrection began, officials searched his pockets, and they found "pamphlets printed in France, filled with commonplaces about the Rights of Man and the Sacred Revolution" (Dubois, 102). Several captured slaves talked of "liberty" and "the rights of man" (105). It seems that events in France had at least partly been an inspiration, as French institutions, including the king, were seen as allies against the white planters. For the free blacks in Le Cap who were called upon to participate in the repression of the rebellion, though, these commonalities had to be swept aside, willingly or not. The rebels tried several times to take the upper part of the city, and they were killed en masse. Some people of color joined the rebels out of desperation—because their property had been destroyed, or they had been condemned in absentia for their role in the Ogé uprising. Free blacks found themselves having choices to make.

It does seem that some nonmixed blacks developed a close connection to the rebels, and one wonders about the role of race in establishing those connections. Reports from witnesses indicate that mixed-race joiners were not always trusted.[67] On the other hand, some blacks were coordinating the rebellion with slaves in Le Cap. In early September, the governor, Vicomte de Blanchelande, wrote: "We had successively discovered and continue daily to discover plots that prove that the revolt is combined between the slaves of the city and those of the plains" (Fick, 102). Shortly after the rebellion started, Jean-Baptiste Cap, a free black, was sentenced to be broken on the wheel after it was revealed that he was a major leader of the rebellion, and the authorities managed to capture him just outside the city. After interrogation, they learned that "in the night of the 25th [August] all the negroes in the plain were to attack the city in different parts; to be seconded by the negroes in the city, who were to set fire to it in several parts at once." Indeed, "in every workshop in the city there were negroes concerned in the plot" (103). Rebels in the eastern part of the northern plain also received help from free blacks. Interestingly, mixed-race men usually occupied inferior positions; in the Grande-Rivière area, for example, southeast of Le Cap, the vast majority of command posts were in the hands of nonmixed blacks. In November, the rebels took Ouinaminthe, an area near the Spanish border, under the military leadership of Jean-Baptiste Marc, a free black, with the help of Cézar, who had recently been emancipated. Both had feigned alliance with the government forces, received military supplies, and then turned back on the district.[68] Another free black was also participating in the rebellion in a leadership role. His name was Toussaint Bréda, the future Louverture.

Even as the northern province saw this participation by some free blacks in the slaves' rebellion, the other two provinces experienced comparatively more violent clashes between free people of color and free whites—and here again, political motivations varied. In the West, rich white planters were willing to forge alliances with free people of color; what mattered to them was that they retained economic power. It was the propertyless whites in Port-au-Prince who resisted. The South, with a frontier-like culture, did not have many rich whites to act as a buffer between people of color and propertyless whites. In both cases, though, the free people of color used the concepts of the Revolution, and the various laws passed by the Assembly, to argue for their civic and political rights. Over against the whites' flirting with political autonomy, they drew their force from the ideologies that came from the metropole. In fact, among their leaders were several men who had been educated in France. At the same time, however, a lot of these men owned property and slaves. They were not fighting for abolition and would not necessarily welcome it when it came.

Through his personal history, as well as his racial, social, and economic status, Belley occupied a unique position. While he did not join the slave rebellion, he had a slave past and strong ties to his black community. His ideological position was different from someone like Ogé, himself a unique figure among free men of color. Wealthy mixed-race men were not in principle opposed to abolition as a long-term strategy. When Thomas Clarkson, a famous British abolitionist, met with six men of color in Paris in the fall of 1789, he was at first anxious about their dedication to the cause. Hearing that they hoped for an eventual abolition of slavery brought him some relief, though the reasons he heard had mostly to do with a hoped-for improvement of relationships between blacks and whites.[69] The men were wearing a National Guard uniform, an emblem of citizenship in revolutionary Paris, and one of them, probably Ogé, was wearing what looked like a cross of

Saint-Louis, a high military honor. As John D. Garrigus argues, while in Paris, Ogé seems to have added a civic, military form of patriotism to the more liberal forms that were more typical of free men of color and that focused on the freedom to vote and to conduct business without impediments—themes he heavily emphasized in his address to the Club Massiac in September 1789.[70] So it seems that Ogé was straddling several ideological worlds. As we will see, Belley embraced civic republicanism fully and was committed to immediate abolition.

It came sooner than expected, in a process that would propel him onto the national stage. On 18 September 1792, three commissioners landed in Saint-Domingue: Léger Félicité Sonthonax, Etienne Polverel, and Jean Antoine Ailhaud. They had been charged by the Assembly with, "among other things, the maintenance of order and public tranquillity," and to achieve these ends, they had been given "all the necessary powers, such as suspending or even dissolving the colonial assemblies now in existence, controlling the public force, and taking all measures necessary to insure the execution of the said Law of April 4" (Stein, 43). Through this law, the Legislative Assembly had given civil and political rights to all free people of color, in a first step toward universalizing the principles of its young constitution, in spite of a clause that stipulated it did not apply to the colonies. A few days after the commissioners landed in Le Cap, the Legislative Assembly was replaced by the National Convention, and France was declared a republic. While these events were immediately caused by an uprising that had taken place in August, they also seemed to be the natural path of the Revolution and the result of an increasingly intense attachment to an ideology that, as we have seen, had made its resurgence in the eighteenth century: republicanism. This ideology now came to the colony through Sonthonax, a man who would have a dramatic impact on Belley's life and thought.

Sonthonax was a lawyer who had moved from the provinces to Paris, and when the Revolution started, he embraced it. It became "a moral crusade" for him, and the republic would mean "the rejuvenation of humanity itself" (Stein, 20). He quickly started writing for *Révolutions de Paris,* a radical journal with an antiroyalist, egalitarian mission. He also became a member of the Jacobin club, one of several political clubs that emerged during the Revolution. The Jacobin club started as a discussion group for deputies during the early days of the National Assembly and became progressively more radical, even as the number of its members grew and many branches were set up throughout the country. Over the course of 1791, it expelled or lost the more moderate members, such as deputies who, in September, voted for a law abrogating the 15 May decree that gave some rights to free men of color. Some of the famous men who remained were Maximilien Robespierre, who would become a symbol of violent radicalism; Jérôme Pétion, a radical lawyer who would become mayor of Paris; the Abbé Grégoire; and Jacques Pierre Brissot de Warville, founder of the Société des Amis des Noirs. Sonthonax attended meetings regularly and became a member of the correspondence committee.

He became known for his focus on colonial issues, and his writings reveal that he approached them from a revolutionary and republican standpoint. In an article published in September 1790, he starts by asserting, like Rousseau, that liberty and tranquility are incompatible: "Do not think that a free state is one where one can taste the pleasures of luxury, where one becomes elated with the pleasures of sensual delights."[71] With this opening, he places the abolitionist fight within the context of a typical republican call for continued vigilance by citizens to eschew the seductions of luxury and to fight enslavement by despots. He then proceeds to analyze the year's events in the colonies. He contrasts the autonomous decisions made by the General Assembly in Saint-Marc with those of the northern assembly, which "has managed to maintain among the colons a spirit of attachment to the mother country."[72] To him, patriotism and revolution go hand in hand, and isolationists are working against the spread of liberty. He ends the essay with a prophetic declaration:

> As far as the slave trade and slavery are concerned, the governments of Europe may well try to resist the cries of philosophy, the principles of universal liberty that are budding and growing among nations. Let them learn that one never exposes the people to the truth in vain. That once the impulse is given, one will have to give way to the torrent that must sweep away the old abuses, and that a new order of things will rise.... Yes! We dare to predict it with confidence: a time will come—and the day is not far off—when we will see an African, with frizzy hair, without any other recommendation than his common sense and his virtue, come to participate in lawmaking in the midst of our national assemblies.[73]

This was a bold statement, at a time when a majority in the Assembly were still willing to accommodate white colons, and an amazingly prophetic one.

Clearly, Sonthonax had absorbed the focus on stoicism and patriotism associated with republicanism. Many of the men who played a role in the Revolution, including Sonthonax, had studied the classics in school. At the Collège Louis-le-Grand, a famous secondary school on the Left Bank attended by Robespierre, teachers told their pupils to "admire the simplicity, frugality, austerity, courage and patriotism of the heroes of the Roman Republic" (Schama, *Citizens,* 170). It was a spartan ideal, and it was strongly linked to a stoical and muscular form of masculinity. While it suffused the culture, it received a striking embodiment in one of Jacques-Louis David's most famous paintings, *The Oath of the Horatii,* which he painted in 1784. The painting draws on a Roman legend, in which three brothers of the Horatius family decide to fight three brothers of the Curiatius family in order to spare the population of the two cities they belong to. Their father stands in the middle of the painting holding up swords, and in the left part of the painting, the brothers are shown taking the oath with their arms extended. The painting speaks to the ideas of masculine courage and sacrifice for the common good that are typical of republicanism. The grieving women on the right side represent a world of female sentiment, but they also feed into the republican ideal if we know that one of them, who is betrothed to a Curiatius, will be killed by her returning brother. David would be a friend of Robespierre and a member of the Jacobin club. At this point, he seemed to be bringing out into the open values that had been latent in the culture, and the painting made a splash.[74]

During his first few months in Saint-Domingue, Sonthonax applied this republican ideal of freedom and civic virtue to all free people in the colony. When he realized that the whites were not willing to work with him, and that for them, revolution meant freedom from metropolitan tyranny, and especially from its moves toward racial equality, he decided to take steps to promote equal citizenship. In October, he and Polverel dissolved the various colonial assemblies and created the Intermediary Commission, six of whose members were to be chosen by the Colonial Assembly before it was dissolved, and six by the two commissioners. As a result, the commission was composed of six whites and six men of color. They also rewrote the laws regarding municipal elections to include free people of color. At the end of that month, Sonthonax organized a huge assembly on the Champ de Mars, a large public space on the west side of the city, during which the armed forces and the local governments swore allegiance to France, after which Polverel left for the western province and Ailhaud for the southern one, in order to establish a metropolitan presence throughout the colony. A few days later, Sonthonax wrote to the Convention: "Count always on an indefatigable zeal, on an invincible courage, on a boundless devotion to the interests of France and the cause of the Revolution" (Stein, 55). As his relationship to the whites soured, he decided to promote a few nonwhites to officer status in the regular forces. On 1 December, he assembled all the troops on the Champ de Mars again, and except for the Régiment du Cap, which had refused to have a nonwhite as an officer, they all swore allegiance to the law of 4 April.[75] All the steps Sonthonax was taking were meant to create the egalitarian, patriotic republic he aspired to.

It is unclear at what point Belley came in close contact with Sonthonax. In an account of the deputies' trip to France, it is said he was serving as an officer in a white line regiment, and he says he had been serving France for more than twenty-five years.[76] Most probably, he was a member of law enforcement when Sonthonax arrived and was then promoted to officer in the regular troops. In a letter to Joseph Georges Boisson, another black deputy in Paris, from February 1798, he asks him to "say many good things to our friend Sonthonax,"[77] a clear indication that they had developed a strong relationship. So if it hadn't been completely developed by the time Sonthonax arrived, Belley's republican worldview certainly received a boost from the commissioner. Indeed, soon after he arrived in Le Cap, most free people of color living there gave Sonthonax their total support. In December, whites, led by a rumor that free men of color were preparing to kill them, led an attack against the barracks of the Sixth Regiment, the regiment of free men of color. These men defended Sonthonax and then retreated to the outskirts of the city. In the next few days, he arrested the leaders of the attack and deported them. On 16 December, he rewarded the free blacks by creating six *compagnies franches,* each composed of fifty free blacks. Soon after, the colony received the news that France had been declared a republic. For Belley and all free blacks in Le Cap, Sonthonax was clearly a symbol of republican ardor and equal citizenship.[78]

Sonthonax's actions over the course of 1793 confirmed this, and Belley would play a part in them. In March, he joined Polverel in the western province, and they moved against Port-au-Prince, which was resisting their authority and condemning the Revolution. After the city surrendered, they created the Legion of Equality, dominated by nonwhites, and they reorganized the National Guard, placing nonwhites in positions of command. On 7 May, Thomas François Galbaud, the new governor of Saint-Domingue, arrived in Le Cap. Seeing hope in him, counterrevolutionaries flocked to the city while Sonthonax was away. When they heard that Galbaud was openly criticizing them, calling them dictators and playing down the idea of racial equality, Sonthonax and Polverel decided to come back to the northern province. After more threatening talk by Galbaud, they dismissed him and sent him back to France to account for himself in front of the Convention. Once again, it seemed as if the Revolution was gaining ground.

But the reaction became more dramatic—and tragic—than the commissioners had anticipated. They put Galbaud on board the *Normandy*, one of the military vessels moored in Le Cap's harbor. These vessels, though, were packed with sailors who had lived in the colony for a while and who often sympathized with the white counterrevolutionaries. On those ships were also a number of whites who were being deported as a consequence of the Port-au-Prince conflict. Galbaud and his brother managed to take control of most of the ships, and on the afternoon of 20 June, they attacked the town, two thousand strong. The commissioners had no time to organize a defense, but several troops lined up to defend the government buildings, including line regiments and men of color commanded by Belley. The assailants retreated, but the next day they came back and captured the arsenal, and the commissioners fled to the outskirts of the city. After someone opened the prisons and hundreds of imprisoned slaves were released, a sort of guerrilla war started, and as a result, most of the city was burned to the ground. The commissioners made a declaration: they would grant freedom to all the slaves who would fight for the republic. Several thousand insurgents then flocked into town, and many whites fled, as well as many of their slaves. When the commissioners came back, the scale of the destruction was shocking, but the republic had gained many new black citizens.[79]

On 29 August, Sonthonax proclaimed general abolition in the northern province. Though not a member of the Société des Amis des Noirs, he had long been an abolitionist and well acquainted with Brissot, whom he knew through the Jacobin club, and who had recommended him for the post of commissioner. In February 1793, he had written to the Convention, urging it to "fix the lot of the slaves" (Stein, 83) as soon as possible. That same month, Britain and Spain declared war on France, and in its answer to Sonthonax, the Convention gave the commissioners virtually unlimited powers. On 5 May, the commissioners issued a proclamation dealing with treatment of the slaves. While the decree still contained a few harsh measures, such as whipping and even death, it clearly sympathized with the slaves and placed the rebellion within the context of slave mistreatment. On 21 June, as promised, Sonthonax gave freedom to all the blacks who had fought for the republic. At the end of August, finally, a few days after he received a petition from an assembly of fifteen thousand people, he issued a proclamation, which he read aloud to a huge assembled crowd. "Men are born and remain free and equal in rights," he said solemnly, finally making public the first principle of the Declaration of the Rights of Man and of the Citizen; "that, citizens, is the gospel of France." After proclaiming general abolition, he made the following clear: "Never forget . . . that of all the whites in the universe, only the French of Europe are your friends" (Stein, 89). All those present—and Belley among them—heard that the universal principles leading to liberty and citizenship were deeply bound up with the ideals of the French Republic. Patriotism and republicanism went hand in hand. For days, festivals and ceremonies were held both in Le Cap and throughout the northern province.

In the western province, Polverel, who had come back by the end of July, issued a decree that was both more conservative and more progressive than Sonthonax's. He freed all the slaves who did not belong to loyal citizens. This means that abolition was not universal, but those who were freed became the owners of the abandoned plantations. Because Polverel's republicanism included a concern for the rights of property, he left the "loyal" planters alone, but in all other cases, he inaugurated a groundbreaking plan of land redistribution. The freedmen were also declared French citizens and would enjoy all the rights of citizenship. By October, he decreed general emancipation for the whole colony, and his plan of redistribution was never put into practice. But it does show the extent to which the notion of equality could be radicalized. Indeed, his final plan did include measures that gave workers a degree of control over their labor, such as participation in workplace elections. The commissioners had definitely given the colony—and France—a taste of what republicanism could look like.[80]

•

Belley soon had a chance to see republicanism in action and to be a part of it. Shortly after his declaration, Sonthonax finally decided to direct local assemblies in the northern province to choose representatives who would elect deputies to the Convention. On 23 September, a meeting took place in the government building of Le Cap in order to proceed with the election of the deputies. After someone remarked that several electors had not arrived yet, the assembly decided to push the meeting back to the next morning, and after two envoys came back with the commissioner's written permission, the meeting was adjourned. The next morning, the remaining electors had finally arrived, and the voting could proceed. Someone suggested that, since the meeting was an important one for the public good, the doors be left open. All agreed, and the doors were opened. The assembly then chose a president, a secretary, and three verifiers. The representatives then proceeded with the election of six deputies and three substitutes. The first deputy to be elected with an absolute majority was "citizen Belley." Five more deputies followed: Louis-Pierre Dufaÿ, white; Joseph Georges Boisson, black; Pierre-Nicolas Garnot, white; Jean-Baptiste Mills, of mixed race; and Réchin, black. After the vote, each of the four deputies present took an individual oath, promising "to be faithful to the French Republic, to obey all the laws of France, already decreed and to be decreed, and to use their power to maintain Liberty and Equality."[81] Because Réchin would be unable to leave Port-de-Paix, which was encircled by British ships, he would be replaced by Etienne Bussière Laforest, of mixed race. But Boisson would be detained, and so when Belley stepped into the Convention in February 1794, he was the only full-blooded black of the delegation.

But before that moment could happen, the deputies had to make the trip to France, and the adventures they had on their way there were a sore reminder that many people were hostile to what they represented. In a letter written to their constituents on 14 December, while stationed in New York, they described what had happened. As soon as they boarded the ship, *Le Citoyen de Marseilles,* they were subjected to disdainful behavior and insults from the passengers. These were whites in exile from Le Cap as a result of the events of the past few months, as well as Captain Planche, who colluded with them. After the ship dropped anchor in the Delaware River, on 6 November, men who had been deported from Saint-Domingue came on board from a French privateer and started insulting the deputies and what they represented. Sailors shouted that the deputation should be hung or shot. Others concurred: "I'll be the executioner!" When they moored before Philadelphia the next day, the deputies learned that French migrants living in the city had boarded an American ship and had insulted and mistreated

Garnot, who was aboard. They asked to be allowed to leave, but the captain refused. The next morning, Dufaÿ jumped into a rowboat full of soldiers and the captain had to let him go, but as soon as he disembarked, he was assailed by several Frenchmen who insulted him and threatened him; they were about to jump on him when a woman intervened and bravely resisted them, and he managed to escape.[82]

Belley was a special target. Most of these whites had left Saint-Domingue after the June battle in Le Cap, which had left the city in flames, and their resentment was still raw, especially against a black man. A group of them boarded the ship, and the captain took them to Belley and Boisson. They beat Boisson, and then "they went to Belley, grabbed his sword, *beat him*, searched him, stole his watch, his money, his papers, all the belongings that were in his room, and insulted him."[83] They were particularly sore about the fact that Belley "dared to serve in a line regiment as an officer, and to command whites."[84] Belley answered that "he only saw in his position his duties *toward France*, that he had served her for twenty-five years, and that anyway, if one was able to save and defend whites, there was no reason one could not command them."[85] Hearing this, they fell upon him, and one of them approached him with a dagger in his hand, asking him to remove his cocarde, saying that a black man should not be allowed to wear it. The cocarde was a round piece of cloth featuring three colors in concentric circles—red, white, and blue—that had become the symbol of one's loyalty to the principles of the Revolution. Belley answered *"that he would not remove it, and that they could strike him."*[86] One of them pulled off his cocarde, but he answered proudly: *"You won't remove the one that I'm wearing in my heart."*[87] After this, they ransacked Dufaÿ's room and took Boisson hostage.

This is the first time we hear Belley speak, and the voice is stunning. Here is a man whose skin color in Saint-Domingue had for so long been associated with slavery and degradation, who was a slave until his late teens, who had to work hard in order to free himself, and who now declared his undying devotion to, and love for, his country. But this is a country symbolized by the tricolor cocarde, and so to him, France signified a revolutionary universalism that had not been attained elsewhere and that had been reinforced for him by the entrance into the colony of a few enlightened and devoted commissioners. Belley's own devotion was also anchored in his military life, which put him in the heart of republican ideology. The pride and patriotism we hear in his responses to the white assailants show that he managed to glean from his environment the ideas and values that best suited his desires and personality.

By doing this, he became one of the most potent spokespersons for the French Revolution.

Aware of his special status within the deputation, Belley added his own individual letter to his black constituents. He tells them that, in other circumstances, he would have been ready to die, but he withstood all the humiliations from those "villainous deported colons" because "I was suffering for my brothers: I had to sacrifice all to the success of our mission."[88] He urges them to join the commissioners in "combatting *all the enemies of the Republic*": "Remember that only France recognizes liberty; that the British and the Spaniards, in coalition with aristocratic or royalist colons, want to throw you back into debasement and slavery, *and that you promised me to all die rather than let the northern province be invaded.*" Finally, he enjoins them to live in peace with the French who stayed, and to obey and protect the commissioners: "My co-citizens, imitate *the French who are fighting for their freedom,* and who not only *know how to die, but also know how to vanquish.*"[89] The man who speaks in this letter has clearly absorbed the ideals of republicanism and urges all to suffer for them. He was now on his way to the beloved country that symbolized them.

Being Black in France

As a black person in Paris in 1794, Belley was bound to encounter a variety of racial attitudes. As in many other European nations, racial thought was in turmoil, but in France, recent events made it even more complex. Like the Dutch and the British, the French in previous centuries had often looked at Africans in positive ways. The eighteenth century saw the slow growth throughout Europe of the kind of biological racism one more commonly associates with the nineteenth and twentieth centuries. At the same time, though, the universalism that characterized the Enlightenment and the egalitarian principles of the French Revolution were at the root of the friendly embrace Belley received on the floor of the Convention. More than any other country, it seemed as if the nation stood on the cusp of a new age. But it could easily be swung in a different direction.

•

The French had only sporadic contact with Africans during the Middle Ages, and the few contacts they had seem to have elicited respect and even admiration. There is the famous story of Ismeria, a black woman from the Sudan who, sometime in the twelfth century, saved three

French knights' lives while they were held in captivity in Cairo as a result of the Crusades. She converted to Catholicism, married Robert d'Eppes, one of the crusaders, and came to live in France. At her death, the knights had a shrine built in her honor, and several French kings, including François I, Henri III, Louis XIII, and Louis XIV, are known to have gone to Liesse, a town in the north of France, to pay their respects to the "Black Madonna." Thousands of people still make the pilgrimage every year.[90]

The early modern period saw a more regular presence of blacks in France, and they seem to have been received without prejudice. François I, who ruled in the first half of the sixteenth century and spearheaded French exploration in the New World, was known to have a black mistress.[91] In his early-twentieth-century history of foreigners in France, Jules Mathorez seems proud to assert that French captains liked to liberate Spanish slaves, highlighting the "benevolent way in which they were received in France," where they were "free and independent."[92] Such is the case of Poix-Blanc, an African liberated from the Spaniards, who had been taken to Dieppe, a port in Normandy, received some instruction, and converted to Christianity. He was said to have fought bravely during the siege of Dieppe in 1567, "his sword in his hand, always leading the defenders, whom he would encourage both by his words and by his example." Guillaume and Jean Daval, writing in the seventeenth century, continue with the sadder part of his story, of how his master agreed to bring him to justice when the hateful leader of the city, Sigongne, felt offended by some remarks he had made; before the master, surprised by the harshness of the persecution, could do anything, Sigongne had the African hung publicly; the master's subsequent financial demise was attributed by many to "divine vengeance, as he had too quickly brought to justice, and consequently led to his death, the poor negro."[93] As the century went on, more and more blacks came into the country, as indicated by baptisms listed in church registries, in towns situated not just on the Atlantic coast but in the interior. A street in Orléans, a city about eighty miles south of Paris, still bears the name "Rue des Africains"; a "collège des Africains" apparently stood on that street.[94]

The next century does not seem to have changed racial attitudes significantly. In 1644, the Count d'Avaux, a French diplomat who was in Münster, Germany, for the lengthy negotiations that would end with the Treaty of Westphalia in 1648, apparently made quite a splash when, one day during the week before Easter, he filled the cathedral with a retinue of 140 blacks. When they entered the cathedral and saw the scene, according to the count's agent Saint-Romain, the three Spanish ambassadors looked horrified and left, a bit confused, through another door.[95] We do not know how the blacks were gathered or what happened to them afterward, but the author of the anecdote clearly aims to flatter his subject by implying a connection between French and Africans that other Europeans did not have.

Over the course of the seventeenth century, the French seem to have become accustomed to the presence of blacks in their midst, a number of whom even became famous. Various black children were baptized and educated in aristocratic households, and others worked as domestics. One woman became famous as "the Mooress of Moret." Rumor had it that this woman was the queen's or the king's illegitimate daughter. She spent most of her life in the convent of Moret, near Paris, and received a pension from the king. Members of the royal family and entourage visited her often. This woman's origins have never been verified, but the rumors certainly did catch on.[96]

The French were particularly taken with Africans of royal blood. In the spring of 1635, a man named Zaga-Christ, supposedly the son of a former king of Ethiopia, made a much-awaited entrance in Paris. Of course, Ethiopia, with its history of Christianity and the never-ending rumors of the presence of Prester John, a legendary Christian ruler, exercised a particular fascination on French minds. But Zaga-Christ himself made quite an impression. Two contemporary accounts tell of the adventures that took him through the desert, to Egypt, to Jerusalem, and to Rome, where he met the French ambassador, who brought him back to France, supposedly so that the French king could help him regain his throne. But soon after his arrival, Zaga-Christ became renowned for being "a valiant champion in the games of Venus"[97] and for using his skills with aristocratic women as a source of income. He died in 1638, in the residence of no less than the Cardinal de Richelieu.

Some Africans also found themselves in France in a diplomatic capacity, and as such, they were received grandly. A much-publicized event was the arrival in late 1670 of Matteo Lopez, ambassador of the king of Ardres, or Allada, in what is currently Benin but was then called the Slave Coast. Since the visit was meant to seal the newly minted commercial relationship between the two kingdoms, Lopez was received with the highest honors. In Jean-Baptiste Labat's account, he was an older man, but still vigorous, with lively eyes and an agreeable appearance. He was accompanied by three wives, three sons, and several servants. During the layover in Martinique, he was received "with all possible magnificence," and in Dieppe, "with honor." In Paris, he was welcomed with two coaches and six horses and was lodged at a luxurious hotel. He had an audience with Louis XIV on 19 December at the Château des Tuileries, and when he and his family arrived, in coaches sent by the king and the queen, several battalions were standing there to receive them. Inside, the stairs leading to the king were lined with the archers of the Grand Prévôt, or chief of the king's police, who was "superbly dressed." The Marquess de Rochefort then led the ambassador and his family through two rows of guards and then through a large crowd of "people of quality." The king was covered with diamonds.[98] While this grand reception was in many ways an acknowledgment of how much French commerce depended on the Africans' willingness to trade with them, it certainly implied a view of Africans as equal partners, deserving of grand ceremonies.

Two other areas on the African coast that were courted by the French sent various representatives, and each time, it is their political identity that seemed to play a prominent role in the way they were perceived, even if racial difference was never forgotten. Two ambassadors sent by the king of Eguafo, an area on the coast of what is now Ghana, arrived in Paris in April 1672. In a letter, an administrator mentions "two blacks, people of quality." The king was away, but they were taken to Paris, *"to let them see the royal houses and fill them with the grandeur of this nation,"* and were then sent back home with presents *"for their king and for them, and to assure him of His Majesty's protection and friendship ... and in order to establish trade with the French in his country."*[99] A more durable memory was left by Aniaba, sent as a teenager by the king of Issiny, in what is now Ivory Coast, and who stayed in France for more than ten years. Both kingdoms thought of him as a good investment in their commercial relationship, but once in France, he became an icon who seamlessly seemed to merge racial difference, cultural assimilation, and political value. He received an education, converted, was baptized in 1691 by the famous theologian Bossuet, met with Louis XIV, and soon took part in the leisurely activities of aristocratic life. He also became a lieutenant in the king's regiment and overall gained such trust and admiration that when he left, he was counted on to take over the throne of Issiny.[100] The fact that a fictionalized treatment of his life published in 1740 marries him off to a white woman gives a sense of France's racial context at the beginning of the eighteenth century.

•

French attitudes toward blacks then went through a clear, if gradual, change over the course of the eighteenth century. By the time Belley arrived in the country, the French were still prone to lionizing exceptional blacks, and the revolutionary discourses of equality and fraternity certainly helped shape racial attitudes, providing the long tradition of open-mindedness just described with an ideological foundation. At the same time, a desire to legislate the black presence in the country, combined with the rise of scientific thought and its push toward racial classification, had led to the first formal and explicit statements of French racism, though they did not go uncontested. More than other European countries, France showed extremes, both positive and negative, in attitudes toward blacks.

Shelby T. McCloy's statement in the introduction to his 1961 study that "France is commonly known throughout the world for friendliness toward the Negro" (3) may be an indirect comment on his own American context, but it is also the result of a reputation that France partly acquired through its visible embrace of a number of blacks throughout history. In the last decades of the eighteenth century, for example, three black men became known for their distinctive careers. Guillaume Guillon Lethière, born in Guadeloupe to a French official and an enslaved mother, was a painter famous for his works in the neoclassical style, often competing with Jacques-Louis David, the most prominent painter of the time. He would later be director of the French Academy in Rome, a member of the Legion of Honor, and a professor at the Ecole des Beaux-Arts.[101] Chevalier de Saint-Georges, also born in Guadeloupe, became famous as a classical composer and an accomplished violinist. He was also a superior swordsman and was named colonel of an all-black regiment. Alexandre Dumas, born in Saint-Domingue, father of the famous author of *The Count of Monte Cristo* and *The Three Musketeers,* became a general in the French army and played an important role during the revolutionary wars. Each of them experienced some forms of rejection because of his race, but the predominant context seems to have been one of acceptance and meritocracy. Unlike Capitein's, their blackness seems to have been embraced rather than erased.

On the other hand, the eighteenth century also saw many French individuals bringing Africans to France as students, servants, or slaves, and while these immigrants added a note of multiracialism to French society, they also contributed to an association of blacks with a dependent status or with the working class. Young Africans also tended to be appreciated for their exotic appeal. Mathorez mentions businessmen from Nantes noticing that young blacks were popular and how "together with parrots and sometimes monkeys, they are part of the family." At one point, one of them asks his agents to bring him women with well-shaped breasts: "He wants black Venuses." At the court, "everybody wanted to have his negro."[102] Probably the most famous black-skinned child, though of Bengali origin, was Zamor, servant to the Countess du Barry, Louis XV's official mistress. Her biographers introduce him as her "pet negro child, something of a human chimera, there to bring serving plates with refreshments, hold the parasol, and roll over on the rugs."[103] The Knight de Boufflers, who was named governor of Senegal in 1785, is known for bringing back several African children, one of whom he gave to Madame de Sabran, his future wife, and another to Marie Antoinette.

Interestingly, these servants were not necessarily made to lose their independent spirit. Zamor would testify against Du Barry during the Revolution, in a trial that sent her to the guillotine. Mercure, servant and messenger to Abraham Gradis, a rich shipowner from Bordeaux, once rode his horse so proudly and so fast through the streets of Paris that he ran over the Count de Choiseul-Praslin, future minister of the navy. The count, full of bruises and subjected to a bleeding, "complained."[104]

In parallel with this phenomenon of inclusion through work, study, or exoticization, a discourse of discrimination and exclusion also developed, first aimed at slaves. One main issue in the course of the century was the legal status of slaves brought to France by their owners. An early case had taken place in 1571, when a Norman slave merchant had arrived in Bordeaux with a cargo of slaves and had tried to sell them; he was arrested and the slaves were declared free.[105] In the eighteenth century, however, a number of measures were taken to accommodate colons. In October 1716, a royal edict allowed colons to bring slaves to France for purposes of religious or skilled trades instruction; these slaves were not allowed to demand their freedom on the ground that they had set foot in France, as such a possibility would cause colons "considerable loss" (Boulle, 248). Still, any administrative error led to automatic freedom. A much stricter edict was put out in December 1738. It starts by stating a concern that slaves brought to France are developing a "spirit of independence" and that those who stay are sometimes becoming "dangerous" (251). As a consequence, it limits the amount of time they can stay in France, as well as the types of cases in which they can go free. But because these edicts were not ratified by the Parlement of Paris, France's highest court, they were not considered official law, and when over 150 slaves sued for their freedom over the next decades, most of them won their suits.[106] At this point, then, the principle of freedom underscoring the 1571 decision trumped the desire on the part of the government to protect the economic well-being of its colonies.

This situation led to a new royal edict, promulgated in August 1777, which struck quite a different tone and stands out through its reliance on racial vocabulary. The new law, called a declaration "concerning the policing of blacks," consistently referred to "black domestics." Its main tenet was to prohibit entry to all people of color. Blacks who accompanied their owners for the voyage had to be detained in one of the *dépôts* set up in each major French port. Moreover, every black person living in France had to go to the authorities and make a declaration containing his or her personal information, such as name, age, profession, and birthplace. The next year, an edict forbade interracial marriage. These measures seem surprising considering the fairly open-minded racial context described above. To Sue Peabody, the phenomenon makes sense in that the rise of the "notion of freedom" (8) naturally gave way to two antithetical responses: the protection and expansion of that freedom for all individuals and the reinforcement of social hierarchy as a reaction. Looked at from a more pragmatic angle, the edict can also be interpreted as not primarily racial in intent. Clearly, the crown's major concern was still that "every day those men most necessary for the cultivation of land in the Colonies are staying away."[107] And the courts' refusal to recognize the status of "slave" in France made recourse to another kind of vocabulary necessary. Indeed, it is clear that the drafters did not want free blacks to leave and infect the colonies with their spirit of independence. Even the proscription of interracial marriage was presented as temporary, until the status of the people involved was cleared up.[108] On the other hand, in the letter that he sent around for comments in order to draft the law, Antoine de Sartine, secretary of state for the navy, mentions that the blacks "get more numerous in the kingdom, the colors are mixing, our blood is deteriorating."[109] The fact that all the French courts agreed to register the law shows that there was no serious query of this way of thinking.

It is also noteworthy that by then, racial theories had become more formalized, at least in certain milieus. Some governmental figures were wielding the vocabulary of "races" and "bloods." As early as 1716, the mayor of Nantes, when asked whether colons could be allowed to bring their slaves to France, wrote that blacks are "naturally inclined to stealing, sex, laziness, and treason. . . . Generally speaking, they belong in servitude."[110] As Pierre H. Boulle notes, though, he had a liberal attitude toward marriage, and his need to justify slavery might indicate a few pangs of conscience. In a 1763 letter, the Duke de Choiseul, secretary of the navy, vented his fears about blacks' "communication with whites, which results in a mixed blood that increases every day."[111] In a 1776 report to a committee on legislation, Guillaume Poncet de la Grave, crown prosecutor at the admiralty court in Paris, complained about blacks' "marriages with Europeans," so that "the colors mix" and "the blood is altered" (McCloy, 46). According to McCloy, none of this new ideology seems to have spread to the French populace, and "mixed couples seem to have faced no hostile public" (53). Moreover, the royal edicts were not applied systematically. Overall, then, a racial discourse was present in social and political life, but its extent and its depth are hard to measure.

In the world of philosophical and scientific writing, in any case, new forms of racial thinking were clearly emerging. Throughout the century, more systematic attempts to account for physical differences between humans led to a number of theories that seemed to underpin the idea of black inferiority. While these ideas did not necessarily reach a wide public, they established a foundation for racist thought that would be built on in the next centuries. The French were major contributors to this attempt at systematized knowledge.[112]

In 1739, the members of the Académie Royale des Sciences of Bordeaux announced a prize for the best essay that would explain the origin of blackness; sixteen submitted essays offer a glimpse of the big ideas that would constitute French racial thought in the rest of the century.[113] One main source of consensus is monogenism, or the idea that human beings belong to one race and therefore have the same origin. Arguments for monogenism in the essays range from the Scriptures to the ability of people of different races to have offspring. The main explanation for differences in skin color is climate: the authors argue that, somehow, it was the hot African climate that caused whites to develop black skin over time. This explanation, which would remain the most popular, clearly assumes that humans were originally white. This assumption would stay in place and be accompanied by the notion that Africans "degenerated" from the original human group. The question posed by the Académie already presumed that much: "what was the physical cause of blackness and African hair, and what was the cause of their degeneration?" (Curran, 81).

A few years later, the naturalist Georges-Louis Leclerc, Count de Buffon, started publishing his own conclusions, and most of them accord with those found in the essays submitted to the Bordeaux academy. He too is a monogenist, and he attributes differences in skin pigmentation to geographical conditions. The fact that blacks and whites can reproduce shows that "all humans derive from the same stock and are of the same family" (Curran, 106). It is the accident of history, the moving across geographical space through the centuries, that has created differences among people. As Andrew S. Curran points out, referring to Swedish naturalist Carl Linnaeus's ranking of human races, "Buffon's understanding of humankind was implicitly *horizontal* whereas Linnaeus's understanding of the genus *Homo* was *vertical* and hierarchical" (107). Still, Buffon does present the passage from white to black as a degeneration and does not shy away from judgments about Africans' social, moral, and intellectual makeup. The result, much like the travel accounts he drew much of his information from, is a mixed discourse, one that combines environmental determinism and essentialized traits, sameness and difference.

Once Buffon had opened the door to essential difference, scientists and philosophers focused on the specifics of blackness and came up with theories that reinforced the idea of fundamentally different bodies. Pierre Barrère, a naturalist who had lived in French Guiana and had supposedly dissected African cadavers there, posited that Africans had black bile. Johann Friedrich Meckel, a German anatomist whose work was read in France but was, as we saw, criticized by Petrus Camper, argued that blacks had darker brains. Claude-Nicolas Le Cat, a surgeon who had performed dissections at the hospital of Rouen, argued for the existence of "an elemental African fluid" (Curran, 125) that darkened Africans' nerves and fluids, including sperm. To Jean-Baptiste-Claude Delisle de Sales, a philosopher, the different brain had led to "a general 'inertia of the mind that differs little from stupidity'" (129). It is clear that these writers and scientists were slowly building a case for fundamental differences between the races and that this case was meant to serve a hierarchical view of moral and cognitive abilities.

Among the *philosophes,* though, we once again find a hodgepodge of egalitarian and racist views. Charles de Secondat, Baron de Montesquieu, is famous for a passage in *The Spirit of the Laws,* first published in

1748, in which he ridicules racist justifications for slavery: "Those concerned are black from head to toe, and they have such flat noses that it is almost impossible to feel sorry for them. One cannot get into one's mind that god, who is a very wise being, should have put a soul, above all a good soul, in a body that was entirely black" (250). Even before the onset of racial theory, Montesquieu was reminding his readers of the dangers of straying from universalist and egalitarian principles. In other parts of the book, though, he develops a climate-based theory of human behavior that comes uncomfortably close to proslavery arguments, as it associates colder climates with qualities such as knowledge and courage and warmer ones with lack of curiosity or of spirit of enterprise. Commentators on Montesquieu are still divided when it comes to the specifics of his positions on race and slavery. Voltaire was much more clear. He rejected monogenism; his theory that human beings belong to essentially separate species was already set in stone in his 1734 *Traité de philosophie*. While he did not condone slavery, his belief in blacks' natural inferiority was grist to the proslavery mill. Denis Diderot, on the other hand, was closer to Buffon in his contributions to the *Encyclopédie*, in that he eschewed classificatory impulses and emphasized monogenism and a dynamic view of human varieties.

Had he been aware of the details of these debates before he arrived in Paris, Belley could still not clearly have predicted how he would be received. In the decades before his arrival, attitudes toward blacks were contradictory, and theories about racial difference were battling it out. Monogenesis prevailed, but polygenesis seemed on the rise. And as we will see, antislavery advocates, inspired by the universalist ideas of the Enlightenment and the Revolution, spread new images of blacks not just as human but as brothers and equal members of the republic.

BLACKS, THE REVOLUTION, AND ABOLITION

The deputies' first two days at the Convention were a dramatic step in the history of the French Revolution. After their entrance was announced, on 3 February 1794, Simon Camboulas declared freedom triumphant and equality consecrated: "A black, a yellow, and a white are going to be seated among you, representing the free citizens of Saint-Domingue."[114] Two other representatives, including Georges Danton, the famous revolutionary, spoke out, and then the three deputies entered. As they were proceeding to take their place on the *Montagne*, the area that seated the Jacobins, so called because they were the highest benches on the ten-tier amphitheater, they were greeted with repeated applause and a "fraternal embrace" from the president.[115] The next day, Dufaÿ made a long speech apprising the Convention of what had been happening in the colony. He was repeatedly interrupted by applause, and as soon as he was done, several members remarked that the new republican constitution, which had been approved in September 1793, said nothing about slavery, and it was time to remedy this inexplicable oversight. Jean-François Delacroix, a Jacobin, exclaimed that a longer discussion of this issue would dishonor the assembly and asked that the abolition of slavery be proclaimed immediately. Another confirmed: "It is time for us to rise to the level of the principles of liberty and equality."[116] And he added: "People of color, just like us, wanted to break their chains; we broke ours, refusing to submit to any master; let us give them the same blessing."[117] All then rose to approve the following declaration: "The national Convention decrees that slavery is abolished in the whole territory of the republic; therefore, all men without distinction of color can enjoy the rights of French citizens."[118] The three deputies were then embraced by their colleagues among applause and shouts of *Vive la République! Vive la Convention! Vive la Montagne!*

It had been a unique, historical, almost magical moment. While the British Parliament had recently passed a few restrictions on the slave trade with much hemming and hawing, and northern American states were passing gradual abolitionist laws that would not free some of their people until well into the nineteenth century, France had removed centuries-old shackles in one clean cut and had declared former slaves French citizens. Clapping and shouting were certainly in order.

Another appearance at the Convention on 3 February coincidentally helped put these events directly in a revolutionary context. According to the *Moniteur universel,* a newspaper that reproduced legislative debates, the deputies did not enter right away. After they were announced, the representatives suddenly heard military music, and a group of "citizens" marched in, carrying big cauldrons of saltpeter, an essential ingredient in gunpowder. The whole room applauded, and several speeches were made, in which the saltpeter was presented as the new gold of the republic, the symbol of a new freedom and its universal reign. The immediate context was war with England, which had awakened a new martial spirit. A few months earlier, the Convention had proceeded to a *levée en masse,* a general conscription of all able-bodied men. It also provided huge resources for arms, food, and clothing. Factories put out cannons and balls, while church bells were melted for their metal. As

Simon Schama notes, "By the spring of 1794, three thousand workers were producing seven hundred guns a day and, according to Bertrand Barère, six thousand workshops were busy making gunpowder" (*Citizens*, 765). The wider context was a republican belief in the duty to export the Revolution and exterminate all the tyrants. So the president of the Convention told the citizens before him: "It is with gold that those monsters had fastened your chains, corrupted your ways, perverted the morals of nations; it is with powder and iron that we will purge the earth of those brigands, and feed the glorious tree of liberty with their blood."[119] The entrance of the three deputies from Saint-Domingue seemed a natural embodiment of this projected extension of freedom through the world by any means necessary.

In many ways, this moment also symbolized the state of the French Revolution in the first months of 1794. Since France had been declared a republic on 21 September 1792, its government had become increasingly radical. The Revolutionary Tribunal and the Committee of Public Safety were set up to enforce the new law, initiating a period known as the Terror. The Jacobins, whose figurehead was Maximilien Robespierre, and who were supported by the Parisian working class, represented a strict republicanism, devoted to social egalitarianism and bent on eradicating what deviated from their own view of patriotic virtue. In June 1793, the Girondin leaders, seen as too moderate, were expelled from the Convention. In July, the murder of Jacobin Jean-Paul Marat by Charlotte Corday, a Girondin, became a rallying point for radical republicans. In September, the Convention passed the Law of Suspects, which enabled it to condemn anybody deemed counterrevolutionary. In the next months, thousands of people were executed, both in Paris and in the provinces. On 31 October, twenty-two Girondins were guillotined. The next year, on 27 March 1794, twenty Hébertistes, who formed a populist faction, also went to the guillotine. On 5 April, Danton himself was executed. In its radical break with the past, the immediate and enthusiastic abolition of slavery on 4 February could also be seen as the positive expression of this ever-expanding zeal for a pure, perfect form of republicanism.

•

Indeed, the case can be made that the growth of French abolitionism was tied to an increased devotion to republicanism and that the great decision commonly referred to as 16 Pluviôse was primarily anchored in this ideology. As we have seen, the language of republicanism that

Belley was exposed to throughout his life did not just entail the embrace of freedom and political representation. It was also specifically anchored in classical republicanism, an ideal that combined notions of liberty and civic virtue, over against the excesses of self-interest, commercialism, and apathy. As Keith Michael Baker argues, "Classical republicanism found recurrent expression in prerevolutionary France," and it was "a critical ingredient in contemporary political debates" (36). It also inflected abolitionist debates. French abolitionism was shaped in the course of the eighteenth century, first through texts that argued against slavery using Enlightenment notions of human rights and universalism. Human nature is the same all over the world, the argument went, and this commonality cannot be erased by cultural difference or economic interest. Enslaving human beings is a fundamental negation of our belonging to one single human family and of the rights members of this family are entitled to. A number of abolitionist texts took a different route and argued from a liberal economic perspective that free labor was much more profitable than slave labor. In fact, many arguments anchored in human rights added this one for good measure. In the last decades of the century, though, the tone changed and became more radical. Several texts envisioned the rise of a black revolutionary who would destroy slavery and the whole colonial system, equating abolitionism with a fight for political liberty and a radical transformation of society. Combined with other political interventions, and with the news of the freedom that the slaves themselves had obtained in Saint-Domingue and that had been made official in Sonthonax's declaration, this discourse contributed to shaping the minds of the men who enthusiastically declared the end of slavery in 1794. For this reason, it is worth taking a closer look at those texts.

Some of the most famous writers of the French Enlightenment spoke out against slavery from a human rights perspective, often in the indirect or ironic way typical of eighteenth-century critical discourse. In his already discussed satirical chapter from *The Spirit of the Laws*, "On the Slavery of Negroes," Montesquieu makes fun not only of racism but also of various arguments used to defend slavery. "Sugar would be too expensive if the plant producing it were not cultivated by slaves," he says, turning the economic argument into a small-minded defense of luxurious pleasures. He also attacks cultural prejudice: "A proof that Negroes do not have common sense is that they make more of a glass necklace than of one of gold, which is of such great consequence among nations having a police."[120] Finally, he turns to the religious argument:

"It is impossible for us to assume that these people are men because if we assumed they were men one would begin to believe that we ourselves were not Christians" (250). A similarly broad attack against slavery takes place in a famous scene from Voltaire's satirical tale *Candide* (1759). On his way to Surinam—in this case, a town—Candide runs into a black man whose left leg and right hand are missing. Asked what happened to him, the man explains that he is a slave and that his hand was cut off because he lost a finger in the sugar mill, and his leg, because he tried to run away. "It is at this price that you eat sugar in Europe" (51), he concludes. With these barbs against slavery's attack on human rights and human dignity, Montesquieu and Voltaire offered no abolitionist programs, but they anchored antislavery thought in a humanist approach.

The *Encyclopédie,* a multivolume "reasoned dictionary" published between 1751 and 1772, also contributed to a philosophical critique of slavery. The entry on slavery, written by prolific contributor Chevalier Louis de Jaucourt, replicated Montesquieu's critique and even, as Jean Ehrard shows, radicalized it.[121] The entry opens with a definition of slavery as "the establishment of a right founded on force, which makes one man as much the property of another man, that this man is the absolute master of his life, his belongings, and his freedom." While this sentence almost reproduces the opening sentence of Montesquieu's chapter on slavery, it adds the notion of "force" and the notion of "freedom," negating from the start any possible interpretation of slavery as voluntary or acceptable. Jaucourt starts the development of his argument by stating that "all men are born free."[122] He then paints a picture of the growth of slavery through the centuries, underlining the mildness of the Greek and early Roman systems, in which slaves received an education and enjoyed a degree of professional independence. But the empire devised cruel laws, through which the slaves' lives were completely dependent on the masters; the Franks, a Germanic tribe that invaded France, were not much more lenient. It took the growth of Christianity to soften customs, and in 1315, Louis X declared that, since all men are born free, the serfs should be free. As Ehrard points out, the article suggests a "philosophy of history," according to which European culture has been gradually progressing toward abolition.[123] The implication is that slavery has no place in contemporary life. It is "an affront to man's liberty," it is "contrary to natural and civil law," and it is "unnecessary."[124]

Since the anchor of his argument is freedom, Jaucourt spends some time defining and discussing it and, in so doing, offers a powerful analysis of the right to freedom. Freedom is "linked so closely with man's preservation that it can only be separated from him by what also destroys his conservation and his life." Anyone who tries to make him submissive is "in a state of war" with him, since what he does is "a manifest attempt on his life." "From the moment that a man wants me to submit to him unwillingly," Jaucourt says, trying to place himself in this situation, "I'm allowed to think that, if he succeeds, he will treat me according to his whims, and will not hesitate to kill me when it fancies him." Therefore, "freedom is what can be called the rampart of my conservation, and the foundation of everything else that belongs to me." Having defended freedom as a natural right, Jaucourt moves to defend it as a civil right. A law accepting slavery is always and in all cases against the slave, and such a law cannot exist because it goes against all fundamental principles of society. Slaves by definition live in a state that is outside of the law; the only law pertaining to them is that of the master, and that's the law of the strongest. Finally, slavery goes against any form of government, whether a monarchy, a democracy, or an aristocracy. Ultimately, everything should contribute to "leaving to man the dignity that is natural to him."[125] Jaucourt used an argument anchored in liberal individualism, devoted to the fundamental right to human freedom and based on an erasing of racial difference.

On the eve of the Revolution, the human rights approach was made most visible by the Société des Amis des Noirs. Founded by Brissot and Etienne Clavière in February 1788, it originally focused on the abolition of the slave trade, in keeping with its British model, the Society for Effecting the Abolition of the Slave Trade, which had been founded in London the year before. But the ultimate goal was the abolition of slavery and an economic restructuring of the colonies. In a speech held at the first meeting, Brissot first underlined the universal human need for freedom, as well as "the prodigious influence of liberty on the development of human reason, and on the establishment of universal peace." He insists that enlightenment and moral growth of the masses—"*la masse entière de la Nation*" ("Adresse," 8)—can only happen when people are free, not under slavery or despotism. He does use economic arguments, referring to the work of Pierre Poivre, who argued that free cultivation of sugar in the east is much more productive, and arguing that an Africa that does not trade in slaves will be more peaceful and commercially inclined. But he makes it clear that the société's main concern is "humanity, the public good" without losing sight of the national interest. The Société's role is thus to inform the public and the government of the conditions of the slaves and to lobby the ministers and even the king "until it has obtained the liberty of our brothers."[126] Though the society remained small, its members kept the issue public by issuing pamphlets, newspaper articles, and translations of British abolitionist writings.

A number of abolitionists did rely on purely economic arguments, and according to Madeleine Dobie, this type of argument became the dominant one in the second half of the eighteenth century. This was the case among the so-called physiocrats, whose economic theory emphasized self-interest and laissez-faire. Over against the until then dominant theory of mercantilism, anchored in monopoly, the hoarding of bullion, and a positive trade balance, the new theory emphasized "the production, circulation, and consumption of goods" (203) as the source of a nation's wealth. Several abolitionists argued that slavery prevented the application of these principles. In a 1771 essay, for example, Pierre Samuel du Pont de Nemours starts by asserting that slavery is morally unjustifiable, even if economically advantageous. Even if abolition raised the price of sugar, "we shouldn't hesitate, we should resign ourselves to paying more for sugar, or even to doing without, rather than violate the rights of humanity so cruelly."[127] But he then proceeds to show in detail how slavery and the slave trade are both less profitable than commonly thought. Dobie concludes that this approach "had limitations" (250) because it "detracted from the urgency of the cause" by "translating what should have been a categorical imperative into a field of calculation" (251). So while this approach no doubt had some impact, it was only one factor among others in the decision of 16 Pluviôse.

A move toward a less theoretical, more gut-wrenching illustration of blacks' desire for freedom took place in the second half of the century and appeared in fictional images of rebellious slaves that often carried a republican message. This message emphasized equality as well as freedom, and it did not necessarily ask readers to forget about racial difference but rather asked that blackness, and the bodies of blacks, be respected and even admired. An early yet powerful figure is Moses Bom Saam, a probably fictional rebellion leader whose speech the Abbé Prévost featured in his review *Le pour et contre* in 1735. As Prévost points out in his introduction, the text is his translation from a speech that appeared in a British magazine.[128] Moses starts by telling his companions that, even though he has been free for many years, he has not ceased to suffer because he had to witness the plight of his brothers. Unlike whites, who live "in luxury and softness," he has used these years to educate himself and has realized that whites are not, as they claim, superior by nature. Indeed—and here the statement is stronger than the English original—they are actually inferior, with their "sickly and disgusting whiteness," compared to blacks' "noble and majestic color," as well as strength and virility. After stating that they have the same freedoms and the same rights as whites, he urges them to flee to the mountains and start a new society. They are not strong enough yet to take over the island, but at least they will be independent. In Prévost's version, Moses envisions a community based on equality: "Let us take possession of this vast highland that from now on we will share, and let us divide it between ourselves without preference and without jealousy"—a definitely more egalitarian statement than the English original, in which he says: "Let us *divide,* and *appropriate,* the Highlands" (22).[129] They will form a strong state and will be feared and respected by the whites. The speech is not just about slavery; it is also about the politics of a good society.

The 1774 multiauthored edition of Guillaume Thomas François Raynal's *Histoire des deux Indes* contains a famous passage about slave rebellion that has a similar republican tenor. After describing the Middle Passage and suggesting reforms to the horrible conditions of slave life, the author, Denis Diderot, declares he will not debase himself by "justifying through politics what morality abhors." He has focused on reforms as a temporary measure, but while waiting for "big revolutions," he asserts that the nation needs to "rise higher." He then critiques slavery by focusing on freedom as a human right but also on fighting for freedom as completely legitimate: "I hold from nature the right to defend myself." After giving graphic descriptions of what this right entails and attacking rationalizations of slavery one after another, he exclaims: "Let us break the chains of so many victims of our cupidity, even if we have to renounce a commerce that only has injustice at its core, and luxury as its object." The slaves have already started acting, and all they need is a courageous leader: "Where is this great man, whom nature perhaps owes the honor of the human race? Where is he, this new Spartacus, who will find no Crassus? Then the *code noir* will disappear, and how terrible the *code blanc* will be, if the victor is only out for vengeance."[130] Reference to the Roman icon Spartacus once again places slave rebellion within a republican framework, and the warning implies that it is still time to create a more equal society.

The inspiration for this passage, which was not in the 1770 edition, may have been a novel by Louis-Sébastien Mercier, *L'an 2440: Rêve s'il en fut jamais* (1770), a utopian novel in which the narrator dreams that he wakes up in the year 2440 and is led around Paris by a friendly guide.

Everything he sees testifies to a society that values the individual but also, although it is still ruled by a king, functions more like a republic, with a senate and various states. This king often walks the streets of Paris, for example, and sometimes spends the night at an artisan's house. All the citizens have equal rights, and while it does not have complete economic equality, the nation tries to minimize differences between rich and poor. The focus is on talent and virtue rather than on self-interest and luxury. At one point, the narrator sees, on a beautiful pedestal, the statue of "a negro, his head naked, his arm stretched out, his eye proud, his attitude noble and imposing." At his feet can be read: "*To the avenger of the new world!*" The narrator's guide explains how this man's courage and "virtuous vengeance" were rewarded. The slaves, suddenly transformed into heroes, killed all their European tyrants; using iron, poison, and fire, they made the soil of the Americas soak up their blood. Standing in front of the statue, the narrator and his guide celebrate the fact that these strong men managed to "reestablish the balance that the iniquity of ferocious ambition had managed to destroy."[131] Rebellion is necessary, the author implies, in order to repair the breaches created by an excessive focus on self-interest and to create the ideal republic of the future.

It may not be surprising that the first full-fledged story of a rebelling slave, *Ziméo* (1769), was written by Jean-François de Saint-Lambert. A poet and a military officer who had ties with famous writers such as Voltaire, Diderot, and Raynal, Saint-Lambert developed ideas very much in keeping with the universalist humanism of the Enlightenment. At the same time, his writings show an engagement with classical republicanism, partly inspired by his study of the Greeks and the Romans. His famous pastoral poem, *The Seasons,* typically praises lives spent tending the earth and enjoying simple pleasures. His article on "luxury" for the *Encyclopédie* displays a republican interest in the subject. After stating that a desire for luxury has moved all societies for centuries, he remarks that it is now being particularly praised by politicians "who speak about it more as merchants or salesmen than as philosophers or men of state." He then rebuts various defenses of luxury, praising Holland for its frugality and simplicity and showing that luxurious nations are not richer, more powerful, more virtuous, or more devoted to science and art. He does refute those who say that luxury leads to inequality, urbanization, and lack of patriotic courage. And he tackles the commonly held opinion that luxury has led to the rise and fall of nations and empires. True, in nascent societies, in which "personal interest" is subservient to "general interest," "patriotic spirit" and "virtues" flourish; as societies grow, while science and art develop, so do luxury and corruption. But corruption is less a consequence of luxury than of tyranny. Ultimately, luxury is only one factor among many in the rise and fall of nations. Still, Saint-Lambert spends much time arguing that, while it can be an incentive to industry and commerce, luxury is a cause of downfall when it is not made subservient "to the spirit of community, to the good of the community." Luxury is only laudable when the government works for "the common good."[132] Saint-Lambert shows both a liberal concern for economic incentives and a republican preoccupation with the excesses of self-interest.

While it may have been influenced by Aphra Behn's *Oroonoko* (1688), the tragic story of an African prince enslaved in the West Indies, *Ziméo* focuses more on the revolt and shows the author's interest in economic and political implications. In a later essay on how to improve the conditions of blacks in the colonies, Saint-Lambert uses two arguments to promote the equality of whites and free blacks. One is that it will increase consumption, which has been undermined by discriminatory legislation such as sumptuary laws. The other is that, as he envisions it, colonial society does not have a marked social hierarchy among its free people, and a common devotion to agricultural productivity will quickly erase all forms of racism among them. Once again, he is preoccupied with both economic progress and the creation of an equalized citizenship.[133] In laying out his plan for abolition, he states that the goal is to transform slaves into "citizens,"[134] by first introducing them to social and moral values. While his plan focuses on reform rather than immediate abolition, he clearly envisions a colony of free and virtuous citizens. Against possible economic doubts, he suggests that Africa itself should start cultivating cotton and sugar—a popular idea among abolitionists at the time, both in England and France. This mix of social, political, and economic concerns already informs *Ziméo*.

The story of *Ziméo* clearly condones rebellion. Told by George Filmer, a fictional American Quaker visiting Jamaica, it starts when Filmer is awakened at dawn by Paul Wilmouth, a Quaker friend at whose plantation he is staying. Wilmouth, who represents a kind master who has earned his slaves' affection, warns him that a rebellion has started; they decide to gather the slaves and arm them. "If I've been a hard master to you," Wilmouth tells them, "kill me, because I deserve it." After receiving confirmation that they will stay with him—some slaves stab their arms to show their loyalty—they decide to defend the plantation. This plebiscite, which momentarily turns the plantation into a minirepublic, contrasts with Filmer's description of the plain below him the next morning: a cloud of dark smoke is slowly rising above the shining sea, the flowers, and the pastures; animals are quietly grazing a short distance away from a scene of human massacre, as blacks are butchering whites under the flowering trees. In the end, after being welcomed and hosted by Wilmouth, the rebels, led by Ziméo, leave for the mountains, ready to live independently as a maroon community. Both in its plot and in its settings, the tale points to the political and economic benefits of small, egalitarian communities. Even the paternalistic model represented by Wilmouth has less appeal than the group of maroons. The tale ends with a tearful scene in which Ziméo and his friends ask the whites to follow them into the mountains. The narrator is looking forward to visiting them and to enjoying once again "the virtues, the great common sense, and the friendship" of Ziméo and his friends.[135]

Ziméo represents a republican leader. He is as beautiful and well proportioned as a Greek statue and seems born to command others. At the same time, and unlike Oroonoko, he is not princely. Though he was the heir of a prince in Benin, he was sent among the peasants for his education. A wise man taught him the value of working the earth, as well as the importance of justice. The love story Ziméo is associated with and the happy reunion with the beloved he had lost after the Middle Passage help convey the author's point that human beings have fundamentally similar emotions and that it is the system of slavery that demoralizes many Africans. But this is more than a story about human rights. It equates slavery with tyranny and presents the rebels as a community linked by solidarity and courage. By contrast, the Europeans are symbolized by one scene during the Middle Passage, when the wind dies down, the ship and the sea remain almost surreally immobile for days, and the crew resorts to cannibalism. Ziméo and his friends are the opposite image of this episode; they represent a movement forward—from the plains to Wilmouth's plantation to the mountains—and a call for a society based on freedom and virtue. Most likely this story, which had been reprinted many times since it appeared in the same volume as the highly popular *Seasons,* left an imprint on French thought about slavery on the eve of the Revolution.

So did Joseph Lavallée's *Le nègre comme il y a peu de blancs,* published in 1789, immediately turned into a play, and reedited in 1791 and 1795. Throughout its complex web of adventures and coincidences, the novel presents blacks as particularly noble and whites as in need of moral regeneration: in Africa, "there is no concept equivalent to the fatal *me*" and no desire for the "pleasures of luxury."[136] Many scenes of interracial mutual embrace help project a future of multiracial affection and brotherhood. The novel also promotes abolition, albeit as a carefully managed process. When Itanoko, the African narrator, inherits a plantation in Saint-Domingue, he frees the slaves, but they remain, guided by affectionate and egalitarian rules. While Itanoko is still the owner, he calls the enterprise "my small republic," emphasizing its combined achievement of equality, virtue, and personal fulfillment.[137] He grows old peacefully in France, with his children and his biracial wife, a sign that a multiracial nation is possible. Lavallée's book, together with the other texts just discussed, contributed to a print culture that associated republicanism with abolition and interracial collaboration. As we will see, this print culture was an ideal preparation for the interventions made by Belley and by other blacks.

•

After the Revolution started, various forces and individuals contributed to a movement toward abolition in fits and starts that, while it did not lead to any significant legislation until 16 Pluviôse, kept the issue alive. During its two years of existence, as we have seen, the Constituent Assembly only legislated on the rights of free people of color, an issue that, while seemingly secondary, unleashed passions because it forced the representatives to argue on whether civic status or race was the primary criterion in conferring citizenship. But the issue of the slave trade also came up regularly. In his speech during the grand opening session of the Estates-General, on 5 May 1789, Jacques Necker, the finance minister, declared that bonuses to slave traders had to be reduced by half. While this modest measure was mentioned quickly, the audience must have been struck when they heard the word "humanity" suddenly pop up from a recital of facts and figures.[138] Much later in this long speech, Necker did come back to the issue, bemoaning that "men similar to us in their thinking and especially in the sad ability to suffer" were now a "barbarian object of traffic."[139] The Société des Amis des Noirs wrote him a month later, both to thank him and to ask for a stronger stance about the trade.[140]

On 21 January 1790, Brissot gave an address to the Assembly. After reminding his listeners that they have been working for the rights and freedom of the French people, he makes it clear that he is not requesting the immediate abolition of slavery, which would be nefarious for the former slaves. But he asks for the immediate abolition of the slave trade, "those markets in human flesh," which is fomenting war and murder in Africa, and leads to the horrors of the Middle Passage, which he describes in detail.[141] He then argues that abolition would be advantageous to the slaves, the colons, and the nation. With this strategy, Brissot was hoping to replicate the efforts that were taking place in Britain, which had led to a report by the Privy Council and a review by the House of Commons. Not until the question of the free men of color was settled, on 4 April 1792, did the Assembly seriously tackle the slave trade again. On 10 April, a motion was brought up and sent to a committee.[142] Finally, on 27 July 1793, a letter from Dominique Joseph Garat, minister of the interior, was read aloud; it asked that the Convention take action regarding bonuses to slave traders. The Abbé Grégoire then spoke: "Until when, citizens, will you allow this odious commerce? Until when will you give encouragement to a traffic that dishonors the human race? Live up to what you've always been, and don't allow any more Frenchmen to go and fetch men, who are the same as us except for their color, in their native country, and to transport them to a foreign soil, where they are treated like beasts."[143] The assembly immediately decided to eliminate bonuses and called for a report in view of abolishing the slave trade.

The issue of slavery was also repeatedly brought up in speeches and publications. As early as July 1789, when a delegation of white colons was requesting twenty representatives at the States-General, Mirabeau asked if someone could explain to him "what principle one follows for the proportional representation of the colonies." "Are the colonies claiming to count their slaves and free men of color as men or as workhorses?" he asked. If the colons don't want to free their slaves, "we ask them to note that, when we decided proportional representation for the people of France, we didn't take into consideration our number of horses or mules."[144] On 25 February 1790, one month after Brissot's speech at the Assembly, an alarmed delegation representing Bordeaux, a thriving port, warned that "the abolition of the slave trade and of slavery would lead to the loss of our colonies"; a delegation representing "the manufactures and the commerce of France" then expressed its anxiety about abolition, arguing in detail that the slave trade and slavery were necessary in order to maintain this grand commercial nation.[145] A few days later, the question of the status of the colonies was sent to a colonial committee that, as we know, would give the colonies much leeway in their political decisions. The question of free men of color would then become the main preoccupation, but voices concerned about slavery continued to be heard. Until February 1794, various publications also maintained the pressure. A number of essays tried to offer pragmatic solutions. Most of them proposed gradualist schemes of abolition, or even plans for the slaves to buy themselves, on the condition that they start receiving salaries. One suggested land redistribution.[146] And as we saw, Sonthonax published fiery and prophetic articles in *Révolutions de Paris*. As Yves Benot puts it, some people will say: "So what? What does that prove? Since nothing was done, these are just words. But these words . . . did have an influence on people's minds, did prepare them to accept and support the 1794 abolition decree."[147]

Influence also came from the people of color themselves, but there were differences of approach in this group. Their most active spokesman, Julien Raimond, started with timid demands and slowly evolved in an abolitionist direction with arguments anchored in the notion of freedom. Raimond was a wealthy mixed-race plantation owner from the southern province of Saint-Domingue who owned slaves. His original concern was with the status of free people of color only. After he arrived in France in 1784, he sent several manuscripts to the Naval Ministry, in which he argued that free people of color were good citizens, that they supported slavery, and that the recent racist laws were unfair. He even proposed that these laws be eliminated for only a minority among the free blacks—the ones who were light skinned.[148] The minister, Anne-César de La Luzerne, wrote back, but nothing came of it.[149] Late in July 1789, as the Revolution was ongoing, and following some pressure from La Luzerne, Raimond paid a courtesy call to the Club Massiac.[150] Once again, he was only pleading for the rights of men of color who had been free for two generations. Still, he quickly became the bugbear of the white colons, especially after he started working with the group around Dejoly, which was lobbying for civil rights for all free people.[151] He was part of the group that addressed the Assembly on 22 October 1789, and on 23 November, he cosigned a long letter to the Credentials Committee pleading for representation in the Assembly.[152] In both cases, the concern seemed to be about the civic status of free men only.

Looking more closely at those texts, one can see that the ones Raimond had a hand in do contain references to slavery.[153] Two earlier texts show the impact the Revolution had on him. Shortly after the first item of the Declaration of the Rights of Man and of the Citizen—"All men are born and remain free and equal in rights"—was approved by the assembly on 21 August 1789, he wrote a "complaint" addressed to the Assembly that required the same rights for men of color, "in the name of the sacred rights of Humanity."[154] He equates the despotism that the Assembly has just erased with the sufferings of the free men of color in the colonies. He requests justice for all free citizens, as a natural extension of the revolutionary measures that have already been passed. He concludes another text, which focuses on his demands for free people of color, by first reemphasizing that the rights of man prescribe that all free men belong to the same group. "And if unfortunately there exists," he continues, "under French domination, a country where one thinks that slavery has to stay in place a little longer," then the only distinction should be between enslaved and free. And it should remain so "until the nation takes strong measures to bring the slaves back to freedom."[155] The 23 November letter contains a similar message buried under the elaborate plea for voting rights. The authors point out that, if the colony, unlike France, never had a "*distinction d'ordre*"—a distinction based on social class—it did have a "*distinction de classes*"—a division into groups. And in order to prove that the criterion for this division was race, they argue: "First they didn't shame away from classing off, and reducing to the status of workhorses, thousands of individuals who are now doomed to groan under the weight of slavery. Then, they created a big difference between free citizens of color and their descendants, however remote, and the white colons."[156] While it was not arguing for abolition, the text implied that the issue of free people of color was only one piece of the colonial puzzle.

Indeed, black pressure, including Raimond's, provoked debates in the Assembly in which the questions of the role of race in the colonies and the more general principles of justice and human rights were kept alive. The question of political rights for free men of color was explored by the Credentials Committee, which, after meeting eleven times, came to the conclusion that it should have two deputies in the Assembly.[157] But as we have seen, the report never made it to the Assembly; decrees passed in 1790 kept colonial voting rights vague under the terms "citizens" or "people"; in October, a consideration gave legislative freedom to the colonies. In May 1791, the Assembly discussed the consideration passionately and at length over several days, after a committee, which had received numerous petitions from blacks—and whites—presented its findings.[158] The fiery discussion flung men such as Grégoire, radical reformer Jérôme Pétion de Villeneuve, and Robespierre, who all appealed to ideas of justice and human rights, against men such as Moreau de Saint-Méry and Louis-Marthe Gouy d'Arcy, representatives of the colons, who raised the specter of the loss of the colonies, and it showed that sympathy for free people of color was growing. Raimond attended these sessions, and he was probably in contact with some of the speakers; on 12 May, a short letter was read aloud, in which he offered to contribute to the debate. On 13 May, the question of slavery finally popped up, when the Abbé Maury dramatically announced that the real issue that had been left unmentioned in all the debates was slavery. Now that the issue was on the table, it had to be dealt with. It was proposed that all initiatives about slavery be left to the colonies. "Perish the colonies," Robespierre famously said, in order to prevent a rewriting of the decree that would have included the word "slaves."[159] By the end of that session, the Assembly had added a clause that had not been part of the original debate—that the colonies were free to legislate about "nonfree" persons—but could still not agree on the section about free people of color.

The next day, Raimond spoke at the tribune. In this speech, he argues that the free people of color are both essential to the colony and not a threat. He first emphasizes the size of their group, pointing out that it is even bigger than officially recorded. He then describes in detail how people of color contribute to the public good, helping to prevent slave rebellion through participating in the militia, working as coastguards, and fighting in wars. He specifically refers to the battle of Savannah. He then points out that the *petits blancs,* or whites who are not landowners, are much more of a threat to the white colons than the people of color. He evokes the image of a poor white fisherman whose only possessions are a cabin, a canoe, and a few nets, and who in times of war, is ready to collude with any enemy or pirate who comes along. Free people of color do not resent the colons; on the contrary, they have a "well-known attachment to the whites."[160] Why would men with property want to shake up the colony? The *petits blancs* are really the ones who are making trouble. They are the ones who killed Ferrand de Baudière, an elderly white man who had helped men of color write a petition. They are the ones who have nothing and are full of resentment against proppertied men, white or black. And so while Raimond is clearly not tackling slavery, he is trying to shift the debate from race to class. Free men of color and whites have the same interests, he implies; they should understand each other, in spite of racial difference.

On 15 May, another letter from Raimond was read aloud in the Assembly. It was brief and sounded like an ultimatum. Raymond asked that, if they were not given the rights they were entitled to, the citizens of color be allowed to leave the "ground that has been steeped in the blood of our brothers"[161] and to emigrate from the colony, taking their fortune with them, without harassment. The letter made a strong impression, as loud clapping could be heard from the left side of the Assembly and from the tribunes. Everything now seemed to go very fast. Someone proposed an amendment that gave voting rights to free men of color who had been born of free parents—the idea had been floated a few times during the debate. Robespierre expressed his disagreement with this dishonorable splitting of liberty. In the end, though, the amendment passed. It was the first victory ever for free men of color, and Raimond had played an undeniable role through his appeals to freedom and equal rights.

Raimond and other blacks also kept spreading ideas in the background. The manuscripts he sent to the Naval Ministry were examined by Saint-Lambert, the author of *Ziméo,* when, as a member of a *comité de législation* set up before the Revolution, he wrote a memoir on colonial policy. While Raimond's ideas at this point were still timid, Saint-Lambert's recommendations are clear: there are only two kinds of men in the colonies, free and enslaved; all free men should have the same rights, and one needs to prepare for abolition of the enslaved.[162] After he arrived in Paris in July 1789, Raimond quickly developed relationships with men such as Brissot and Grégoire, although it is not quite clear when he met them personally for the first time. Gabriel Debien suggests that it is Brissot who introduced the men of color to Dejoly in October.[163] Brissot already broached the question of their voting rights in the 9 October issue of his review, *Le patriote françois*. Even more striking is that he does so by quoting a passage from Bernardin de Saint-Pierre's *Voeux d'un solitaire,* published the month before, in which the author argued that free blacks should be allowed to "deliberate about the interests concerning their metropole" and that this would "prepare the abolition of slavery in the colonies."[164] So it seems that the issue of slavery was very early on a topic of conversation in certain circles. Raimond probably met Grégoire at the Assembly on 22 October, when Dejoly presented their requests. From then on, Grégoire became an incessant defender of their cause and of abolition in general.

The blacks also made contacts with groups that seemed likely to support their arguments. On 24 November 1789, five men of color, including Raimond and Ogé, became members of the Société des Amis des Noirs. After Dejoly, who accompanied them, made a speech, the members decided that the society would include the defense of their rights among its objectives. On 11 December, the members discussed the possibility of putting pressure on the president of the Assembly about the issues of abolition and voting rights for free blacks. Raimond intervened, arguing that "making two requests at the same time could undermine both."¹⁶⁵ It is possible that he did not want his own issue to be connected to that of the slaves, but he may also have been thinking strategically. After deliberation, the group decided to go for abolition. On 1 and 11 February 1790, Dejoly and a group of thirty men of color addressed the general assembly of the Paris *commune,* or city hall, asking the members to work on their behalf. On the second day, Brissot took over and talked about abolition.¹⁶⁶ But because of a speech from a representative of the white colons, who argued, rather disingenuously, that the men of color could not act as a separate party because such distinctions had been abolished, Dejoly withdrew the petition.

Finally, from thousands of miles away, it was the slaves themselves who put pressure on France. The Assembly heard of the insurrection in Saint-Domingue on 27 October 1991. A letter read aloud reminded all that "the crisis in the colony is . . . a national crisis."¹⁶⁷ Two days later, an article in *Révolutions de Paris* celebrated the rebellion and "the independence of five hundred thousand blacks." "There is no hesitating," it continues; "the laws of justice come before those of commercial convenience, and our interests come after those of the human race that have been violated for so long."¹⁶⁸ The author then launches into a passionate defense of the rebellion, equating it with the French Revolution. Pushing aside all economic arguments, he ends by imagining a scene in which French commissioners arrive in the colony and side with the rebels. Other journals would make similar calls in the next few years. In a long speech he gave at the Convention on 1 December, Brissot attributed the troubles of Saint-Domingue to white prejudice and violence and to the whites' desire to separate from the revolutionary motherland. "The heart of a black," he exclaimed to loud clapping, "also beats for liberty."¹⁶⁹

•

From then until 16 Pluviôse, blacks in Paris continued their pressure through their writings, their acts, or their presence, but now their contributions emphasized their growing republicanism. Early in 1792, Raimond wrote an address to the Legislative Assembly. In it, he argues that if the Assembly chooses to give free men of color their full political rights, they will "preserve the colonies, maintain calm, contain the slaves."¹⁷⁰ But this quietist message is laced with republican feeling; as he keeps emphasizing the free blacks' patriotism and devotion to the mother country, he represents Ogé's rebellion as a natural demand for the realization of the decree's promise, and he presents the whites as separatists who want to transform free blacks into "pure machines" (*Véritable origine*, 27). Indeed, he presents the deputies of the white colons as agents of the "counter-revolution" (43) and the free men of color as the real inheritors of the Revolution.

On 4 April 1792, the Assembly finally gave full political rights to free men of color; by the end of summer 1792, as France was turning into a republic and was also at war with Prussia and Austria, blacks made it clear they were ready to fight for it. War with Britain would break out a few months later, and this military context would give the movement toward abolition a nudge. On 7 September, Raimond led a large delegation of men of color in front of the Assembly. Declaring that they were ready to spill their blood for the fatherland, he asked for authorization to organize a legion—a mixed unit of light troops. The request did not come totally out of the blue: the atmosphere in the country was one of urgent rallying against the enemy, and since the beginning of the year, the government had been planning the creation of several legions. More nimble than traditional line regiments, legions could do reconnaissance missions, spy on the enemy, intercept convoys, try some bold action, and overall, force the enemy to stay on its guard.[171] Moreover, black troops in the French army were not unheard of. A few decades earlier, the marshal of Saxony, a famous military leader, had a company of cavalry made up of about a hundred men, about eighty of whom were black. Nothing indicates that they were treated differently from white soldiers.[172] The black soldiers standing in front of the Assembly had reason to hope this would also apply to them.

The event was a display of French citizenship. "If nature," Raimond stated, "inexhaustible in its combinations, outwardly differentiates us from the French, on the other hand, it has made us perfectly similar, by giving us, as it did them, a heart burning to fight the enemies of the State." The president, Marie-Jean Hérault de Séchelles, known as a radical republican, used the opportunity for grand statements: virtue was independent from color; their service was not just to France but to the human race; the love of liberty and equality was no doubt stronger for those who had suffered through the shackles of servitude. He concluded that "it is impossible that France does not soon become the capital of the free world and the tomb of all the thrones in the universe."[173] One deputy ventured to ask if the men of color should really be separated from regular French soldiers. Another argued that this separation made them more visible and gave them more opportunity to display their public virtue. Enthusiasm was palpable in the room.

The next day, the assembly approved the creation of the Légion nationale du midi, or National Legion of the South, which would be made up of eight hundred foot and two hundred mounted troops.[174] On 6 December, it was referred to as the Légion des Américains,[175] and it would soon become known as the Légion de Saint-George, after the famous composer who took its command. Bernard Gainot estimates that the size of the black community had been overestimated and that recruitment did not go over two hundred men, who thus formed a cavalry unit. Their profiles show a diversity of men, both full-blooded blacks and men of mixed race, some former slaves, many with a military background, either in the colonies or in France.[176] The legion would end up being split into several units: one was sent to fight the counterrevolutionary resistance in the Vendée, another went to the West Indies, and another fought in the north of the country. Alexandre Dumas, father of the future novelist, distinguished himself.[177] Raimond was too old to fight, but as a resident of the Tuileries neighborhood, he participated in that section of the militia, and he donated money to help in the Vendée, a bloody struggle that lasted several years.[178]

In the meantime, as the political atmosphere in Paris was radicalizing, blacks started turning their attention to slavery. On 17 May 1793, Julien Labuissonnière, a black man from Martinique, put his signature, together with seventeen others, to an "address" to the Convention and to all political clubs. In it, he asks the French, who risked so much for "the sacred rights of man," to listen to "the cries of a million slaves." Using metaphors of degeneration and rebirth, he first depicts tyranny as a tree that slowly grows and covers everything with its shadow; a wise government can cut it at the root, and humanity will flourish. He then speaks in the name of the slaves: "We see the beauty of a sunrise, we feel the softness of the zephyr, we harvest for men who haven't sown, we gather treasures that we can't enjoy, we serve without hope for freedom." But now, thanks to France's new commitment to liberty, equality, and the rights of man, the slaves will be enlightened, and they will "fertilize the rich earth." A man is like a plant that can only grow in good conditions; without freedom, this land will remain sterile. The laws of the Revolution will "regenerate the destinies of men" because they should also apply to the slaves. Why should there be a difference in rights "between men who are equal"? He then asks for immediate abolition in all the colonies of the republic.[179] With his metaphor of regeneration, Labuissonnière was clearly appealing to republican feelings.

Abolition was then dramatically brought up in the Convention on 4 June, when a delegation of free blacks asked if they could parade in front of the assembly. The same group had visited the Jacobin club the previous day and had been well received.[180] The leader reminded the deputies that they belonged to a great nation that had been called upon to spread freedom in the world, and he laid an abolitionist petition on the desk—it was Labuissonnière's.[181] Five of the signatories, probably also present that day, were members of the American company, a unit of the Légion des Américains, come to Paris to question their proposed reassignment to the colonies.[182] The group then marched to the sound of military music, bearing a tricolor flag that featured three men—a white, a mulatto, and a black—armed with a pike that bore a liberty bonnet. An inscription read: "Our union will be our force." With this flag, the blacks had ingeniously conflated devotion to the republic and the universalism of the Revolution; it was also an eerie anticipation of the three-man delegation that would walk into the room the next February.[183] Among the group was a black woman who was 114 years old, who marched holding the arms of two petitioners. Her name was Jeanne Odo, the leader informed them, and she was born in Port-au-Prince. The whole assembly stood up, and the president gave her the fraternal embrace. Grégoire spoke, first reminiscing that a few years ago, an older man from the Jura, a region in eastern France, had also stood before the Assembly in order to thank its members for breaking feudal bonds. Then all the deputies stood up to honor old age. Grégoire then made his point: "There still exists an aristocracy, that of the skin." "I hope," he continued, "that the national Convention will apply the principles of equality to our brothers in the colonies . . . and that very soon you will be presented with a report that will recommend freedom for the blacks."[184] While the petition was sent to die in a committee, the whole episode seems like a rehearsal for 16 Pluviôse.

The next day, as Benot puts it, Labuissonnière "didn't go to sleep." He wrote a flier in which he addresses the *sans-culottes,* or radical working-class revolutionaries, in combative language. Yesterday, he says, their black brothers paid a visit to their deputies, and said: "Give us liberty, or give us death." Such was their cry of pain, but then the assembly "pulled the veil of oblivion over the wounds we were showing them" and relegated the petition to the darkness of a committee. He urges the real republicans to help them in this fight, to come and "plant with us the tree of liberty," promising that the slaves will be forever grateful.[185] On 8 June, a black delegation was received by the *commune* of Paris. The delegates then proceeded to the Champ de Mars to take a civic oath in front of the "altar to the fatherland," which had been erected for the Feast of the Federation, an event that took place on 14 July 1790 to commemorate the fall of the Bastille. Back at the town hall, they read an address in which they asked for "liberty for America," and they were assured that they would receive help.[186] The president then put a crown on Jeanne Odo's head. A few days later, the *commune* of Paris, which had promised the blacks a banner, decided that it would feature, on one side, a white, a black, and a mulatto, with the inscription "Men of color, you will be free" and, on the other, Liberty and Equality holding a globe, with the words "Universal liberty and equality."[187] But they heard that Labuissonnière had been arrested, in a process that remains murky. Whatever the reasons, it is clear that, as blacks made an increasingly vocal show of their attachment to republican liberty, the white colons increased their efforts against them in the background. Raimond would be arrested in September.

In the end, the first great abolition of slavery happened thanks to a speech—the one Dufaÿ made in front of the Convention—that derived its power not just from ideology but from its emphasis on black agency. In this long speech, which apparently swayed all the members of the Convention, Dufaÿ first devotes much time to defending the decisions made by Sonthonax and Polverel. He presents Galbaud, the governor who stoked the conflict that led to the burning of Le Cap, as a traitor, a counterrevolutionary bent on serving "the pride of whites"—especially all the whites who wanted to "shake off the yoke of France"—and on giving the colony to Spain or England. Then he shows how the men of color, who are "the people, the true *sans-culottes* in the colonies," immediately rallied around the commissioners: "They defended your colleagues with the greatest courage, they fought like heroes." Then, when they realized that the commissioners had been forced to retreat and that the men of color were fighting for their lives, the slaves decided to join the fray—first the city slaves, then the rebelling slaves who came running from the plains and the mountains. They fought bravely, but in return, they asked for freedom—"they even added: *the Rights of Man.*"[188] The blacks had the upper hand; they knew they were needed and had the commissioners in their power. So freedom had to be promised, as the only way to preserve the colony was to free all the slaves.

Ultimately, Dufaÿ argues that the blacks are the true republican patriots. Their desire for liberty is anchored in their love of France, the "mother country." When they decided to defend Le Cap, they were fighting for France and for the freedom and the equality that, to them, it represents. When they demanded freedom for their wives, they argued that they would join the fold of the republic: "They share our feelings; while we fight for France, they will instill them into our children; they will work to feed the warriors."[189] Children, being of their blood, could not remain slaves either. And so Dufaÿ paints the picture of valiant republican families, inspired by public virtue, and completely devoted to France, while the British and the Spaniards were waiting in the shadows and beckoning to them. In these conditions, Dufaÿ argues, the cause of humanity was joined to the cause of France, and the commissioners made a glorious decision. While he adds that it came with a strict regulation of labor conditions, the image that emerges is one of discipline and contentment. The idea is that freedom will make the colony flourish again.

And so Dufaÿ presents the events in Saint-Domingue as a natural extension of the ideals of French revolutionary republicanism, and he presents himself as one of the channels that helped ideas flow from the metropole to the colony. He tells of his frequent conversations with the slaves, in which he would recount the portentous events happening in the metropole. He had always carried the "germs of liberty and equality" in his heart, but in Paris, he learned from the Revolution and from popular societies: "I only saw in the revolution that took place in Saint-Domingue the realization of my wishes for the human race." Now he could finally "see all the men equal and embrace them as brothers." He stands before the deputies, proud to relay these men's "devotion to the republic, one and indivisible: Europeans, creoles, Africans, don't know any other color, any other name than that of Frenchman." He urges them: "Please create a new world once again."[190] The assembly was ready to do just that.

•

If the achievement of 16 Pluviôse was a total loss for the white colons, it seems that for the rest of the country, it was cause for celebration. That evening, the three deputies were warmly received at the Jacobin club. Each of them made a speech and received the fraternal embrace from the president. They then presented the assembly with a tricolor flag bearing a white, a black, and a mulatto, a sure sign that they had established contacts with the black community in the capital.[191] On 11 February, they were welcomed at the Paris *commune,* with applause from the room and embraces from the president. Mills declared that, as the delegate of black constituents, he expressed "the most ardent feelings for liberty." Belley then spoke: "I was a slave since my childhood." With these opening words, he dramatically conveyed the meaning of abolition, for an audience that had rarely been in direct contact with slavery. "In the course of my life," he continued, "I have felt deserving of being French, and my blood has been spilled for the French Republic." He promises that the tricolor flag will always "fly on our shores and in our mountains."[192] With these words, he was inserting himself in this historical and ideological moment, as one of its most stellar representatives. On 18 February, a huge celebration took place at the "Temple of Reason," as Notre-Dame had been renamed. Hundreds of people attended, including *sans-culottes,* popular societies, and deputies from the Convention. The three deputies from Saint-Domingue made quite an impression.[193] Pierre Gaspard Chaumette, representing the *commune,* gave a grand speech celebrating the advent of reason and justice over tyranny and the search for pleasure and luxury. After showing that slavery is the opposite of civic and personal virtue, that it has brought down empires throughout history, that it offends the laws of nature and civilization, he invites his audience to celebrate because "SLAVERY IS ABOLISHED."[194] His concluding shout, "VIVE L'ÉGALITÉ! VIVE LA LIBERTÉ!" would resonate throughout the country in the next few months, as hundreds of congratulations would be sent to the Convention, and at least twenty towns would celebrate revolution and abolition as synonymous and forever linked. The message was clear: blacks were the real republicans, and they had helped complete the work of the Revolution.[195]

REPUBLICAN AND COSMOPOLITAN

In 1797, an unusual painting was exhibited at the Elysée hotel, a beautiful neoclassical building situated in the heart of the city. It was titled *Portrait of a Negro;* the painter was Anne-Louis Girodet de Roussy-Trioson. The next year, the portrait was exhibited at the Salon, an internationally known exhibition that took place in the Louvre, and this time it was titled *Portrait of C. Belley, Former Representative of the Colonies.* The *C* stood for *Citizen.* The painting is about five by four feet, and it shows a tall, handsome, middle-aged black man who looks rather formidable. His dark blue coat opens at the neck to leave room for a thick white neckpiece, which contrasts with the smooth black skin of his face. It is also held together at the waist by an elaborate tricolor sash. In his left hand, Belley holds a hat with a tricolor cocarde; his right elbow leans comfortably against a plinth, which bears the white marble head of an older man, and the inscription "G. T. Raynal." Belley looks upward and to the right, so we can see his salt-and-pepper, frizzy hair and a gold earring. He looks both masculine and elegant, both sensual and intelligent.

It is unclear whether Belley commissioned the painting or Girodet approached him, but in any case, it shows an ideal that Belley was striving for. He seems to be the living embodiment of what the Revolution signified for him. He comes across as a man of both thought and action, proud to be French, eager to serve. He has traveled to France to remind her that her national identity now embraces all races, and he can now stand leisurely, without humility or gratitude, besides a bust of Raynal, widely seen as an abolitionist and a defender of the rights of blacks. At the same time, though, the painter does not want the white viewer to forget Belley's racial difference. Unlike abolitionist imagery, which often asks the viewer to forget about racial difference for the sake of empathic identification, Belley's blackness is highlighted and made alive. His attitude, moreover, is one of relaxed independence, as he is lounging by a marble bust he at the same time seems to ignore. As Darcy Grimaldo Grigsby argues, the portrait "enhances our sense of the personal autonomy and psychological independence of a specific black man precisely because it insists, with extraordinary intensity and detail, upon his irreducible distinctness" (*Extremities*, 49). In this sense, the portrait expresses Belley's political philosophy: a universalism that is anchored in national identity, a cosmopolitanism that does not preclude racial pride. The past three years had seen him acting it out—and finding many allies and enemies along the way.

Belley found enemies because, of course, as soon as the abolition decree was pronounced, many people started working against it, and Belley played a role in countering them, both by his presence and by taking part in the conversations, sometimes belligerently. He spoke at least twice in front of the Convention. On 23 August 1794, he published an essay directed against two white colons who had agitated against Sonthonax and Polverel and who had also tried to make the lives of the deputies from Saint-Domingue miserable. In 1795, he published an essay against another white colon. He also put his signature to various statements issued by the deputation. In all these contributions, it is clear that Belley has absorbed the ideas and the vocabulary of French republicanism, particularly the emphasis on patriotism and unconditional devotion to the republic that marked its second phase. At the same time, he is always careful to place his arguments within the larger context of universal freedom and equality. The voice that comes across is that of a French revolutionary, a republican, and a black cosmopolitan all at once.

•

Ever since they had arrived in France in July 1792, after their election as commissaries by the Colonial Assembly in Le Cap, the white plantation owners Pierre-François Page and Augustin-Jean Brulley had devoted their energy to lobbying government, defending white colons, undermining Sonthonax and Polverel, and, after they arrived, harassing the three deputies.[196] Having to deal with the Convention, a new, more radical assembly with no representatives for white colonial interests, they tried to ally themselves with the Jacobins by appealing to their shared hate for the Girondins, also called Brissotins because the group had originally grown under Brissot's leadership. They knew that emphasizing the friendship between Brissot and Sonthonax was a good strategy. As a result, in the fall of 1792, the Jacobin club expelled Sonthonax and Polverel.[197] On 15 March 1793, ten days after the Convention issued a decree that gave more powers to the two commissioners in Saint-Domingue, Page and Brulley were part of a delegation of white colons who submitted a petition to the Convention, warning that the decree would turn them into dictators who were not to be trusted.[198] On 19 March, they protested again, and the Convention suspended the decree. On 29 April, the criminal tribunal acquitted an ex-governor of Saint-Domingue after hearing witnesses who declared that Sonthonax and Polverel were "counterrevolutionary agents belonging to a faction led by Brissot."[199] Finally, on 16 July 1793, a letter from the colons was read aloud to the Convention. It accused the commissioners of sowing anarchy on the island and of planning to welcome the British and the Spaniards into the colony; the colons, "bound by interest and affection to the metropole," were asking for help.[200] The Convention, seemingly convinced by this war of attrition, and still dealing with the recent death of Marat, proceeded to vote on a decree of accusation against the commissioners, recalling them to France for a trial. "These commissioners are the agents and creatures of people like Brissot, like Clavière," declared Jacques Nicolas Billaud-Varenne, a future member of the Committee of Public Safety and one of the architects of the Reign of Terror.[201]

After the news of the burning of Le Cap reached France in August 1793, Page and Brulley used all the means in their political repertoire to spread their version of the story, which was an indictment of Sonthonax and Polverel. They swayed Jean Bon Saint-André, minister of the navy, who presented a report to the Convention that was very critical of the commissioners: they had ordered "the murder of whites," and they were planning to "either usurp the sovereign power on the island or give it to the enemy."[202] He asks that the arrest decree decided in July be executed, and the Convention agrees. In the next few months, Page and Brulley had many meetings with Jean-Pierre-André Amar, member of the Committee of General Security, and they persuaded him to arrest Julien Raimond. When the Girondins were executed in October, it looked like the only voices that had kept abolitionism alive had been silenced. In January, Page and Brulley felt confident enough to provide the War Ministry with a list of "counterrevolutionaries" (Popkin, 352), asking that they be arrested. While overall, probably preoccupied with what they considered more urgent issues, the Convention seemed to show little enthusiasm for Page and Brulley's shenanigans, it did agree to all the proposals that came before them bearing the mark of the white colons. Abolitionism, though kept alive by interventions such as the black parade in the Convention on 4 June, was being undermined from the other side, and it is likely that things would have run their course if the three deputies from Saint-Domingue had not arrived and shaken things up.

On the day that Belley and his fellow deputies finally made it to Paris, Page and Brulley asked Amar to arrest them. After they gave him a written request signed by other colons, whom they had misled about the nature of the deputation, Amar agreed.[203] The next day, before the arrest could be executed, the three deputies testified before the Committee of Public Safety and made a strong impression. A few days later, four policemen visited them, and after they interrogated Dufaÿ and Mills, the deputies were arrested and imprisoned. On 31 January, Dufaÿ and Mills wrote a letter to the Convention from the prison, complaining about their treatment, as they had been left without beds or heat, and swearing their fidelity to the motherland and to the republic. "There is in this horrible affair," they concluded, "a hatred of France, a hatred of equality, and racial prejudice, because this deputation has two men of color, and there are more in the deputation that is on its way here."[204] It is not clear why Belley did not sign the letter. On 2 February, however, Page and Brulley heard from Barère, a member of the Committee of Public Safety, that the committee was very angry about the arrest of the deputies, whom they had released. "Everybody knows," he declared, "that the whites are the aristocrats in this colony, and that blacks and men of color are the patriots."[205] The next day, Page and Brulley heard that the deputies had been seated in the Convention. They sent a letter of protest, in which they said that Belley was not even French but came from "an African Bambara nation,"[206] but this attempt at intervention had no effect. The Convention had clearly sided with the deputies. Still, the fact that they had been imprisoned was a sign that there was no complete unity on the question of slavery.

Indeed, the enthusiasm and acclamations that marked the abolition of slavery on 4 February may have masked voices that were reticent or critical. As Yves Benot has shown, official accounts of the event give hints that that may have been the case. After the wording of the decree was agreed on, a few members argued that the word "slavery" was a "stain" on such a noble text, and it should be removed. It took an intervention from Grégoire, the same person who, during the debates on the 28 March 1790 law had argued that it should refer specifically to free men of color unless the colony interpret it narrowly, to plead for keeping the word "slavery" in the decree: "otherwise one would claim once again that you meant something else."[207] Moreover, the fact that Delacroix closed the discussion indicates that some members had asked to send the proposal to a committee, a sure way to bury it. The next day, after the president read the minutes, one representative came back to the question of the use of the word "slavery"; the proposal was again put down, this time by several representatives, including Dufaÿ. Ultimately, it was the original text that was published, but the discussion had made a few cracks appear in the surface of unanimity.[208]

Aware of these velleities, Belley intervened and made his voice heard. On 8 February, a group of people of color living in Paris came before the Convention in order to offer thanks for the decree. César Télémaque, who a few years later would be mayor of Le Cap and play a role in the Haitian Revolution, stated that they had come to congratulate the deputies for the service they had rendered to equality "by adopting among you our brothers."[209] This wise decree would make them forget two centuries of suffering and hardships, as well as the hated word "colon." It was the true legacy of the Revolution and augured universal happiness. Moved, the president answered that France now only knew free men: "*Your rights have been given back to you,* because you should never have lost them."[210] A few minutes later, Belley stood up, walked to the tribune, and addressed the assembly. "I am sure you don't expect from me brilliant eloquence," he started bluntly, both reminding them of his racial difference, which was plain to see, and acknowledging the possibility of racial prejudice among his colleagues. He went on: "I will speak according to my heart; and naked truth shall be my whole talent."[211] Just as he had done when answering his white attackers in Philadelphia, Belley was emphasizing his emotional connection to the nation. He is both black and a child of the republic speaking to his brothers, he implied, and his straightforwardness is a token of his affection, as well as of his republican virtue. In a few strokes, Belley established himself as the one element in the assembly that gave their patriotism a larger meaning—that made its members consciously see racial difference and embrace it. "The tribune of the Convention is now really the tribune of Equality," wrote *Le Journal de Paris,* "since a black citizen, deputy of Saint-Domingue, has finally spoken at it for the first time. His name is Jean-Baptiste Belley."[212]

As a good republican, Belley then went for the jugular. He reminded the assembly of all the vexations he and his two colleagues had suffered at the hands of Page and Brulley. Implicitly presenting them as traitors, he accused them of undermining the colony—a dangerous accusation considering that, the year before, a governor had been executed for the same reason. After all, he continued, "It is they who managed to have us thrown in prison, my colleagues and myself, when we arrived."[213] As a consequence, he asked "that these dangerous schemers be arrested."[214] Though the Convention did not act right away, Belley had made it clear that he would use his position as a deputy to undermine white colonial power. Accusations at the time were often a stepping-stone to the guillotine, and he knew that Sonthonax and Polverel, who were still in Saint-Domingue, would have to come home to be tried. He may also have had a thought for Brissot, who had been executed in October. The only way to maintain liberty and equality, he knew, was to hold the pressure on the Convention and keep reminding the delegates that a multiracial nation requires constant vigilance. More important, he made it clear to the deputies that he, and not the colons, represented the true republican revolutionaries.

In the next few months, the deputies engaged in a public exchange of accusations with Page and Brulley; the attacks were personal, but the broader context was the meaning of the Revolution and the question of who were its true inheritors. On 24 February, the deputies wrote a letter to the Committee of Public Safety, in which they emphasized that Page and Brulley were not official representatives of the colony, since they had been chosen by a colonial assembly that excluded people of color, even though the law of 4 April 1792 had already been passed. Moreover, they were sent *"to the tyrant only, with a specific order to treat with him exclusively, and to bypass any national assembly."*[215] Unlike these royalist usurpers, the implication was that the three deputies had been elected in a democratic process that reflected the goals of the Revolution. They asked that the colons' papers be seized and that all the counterrevolutionaries, such as the members of the separatist Saint-Marc assembly, be arrested. On 7 March, Page and Brulley were arrested. Two days later, the Convention issued a decree ordering the arrest of counterrevolutionary colons—most of the white colons living in Paris—and the seizure of all their papers.[216] Clearly, the Convention adhered to the philosophy expounded by the deputies, which entailed that real devotion to abolition meant not just the passing of a decree but a continued dedication to its defense.

As the colons kept putting out accusatory letters, even from prison, Belley made an important contribution to these public exchanges. On 23 August, he published an essay "to his colleagues" of the Convention. Once again, he starts the essay by stating that he has no eloquence: "I am one of those men of nature whom the wisdom and the principles of the French nation have snatched from the yoke of despotism." Again holding up the image of a black man who speaks from the heart, he emphasizes the fusion of his love of liberty and his national feelings. But this love of liberty is not just personal or passive. Because he also feels the need to defend the dignity of his constituents, he attacks Page and Brulley as enemies of the republic, as men who have always rejected what came from the motherland, as men sold out to Louis XVI. The only reason they came to France was to submit to the king a decree from the Colonial Assembly that declared slavery inviolable—an assembly that, moreover, "had refused to admit citizens of color and blacks, who at the time were not considered *persons*." Once in France, they fought anybody who wanted to bring the Revolution to the colonies and install "liberty and equality among all men without distinction." It is clear, Belley says, that these men were aiming at separation and federalism so that the colony could be left to its own devices. These men were "against national assemblies and the convention, Jacobins, the civil commissioners, and everything else that came from France."[217] He knows that this accusation of separatism conveys the image of a white clique turning away from universalist principles in order to keep their privileges. Once again, patriotism is equated with principles of racial equality.

He then adjusts his critique to the immediate political context. He connects the colons to the Terror by pointing out that the famous *conspiration des prisons,* or prison conspiracy, through which the Revolutionary Tribunal "purged" the prisons of hundreds of prisoners, bypassed them. Obviously Antoine Fouquier-Thinville, the public prosecutor who sent so many people to the guillotine, was their "intimate friend." No doubt Belley is aware that this connection can hurt them, since by the time he is writing, Robespierre has been executed following the so-called Thermidorian reaction that took place on 27 July, Fouquier-Thinville has been arrested, and the new mood is critical of the Terror. Page and Brulley displayed the mind-set of the Terror, he implies, when they asked the Convention that Sonthonax and Polverel "be declared outlaws, *and this without being heard,* and on their own special denunciation." Belley then turns the legal table against them, arguing that they are not valid delegates, and they do not know anything about what happened in the colony, since they have been in France since 1792. He points out that Sonthonax and Polverel have been honest enough to come back to France and face their accusers and submit themselves to the law, something Page and Brulley would most certainly not have done. So—and this is the climax of the piece—he asks that the men be judged on the basis of the documents that "attest to their crime and their treachery." Placing himself within an attachment to the legal realm, Belley knows how to use the revolutionary language appropriate for this more bureaucratic time period. At the same time, he is aware that his readers know he is black, and he keeps emphasizing that his enemies have "a profound hate for liberty and equality."[218] In this contribution, Belley shows that, more than the specific characteristics of the French Revolution he is espousing, it is the wider, more universal principles of freedom and equality that he wants to serve.

The day before this essay was published, he had made a similar case in the Convention. That day, a group of white colons had appeared before the assembly, led by Louis François René Verneuil, a former plantation owner who had been expelled by Sonthonax during the December 1792 troubles, and who would be one of the official accusers of Sonthonax and Polverel in front of the colonial commission set up to untangle what happened in Saint-Domingue.[219] In his speech, Verneuil presents the white colons as patriots, arguing that they are the ones who have been "oppressed, assassinated." Sonthonax and Polverel are the cause of all the horrors that took place in the colony, and their sole goal was to amass as much gold as possible. And yet they are walking around free, while the colons are in prison! He asks that Page and Brulley be released and that their testimony be heard against that of the commissioners. The Convention decided that such a procedure was fair and immediately decreed the release of the colons. At this point, Belley intervened: "You must know that the colonies are lost. Who lost them? Is it the colons? Is it their agents? Yes." To him, releasing the colons had nothing to do with justice: "Page and Brulley are villains. Justice and fairness are certainly in order, but not indulgence for men covered with crimes." Once again, he knew that as a black man—and the report of the debate refers to him as "BELLEY, *man of color*"—he brought a particular meaning to the notions of "justice" and "crime."[220] In the next few months, Page and Brulley would print several responses, but a year later, Sonthonax and Polverel would be vindicated by the colonial commission.

•

In the next few years, Belley settled into his life as a deputy in Paris, and together with his colleagues, kept applying pressure to make sure that the republic would live up to its ideals. By summer 1794, the other two deputies from Saint-Domingue had arrived. Born in France, Nicolas-Pierre Garnot, white, had lived in the colony for twenty years as a plantation owner. A biographer describes him as a kind slaveowner who freed his slaves as soon as the troubles started. Back in France, he became reacquainted with old friends, including Jacques-Alexis Thuriot de la Rosière, a radical republican, as well as Alexandre Dumas, by now a famous general. He could feel the political winds were turning. When he asked Thuriot if he should pay a visit to all-powerful Robespierre, Thuriot answered: *"Avoid that by all means. The bugger doesn't have a month to live!"*[221] The other deputy, Joseph Georges Boisson, black, was born in Le Cap. Together, the five deputies fended off more attacks from Page and Brulley, who, in June 1795, were still penning screeds arguing that the deputies were illegitimate and colluding with England. In a now more sedate political climate, they also attacked them as friends of Robespierre and Thuriot and as "executioners of the colons, exterminators of their families, destroyers of their property."[222] In their own statement, the deputies argued that the colons wanted to "make people of color worry about their rights, and blacks about their status and their freedom, in order to pull them away from France."[223] Equality and freedom were still tightly linked to patriotism.

Toward the end of 1794, Belley defended these same principles vehemently against another white colon, Benoît-Louis Gouly, representative of Isle de France, the French island colony in the Indian Ocean that had been the setting of *Paul et Virginie*. In the months after 16 Pluviôse, the Convention's main task regarding the colonies was to decide on the measures to take in order to apply the decree. After a series of long and passionate discussions in February 1795, it would decide to send representatives to the colonies. In the meantime, Gouly applied constant pressure on various committees in order to slow down the process, and on 27 November 1794, he published a long pamphlet expounding his views. The pamphlet was strikingly conservative compared to the pragmatism he had exhibited until then.[224] He starts by emphasizing the vital role played by the colonies in French commerce and prosperity. But he then reassures colons that this connection does not mean political oversight: "The Nation is not gathered today to make laws for the universe; it will only be concerned with France"; in order to maintain the colonies and make them flourish, the representatives "will educate themselves about the character of the colons and of the foreigners who live there, the influence of the climate, the nature of property, the means to preserve it." Later on, he asserts that there can be two constitutions in the same empire, since "the constitution and the laws are relative to people, land, and things."[225] Gouly is energetically endorsing the traditional white colons' defense of particularism for the colonies, rejecting the universalism that had led to 16 Pluviôse in the first place.

More shocking is his description of blacks in the colonies, which can be seen as an early example of full-blown biological racism. He starts by saying that the white colons are not against freedom and political rights, but these should be determined by the "individual faculties" of the people in question. Rejecting the blanket assertion of freedom and equality derived from the republican perspective, he uses this notion of individualism in order to paint a devastating portrait of blacks. He starts by asserting physical difference, "in the color of his skin, in the habits of his body, in the shape of his members, in the form of his head, in the shape and arrangement of the various parts of his face." He then launches into an accumulation of negative statements about blacks' faculties, stating that blacks act and don't think, have no deep feelings of joy or pain, have no shame or desire, hate work, have no constancy in love, have no memory or concept of the future, have no talent of invention. He concludes: "Thus is the African whom today you affectionately call your brother, your friend, but who will never be your equal." To him, republicanism applies in France, where "the character, the genius, the intellectual faculties of the French are the same," but cannot work in a multiracial and multicultural society.[226] Political principles cannot be universal.

Belley published his answer shortly thereafter, and while he rebuts Gouly's racist assertions, his main concern is to maintain that republican principles are universal. He reasserts his attachment to the French Republic precisely because it stands for those principles. What Gouly writes contradicts "the sacred rights of man" and "the sublime morality of our constitution." Who are these tyrants, he asks, who are rejecting the laws of the republic? Clearly they are white colons who want to maintain slavery, arguing that the laws of the colonies should be independent from those of France. If all the deputies asked for their own special laws, what would happen to the "indivisible Republic"? To him, the unity of the republic symbolizes the universality of its principles. Then he asks: "Who is not full of indignation and of pity when they read the bizarre portrait that Gouly draws of blacks?" He asks his reader to think of the conditions in which slaves live and to realize that slaves are not degraded by nature but by slavery itself. He asks: "Do you believe, citizen colleagues, that nature is unjust, that it has, as the colons affirm, made men to be the slaves of others?"[227] Using himself as an example, he says he was born in Africa, and gained his liberty thanks to his hard work. Slaves are not brutes; they are thankful to France and ready to fight for it. He then asks that the decree of 16 Pluviôse be sent to the colonies as soon as possible. Through this last published writing, Belley reasserted his principles: a belief in human rights without negating difference, a universalism anchored in republican nationalism.

Gouly quickly published a response that, while its tone is often conciliatory, confirms Belley's attacks. He keeps calling the slaves "foreigners," denying the very attachment to France that motivates Belley. He says he does not want to repeal the decree of 16 Pluviôse, "only to regulate its application, taking into account *the place, the things, and the different races of men*," thereby confirming that he is asking for a particular status for the colonies. He evokes the loss of the colonies. He asserts that he is fighting for the blacks' well-being, but he also states that he was not sent to France to represent "a race of foreign men to the detriment of the indigenous race."[228] The whole argument speaks to a vision that is opposite to Belley's, in its particularism, racism, and lack of egalitarianism. On 29 November, Dufaÿ spoke in front of the Convention, officially to complain that Gouly's pamphlet had been published in its name. He then launches into a critique, arguing that Gouly's views are "anti-social, anti-republican, anti-political," and "contrary to the unity, the indivisibility of the republic."[229] If the colonies are left to their own devices, he continues, they will be in the hands of white plantation owners, but if they belong to the people, as national sovereignty would have it, then they belong to the blacks. He then praises the decree of 16 Pluviôse, which has been translated into several languages, and has been acclaimed everywhere. The universal tide of liberty cannot be turned back. He asks that the Convention declare it does not approve of the pamphlet, and after a discussion reiterating the rights of all men, white and black, the Convention approved Dufaÿ's proposal.

Belley continued his work as a deputy for the next few years, even as France's political structure was changing. From November 1795, the government was organized as a bicameral legislature, composed of a Council of Elders and a Council of 500 and led by a five-member Directory. While more conservative than its predecessor and often derided as the unexciting tail end of the Revolution, this government continued the fight against racial inequality; it kept the abolition of slavery enshrined in its constitution, and it significantly increased the number of black deputies seated in the legislature. Belley now sat on the Council of 500; also reelected were four of the other Saint-Domingue deputies who had been with him since 1794: Boisson, Dufaÿ, Garnot, and Laforest. In 1796, six new deputies were added to the delegation: Etienne Laveaux, Martin Noël Brothier, and Sonthonax, white; Pierre Thomany, black; Louis François Boisrond and François Pétiniaud, of mixed race. After elections in the spring of 1797, two more black deputies arrived: Etienne Mentor sat on the Council of 500, Jean-Louis Annecy on the Council of Elders. Together the black deputies would form an active group, on both the political and the social scene. But by May 1797, Belley was done with his work as a deputy. On 5 March, the Council of 500 had proceeded to a sort of raffle for former Convention members, and Belley had picked the note that said: "Member of the Council of 500 until this coming May."[230] Soon, though, he would have a different sort of job to do.

•

Saint-Domingue had gone through major changes since Belley left in 1793. In the course of 1794, a new black military leader had emerged; his name was Toussaint Louverture. Over the next few years, Louverture retook the northern and the western provinces from the Spaniards and the British, respectively. Even as he gained ground, he tried to bring the plantation economy back. After he drove the British out of Mirebalais, an important position in the western province, he was named commander in chief of the French forces in the colony. He then grew increasingly powerful, sending Sonthonax, who had come as part of a new commission, back home, and initiating negotiations with the British. So the French government decided to send another commissioner, Gabriel Hédouville, in order to reassert French authority. Hédouville arrived in Le Cap in March 1798. Accompanying him was Belley.

General Hédouville was known for his taming of the Vendée rebellion, and one may wonder why Belley chose to be part of this expedition against Louverture. It probably had to do with what he had been hearing about Louverture in Paris and may have been confirmed by Sonthonax if they had a chance to meet before his departure. Sonthonax had recently come back from Saint-Domingue, where he had been sent as part of a third commission in order to confirm the abolition of slavery, set up color-blind institutions, and work on reestablishing prosperity under new labor conditions. The choice of Sonthonax had been obvious; he was the first emancipator, he had been vindicated, and many former slaves loved and respected him. According to Madiou, when he disembarked in Saint-Domingue in May 1796, blacks had flocked to him, showing signs of their love.[231] As soon as he arrived, Sonthonax tried to "establish a viable, peaceful, and prosperous multi-racial society" (Stein, 135), leasing plantations, setting up schools, trying to get rid of the British in the western province. But establishing civilian control over the military leaders proved difficult, and in summer 1797, Louverture asked him to leave. The source of the conflict is unclear—after all, Sonthonax had promoted Louverture just a few months earlier. Sonthonax alleged that Louverture wanted to become the sole ruler of Saint-Domingue. This version of events must have riled Belley.

Indeed, like Sonthonax, Belley thought of French republican control as the best way to preserve liberty in Saint-Domingue and to spread it far and wide. Writing from the port of Brest on 4 February 1798, as he was awaiting departure, he was thinking about Sonthonax, who that very same day was testifying before the Council of 500 to respond to criticism from conservatives and royalists, whose influence was growing. The symbolism of the date was pregnant. "I am convinced," he writes Boisson, "that he will have been heard with some interest in his justification, and that he will prove easily that he has only been slandered by the enemies of liberty."²³² And indeed, in his speech, Sonthonax reminded his listeners that "emancipation was the Convention's most glorious act." He then described his mission as successful, but one remaining problem was Louverture, who "was guilty of being led by counter-revolutionaries into supporting independence" (Stein, 180). For Sonthonax, as for Belley, independence meant an inevitable retreat from the values of liberty and equality represented by France. Sonthonax made his philosophy public again the next year, on the same date, when in a speech, he said that slavery and the slave trade still flourished, and he urged his audience to fight for complete black freedom "so that, eventually, France's example would spread to the rest of the world" (Necheles, 162). Belley, who had returned to France a month before and was no doubt among the audience, must have approved wholeheartedly.

What Belley writes of Louverture confirms that he had no admiration for the man. Writing from Le Cap on 17 August, he tells Boisson that he, Hédouville, and a few others had landed in Santo Domingo in April and then made their way west: "We found the whole northern province in a surprising state of poverty." He continues: "Toussaint Louverture was in Gonaïves when we arrived. He didn't hurry to join us since, after waiting for fifteen days, the commissioner wrote to ask him to come since he didn't want to do anything without consulting with him." Louverture deigned to arrive five weeks later. There were galas, and he received presents from the Directory. "Would you believe, my friend," Belley asks Boisson, "that I didn't manage to have a single private conversation with him?" Still, Louverture was very much aware of Belley's role and presence. Belley had been led to believe that he would be in charge of the *gendarmerie,* or police force, in the whole colony. But Louverture "persuaded the commissioner to only give me the commandment of the northern province, out of fear, he said, that it would give me too much influence." Hédouville agreed, though he feared slighting Belley. Belley remained stoic and true to his principles, hoping that the commissioner would now "start to distinguish the friends of tranquility from those who are full of intrigue and ambition."²³³ And so Belley places himself clearly within the republican tradition of civic virtue, in order to distinguish himself from what he considers localized and self-interested. He may have felt vindicated: the mission only lasted a few months, as toward the end of October, Hédouville, Belley, and most of the officers who had come on the mission boarded a ship in the harbor of Le Cap, fleeing from thousands of troops under Louverture's command.²³⁴

After he returned to Paris, Belley continued to work with his colleagues. More than ever, this work now consisted in preserving the rights that had already been granted and promoting the idea of these rights as widely as possible, especially since an upsurge in royalism, foiled by a coup later in the year, showed that those rights could not be taken for granted. In January 1798, an important law had been passed. It confirmed an earlier law, passed the previous October, that officially declared the colonies French departments.[235] It also stated that blacks born elsewhere "are not considered foreigners; they enjoy the same rights as an individual born on French territory,"[236] provided they have an occupation. The law also provided for public instruction in the colonies. As soon as he came back, Belley joined the revamped Société des Amis des Noirs et des Colonies. Re-created in late 1797, the Société now had two main objectives: making sure that general liberty would not be revoked and keeping the colonies within the republic.[237] Belley managed to attend only two meetings, but it is clear that he was considered an important member, since at the second of these meetings, he introduced Dufaÿ. A black man sponsoring a white man—here was an example of the kind of equal treatment he had been fighting for. The Société also inherited from its predecessor an international consciousness. Several members read foreign works or had relationships with foreign abolitionists, particularly British. An important member was now Carl Bernhard Wadtsröm, a Swedish abolitionist who advocated the creation of colonies based on the abolition of slavery and the promotion of free commerce. So Belley was part of social circles that aimed to promote the internationalization of liberty.

He was also part of a black cosmopolitan community that fought for the same republican ideals. He seems to have had most in common with Pierre Thomany and Etienne Mentor. Thomany was quite active, both in the Société and in the legislature. He attended almost all the meetings of the Société and was its president for a while. On 4 February 1799, he gave a speech in the Council of 500 celebrating abolition. In it, he praises the Convention's decision, which dared to make philosophical principle trump commercial considerations so that Africans and their descendants could enjoy the freedom that was their due. As a result, the republic gained new children, ready to defend it against its enemies. He invites his audience to observe the new happiness of the freedmen's families. He urges them to envision the most moving portrait: "It is the spectacle of two million men to whom today's most beautiful celebration brings the highest joy; who, now looking at heaven, now at the shore that brings the vessels of the liberating nation, merge thanks to the divinity with feelings of gratitude toward their generous benefactors."[238] He then proposes that 16 Pluviôse be made a national holiday in the colonies, a symbol of the equivalency of love of freedom and national feeling.

Thomany was also a member of a legislative committee put together to evaluate the claims of former slave traders, and as such, he had the chance to defend the principle of equality against commerce. Ever since the decision of 16 Pluviôse, slave traders had inundated the government with petitions, asking that they be compensated for the debts still owed them by merchants or colons. Their argument was that the law of abolition should not be retroactive. But the committee argued that the slave trade was an unusual commercial transaction and that any debt connected to it disappeared once the law was passed. On 15 October 1798, the committee presented its conclusions: "All debts derived from the sale of slaves are now moot and abolished. It is forbidden for tribunals, either on the continent of the Republic, or in its islands and colonies, to pronounce any condemnation in this respect, and all judgments passed but not yet executed will be considered invalid."[239] This was a strong statement of principle, and it showed that the spirit of the Revolution was still alive and well among some legislators.

Etienne Mentor, though younger than his colleagues, often spoke in front of the legislature, emphasizing the values of universal equality and fraternity he saw embodied in the French Republic, and considering his personal history, this is not surprising. Born in Martinique, where his father was a blacksmith and a member of the National Guard, he was captain of a Chasseurs unit in Guadeloupe. When the island was taken by the British in 1794, they deported him, and after arriving in Brest, he was placed in the Arras battalion. From there he made his way to Paris, but he soon after embarked for Saint-Domingue to accompany the third commission led by Sonthonax. Once there, Sonthonax, praising Mentor's "zeal, patriotism, and talents," promoted him to *chef de bataillon*. In May 1797, Mentor was named adjutant general; commander in chief Louverture praised his "zeal and talents" in a letter to Sonthonax. Soon he was elected deputy and went back to Paris. After his term ended, he had his title of adjutant general confirmed by the Directory and asked to be assigned to the Army of the West. He needed work: "Without any means of existence, with a wife, a child, and a sister, he hasn't deserved this fate, and his dedication to the republican government remains steadfast," he wrote to the government.[240] In the end, he was sent back to Saint-Domingue, though he warned the authorities that he had publicly spoken against Louverture, and he did not want to undermine the success of the operation. He was sent anyway, but not without rescuing a sailor who had fallen into a stormy sea and being hospitalized as a result. Much about this man seemed to be a materialization of the principles he espoused.[241]

Like Belley, in his speeches he applied his republican principles to several levels, using the concept of brotherhood to refer to his black constituents, to his French compatriots, and to human beings all over the world. The blacks of Saint-Domingue, he said in May 1798, who have found "a fatherland, protectors, brothers" in France, swear attachment to it, and there is now universal hope, as "the link of the same interests, the same feelings, is starting to unite Europe to America, to Africa, to Asia." He ends the speech with a dig at "those who, motivated by personal ambition, could become traitors to the Republic."[242] Since he has just referred to black republicans, it is clear he means Louverture, and his placing of civic virtue above personal ambition mirrors Belley's. On 15 October of that year, he spoke in support of the committee that had evaluated the claims of former slave traders. The main idea that emerges from his speech is that those claims belong to a dark past that has now been revoked. "Those days are over," he says, "when the French used to have slaves; now he can only have equals and brothers." The petitioners "should not dishonor humanity by reviving memories that are as painful as humiliating for the unfortunate Africans and their descendants." These tyrants "should try to make us forget their wrongs instead of reminding us of them through a request that is as strange as it is unjust."[243] To Mentor, the equality of men and of their rights has now been established, and the march of progress, whether in time or space, is irrevocable. The next year, he would appear listed by a conservative "someone" as a neo-Jacobin and compared to Hébert, the radical republican, and to Robespierre.[244]

These black men were linked in other ways. For many of them, experience in the military was an important contributor to their notion of French citizenship, their cosmopolitanism, and their sense of racial solidarity. As we saw, Mentor was adjutant general in Saint-Domingue before he was elected. As a deputy, he supported the petitions of two men, Isaac Bazonga and Charles Soubise, who had been officers in the Légion des Américains and were asking the government for reinstatement in the military. An official document describes each of these men as uneducated and immoral,[245] but Mentor praised Soubise's "patriotism, good behavior, courage,"[246] and Thomany also signed Bazonga's petition. Bazonga had been born in Africa, enslaved in the West Indies, was an officer in France, and was obviously down and out after his service ended. The deputies' support may simply have been a form of racial solidarity; it may also have been the result of a broader vision, a desire for a racially integrated France that would symbolize the social transformation brought about by millions of Atlantic crossings. On 23 June 1799, Mentor spoke out about the treatment of two companies of men of color who had been made prisoner by the British in the West Indies and deported and were now confined on a small island on the French west coast in miserable living conditions. What Mentor mostly condemns, though, is their segregation from the regular army, since these men were "isolated from their European comrades in arms." Their sequestration reeked of the Ancien Régime and was contrary to the principles of the republic. They had been "relegated" to a corner of land, "far from their brothers in arms." He asks his colleagues to end "an exile that degrades them, that isolates them from other Frenchmen."[247] Once again, the military context provides the substance for a republican, transatlantic, multiracial equality.

If we are to judge from their letters, these men were also a tightly knit group of friends; they knew each other's families, and they helped each other become what Bernard Gainot calls "a social group in full ascension."[248] On 11 February 1798, while he was in Brest waiting to embark for Saint-Domingue, Belley wrote Boisson, asking him to keep him informed of all that will happen in the capital concerning the colonies. He then wishes him good health, "as well as your dear Adelle, to whom I'm asking you to say a thousand nice things." He then tells him he has just received a letter from Thomany, who tells him about the death of his grandson, Roy: "You can imagine how painful that is for me." He also sends greetings to "our brothers," including Mentor, as well as to their wives. He signs: "I am your friend, Belley." When he writes him from Saint-Domingue, he tells him that he has seen Boisson's mother and sister. In another letter, he says: "No, my friend, I don't expect you to see me as a father. You can be certain that I am your friend and that I will seize every opportunity to prove it to you."[249] In spite of their deputies' salaries, most of these men seem to have scrambled for a living, and they offered each other support. Belley was trying to help Boisson obtain a military commission. Boisson apparently liked the good life and owed people money, including Thomany. Thomany himself wrote that he was "embarrassed." Once back in Saint-Domingue, Belley himself said he had not been paid, and had to rely on friends.[250] Clearly, besides the interracial, republican feelings, there was also the sense that one could turn to one's black community for various forms of solidarity.

Another way in which these families created bonds is through the education of their children. We know through Belley's official declaration that he was not married.[251] But he had a son, whom he brought to France with him. In his dramatic speech on 16 Pluviôse, Dufaÿ had described the way Belley had been assailed by white colons on the ship docked at Philadelphia. Detailing their doings to the Convention, he told how they tried to pull off his cocarde and then "stole his watch, his money, all his belongings, even those of his child."[252] In Paris, this son attended a boarding school called the National Institution of the Colonies, which was a perfect example of what Gainot calls "republican integration." Created by the government to educate the children of colonial leaders, it occupied the space of a former college on the Left Bank and was directed by an abbey. The school opened in September 1798, and by 1800, thanks to the January 1798 law, which directed the colonies to send children every year to be educated in France, it counted almost eighty students. Louverture's sons, Isaac and Placide, attended, as well as Thomany's and those of Sonthonax and his mixed-race partner. White children also attended, including the sons of Brissot.[253] The school would turn into a symbol of the new times when it had to close its doors as the new century began.

On 18 Brumaire of year VIII, or 9 November 1799, a coup d'état brought General Napoleon Bonaparte to power. By this time, Louverture controlled the whole island of Hispaniola. Soon Napoleon promoted a constitution that allowed the colonies their particular laws, abandoning the universalism that had been the hallmark of the Revolution. In July 1801, Louverture himself promulgated a constitution for Saint-Domingue; while it proclaimed freedom from slavery and racial hierarchy, it also contained strict labor laws that, among others, severely limited workers' freedom of movement. It also had a dictatorial streak and helped Louverture turn the colony into a police state. In January 1802, a fleet of fifty ships, carrying twenty-two thousand soldiers and twenty thousand sailors, arrived in sight of the island. Leading it was General Charles Victor Emmanuel Leclerc, Napoleon's brother-in-law, charged with wresting power from Louverture. Soon it was all-out war. In June, Louverture was arrested, together with his wife and sons, who had come back with Leclerc, and all were taken to France. When Napoleon had signed a decree the month before reestablishing slavery in some colonies and allowing the slave trade, it was clear that the metropole had taken a sharp turn backward.

Leclerc found himself increasingly on the losing side, as thousands of his men died of yellow fever, and many blacks fighting with him switched sides and joined the rebels. His solution: genocide. "We must destroy all the blacks of the mountains—men and women—and spare only children under twelve years of age," he wrote Napoleon in October. "We must destroy half of those in the plains," he continued, "and must not leave a single colored person in the colony who has worn an epaulette" (Dubois, 291–92). Leclerc himself soon died of yellow fever, and he was replaced by the Viscount de Rochambeau, who gleefully continued his reign of terror. These practices led the rebels to unite, and by November 1803, Rochambeau surrendered to their leader, Jean-Jacques Dessalines. France had lost its republican symbolism by now, and on 1 January 1804, Dessalines declared an independent Haiti.

Belley was caught up in this new onslaught of imperialistic and racial violence. When in December 1799 he was asked his opinion about the best way forward for Saint-Domingue, he advocated strong military action, in keeping with his principled opposition to independence.[254] So he came with Leclerc. But he was suddenly slated for deportation a few months later, purportedly because he made "anti-European remarks."[255] It is possible that Leclerc decided he did not want strong black leaders around, since he sent many others along with him. The difference is that, after he disembarked in Brest in June 1802, Belley was sent to Belle-Ile, a small island off the coast of Brittany. He died there, in the military hospital, on 6 August 1805. He left a testament, which ceded his few belongings to his half brother, Joseph Domingue, "so that they could in part be given to his family in Saint-Domingue."[256] Joseph was twenty years younger and, like Belley, a military man and a patriot. A little more than a month later, he came from Rochefort, a coastal town about three hundred miles south, to gather a few clothes, shoes, silverware, and jewels—a few valuables left over by a man who had lived his life for an ideal.

3

John Marrant

From Methodism to Freemasonry

Of the three men who are the subjects of this book, John Marrant is the one who had the most peripatetic life. Born free in New York on 15 June 1755, he moved with his mother to Florida at the age of four. They were briefly in Georgia and then moved to Charleston, South Carolina, when he was eleven. According to his autobiography, he was impressed in the Royal Navy during the American Revolution, then lived in London for a few years, until he was ordained as a Methodist minister on 15 May 1785 and left for Nova Scotia, recently settled by American loyalists. He moved to Boston in 1787 and became chaplain of the black Freemasons. He returned to London in 1790, where he died a year later.

Marrant's three major pieces of writing trace the gradual growth of an urban free black from a musician to a Methodist to a cosmopolitan. The *Narrative of the Lord's Wonderful Dealings with John Marrant,* published in London just as he was about to sail for Nova Scotia, focuses on his dramatic conversion in Charleston, his stay with Cherokees, and his subsequent preaching among slaves. His *Journal,* published after he came back to London, is a detailed record of his ministering in Nova Scotia. A separately published sermon is an address to the Boston Freemasons. Like Capitein's, Marrant's Calvinism led him toward a revitalized vision of world community. But the vision itself, as well as the path toward it, differs significantly from Capitein's.

Marrant's growth started with a flash—his quick conversion in the days after he attended a revival meeting. To him, and in the words of this new brand of Christianity he was experiencing, it symbolized a new birth. This concept of new birth, or of a new, individual relationship with God, motivated his preaching in the next few years, whether in

John Marrant. Published by Daniel Boulter, 1795. (Fitzwilliam Museum, England)

the American colonies or in London. What mattered was a revitalized sense of self-worth fostered by religious fervor. Once in Nova Scotia, he started using the notion of a special relationship with the deity to give strength, hope, and a sense of social harmony to the communities he addressed. His religious and intellectual journey continued in Boston, where thanks to Freemasonry, his vision of community bloomed into a republican, cosmopolitan one. More than for Capitein or Belley, though, black identity would form an essential component of his cosmopolitan outlook as he faced the constant pull of communal and universal ideals.

And the fact that he traced this growth in a number of published works shows that, besides offering a record of his individual experience, Marrant felt he had a contribution to make to the public discourse by and about blacks in the late eighteenth century. Indeed, his variations on some major literary genres, such as the conversion narrative and the captivity narrative, imply a self-conscious desire to participate in the print culture of his time, and a fundamentally cosmopolitan sensibility.

Conversion and Captivity in South Carolina

John Marrant's *Narrative* is an evangelical conversion narrative with a difference. It features typical components of the genre, including a dissolute youth, a dramatic moment of conversion and acknowledgment of previous sin, a period of struggle, and a final sense of redemption or grace, signaling the beginning of a dedication to religious work. At the same time, it places the growth of this individual relationship to the deity within the racial and revolutionary context of the late-eighteenth-century American South. Looking back on his life from London in 1785, Marrant carved out a space for himself as a black man in the combined stories of religious and political individualism. The popularity of the *Narrative*—it went through as many as ten printings that year—was probably partly due to this novelty.[1]

•

Even for a religious culture that promoted dramatic conversions, Marrant's was pretty spectacular. Walking with a friend through the streets of Charleston one evening in spring 1770, he went by a crowded meeting house. Curious about the "crazy man" who was "hallooing" inside, he agreed with his friend that he would go in and start playing his French horn, which he was carrying with him. After he entered and was about to start blowing, the preacher, who as he later found out was the famous George Whitefield, turned to him and, seeming to look directly at him, said: "PREPARE TO MEET THY GOD, O ISRAEL." At this point, Marrant "was struck to the ground, and lay both speechless and senseless near half an hour." He was taken to the vestry, where Whitefield came to see him a bit later and immediately said: "JESUS CHRIST HAS GOT THEE AT LAST" (*Narrative*, 113). That evening Marrant was taken home to his sister's, where he lay three days without food. A minister sent by Whitefield then visited him and made him kneel to pray three times. The third time, "the Lord was pleased to set my soul at perfect liberty, and being filled with joy I began to praise the Lord immediately; my sorrows were turned into peace, and joy, and love" (114). Marrant's faith would be tested, but he had successfully undergone the single most defining moment of an evangelical Christian's experience.

No doubt Marrant's conversion narrative was inspired by the Ur-text of Christian conversion, Paul's conversion on his way to Damascus, as recounted in the Acts of the Apostles. The similarities are striking. As Paul is approaching Damascus, where he plans to take converts prisoner and bring them back to Jerusalem, "suddenly a light from heaven flashed around him." At this moment, he "fell to the ground and heard a voice say to him, 'Saul, Saul, why do you persecute me?'" When he asks who is speaking, he receives a resounding answer: "I am Jesus, whom you are persecuting." After he gets up, he finds that he is blind, and so his fellow travelers "led him by the hand into Damascus." Once there, "for three days he was blind, and did not eat or drink anything." Then suddenly, on being touched by Ananias, a disciple sent by God, "something like scales fell from Saul's eyes, and he could see again" (Acts 9:3-18). Soon he is baptized and starts the work of evangelization. Through his account, Marrant was clearly placing himself within this Pauline tradition of spectacular conversion.

By 1785, moreover, Anglo-American religious culture was awash with dramatic conversion narratives. The genre had received a boost in the course of the seventeenth century, when dozens of these narratives were published, as people seeking admittance to the Protestant churches had to testify that they had received a personal, saving grace, and they wrote down their testimonies.[2] The model for many after 1672 was the famous *Grace Abounding to the Chief of Sinners,* by John Bunyan, which he wrote while in prison for being a nonconformist, or someone who did not adhere to all the principles of the Church of England. In it, Bunyan describes a youthful period in which he has few equals "for cursing, swearing, lying and blaspheming in the holy name of God" (8). One day, he feels guilt after listening to a priest's sermon, "thinking and believing that he made that sermon on purpose to show me my evil-doing" (10), but soon he forgets about it. Some time later, though, as he is playing sports outside, "a voice did suddenly dart from heaven into my soul, which said: '*Wilt thou leave thy sins, and go to heaven? Or have thy sins, and go to hell?*'" (11). Convinced that it is already too late for him, he decides to ignore the voice. One day, though, while walking through the streets of Bedford, he hears a few poor women talking, and he is struck by what he hears: they are talking about "a new birth, the work of God on their hearts" and "how God had visited their souls with his love in the Lord Jesus" (14). The rest of the book describes his search for this new birth, through a complex maze of temptations and doubts, until he reaches full conversion and starts working as a minister. While Paul's conversion had been almost instantaneous, Bunyan's text became the paradigm for a convoluted, gradual movement toward a new birth.

These models then inspired the many narratives that were published in the first half of the eighteenth century, during an international movement of evangelical revival now commonly referred to as the Great Awakening. Not surprisingly, George Whitefield, the major figure in the spread of this revival, published his own. Its title, *A Short Account of God's Dealings with the Reverend Mr. George Whitefield,* is echoed in Marrant's. Like its models, the account first stresses an immoral youth. "It would be endless to recount the sins and offences of my younger days," Whitefield warns. Of the ten commandments, he can say that "I have broken them all from my youth" (28). At one point, he receives "unspeakable raptures" (31) in church and becomes interested in things religious, but this soon fades. He continues a sinful life and "went to public service only to make sport and walk about" (33). Gradually, though, he acquires devotion. At Oxford, he meets a group of Methodists, including Charles Wesley, who together with his brother John, had founded this new evangelical movement within the Church of England. Finally, upon reading Henry Scougal's *The Life of God in the Soul of Man,* a book that focused on a deep spiritual relationship with God, "a ray of Divine light was instantaneously darted in upon my soul." He starts writing letters to his family, letting them know that "there was such a thing as the new birth" (37), but their answers make it clear they think he has gone mad. After going through a series of temptations, and a meeting with John Wesley, he feels relieved of his burden and realizes that God has finally "taken possession of my soul" (49). He can now start his work as a preacher. In this work, he would focus on conversion as a moment or process of radical transformation or rebirth and become "the most important popularizer of the concept in Anglo-American history, at least until Billy Graham's revivals of the twentieth century" (Kidd, 48).[3] Because of his emphasis on the idea that conversion and grace only happen to those elected by God, he would also become the major representative of Calvinist Methodism.

While more dramatic than Whitefield's, Marrant's account of his conversion can still be seen as standing in the long line of spiritual narratives studded by best sellers such as Bunyan's and Whitefield's. He too presents his youth as dissolute. After convincing his reluctant mother that he should learn to play music rather than a trade, he learns to play the violin as well as the French horn. "This opened to me a large door of vanity and vice," he remembers, "for I was invited to all the balls and assemblies that were held in the town." Now thirteen and with plenty of pocket money, he is "devoted to pleasure, and drinking in iniquity like water" (*Narrative,* 112). After his dramatic conversion, he leaves the city and goes to live with his mother in the backcountry. Being persecuted by his mother, his siblings, and his neighbors for what they perceive as strange behavior, he goes through a period of temptation, but then one day, he grabs a pocket Bible and a book of hymns, and "went over the fence, about half a mile from our house, which divided the inhabited and cultivated parts of the country from the wilderness" (115). There he goes through a number of trials, including hunger, thirst, wild animals, and capture by Cherokees. He is then rewarded by his successful conversion of various people along his travels.

In many ways, then, Marrant's *Narrative* reflects his exposure to, and endorsement of, the focus of Anglo-American evangelical Christianity on an individual new birth through a new sense of deep personal faith. In Charleston, it happened through Whitefield and his minister, who also introduced him to the Bible, as he "now read the Scriptures very much" (114). In London, where he lived for several years before he published the *Narrative*, he made connections with evangelical circles. He lived for about three years with "a respectable and pious merchant" (126). In an affidavit appended to one of the *Narrative*'s editions, this merchant, John Marsden, testifies to Marrant's character in language typical of evangelicals, saying he lived "with honesty and sobriety," "had a desire to save his soul before he ever came to live with us," and attended "the means of Grace diligently" (131). After several years of roaming during the American Revolution, Marrant had clearly reconnected with his faith and its representatives by the time he started writing.

The fact that William Aldridge, a minister, took down the narrative and edited it also shows that Marrant was frequenting Methodist circles. Aldridge had long worked with Selina Hastings, Countess of Huntingdon, who, together with Whitefield, came to symbolize Calvinist Methodism. As a young adult, the countess had gone on a spiritual search, coming under the influence first of the Moravians, a group that stressed piety, then of John Wesley, who emphasized asceticism and striving for perfection in a methodical way, and finally of Whitefield, who believed in predestination. Toward the end of the 1740s, she asked Whitefield to be one of her personal chaplains.[4] From then on, she almost single-handedly built up the movement, founding dozens of chapels, appointing itinerant preachers, securing their ordinations in the Anglican Church, and setting up a ministers' college in Trevecca, in Wales. Aldridge had been trained at Trevecca and had preached in various places, including with Joseph Cook, another Trevecca student, who later moved to South Carolina. After separating from Hastings in 1776, he became the minister at the Independent congregation on

Jewry street, and he developed a good reputation as a preacher.[5] So for Marrant, Aldridge represented an important connection to the religious awakening he had experienced in his youth.

Indeed, the connection between his life in London and his previous life in the American colonies was strengthened by the fact that Marrant seems to have been at the confluence of various evangelical preachers' lives. It is unclear how he and Aldridge met, but possibly Marrant, who lived with John Marsden on Dowgate Hill, attended Aldridge's church on Jewry Street, only a few blocks away. According to Samuel Whitchurch, a poet who took down Marrant's testimony during his ordination and turned it into a poem, Marrant was eager to hear various preachers after he arrived in London: "To learn what things our gracious Lord had done,/To hear his word, from place to place I run" (21). Aldridge may also have been corresponding with Cook who, in South Carolina, met Oliver Hart, the prominent Baptist preacher who had visited Marrant and helped him complete his conversion.[6] Hart himself had often heard Whitefield speak while growing up in Pennsylvania, and "in his religious principles, he was a fixed Calvinist" who believed in "the doctrines of *free efficacious grace*" (Sprague, 49). In his search for spiritual sustenance, Marrant also heard Thomas Wills, an evangelical preacher who had married Lady Huntingdon's niece, and one of the few to stick with her when she dissented, and William Romaine, an evangelical Anglican who had been one of her chaplains. Once he decided to go to Nova Scotia, he applied to Wills for help in receiving his ordination.[7]

Marrant himself was also clearly participating in the evangelical discourse that continued to spread. He preached regularly at the Spa Fields Chapel, a pantheon-like building in Clerkenwell, an area in central London, which Lady Huntingdon had taken possession of a few years before, and which she had been forced to register as a Dissenting chapel.[8] Although she lived in the house attached to it, it seems that the two never met.[9] Still, he was ordained at her famous neo-Gothic chapel in Bath.[10] According to Whitchurch, he also preached "much to their satisfaction before some of the most numerous and respectable congregations in Bath and Bristol" (3). The fact that, in his preface, Whitchurch finds the need to defend his subject against accusations of "enthusiasm"—a common attack against the evangelical style of preaching—indicates that Marrant was part of that cohort.

•

If Marrant's *Narrative* shows that he was definitely part of a movement and followed its conventions, it is also unique, partly because he was black and because his evangelical experience in the American colonies as he recalls it pertains mostly to Indians and to blacks, and partly because his account of his religious development is written after, and informed by, the events and ideas of the American Revolution. Indeed, as he describes both his religious and his secular experiences, it almost seems as if he is rewriting the story of American individualism, expanding and enriching it for his British audience. So while he makes no statements overtly critical of slavery and offers no radical social or political critique, Marrant's *Narrative* draws on the religious and revolutionary sensibility of the age to place racial minorities, including himself, within the growing story of eighteenth-century liberalism. Philosophically, he is not a cosmopolitan yet, but he already shows a desire and an ability to make the ideas surrounding him more inclusive and progressive.

The first image of himself Marrant provides is that of a confident black teenager freely taking advantage of the social and economic opportunities available to him in Charleston. Charleston in the 1760s was a city of almost ten thousand people with an intricate racial and social hierarchy. Established in the 1680s at the tip of a small peninsula, it had grown into a major port and commercial hub and was known for its wealth, architecture, and social and cultural life. Charlestonians loved to dine, dance, go to the theater, play billiards, gamble, hunt, and fish. As Robert N. Rosen puts it, "A more hedonistic, pleasure-oriented society never lived on the North American continent" (32). At the time Marrant lived there, the city's population was almost equally divided between blacks and whites, and most of the blacks were enslaved. But slavery in Charleston had its own unique flavor. Many slaves were allowed to hire their time out and enjoyed a certain degree of independence. Blacks dominated the public markets as vendors, fish was provided by slave fishermen, schooner services were in the hands of slaves, and many skilled artisan workshops employed slaves. There were many opportunities for blacks to congregate, and whites often attended. Attitudes toward interracial liaisons seem to have been quite liberal. Clearly, the city was unique for "the latitude, diversity, and fluidity of urban slavery" (Morgan, 220) it displayed.[11] Marrant arrived there at the age of eleven, after having moved from New York to Florida and then to Georgia with his family. As one of the very few free blacks, he quickly developed a sense of choice and possibility.

The *Narrative* shows him embracing opportunity. His family puts him as an apprentice to "some trade." Soon afterward, as he is walking by a school, he "heard music and dancing, which took my fancy very much." He goes home and informs his sister—who is guarding him while his mother lives in the backcountry—that he would rather learn music than a trade. Disapproving, the sister writes a letter to their mother who, after receiving it, "came to Charles-Town to prevent it." In a few strokes, Marrant creates the image of a family that is literate and upwardly mobile, concerned as it is about his welfare and success in life. Unable to convince him otherwise, the mother makes arrangements with a music teacher, whom she agrees to pay to train her son for eighteen months. Marrant quickly masters the violin. He also "used to resort to the bottom of our garden, where it was customary for some musicians to assemble to blow the French-horn," and he also quickly learns to play this instrument. From then on, he not only plays at the school but is also "invited to all the balls and assemblies that were held in the town, and met with the general applause of the inhabitants." As a consequence, he "was a stranger to want, being supplied with as much money as I had any occasion for" (112). He then decides he wants to learn a trade after all, and his sister's husband finds a master carpenter willing to take him on as an apprentice. He continues to play music while learning carpentry, and it is on his way to "go and play for some Gentlemen" (113) that he walks by the meeting house that will trigger his conversion. Marrant never designates people by race, and the image that emerges is that of a multiracial community linked by social and economic ties. He nimbly navigates this community as a young black man, freely pursuing his self-interest.

While it reproduces several tropes of the conventional conversion narrative, the story of his subsequent conversion also recalls another black text, one that, as we saw in chapter 1, also clearly places itself within the individualistic, new-birth strand of Calvinism. Indeed, several moments in Marrant's *Narrative* recall similar passages in the only self-authored text published by a black person in England before him, James Albert Ukawsaw Gronniosaw's *Narrative*. This narrative, whose first dated version was published at Bath in 1772, saw at least twelve editions before the end of the eighteenth century.[12] Dedicated to Lady Huntingdon, with a preface by Walter Shirley, who had become one of Lady Huntingdon's chaplains after the death of George Whitefield in 1770, and taken down by a Calvinist amanuensis also connected to her, this narrative was bound to have caught Marrant's attention.[13] Like

Marrant's, Gronniosaw's conversion process starts when he thinks the minister—who is also his master—is addressing his words to him, and he is deeply affected: "I was in great agonies because I thought my master directed them only to me; and, I fancied, that he observ'd me with unusual earnestness" (40). During his subsequent spiritual struggle, he finds himself in "extreme distress," and like Marrant, he "continued very ill for three Days and Nights; and would admit of no means to be taken for my recovery" (41). While the latter occurrence also echoes Paul's, one wonders to what extent Marrant was deliberately making links with a previous black text that, like his, created a new sense of black self-definition.

So it may not be surprising that the story of what happens after Marrant's conversion contains more elements that recall Gronniosaw's *Narrative* and that continue the theme of exceptional experience and exceptional relationships. Marrant decides to go and stay with his mother, who lives eighty-four miles from Charleston. Once there, his strict religious behavior alienates the family and the neighbors, and he finds himself persecuted, in a way that is reminiscent of Gronniosaw as a young inquisitive boy, whose siblings "disliked me, as they supposed that I was either foolish, or insane" (34). Interestingly, both passages are also similar to one in Whitefield's *Short Account*: "My relations were quickly alarmed at the alteration of my behaviour, conceived strong prejudices against me, and, for some time, counted my life madness" (41). Marrant decides to leave his family and walks into the backcountry, where he wanders for about two weeks, suffering from hunger and thirst, until he meets an Indian hunter, with whom he spends about ten weeks, learning how to hunt and survive. The hunter then takes him to a large Indian town, where he is thrown into prison and learns he is going to be executed in a gruesome manner. But the Cherokee king relents, seemingly converted on the spot: "The Lord appeared most lovely and glorious; the king himself was awakened, and the others set at liberty" (120). In the same way, when held prisoner after he has arrived on the Gold Coast, Gronniosaw is saved at the last minute when "it pleased GOD to melt the heart of the King, who sat with his scymitar in his hand ready to behead me" (37). In these passages, Marrant and Gronniosaw project themselves as exceptional black men whose lives are worth saving, and whose redemption occurs because their personal relationship with God is suddenly and beneficially replicated in the individuals holding their fates in their hands. Not only are these scenes of personal transformation and preservation exceptionally dramatic, but the fact that the four characters involved are either black or Indian gives a new face to the images of conversion that suffused Anglo-American culture at the time. And Marrant's revision of the earlier text also implies a desire to make his text resonate in the wider print culture.

Indeed, in many ways, Marrant's *Narrative* expands on three genres that had become canonical by the time he was writing: the conversion, the captivity, and the mission narratives. Like the conversion narratives, captivity and mission narratives were quite popular in the American colonies and in England throughout the eighteenth century. Captivity narratives were accounts of American colonists taken prisoner by Indians, usually during the French and Indian wars that took place at regular intervals during the seventeenth and eighteenth centuries, and who had gone through extreme sufferings before finally becoming free again. Mission narratives told of efforts to evangelize the Indians. Culturally, these narratives served different ends. The captivity narratives published before Marrant's usually contrasted savage natives with a civilized, Christian captive and celebrated the benevolence and power of a god who had allowed the captive to survive. Mission narratives or journals, on the other hand, showed the possibility of cultural transmission, albeit mostly in one direction. By merging these genres and altering them, Marrant's *Narrative* creates a sense of cultures in flux, where transformation is brought about by sheer individual decision.

The *Narrative* first sets itself off by showing the young Marrant wandering in the wilderness for two weeks, sustained only by God's apparent intervention. The echoes of biblical texts are multiple, including Exodus, or the story of the wanderings of the Israelites from their captivity in Egypt to their settlement in the land of Canaan; of Jesus staying in the wilderness for forty days and forty nights; and of John the Baptist, the itinerant preacher living in the wilderness. Whitefield himself describes a period during his conversion process when he remembers that "Jesus Christ was amongst the wild beasts" and that he "ought to follow His example" (*Short Account,* 46). Another echo is the physical suffering described in many captivity narratives, in which the captive tries to keep up with the nomadic tribe that is holding him or her prisoner. Because Marrant is alone, though, his story freely merges evidence of God's providence with rugged individualism. During the first few days, he does not eat or drink, and he sleeps in trees because he is "surrounded with wolves" (115). On the fourth day, as he is crawling on his "hands and knees," he happens to find some "deer-grass," "bit it off like a horse" (115), and "thought it the best meal I ever had in my life."

Feeling extremely thirsty, he happens to see some bushes, whose "large hollow leaves . . . contained the dews of the night," but as he tries to drink them, they fall on the ground. Finally, he finds "a puddle of water very muddy, which some wild pigs had just left" (116) and drinks water and mud together. One day, he passes between two bears, who seem to pay no attention to him. And so he survives his ordeal, being all at once the frontiersman, the Israelite receiving manna from heaven, John the Baptist living off "locusts and wild honey" (Mark 1:6), and Jesus "fasting forty days and forty nights" (Matthew 4:2) while surrounded with "wild animals" (Mark 1:13). He has undergone both the obligatory trial of his faith and a quintessential American experience.

His subsequent first contact with an Indian has nothing of the barbaric violence through which colonists usually ended up in the hands of their Indian captors. On the contrary, one day an Indian hunter bolts from behind a tree, "put his hands on my breast" (116), and starts interrogating him on his whereabouts, his means of survival, and this "Lord" Marrant keeps referring to. It turns out that this hunter knows Marrant's mother and sister, "having been used in winter to sell skins in our Town." Upon hearing this, Marrant starts crying for fear that the hunter will force this hapless young man to go back home. And so, ironically, it is the Indian in this scene who, a bit like Aunt Sally in *Huckleberry Finn,* represents the forces that are trying to push Marrant back to civilization. And when, probably out of concern for his chances of survival, he promises not to take Marrant home if he agrees to go with him, Marrant once again refuses "for fear he would rob me of my comfort and communion with God." He is finally convinced, and the two spend the next ten weeks killing and skinning deer. For Marrant, it is a period of schooling in the ways of the wilderness, as he learns how to take off the skins and dry them, build shelters in the evenings, kindle and feed a fire, and keep watch while the hunter sleeps. And so while he asserts that he was still able to maintain a "sweet communion" (117) with God, his tale of survival in the wilderness gradually turns into one of initiation and acculturation.

The subsequent episode of captivity then takes on a unique meaning, in which the themes of captivity, Indian conversion, and acculturation freely flow into each other. The hunter takes Marrant to "a large Indian town, belonging to the Cherokee nation" (117). But against the hunter's wishes, Marrant is immediately imprisoned and condemned to death for trespassing without a good reason. The next morning, the executioner, who has heard him pray aloud during the night, asks Marrant whom he has been conversing with. After he shows him the torture he is about to undergo and he hears him again pray at length, in English and then in Cherokee, "the executioner was savingly converted to God" (118). He embraces Marrant and takes him to the king in order to plead for his life. During the interview, the king's eldest daughter walks into the chamber and kisses Marrant's Bible. Marrant is then allowed to pray, and when he starts, "we all went upon our knees, and now the Lord displayed his glorious power" (119), as "in the midst of the prayer some of them cried out, particularly the king's daughter" (118–19). Angry and accusing him of being a witch, the king throws Marrant back into prison. But the next day, he calls Marrant back to him, ordering him to make his daughter and another man well again. After several attempts, "the Lord appeared most lovely and glorious; the king himself was awakened, and the others set at liberty." From that moment on, Marrant is "treated like a prince": "I had assumed the habit of the country, and was dressed much like the king, and nothing was too good for me" (120). After nine weeks, he visits other tribes to try and convert them, but in vain. He finally decides to return to his family, and a group of Indians takes him home safely. His family does not at first recognize him, but after they do, he is welcomed, and he "remained with my relations till the commencement of the American troubles" (123). And so Marrant weaves a unique tale with himself at the center, as he shows his almost seamless transformation from captive to missionary to native back to a black man on the eve of the American Revolution.

Most of the captivity narratives published before Marrant's certainly did, like his, present the captive's sufferings and deliverance as the work of a powerful and benevolent providence. Mary Rowlandson, a Puritan who for eleven weeks in 1675 was held captive by Wampanoags, keeps thanking the Lord for his "power" (237) and his "wonderful mercy" (241). Jonathan Dickinson, a Quaker merchant shipwrecked with others on the coast of Florida in 1696, describes a harrowing trip up the coast to Saint Augustine, partly as captives of local Indians, and at great exposure to the elements. The first scene heralds the rest of the journey: shipwrecked on the beach, the group is suddenly surrounded by Indians, who place themselves behind them, grab their heads, and extend their arms "with their knives in their hands," clearly ready to strike; but suddenly, "it pleased the Lord to work wonderfully for our preservation" (30), and the Indians desist. John Williams, a Puritan minister who was captured by Mohawks in 1704, describes horrible sufferings during the trek north, including murders, torture, physical hardship, and the loss of his wife. Any small comfort he receives is seen as God's work. "We should never distrust the care and compassion of God" (33), he declares, after describing a long and arduous hike on a frozen river. Elizabeth Hanson was captured by Abenakis in 1725. During the exhausting travel through the mountains, her Indian "master" would sometimes carry her infant. "This," she says, "I esteemed as a favour from the Almighty" (135). The same religious sensibility seems to inform all these narratives, as suggested by titles that often announce "deliverance" or "redemption."

Marrant's *Narrative* subscribes to a similar vision of an interventionist and ultimately benevolent god, but his focus is always on an intense, personal relationship. During his trials in the wilderness, he repeatedly asks God to deliver him to his fate, but he understands each time he is saved that God has chosen to preserve him. When he finds himself crawling on his hands and knees, he prays "that the Lord would take me to himself." When he explains that "such nearness to God I then enjoyed, that I willingly resigned myself into his hands" (115), his sufferings seem merely an opportunity to experience communion or ecstasy. He often feels that Jesus is "very present" (116, 118). In fact, his account of the anxieties he goes through before the Indian king's conversion subtly suggests he is turning into a Christ figure. The executioner describes the tortures he will be subjected to: pegs will be stuck into his body and their ends set on fire, then the same will be applied to the other side of his body, and then his body will be thrown into the fire. While some historical accounts confirm that this form of torture was practiced by some Indian tribes, in Marrant's text the religious subtext immediately calls up the crucifixion.[14] It is not surprising, then, that, when allowed to read from the Bible, Marrant chooses Isaiah 53, a famous passage that announces the coming of a "man of suffering," and Matthew 26, about Jesus's betrayal and trial by the Jewish court. Marrant's account of his captivity is about more than God's physical deliverance; it is about his own gradual achievement of a state of grace through suffering.

Interestingly, moreover, the kind of Calvinist sensibility one finds in the Puritan captivity narratives is absent from Marrant's. What makes Rowlandson's and Williams's texts characteristic is that they place their deliverance within the wider framework of their community's renewal. In Puritan terms, their suffering and release is a warning from God that the covenant with him must be kept. The suffering that is the result of "sinning," or failing the deity, is also the means by which humans will achieve a more perfect world under his guidance. As John Saillant puts it, the captivity narrative was thus "a civic document concerned with the virtue of the commonwealth" ("Remarkably Emancipated," 124). Toward the end of her narrative, Rowlandson thinks she can say: "It is good for me that I have been afflicted" (266), as her primary concerns are now redirected away from the small matters of the self. Like Rowlandson, Williams ends his narrative by praising the people who helped him and his family when they came back to Boston: these were "acts of charity performed out of a right Christian spirit, from a spirit of thankfulness to God, out of obedience to God's command, and unfeigned love and charity to them that are of the same family and household of faith" (143). To him, it is this exceptional community that, unlike the Catholic ones he has seen in Canada, represents the perfect commonwealth. This sense of exceptional virtuous community is absent from Marrant's text. He describes some conversion work he did after his return to his family, but the religious sensibility exhibited in those passages is different from his Calvinist predecessors', as this work happens haphazardly and without a conscious communal goal. Marrant's Calvinism at this point in his life is informed by the Great Awakening; it does not display the civic consciousness that guided the Puritans and is much more concerned with individual salvation.

In fact, the episode about his captivity and his conversion of the Indians owes much more to Whitefield than to the Puritans, particularly in the way he turns himself into a spectacle. Nancy Ruttenburg has argued that Whitefield contributed to the growth of a democratic sensibility in the American colonies through his sheer emphasis on the importance of the individual self—his own, and that of the people converting. Conversions became theatrical events, brought about by this "entrepreneur of the self" (435). She points out that when Charles Chauncy, a prominent Congregationalist clergyman from Boston—Congregationalism being the official form Calvinism had taken in the colonies—criticized him in an open letter, his main accusation was that he performed "a sanctified enlargement of the self" (436). In the same vein, throughout the scene of captivity, conversion, and deliverance, Marrant emphasizes self-created drama: he regularly bursts into tears; he performs acts that seem magical; he starts singing; he is taken to the king "guarded by two hundred men with bows and arrows" (119); and overall, he is the cause of "a great change . . . among the people" (120). It is undeniable that the whole scene conveys a sense of his exceptional power and presence.

This emphasis Marrant puts on the self in his deliverance and his conversion of the Indians can also be found in the secular themes of the *Narrative*. Probably the most striking one is the Pocahontas theme. As he is standing in front of the king, twice the king's daughter takes the Bible from Marrant's hands, and twice she kisses it. It is thanks to her intervention that Marrant is allowed to pray aloud, that people and particularly the daughter are spiritually and physically affected, that Marrant is ordered to cure her, and that her miraculous recovery changes his status in the community. It is probable that Marrant knew about the story of John Smith, the first leader of the Virginia colony who, as he was about to be put to death by the Powhatans, was saved by the chief's daughter, who placed her head on top of his to receive the blows destined for him.[15] At the time Marrant was writing, the story of Pocahontas was undergoing a transformation. For most of the eighteenth century, it was her status as the wife of John Rolfe, who had come to England, met with the king and queen, and died soon after, that predominated in English culture.[16] But soon after Marrant's publication, her role in John Smith's rescue would come to receive more and more emphasis. Among a number of versions, the account by John Davis, in his book of travels about the newly founded United States, injected the story with all the paraphernalia of sentimental fiction. Smith is "extremely prepossessing" (296); Pocahontas "could not conceal those soft emotions of which the female bosom is so susceptible" (297); when she saves him, "every heart melted into tenderness at the scene" (298); when she visits him at Jamestown, they walk along the river, and "it was then she gave loose to all the tumultuous extasy of love" (303). Marrant's *Narrative* has no romantic connotation, but the role played by the king's daughter may be a sign that the theme of the young Indian woman savior was in vogue. In 1755, in fact, the *London Magazine* had already published an account of the birth of the Virginia colony that attributed Smith's deliverance to the "surprising tenderness and affection of Pocahontas."[17] Creating a parallel between himself and John Smith was bound to connote the presence of an exceptional individual.

Taking up another theme that was not uncommon by then, Marrant's *Narrative* also attributes his deliverance to his literacy. The second time that the king's daughter takes the Bible from his hands, "she opened it, and kissed it again"; when her father tells her to return it, she does, "but said, with much sorrow, the book would not speak to her" (119). Here Marrant uses what Henry Louis Gates Jr., has called the "trope of the talking book," in which an illiterate person wonders at the seemingly magic power of an object that seems to be talking to the person who handles it. Once again, Marrant must have known that Gronniosaw uses this trope in his own narrative, when he describes being on the ship that is taking him away from Africa and seeing "the book talk" to his master, after which he "open'd it, and put my ear down close upon it, in great hope that it wou'd say something to me"; when the book will not speak to him, he thinks that "every body and every thing despis'd me because I was black" (38). In his analysis, Gates shows that Marrant offers an important revision of the trope, since "in this Kingdom of the Cherokee, it is only the black man who can make the text speak" (144). So Marrant's deliverance is prompted by his difference from, and superiority to, the Cherokees, as the only individual in the group who has access to God's word—and to God's presence.

And once again, Marrant seems to self-consciously place himself within the broader print culture by participating in the revision of a genre. The image of an Indian unable to make a book speak has a long history. As early as 1581, Thomas Nicholas published a translation of Augustin de Zarate's *History of the Discovery and Conquest of Peru,* in which is recounted the encounter between Atahualpa, the Inca emperor, and the ambassadors of Francisco Pizarro, the famous conquistador. After the priest, Vincent Valverde, gives the Inca a quick overview of the major Christian beliefs and concludes by saying that God has given this country to King Charles and so the Indian had better surrender if he wants to avoid a "cruell warre" (70), Atahualpa answers that this country is his and nobody else's and that as far as Jesus Christ is concerned, he wonders where Valverde gets his knowledge from. When the priest hands over his book, Atahualpa turns it "from leafe to leafe": "Why (quoth he) this booke speaketh not one word to me, and there with threw it on the ground" (71). In his 1777 *History of America,* William Robertson repeats the incident, adding the detail that the Inca took the book and "lifted it to his ear" (305). John Smith himself must have been familiar with the story. In his account of his captivity, he sends Indian messengers to Jamestown with a written message. When the messengers come back, they express their amazement "to the wonder of them all that heard it, that he could either divine or the paper could speak" (63). So it is not surprising that this trope found its way into Marrant's text, as it places him in a long line of exceptional holders of knowledge and, more broadly, of exceptional men.

•

The trope of the talking book is also interesting because it offers a good point of entry into the question of Marrant's portrayal of the Indians and of his relationship to them. The most apt comparison is with the mission narrative or journal. As a mission narrative, Marrant's is idiosyncratic. His emphasis is clearly on how Indians go through the same dramatic process that he went through in Charleston, as he shows individual Indians suddenly receiving the light and converting. In this, he follows Whitefield's emphasis on the immediacy and inner depth of the conversion experience. The executioner is a case in point. He asks Marrant twice whom he is addressing in his prayers; the first time Marrant answers, he makes no reply, and the second time, he allows him to pray. When Marrant starts praying in Cherokee, which "wonderfully affected the people," the executioner is "savingly converted to God." He embraces Marrant, "was unable to speak for about five minutes" (118), and decides to take him to the king. We have seen what happens to the king, to his daughter, and to several attendants. Toward the end of the *Narrative,* Marrant mentions how, after the siege of Charleston, he saw the king riding into town: "He alighted off his horse, and came to me; said he was glad to see me; that his daughter was very happy, and sometimes longed to get out of the body" (126). So Marrant's last reference to his mission work among the Indians is to the experience of ecstasy he elicited among them. By showing how the notion of individual spiritual transformation applies equally to Indians, Marrant places them in the same spiritual realm, creating an image of transmission and subsequent ownership of one's special relationship to the deity.

Some critics see Marrant's relation to the Indians as necessarily marred by his position as a colonizer. Tiya Miles argues that, because he follows the ethnocentric model of redemptive suffering typical of the captivity narrative, he is "reinforcing an English moral authority that was linked to the enforcement of imperial power over indigenous Americans" (177). Moreover, she points out, when the king's daughter kisses the Bible, the narrative "refigures conquest as the fulfillment of native desires" (180). It is true that, to some extent, Marrant cannot avoid a dimension of cultural imposition typical of any evangelical enterprise and that the repeated interrogations and displays of curiosity on the part of the Indians regarding his faith imply a longing or even a need for conversion. While we now have an interracial cast, one could say that Marrant has just taken the place of the white man in the scheme of ideological imperialism. The trope of the talking book has just shifted to another group of people who cannot hear the book because they are different—and inferior.

To some extent, Marrant's *Narrative* also fits within the ethnocentric myths that are usually associated with the captivity narrative. To John Sekora, captivity has provided a "theologically powerful as well as physically useful version of manifest destiny" (95); the captives may be maltreated or tortured, but in the end, their survival and rescue justify the European presence and expansion in a land inhabited by savages. To Richard Slotkin, the captivity narrative features the central American myth of "regeneration through violence" in the wilderness; the most representative story is that of Daniel Boone, the famous frontiersman who explored and started the settlement of Kentucky west of the Appalachians, and who was temporarily held captive by Shawnees. The captivity narrative has also been seen as a variation on the myth of the hero as described by Joseph Campbell in *The Hero with a Thousand Faces,* according to which the hero goes on a quest or a journey of initiation and returns transformed.[18] Marrant's *Narrative* contains all of these elements.

Because it freely mixes different genres, though, I find that the *Narrative* ultimately undermines the imperialistic element, if it does not totally erase it. On the one hand, it is never completely a mission narrative. Marrant does not originally intend to convert the Indians. His story sounds more like the legend of Saint Alban, the famous British martyr whose executioner suddenly converted at the moment of execution. Once Marrant decides to actively go on a mission, he visits the Creeks, the Choctaws, and the Chickasaws but fails, as he "had not much reason to believe any of these three nations were savingly wrought upon" (121). This last episode feels like a sort of coda, though, and what the reader remembers is the dramatic scene of near martyrdom, where the emphasis is not so much on conversion as on Marrant's own spiritual state, as the Indians seem to willingly step into his world. Similarly, it is not completely a captivity narrative. Marrant stays with the Cherokees as a guest and makes free decisions while with them: he "began now to feel an inclination growing upon me" (120) to visit other tribes, and the king agrees and sends fifty men with him; he feels an "invincible desire of returning home" (121), and the king consents and also sends men with him for protection. While most captivity narratives end with an escape, an exchange, or ransom, this one highlights Marrant's surplus value to the Indians, who come across as independent evaluators of their cultural assets.

As we have seen, most captivity narratives published before Marrant's are also stories of initiation, in which captives have to adapt to Indian ways in order to survive. Elizabeth Hanson got used to eating "guts and garbage" and was thankful for it, while in normal times she "could by no means have dispensed with it" (142). John Gyles, who was captured by Indians during King William's War and was held for six years, develops the same hopes and fears as his captors, as they lay up canoes in the winter and live off hunting, rejoice over taking a moose or a bear, smoke the meat to preserve it, make canoes from moose hides, plant corn in the spring, harvest it, and store it. Thomas Brown, taken captive for almost four years during the same war, learns to survive with the Indians by "Hunting, dressing Leather, &c., being cloath'd after the Indian Fashion" (14). But these kinds of acculturation are temporary, and the return of the captives to their community usually signifies a relinquishing of these customs. That is certainly the case for Daniel Boone who, at one point in John Filson's telling, is "adopted" by an Indian family, but at the end of the narrative makes it clear that, to him, Indians are "savages" (74) who are out to "destroy us, and entirely depopulate the country" (75). When they return unexpectedly, captives are not always immediately recognized, but these short scenes actually end up reinforcing the captives' original identity when recognition takes place. Peter Williamson, captured by Indians during the French and Indian War, manages to escape, but when he finally knocks on a friend's door and his wife opens, her screams "alarmed the whole family, who immediately fled to their arms, and I was soon accosted by the master with his gun in his hand" (30). Once he makes himself known, though, he is embraced and affectionately taken care of. Similarly, the white man who first sees Elizabeth Fleming at the end of her wanderings is so frightened by the "strange figure I cut" that he first shoots at her; another man cries out that "*she is a white Woman by her Voice*" (20), and she is taken care of. The initiation in these stories is less in the ways of the Indians than in the knowledge that comes from encountering another culture and returning to embrace one's own with even more conviction.

Initiation and acculturation in Marrant's *Narrative* come across somewhat differently, in that they take place in a nonviolent context, and the cultural categories are less sharply drawn. Marrant acknowledges that, after a lengthy stay with the Indians, "my affections to my family and country were not dead" (121). Unlike some famous cases of white captives who ended up becoming Indian, Marrant still has a clear feeling of affiliation. Still, he makes his sympathy with the Indian point of view clear: "When they recollect, that the white people drove them from the American shores, they are full of resentment" (120). So Marrant presents himself as his own man, ready to acknowledge that Indians kill "men, women, and children" (121), but equally ready, in one of the few passages that contains racial vocabulary, to condemn white encroachment on Indian land. The scene of his return is equally double edged. He is told by his uncle, then by a friend, then by his mother, that John Marrant is dead and buried, and each time he cries. The tears seem to signify the loss of an older, more innocent self. But then his younger sister comes home, and she recognizes him immediately, as if he had kept an essence of himself that a child could easily spot. His return has none of the triumphalist vindication of Western culture we find in other narratives. He mentions that, after his return, he travels to listen to "Gospel ministers" (123) once in a while and finds some communion with others, but he gives no sense of a rejuvenated community. Indeed, some earlier editions mention that his "soul was got into a declining state" (130). He seems to imply that he is in many ways in a state of emotional and cultural limbo.

In the whole Indian section, then, Marrant is less an imperialist than a man in search of himself. By the time he is telling this story to Aldridge somewhere in London or Bath in 1785, he is retracing his spiritual growth, emphasizing the ups and downs of an individual's relationship to his god. He is aware that it is this individual experience that matters to his religious audience. He is about to leave for Nova Scotia, on a new voyage of exploration and discovery, and is not trying to create a sense of community where he is. Indeed, most of the characters in his *Narrative* are themselves on a search, or open to new experiences. It is as if the text is infused with the sense of freedom and renewal that drove the Revolution that had just come to a close.

Marrant is also aware that British attitudes toward Indians in these postrevolutionary days may accommodate positive images. Relationships between the Cherokees and the South Carolina colonists had had their ups and downs in the course of the eighteenth century. In the decades after the bloody Yamassee War of 1715, the two communities had a period of relative calm, during which trade increased, forts were built, a conference was organized. But tensions increased again, and another conflict took place during the French and Indian War, during which the governor organized three campaigns against the Cherokees. Then, during the Revolutionary War, the Cherokees gave their allegiance to the British against the rebels, which led to ruthless punitive expeditions in what is called the Indian War of 1776.[19] To Tom Hatley, Marrant is a "Carolina Everyman" who knows the "perceptual landscape of Carolinians" (237) and who shows them that "the old and frightening terrain across the fence, in the mountains to the west, had been tamed" (238). But Marrant is also addressing a British audience, one whose main idea of Indians may have come from seeing some of them received in style when they visited London: seven Cherokees came with Alexander Cuming in 1730; a group of Creeks accompanied James Oglethorpe in 1734; three Cherokees came with Henry Timberlake in 1762. Indeed, he reminds them that Cherokees are allies when, toward the end of the *Narrative,* he mentions seeing the Indian king riding into town with General Henry Clinton just after the siege of Charleston. And after all, he too fought on the British side. Marrant's sense of national affiliation has begun to loosen, and his sense of categories to erode. Black, white, red, American, British—to him, these concepts do not seem to matter as much as what an individual contributes through his faith.

•

Because of its emphasis on individual new birth, the Great Awakening is often associated with an opening up of conversion to more diverse audiences, such as Indians and blacks, but this development happened slowly. Before the eighteenth century, conversion of Indians by English Protestants was less successful compared to the work of Jesuits in the French territories. Jesuits tended to work in "flying missions," living in Indian communities and adding Christianity to the already existing culture; Protestants aimed at bringing Indians into their notion of a good commonwealth and worked through the creation of schools and separate "praying towns."[20] Similarly, until the middle of the eighteenth century, missionary work with slaves in the American South, which was almost completely in the hands of the Anglican Society for the Propagation of the Gospel, founded in 1701, achieved little success.[21] Peter Wood calls the time of the Great Awakening a period of "initial convergence," during which some slaves became acquainted with a form of Christianity that "stressed emotional preaching over learned discourse, spontaneous response over rote learning" (5) and started to show some interest. Not until the last third of the century, though, did a number of black preachers emerge to create a few thicker pockets of black Christian communities.

Whitefield certainly favored the conversion of slaves, but to what extent he was successful during his seven tours of the American colonies is uncertain. According to Thomas Kidd, "He and his Methodist friends recorded numerous instances of speaking individually with African American seekers" (112). It is clear that blacks were often in attendance when he preached to large crowds. In May 1740, for example, he preached in Philadelphia to about fifteen hundred people. Later that day, many came to visit him in his lodgings, among whom were "near fifty negroes." Whitefield then notes in his journal that "some of them have been effectually wrought upon" (*Journals,* 420). But Whitefield rarely singled out slave communities. One exception is when, in the spring of 1748, he went to Bermuda, a Caribbean island with a population of about eight thousand people at the time, almost equally divided between whites and blacks. On May 1, he preached to an assembly of slaves in a field, and a few whites came to hear him. "As the sermon was intended for the negroes," he writes, "I gave the auditory warning, that my discourse would be chiefly directed to them, and that I should endeavor to imitate the example of Elijah, who, when he was about to raise the child, contracted himself to its length" (*Memoirs,* 113). He hears later that the slaves did not like his sermon because it focused on their "cursing, swearing, thieving, and lying," while they expected "to hear me speak against their masters." He then congratulates himself on not having done that. He also hears that the slaves were perplexed and wondered why he had told them they had "black hearts" (114). And while Whitefield optimistically infers from all these comments that the blacks are opening up to his message, what clearly comes through for us is the slaves' skepticism about a religion that denigrates them and condones their enslavement.

Indeed, Whitefield was never an abolitionist. After visiting a slave family in North Carolina toward the end of 1739, he wrote to a correspondent in London that slaves "were much on his 'heart'" (Kidd, 98). The next April, he delivered three letters to Benjamin Franklin to be published in the *Pennsylvania Gazette,* one of which was addressed to the inhabitants of "Maryland, Virginia, North and South-Carolina." The letter, he announces at the beginning, is about the "Miseries of the poor Negroes." He thinks that "God has a Quarrel with you for your Abuse of and Cruelty to the poor Negroes." He does not want to decide whether "it be lawful for Christians to buy Slaves," but he knows it is "sinful, when bought, to use them as bad, nay worse, than as though they were Brutes" (*Three Letters,* 13). After describing examples of violence and neglect, he brings up the fact that most masters "keep your Negroes ignorant of Christianity" (14). To the argument that teaching them Christianity "would make them proud," he answers that these "blasphemous Notions" go against the very "Precepts of Christianity": "Do you find any one Command in the Gospel, that has the least Tendency to make People forget their relative Duties?" (15). If slaves are introduced to true Christianity, their obedience will be assured. Preaching in Philadelphia that same month, and in an argument reminiscent of Capitein, he emphasized the importance for blacks above all to be delivered from "the slavery of sin" (Kidd, 111). To Whitefield, "benevolence to slaves primarily entailed introducing them to the gospel" (112). Once his plans for the orphanage started to firm up, he advised the trustees to buy slaves; in 1747, he himself bought a plantation—and slaves.[22]

Marrant's emphases in the *Narrative* are similar, in that he criticizes a despicable and violent slaveholder, while ultimately focusing on the slaves' spiritual salvation. Of course, there was hardly any organized abolitionism at the time the *Narrative* was published; the clearest statements came from Quakers and from several northern states' passage of abolitionist bills. Eliciting a reader's sympathy about the condition of blacks was still the best way to criticize the institution. But in the *Narrative,* this institution is not clearly his focus. Some time after he has come back home, Marrant works as a carpenter on a plantation about seventy miles from Charleston, and he gradually starts teaching the slaves his religion. When the mistress finds out, she forces her husband to punish "the poor creatures": the "men, women, and children were strip'd naked and tied, their feet to a stake, their hands to the arm of a tree, and so savagely flogg'd that the blood ran from their backs and sides to the floor" (123). The fact that Marrant added this section to the original edition shows that he wanted to make a public statement about slavery. At the same time, the emphasis in the passage is on the blacks' persistence, in spite of the violence, in seeking religious instruction. What seems to matter most is the slaves' spiritual well-being. The plantation owner tells him that "I had spoiled all his Negroes," but cannot help acknowledging that "they did their tasks sooner than the others." When he expresses fear that he will be unable to keep them "in subjection," Marrant asks him "whether he did not think they had Souls to be saved?" (124). He leaves the plantation soon afterward but tells us with great satisfaction that the slaves kept their gatherings going in spite of persecution by the mistress. The next segment of the *Narrative* is about a little girl who, like Little Eva in *Uncle Tom's Cabin,* displays strong faith as she approaches death. These two episodes, which Marrant added to the fourth edition, seem to place him within a Whitefieldian circle of grace, as he moves from eager converts to a deep believer, from black to—probably—white, from being a teacher to being a comforter. There is no theatricality here, but there is also no real sense of community—just a concern for individual souls.

Clearly Marrant's *Narrative* was written to establish his credentials as a Methodist preacher, but it also says a lot about his understanding of himself in the world. The moment of conversion or new birth at the center of it shows that he adheres to a Calvinist concept of man as the receptacle of God's will. It is the intensity of this individual relationship to the deity that prevails over social or political considerations. As a consequence, he makes seemingly easy contacts across race, class, and social status but rarely presents himself as part of a community. In the next episode of his life, he is drawn into the events of the American Revolution as if by chance: "In those troublesome times, I was pressed on board the Scorpion, sloop of war, as their musician, as they were told I could play on music" (125). He seems to have no specific allegiance and is recruited as an artist, an outsider. While as we have seen, he is not unmindful of the fact that his audience is British, he comes across as a free agent, tied only to the faith he is about to go spread. He knows he is black and American, but above all, he is a Christian man in a world in turmoil.

Being Black in England

Marrant stayed in London for three years, at the end of which he saw his "call to the ministry fuller and clearer," and, concerned about "the salvation of my countrymen," he started feeling great sorrow "for my brethren, for my kinsmen, according to the flesh" (126). He wrote a letter to his brother, who was in Nova Scotia, and who answered that his community needed ministers. Marrant then decided to be ordained and to leave for Canada as soon as possible. Just as, when he lived with the Cherokees, he had realized that "my affections to my family and country were not dead" (121), Marrant once again felt the desire to return to a familiar community. In Romans 9: 2–3, the "kinsmen" Paul refers to are the people of Israel who are still unconverted. When he refers to "kinsmen, according to the flesh," Marrant seems to mean a specifically racial community: the black loyalists who had relocated from the newly formed United States to Canada at the end of American Revolution. What motivated Marrant to make this move? After spending seven years "in his majesty's service" (125) and three years in London, what drove him to radically change the course of his life, and devote himself to a particular community? In this interesting development, Marrant seems to have both entered a cosmopolitan world, and then, in an apparent recoil from its vertiginous reach, picked an allegiance.

•

From the moment he was impressed in the Royal Navy, Marrant entered one of the most multinational and multicultural worlds in existence at the time. By 1775, the navy counted almost thirty thousand men, a number that would more than triple in the course of the war. "There were men from every nation under heaven in the Navy," N. A. M. Rodger says, including "Americans of every colony and every colour" (158). When abroad, British ships could not rely just on British merchant ships for impressment, and so they picked up seamen stranded in various ports, including foreigners. As British scholar Michael Lewis points out, foreign sailors "were in larger numbers than is sometimes supposed because, then, as in most other periods, the merchant marines of the various sea-using nations, our own included, were a very cosmopolitan lot" (128). The microcosm of the ship made engagement with this cosmopolitan world necessary.

Ships were also a place of unusual racial egalitarianism. "At sea," as W. Jeffrey Bolster puts it, "black and white sailors faced down the same captains, weathered the same gales, and pumped the same infernally leaking ships" (69). Because of harsh discipline, impressment, or the possibility of being traded out to other ships, white sailors often felt deprived of their liberty in a way that made them sympathize with slaves. Of course racism never completely disappeared, but divisions were less by race than by level of skill, extent of experience, and status in the crews' hierarchy. Much of the work on ships was collective work, such as operating windlasses, heaving the anchor, or taking sails up and down, and this kind of collaboration transcended race. Blacks sometimes even assumed positions of leadership, as in the case of some able seamen, pilots, or salvage masters.[23]

While Marrant says he was pressed, blacks in Charleston had good reason to find life at sea attractive, as white rebels, or patriots, were watching their every move. After the first military engagements between British soldiers and American militia in Lexington and Concord, Massachusetts, in April 1775, and the Battle of Bunker Hill in Boston in June, the state of hostility became official and British institutions continued to unravel. In South Carolina, white patriots became increasingly suspicious of blacks and Indians, as they believed that the British were encouraging loyalist allegiance among them. The year before, as the first Continental Congress was meeting in Philadelphia, whites had already lodged numerous complaints about what they saw as increasingly disorderly conduct among Charleston's blacks.[24] In October, the *South Carolina Gazette and Country Journal* had published an account of a slave insurrection aboard a ship off the coast of Africa. And toward the end of the year, an arrest warrant had been issued for David Margrett, a black man who had been preaching openly against slavery.[25] White fears only grew in the course of the next year. When they drafted an "Association" in May, South Carolina's patriot leaders explicitly referred to "the dread of instigated insurrections at home," and on 5 June, the Provincial Congress, created to replace the Commons House of Assembly, formed a committee to investigate slave revolts.[26] When the new governor, Lord Campbell, arrived later that month, he received a chilly reception, partly because a letter from a patriot correspondent in London had asserted that Campbell was out to instigate slave insurrections. Blacks could definitely feel white anxiety mounting.

This anxiety came to a shocking expression when, at the end of the summer, leaders executed Thomas Jeremiah, a free black. Jeremiah, a wealthy, skilled pilot, was accused of colluding with the British and of fomenting a slave rebellion. As rumors of slave unrest had begun to circulate, a slave accused Jeremiah of asking him to smuggle guns in order to help organize a slave rebellion, and another one asserted that Jeremiah had told him that war was coming to help the blacks. Jeremiah was arrested and put into solitary confinement.[27] A few weeks later, a slave named George was executed in a parish outside of Charleston after authorities heard that he and a number of slaves were preaching that the British king was about to set them free and that blacks "were equally intitled to the Good things of this Life in common with the Whites" (Laurens, 208). In August, Jeremiah was tried a second time; he was hanged and burned a week later.

We do not know how Marrant felt about what he calls "the troubles," but it is hard to imagine that he remained indifferent. He was apparently living in Charleston that year, as he mentions visiting a little girl whose parents "lived in the house adjoining to my sister's" (124). His social contacts must have provided very different ideological viewpoints. On the one hand, Oliver Hart, the Baptist minister who helped bring about his conversion, was a patriot, whose help had been enlisted by the patriots; he agreed to go into the backcountry in order to explain "to the inhabitants, in a proper and true light, the nature of the present dispute unhappily subsisting between Great Britain and the American colonies" (Owens, 16). He owned at least one slave, whom he was ready to hand over to patriot authorities on the lookout for information, since he wrote Henry Laurens, president of the Committee of Safety, that she and another slave "could make very ample discoveries" (Laurens, 185). On the other hand, some blacks must have known that Campbell had been sympathetic to Jeremiah's plight and thought the trial unfair. Appalled by the proceedings, he had appealed to the Committee of Public Safety. On 15 September, when it became clear that the patriots were about to seize him, he removed himself to the HMS *Tamar,* which lay in Charleston's harbor. On 14 November, from a warship off Yorktown, the governor of Virginia, Lord Dunmore, published a proclamation in which he offered slaves and indentured servants of patriots freedom in return for their allegiance and their readiness to fight for the Crown. Word spread quickly, and soon hundreds of Charleston's blacks made their way to Sullivan's Island, close to the British ships. Clearly, this was a moment for blacks to take sides.

This is also the moment when Marrant was pressed into service by the British. At the end of November, the HMS *Scorpion* arrived from North Carolina, commanded by John Tollemache. Tollemache had been in Charleston that summer and had left carrying away a black pilot.[28] In a conversation reported to a patriot some time after arriving, he acknowledged having some blacks on board and added that "they came as freemen, and demanding protection; that he could have had near five hundred, who had offered" (Ryan, 114). On 16 December, patriot leaders met to discuss the issue of blacks flocking to the British side. Alarmed, they considered possible measures, such as another public execution or using Catawba Indians to frighten the blacks. A few days later, a number of patriot soldiers dressed as Indians descended on Sullivan's Island, but they only managed to take a few people.[29] On 18 December, the *Scorpion* sailed away, with "thirty or forty negroes" (Laurens, 609) on board. Marrant was one of them.[30]

Telling his narrative almost seven years later, Marrant does not give any indication about his allegiance. Clearly he had made a name for himself as a musician, since "they [the British] were told I could play on music" (125); he had a job in the city, since his young neighbor attended a school he passed as he was "returning from my work" (124). So he had contacts with blacks and whites but no apparent strong sense of American identity. The length of his stay in the navy then gave him extended exposure to a cosmopolitan Atlantic culture that, while brought together under the British flag, existed and grew outside of national boundaries. That he was susceptible to its influence comes through when he says that a "lamentable stupor crept over all my spiritual vivacity, life and vigour" (126). Of course, the context and the genre of the *Narrative* demand that he look back negatively on a period of his life that was not guided by faith. At the same time, though, the implication is that he gave himself over to the rowdy and intense multicultural life that was typical of sailors in the British navy at the end of the eighteenth century. Indeed, after he was discharged from the *Scorpion*, he decided to stay in the Royal Navy, since he ended up at the siege of Charleston in 1780.[31]

Of that siege, he only says that he "passed through many dangers" (126) and that it allowed him to see his old friend again, the Cherokee king. So his last mention of his old home is associated with people who were outsiders to American culture, and with an American defeat. It is not known whether he participated in the ground siege or stayed on the ships in the Charleston harbor, but during this six-week siege, all the members of the British army and navy became actors in a strategically planned and executed assault against the American colonists. The more than eight thousand troops who sailed south from New York in December 1779 were quite diverse, as they included British infantry, cavalry, and artillery, German soldiers, and loyalists from various provinces.[32] Less than a year before, Jean-Baptiste Belley had been part of equally diverse French and American forces for the assault on Savannah. In this case, Marrant was part of a force that masterfully encircled the Americans and forced them to surrender. Clinton and his men first landed on an island about twenty miles south of Charleston and gradually made their way to the mainland, across the Ashley River, and to a plantation just two miles north of the city, as well as to the area east of the Cooper River. In the meantime, several ships sailed through the bar unhindered, but Admiral Marriot Arbuthnot decided not to go any further. Since Marrant mentions danger, he may have been part of the ground forces, which engaged in some trench warfare before the Americans finally capitulated. He must have looked on the city with a different eye when he entered it with the British troops.

But he did not stay there long. The next year, he was fighting in a battle against the Dutch in the English Channel. Marrant says that he was "in the engagement with the Dutch off the Dogger Bank, on board the Princess Amelia, of eighty-four guns." This encounter, which took place on 5 August 1781, caused heavy casualties on both sides. He describes it as a real brush with death: "We had a great number killed and wounded; the deck was running with blood; six men were killed, and three wounded, stationed at the same gun with me; my head and face were covered with the blood and brains of the slain." He adds: "I was wounded, but did not fall, till a quarter of an hour before the engagement ended." He stayed in a hospital for almost four months, was sent to the West Indies on a ship of war, came back, and, "being taken ill of my old wounds" (126), stayed at a hospital in Plymouth. Declared incapable of serving the king, he was discharged and made his way to London. The city meant a change of pace for a man who for the past seven years had lived in the world of ships, caught in a transatlantic war, having passed through many dangers. Once again he faced a fight for survival, but one of a different kind.

•

Once in London, Marrant established relationships with white evangelicals, particularly the Methodist circle around the Countess of Huntingdon. His conversion by Whitefield back in Charleston made him a natural fit. A few months before he arrived, the countess had officially severed ties with the Church of England, registered the Spa Fields Chapel as a dissident chapel, and baptized her movement the "Countess of Huntingdon's Connexion." On 9 March 1783, Thomas Wills and William Taylor, two Anglican ministers who had followed her in secession, ordained six students of her Trevecca school at the Spa Fields Chapel. As part of the ordination, the new ministers had to subscribe to the Connexion's Fifteen Articles, which read as a compounding of the Thirty-Nine Articles of the Church of England with the Westminster Confession of Faith, a Reformed document drawn up at Westminster Abbey and adopted by Parliament in 1648, during the English Civil War. The resulting document emphasizes original sin, predestination, and justification by faith alone.[33] The need to enlist and ordain new ministers for the dissident movement was now urgent, and Marrant must have seemed a prime candidate.

Moreover, with the end of the War of Independence, sealed by the Treaty of Paris in 1783, the countess could think again about expanding the reach of the Connexion overseas. Ordaining a black minister was not unheard of. In 1765, the *Gentleman's Magazine* noted that "at the chapel royal at St. *James*'s by the Hon. and Rev. Dr *Keppel,* Bishop of *Exeter,* a black was ordained, whose devout behaviour attracted the notice of the whole congregation" (145). Brought from Africa by the Society for the Propagation of the Gospel, Philip Quaque would go back to the Gold Coast, where he worked as a chaplain and missionary for the next forty years. In 1774, the countess herself agreed, on the advice of several ministers, to send David Margrett, who had studied at Trevecca and had done some preaching in the counties around London, to Georgia, where she had inherited the Bethesda orphanage from Whitefield. The orphanage used slave labor, and the countess was advised to send Margrett in the hope that he might be better able to communicate with the slaves.[34] Though it all turned out to be an unfortunate experiment for her—Margrett ended up inciting the slaves to rebellion—it showed that the countess was willing to invest in overseas evangelization by a black preacher. The narrowing of her circle after the secession, as minister after minister refused to join her, made it even more likely.

The countess's missionary zeal had had its ups and downs throughout the decade before Marrant's arrival. As Boyd Stanley Schlenther puts it, "The romance of overseas missions had always taken Lady Huntingdon's fancy" (*Queen*, 83). She had a complicated relationship with the Moravians, a religious group famous for its missionary activities around the world, and decided to work independently. Early in 1770, she sent two young men on a mission to the East Indies, at the cost of £600, but the mission failed, as one of them remained with the British garrison in Sumatra, and the other came back to England suspected of criminal activity.[35] After Whitefield's death later that year, her overseas interest focused mostly on the orphanage at Bethesda, which she began to see as a springboard for itinerant missionaries in America. She sent William Piercy, an ordained minister, to Georgia, as well as five Trevecca students. But things did not go well, and in May 1773, the orphanage was burned to the ground, in an apparent act of arson. The five students dispersed, back to England or throughout Georgia and South Carolina. In July of that year, she wrote to James Habersham, a Georgia merchant and statesman, that events "must exceedingly discourage all my future attempts" (Tyson with Schlenther, 223). Yet she persisted, pouring more money into rebuilding and buying slaves for the establishment.[36]

The secession from the Church of England revived her interest in missions. She must have realized by then that a Dissenting group would appeal to Americans much more than the Anglican establishment that Bethesda had represented to most people in Georgia a decade before. In February 1783, she personally wrote to George Washington, telling him that she had "taken the liberty of naming you as one of my executors for establishing a foundation in America principally intended as a College for a mission to the Indian Nations" (Tyson with Schlenther, 230). In this and subsequent letters to Washington, we see some of her strongest expressions of emotional investment in missionary activity to nonwhites. She speaks of "my heart which stands so connected with the service of the Indian Nations" and of "the eternal good of that miserably neglected and despised Nations [*sic*]" (231). In a 1784 proposal, she intends to sell the land in Georgia in order to buy up land elsewhere for "the introduction of the Gospel in to the Indian Nations." Her goal is to create a "College for forty young men" (236), some of whom would learn Indian languages for purposes of evangelization. Interestingly, even though she is looking for land in a more moderate climate than Georgia, she assumes that slavery will be practiced there, since she speaks of buying "land and Negroes" (236). Converting blacks does not seem to be a priority for her, though. Writing Piercy in 1773 about students who wanted to leave Bethesda, she seemed indulgent, understanding that "as to their teaching the children or Negros I find they are not willing, and I think a poor common Master that can do nothing else might do that" (224). When it came to promoting missionary work in the Americas, she had certain priorities.

This was her state of mind at the time she approved Marrant's mission to Nova Scotia, and it undoubtedly shaped his own understanding of it. Marrant did make connections with ministers outside of her circle while in London. William Romaine, one of London's most prominent evangelical preachers, whom he often went to hear, had severed relations with her in the late 1770s.[37] William Aldridge, who took down and published Marrant's *Narrative,* broke off his relationship with her in 1776.[38] But Thomas Wills, one of her chaplains, who had married her niece, had followed her in secession and had been appointed resident minister at the Spa Fields Chapel. His preaching was so popular that the chapel, which could hold several thousand people, became too small for the crowds, as "people packed the aisles, crowded the pulpit, and spilled onto the road."[39] Marrant went to hear him, and Wills became the link between him and the countess. So, unsurprisingly, evangelizing the Indians became part of Marrant's mission. In the *Narrative*'s conclusion, Marrant wishes that "Indian tribes may stretch out their hands to God" (127). And in his letters from Nova Scotia to England, he mentions that he "has visited the Indians in their Wigwams" (132). That "the sable youth Shall to Barbarians preach the Word of Truth" (Whitchurch, 8) seems to have been the condition for the young black man to receive the patroness's support. Unlike David Margrett, Marrant had been hired for his multicultural, cosmopolitan credentials.

•

At his ordination, though, Marrant had his brother's letter from Nova Scotia read aloud, a sure sign that he wanted his mission to be associated with the black community that had recently sprung up in Canada.[40] "This shall the *Negro Convert* publish still / To fellow blacks, the great Jehovah's will" (9), says Samuel Whitchurch in his poetic description of the task that awaits him. Indeed, the poem—which reflects Marrant's ordination speech—implies that Marrant is looking for a kind of emotional and social sustenance he did not find either during his seven years on His Majesty's ships or over the past three years in London. His naval service is described as "a tedious servitude" (Whitchurch, 16), as the young man is bullied for his religious bent, so much so that "from the bow port I thrice essay'd to find / A wat'ry grave to ease my troubled mind." After continuously facing "the dangers of the deep" (17) and "war's tumultuous thunders" (18) and after, back in England, his wounds have finally healed, he has only one dream: "My wages paid—recross'd the western main—/ My native shores, my friends, I greet again!" But the dream is quickly shattered, as he makes his way to London "to claim my shares of captures from the foe," but without success: "I urge my claim—but ah! I urge in vain; / I plead my cause—but scarce a hearing gain" (20). He stays in the city, but his "dear connexions hang upon my mind." One night, finally, he is awakened by a vision: "Go forth! Go forth!" (21), it says. He gets up and spends the rest of the night writing a letter to his brother. Shortly after, he turns to Wills for help, and the result is his present ordination. The "salvation" of "distant Negroes" (24) is presented as what guided his steps all along.

One wonders what connections Marrant made with London's black community. Blacks had been sparsely present in England since the age of exploration, but they had become an unremarkable presence by the end of the eighteenth century, at least in London. Estimates put their numbers between five and fifteen thousand in London at the time Marrant was there. Most of them were either members of the working class, such as servants, performers, and seamen, or part of a poor underworld that survived by prostitution, begging, or crime. According to Gretchen Gerzina, they had "become a community, with a concern for joint action and solidarity." They would meet regularly in pubs, churches, and other gathering places, and formed a "thriving and structured black community" (*Black London,* 6). According to the 1764 *London Chronicle,* for example, fifty-seven blacks gathered one evening: they "supped, drank, and entertained themselves with dancing and music, consisting of violins, French horns, and other instruments, at a public-house in Fleet-Street, till four in the morning" (Hecht, 49). In 1772, the *London Chronicle* reported that, after Lord Mansfield issued his famous judgment in the Somerset case, in which he declared that a man purchased in the colonies and brought to England could not be taken out of the country against his will, the blacks present in the packed courtroom at Westminster Hall "bowed with profound respect to the Judges, and shaking each other by the hand, congratulated themselves upon their recovery of the rights of human nature, and their happy lot that permitted them to breathe the free air of England" (48). Nearly two hundred people attended the black ball held "at a public house in Westminster" (49) shortly afterward. In 1773, the *London Packet* reported that two blacks committed to Bridewell prison for begging were "visited by upwards of 300 of their countrymen" and that the black community "contributed largely towards their support during their confinement" (48). Clearly there was a well-organized, politically aware, and mutually supportive community of blacks in London.

The fortunes of many blacks were naturally tied to whites, and some individual blacks managed to get ahead thanks to their connections to the white world. Jack Beef, servant of the magistrate John Baker, was an important and trusted member of the household, who ran errands, bought and sold horses, and traveled. Ignatius Sancho occupied important positions in aristocratic households, first as a butler, then as a valet. He opened a grocery shop with financial help from a former employer. Francis Barber was Samuel Johnson's servant, and he used his inheritance money to open a draper's shop. Quobna Ottobah Cugoano worked for fashionable painters. Gronniosaw and his family managed to survive thanks to the generosity of various gentlemen who regularly showed up when all seemed lost. In one unexpected episode, an employer asked to speak with him because he had heard that he was black and, at the end of their conversation, decided to give him a raise.[41] The young Soubise was famously a protégé of the Duchess of Queensbury. Given a good education, he quickly became famous for fencing, riding, and swordsmanship. While skilled and good natured, it seems that he turned into a fop, whose extravagant style of living was a regular source of gossip.[42] Marrant himself managed to make a connection with a "respectable and pious merchant" for whom he worked and with whom he lived for three years and who was "unwilling to part with me" (*Narrative*, 126). Clearly, trusting and mutually beneficial interracial relationships were not uncommon, and for blacks, dependence on whites was a means to survive or move up.

Black community building could be made difficult by the lack of stable, well-paying employment. As Peter Fryer points out, blacks "were atomized in separate households, cut off from the cultural nourishment and reinforcement made possible by even the most inhumane plantation system" (70). For most of the century, this dispersion hampered the kind of rise in self-consciousness that, as we saw, occurred among free blacks in Saint-Domingue. Many blacks were also struggling to make ends meet. The last part of Gronniosaw's narrative is a litany of the suffering caused by the vagaries of employment and of how they take him and his family away from London. Olaudah Equiano's peregrinations can partly be explained by the fact that he was not satisfied with his paltry salary as a hairdresser—twelve pounds a year. Marrant himself was certainly not well off, even if he managed to save a little money.[43] In an affidavit, the cotton merchant he lived with testifies that Marrant lived "with honesty and sobriety," and that he was "tender hearted to the poor," and gave them "money and victuals if he had left himself none" (*Narrative*, 131). While he must have known he would not strike it rich in Nova Scotia, the material and emotional ties to London were not strong enough to hold him back.

It is possible that, if anything, religion brought a number of blacks together. It is hard to quantify church attendance for blacks, but baptism certainly seems to have been popular. Equiano stayed with two kind sisters in London when he was about twelve years old. Some servants told him he would not go to heaven unless he was baptized, and so in February 1759, he was baptized at St. Margaret's church in Westminster.[44] Interestingly, some people at the time thought that baptism automatically freed a slave, and so baptism was an important symbolic act. Equiano's master's first reaction when the boy asked to be baptized was to refuse. Moreover, baptism allowed indigents to receive relief from the parish where they were baptized.[45] In his list of subversive activities slaves engaged in once they started living in England, Sir John Fielding mentions that they "become intoxicated with liberty" and then "enter into Societies, and make it their Business to corrupt and dissatisfy the Mind of every fresh black Servant that comes to *England;* first by getting them christened or married" (143). According to Michael Bundock, the London baptismal records contain numerous entries referring to people of color, some of whom are quite advanced in age.[46] Baptisms, weddings, and funerals were not just an opportunity for blacks to get together and build ties; they signified blacks' access to a liberal political system.

Whether their ties were religious, social, or political, the group of blacks who started speaking publicly against the slave trade in the second half of the 1780s showed that a self-conscious black community was finally emerging. As early as March 1783, Equiano called on Granville Sharp, the notorious defender of blacks, to discuss the recent court hearing on the *Zong* case.[47] Two years before, the captain of a slave ship had ordered 133 Africans thrown overboard, and the ship's owners had just won compensation from the insurers. In July 1786, Cugoano informed Sharp that a black man was being held on a ship bound for the West Indies and asked him for help.[48] In 1787 and 1788, more than twenty black men, who dubbed themselves "Sons of Africa," cosigned various antislavery letters, which were either written privately to Sharp or published in newspapers. Cugoano published his *Thoughts and Sentiments on the Evil of Slavery* in 1787, and Equiano published his *Interesting Narrative* in 1789. A black abolitionist movement had sprung up in only a few years.

It is impossible to know if Marrant had any connection to those circles. The public letters are infused with Christian belief, so it is quite possible that Marrant and some of these men happened to attend the same churches. Equiano was only intermittently in London during the years Marrant was there. But he knew William Romaine, who was rector of St. Andrew-by-the Wardrobe in Blackfriars, and who had helped him in the last stage of his conversion, when his sermon "clearly shewed the difference between human works and free election" (Equiano, 192). He also knew Henry Peckwell, the Methodist preacher who had long been part of Lady Huntingdon's Connexion, and whose sermon at a Westminster chapel "evidently justified the Lord in all his dealings with the sons of men" (187). Did he go back to hear them regularly? Did he take his friend Cugoano with him? Did Marrant sometimes find his way to Westminster? Toward the end of his *Narrative,* he refers to "all my kind Christian friends" and "my very dear London friends" (127), so he clearly did create a community for himself. Still, he left England in 1785. Did he hear about the *Zong* case? Did he have a chance to read the first antislavery tracts coming out, such as Joseph Woods's *Thoughts on the Slavery of Negroes* (1784), or James Ramsay's *Essay on the Treatment and*

Conversion of African Slaves (1784)? Would he have joined those letter writers, had he stayed? Maybe. In any case, he knew about a black community forming in Nova Scotia, and that is where he would rather be.

Nova Scotia and the Black Loyalists

Standing on the ship *Peggy* bound for Halifax, Nova Scotia, in August 1785, Marrant had some reasons to be optimistic. He had arrived at Gravesend, the famous port town on the River Thames, one hour after the ship had sailed, but had managed to get on board anyway—not without having to pay two guineas, or a bit more than two pounds. Then that night, the ship was hailed by a boat that enquired what ship it was: "They then asked, if Mr. Marrant was on board? and was answered, yes; so she came along side, and I was called up. A man came on board, and presented to me a pocket book, which, when I opened, I found a twenty pound bank note" (*Journal*, 98). This generosity from a friend Marrant refuses to name was perhaps a sign that his new mission would continue to receive financial support. He was also bound for a place that he thought needed spiritual guidance, and where he could finally exercise his calling in visibly beneficial ways. In the months since his ordination, he had preached "many sermons" in Bath, Bristol, and London and had found receptive congregations, a sure sign to him that God had chosen him as "an instrument" for "his glory" (97). Finally, he would be part of a tight black community. This was a decisive turn in his life.

But he probably also anticipated the extent to which his work would be fraught with difficulties. He knew that it would be physically rigorous, as the usual hardships of itinerant preaching would be combined with the challenges of what was basically frontier life in a forbidding climate. Moreover, people who were busy building new lives might not look kindly on someone reminding them of the judgment of an all-powerful God. And if they were open to religion at all, they might prefer more emotional, elation-inducing performances, or a message that promised rewards for good works. Indeed, Marrant would find out that other preachers besides himself were vying for the settlers' attention. He would need to make it clear that his own message was not just worthwhile but unique.

•

As Marrant knew, the blacks he would find in Nova Scotia were already people with an amazing history. Most of them were former slaves who had decided to join the British side during the Revolutionary War—they were black loyalists. That process had taken place in the course of the war, as the British made various official appeals to them. In November 1775, Lord Dunmore, governor of Virginia, issued a proclamation from his ship in the harbor that declared slaves of rebels "free that are able and willing to bear Arms, they joining His Majesty's Troops as soon as may be" (Clark et al., 920). The news spread fast, and in the next few months, hundreds of blacks flocked to the governor's fleet and immediately started serving as soldiers, pilots, diggers, and foragers. If this was mostly grunt work, it also symbolized a new status and a new purpose. It was even said that the men wore an "inscription on their breasts": "Liberty to Slaves."[49] But freedom also meant sacrifice. In a 6 December letter, Dunmore announced his intention to raise two regiments; the black one would be called "Lord Dunmore's Ethiopian Regiment" (1311). Blacks fought at the bloody battle of Great Bridge a few days later, in which the British forces were overwhelmed. Then in the early months of 1776, many of them were decimated by smallpox. By the time the British left the Virginia coast, after dismantling or burning 63 of their 103 vessels, only three hundred blacks accompanied them to New York.[50] Of these, twenty-two—eight women, ten men, and four children—later found their way to Nova Scotia.[51]

After more proclamations, and especially after Britain switched to its southern strategy in 1778, many more blacks ended up behind British lines. Some slaves were carried off as war booty, but most of them joined the British voluntarily. Especially after the British took Savannah in December 1778 and Charleston in May 1780, blacks ran to them, by foot and on waterways—in the end, tens of thousands of them.[52] In Savannah, blacks helped repulse the attack led by French and American forces in 1779. Blacks were essential to Charles Cornwallis who, left in command of the South, tried to strengthen his hold in South Carolina after the capture of Charleston and then marched northward to Virginia. Through this long march all the way to Cornwallis's surrender at Yorktown on 19 October 1781, blacks spied, foraged, cooked, built fortifications, and impressed horses. One German officer commented: "This multitude always hunted at a gallop, and behind the baggage followed well over four thousand Negroes of both sexes and all ages. Any place this horde approached was eaten clean, like an acre invaded by a swarm of locusts. Where all these people lived was a riddle to me" (Ewald, 305). A number of them fought as soldiers. Many more died of smallpox or even starvation.

Once the British capitulated, the question of the status of the blacks who had joined them throughout the war became an issue for the Americans, and it would remain one for many years. While the Articles of Capitulation, and the Treaty of Paris, stipulated that American property had to be returned, most black loyalists managed to leave with the British. In the summer of 1782, thousands of blacks—some free, some the slaves of loyalists—left Savannah for the West Indies and St. Augustine. Later that year, thousands of them left Charleston for the same destinations, as well as for London and New York. Finally, throughout the summer of 1783, three thousand blacks left New York for Nova Scotia. Of these, about twenty-six hundred were free.[53] As part of an agreement between Sir Guy Carleton and George Washington, the British kept a register of the people who embarked. This register, commonly called the *Book of Negroes,* gives a brief description of each passenger's personal history and is a testament to the determination and independent spirit of people who, in the face of danger and deprivation, decided to dramatically change the course of their lives.[54] It is the symbol of the fundamental drive for freedom that motivated countless blacks during the Revolution and that led them to leave their country to face an uncertain future.

These are the people whom Marrant was on his way to meet. Himself an independent agent, he had not completely lost touch with enterprising American blacks. While in Charleston just after the siege, he probably reconnected with friends and family, at a time when decisions about allegiance were urgently being made. While in London, he stayed informed about the various stages of the Revolutionary War, and he probably came in contact with some of the four hundred black loyalists who emigrated to London. Of these, forty-seven men formally applied for a pension or for property compensation, and even though what they received was minimal, the fact that they went through the application process shows that they were aware of their rights as British citizens and were taking steps accordingly.[55] Did Marrant know Scipio Handley, for instance, who had been a free man in Charleston—a fisherman, who owned a boat—had fought for the British, and got baptized once he arrived in England?[56] Or George Peters, who "supported himself by his Trade as a Miller" in Pennsylvania, had served under Sir William Howe, had come to England at the New York evacuation, and was now a servant at a "Gentlemans House" (Gerzina, "Black Loyalists," 93)? It seemed as if any black person you ran into in London had an amazing story to tell. Marrant knew that there were many more like that in Nova Scotia.

By the time he arrived, though, quite a few were already demoralized, certainly in the area where he would spend the next two years, around the towns of Shelburne and Birchtown, on the southeastern coast. More than one thousand blacks recorded in the *Book of Negroes* had settled there, but there were many more, who had arrived earlier or on other ships.[57] Each family was supposed to receive a plot of land, but only a few black families did, and the plots were smaller than the ones allocated to whites. They also received fewer provisions and often had to work for them. Some of it was due to lack of administrative staff, some to racist neglect. The fact that Nova Scotian society still practiced slavery, with a number of slaves living in Shelburne, also helped perpetuate racial prejudice. Since so few blacks owned land, most of them became members of the skilled working class, dependent on white employers, whether private or governmental. Others were sharecroppers, servants, fishermen, or sailors. Indeed, blacks came to form, "in many Parts of this Province, the Principal Sources for Labour and Improvement" (Walker, 42). Harsh living conditions, the struggle for survival, occasional racial violence, disease, an unequal justice system—all this was enough for some of these migrants to start questioning the choices they had made.

Still, they did have a sense of their capabilities and desires as a community. As James W. St. G. Walker puts it, the loyalist's object was "to become self-sufficient and secured by British justice in his rights as a subject of the Crown"; the passage to Nova Scotia was "an entry into a new world where the dignity and independence that came of equal citizenship were to be his" (18). Armed with this profoundly republican ideal, the black migrants got to work and founded Birchtown when allocated land in August 1783. A year later, there were about fifteen hundred people living in the town. Very soon, with the help of philanthropists, schools were set up, and teachers were found. In spite of all its hardships, this was a community with resilience and cohesion, busily in the process of giving meaning to its experience. When Marrant arrived, religion was already providing an important part of this meaning. It would be up to him to see how he could contribute to the community's already complex and intertwined racial and spiritual consciousness.

•

Before the end of the Revolution, Nova Scotia, which had seen its first influx of immigrants just after the middle of the century, had gone through a first religious revival as a result of the work of Henry Alline. Raised a Calvinist, Alline went through a strong conversion experience, during which he "felt himself overwhelmed and possessed by a power greater and mightier than himself" (Armstrong, 64). Even though he had no training and hardly any education, he started preaching, emphasizing the importance of a personal religious experience and the finding of an inner light. His emotional delivery soon led to a revival that spread like wildfire throughout the peninsula. He did not care about denominations, and the churches he created were commonly referred to as New Light, in a recognition that Alline's enthusiasm had much in common with the one generated by George Whitefield during the Great Awakening. He left Nova Scotia in 1783, the year thousands of loyalists arrived. In many ways, Alline prepared the ground for what would be a series of religious revivals that would last until the end of the century.

Soon after they arrived, some black loyalists joined the Church of England, which was funded by the government and by the Society for the Propagation of the Gospel and had all the trappings of an established church. Most of the white loyalist migrants were Anglicans—thirty-one of them were clergymen[58]—and by 1787, Nova Scotia had a bishop. In a letter, he expressed what most people probably thought when he said that "wherever the principles of our church prevail, they naturally byass the mind towards the constitution, and incline it to loyalty" (Walker, 65). Interestingly, this connection between Anglicanism and the power of the state may have been one reason that it attracted a number of blacks. As Walker points out, many must have associated the free exercise of a religion with the status of freeman.[59] To former southern slaves who had seen it sustain and inspire powerful whites, Anglicanism symbolized their new identity as equal subjects of the king. It is also possible that, as they were focused on survival, it offered them easy access to a religious identity, one that provided them with an official worldview while making few emotional demands.

For blacks used to objectification and abuse, moreover, the Anglican priests' willingness to welcome them into the church may have augured a new day for cross-racial relations. Anglicanism had a spotty record when it came to evangelization of slaves in the South. Anglican priests were often dependent on the power of the vestries, church-governing bodies that were in the hands of planters. So for most of the eighteenth century, slaves' religious instruction was left to the will of the masters, with predictable results.⁶⁰ The situation in Nova Scotia was different. During the first year, John Breynton, rector of St. Paul's in Halifax, baptized "many hundreds" of blacks. Breynton, a kind Briton in his sixties who had lived in Nova Scotia for thirty years, and who was used to navigating relationships with dissenters and even with a small Dutch church in Halifax, showed some concern for blacks' education and employment.⁶¹ In November 1783, William Walter, a minister from Shelburne, held a mass baptism of seventy blacks in Birchtown, and the following year, he baptized seventy-nine. Walter was a former rector of Trinity Church in Boston and, according to a contemporary, his "countenance was always serene," "his temper always cheerful" (Eaton, 184). Not long after, George Panton—who was competing with Walter for the post of Anglican clergyman in Shelburne—baptized 125 blacks.⁶² So it seems that, from early on, the Church of England attracted plenty of black converts, and valued them.

But very soon, experience and inclination stoked awareness of racial identity. The blacks attending St. Paul's were relegated to a gallery, and when that space was needed for whites, they were asked to meet in private homes. Birchtown Anglicans received an occasional visit from a white pastor but otherwise became fairly independent, and until late 1786, services were held by Isaac Limerick, who was also a teacher in Birchtown, would later teach black children in Halifax, and would be among the 1,190 blacks who left for Sierra Leone in 1791.⁶³ Few blacks attended the Anglican churches in Shelburne, possibly because of high pew fees. Other black communities, such as Brindley Town and Little Tracadie, were similarly left to their own devices. So while it may have given black congregations a feeling of belonging as equal subjects of the empire, Anglicanism also gradually helped foster a sense of racial separateness.

The Baptists, while trying to appeal to all people, also promoted the rise of black churches. When the loyalists arrived, there were no Baptist churches in Nova Scotia, but the enthusiasm created by Alline was still simmering. One person managed to rekindle it: David George, who arrived late in 1782 and would help make the Baptists one of the most successful denominations in the peninsula. While a slave in South Carolina, George had been encouraged in his conversion by George Liele, a black Baptist who would later found the first Baptist church in Jamaica, and by Wait Palmer, a white Baptist from Connecticut; he became a preacher in the newly founded Silver Bluff Baptist Church, now considered one of the first black congregations in the American colonies. At the end of the war, George and his family were among the few blacks who sailed directly from Charleston to Halifax. As soon as he arrived there, he realized that "no way was open for me to preach to my own color," and so he moved to what would soon be called Shelburne a few months later, and started preaching in the woods: "The Black People came far and near, it was so new to them."[64] While both blacks and whites went to hear his sermons, he started a church with six black members, and when he decided to build a meeting house, "the worldly Blacks, as well as the members of the church, assisted in cutting timber in the woods" (337). Soon the church grew to fifty members. The next year, in July 1784, a gang of disbanded and unemployed soldiers drove him out during what can be called a race riot, and he settled down in Birchtown, where he started preaching from house to house and baptizing people. Clearly, while he was happy to preach to and to baptize all who were willing, including a few whites who specifically appealed to him, George was driven by a desire to create a source of identity and spiritual sustenance for blacks.

Indeed, his *Narrative,* which he dictated during a visit to London after his move to Sierra Leone, displays a racial consciousness that is rare among eighteenth-century black texts. He often refers to specific persons, or to crowds, by indicating their race. He also regularly points out who would later choose to go to Sierra Leone, implying that such persons had a particular concern for the fate of their black community. When he started his church at Shelburne, he "received four of my own color; brother Sampson [Colbert], brother John, sister Offee, and sister Dinah; these all wear well, at Sierra Leone, except brother Sampson, an excellent man, who died on his voyage to that place" (337). During his preaching tour in New Brunswick, he preached in St. John's, and "numerous spectators, White and Black, were present." He appointed Peter Richards there to continue the work. Richards, who was from South Carolina, and is listed in the *Book of Negroes* together with his wife, "afterwards died on the passage, just going into Sierra Leone, and we buried him there" (339). George also notes that he appointed Hector Peters at Preston, a town just east of Halifax with a sizable black community; Peters would also choose to emigrate to Sierra Leone. So George leaves no doubt that race was a binding element, over against whites who "had been very cruel to us, and treated many of us as bad as though we had been slaves" (340). He even seems to express surprise that those whites did not want them to leave.

Still, racial solidarity did not necessarily mean similar spiritual needs. George found out the hard way when, after he had been driven out of Shelburne and had been preaching in Birchtown for some time, he had to leave Birchtown because "my own color persecuted me there." It is possible that George's preaching style or his baptisms by full immersion were unwelcome. Once, when he had been in the process of baptizing a couple in Shelburne, an angry mob had come to prevent it, and the woman's sister even pulled her by the hair "to keep her from going down into the water" (338). While these reactions may have been racially motivated, since the couple was white, there is no doubt that the ritual itself felt alien and intrusive enough to stoke this kind of anger. The history of Baptists is replete with aggressive reactions to their emphasis on adult baptism. George had also inherited a faith marked by the revivals of the Great Awakening. In the 1740s and the 1750s, the Philadelphia Association had worked on spreading what was called "Separate" Baptist influence into the Carolinas, and several churches had been founded.[65] Oliver Hart, the pastor who converted Marrant, was part of this spread of evangelical Baptism. So was Shubal Stearns, who was baptized and ordained by the same Wait Palmer who baptized George. So when he started preaching at Birchtown, George was introducing a brand of faith that may not have won approval from all.

But apart from this rejection, most blacks embraced this representative of evangelical Christianity. True to its most fundamental tenet, his faith was anchored in the idea of the new birth, and this overwhelming moment of conversion had to be brought about through a complete emotional transformation. So he acquired popularity as a fiery, passionate preacher. In a June 1786 diary entry, Simeon Perkins, a merchant and colonel who lived in Liverpool, a town on the coast to the east of Shelburne, wrote: "A Black man from Shelburne, Said to be a Babpist Teacher, holds forth at the New Light Meeting House. He Speaks Very Loud and the people of that meeting, I understand, like him Very well" (320). In 1791, Harris Harding, a disciple of Alline, gave the following description of a meeting held by George: "Several of them frequently was obligd'd to stop and rejoice, soon after David began prayer, But was so overcome with joy was likewise obligded to stop, and turn'd to me with many tears like brooks rolling down his cheeks" (Rawlyk, 41). George ended up having more black followers than any other preacher at the time, and in the nineteenth century, most Maritime blacks would be New Light Baptists.[66] Whether or not he promoted racial solidarity, it seems that George managed to open an emotional and spiritual space where blacks felt "at liberty," a phrase that meant both a feeling of spiritual rebirth and a new sense of freedom.

It is possible that the rejection George experienced at Birchtown was in fact the work of other denominations. Most of the ministers who preached there were Methodists, and it was against them that Marrant would have to stand out, as there was one major difference between them: these were Wesleyan Methodists. The rift between John Wesley and Whitefield had been one of the major divisions during the Great Awakening, as Wesley rejected predestination and embraced the idea of free grace, as well as an emphasis on continued work toward spiritual perfection. In the second half of the eighteenth century, many Wesleyan Methodist missionaries fanned out across the American colonies, which had officially become the fiftieth Methodist circuit. According to Sylvia R. Frey and Betty Wood, "The predominantly British itinerancy achieved an almost charismatic rapport with enslaved Africans" (107). Very soon, a mass biracial Methodist revival spread throughout the South. In 1784, the Methodist Episcopal Church was founded, and Francis Asbury was ordained as its bishop. Most of the Methodists in Nova Scotia had been influenced by major figures in the movement, and all knew that they had a vast organization behind them.

William Black, a young white man who first visited Shelburne in June 1783—just a few weeks before George arrived—brought with him the emotional new-birth experience that was also typical of the Methodists. Born in Yorkshire, he had moved to Nova Scotia with his parents as a teenager and started attending meetings led by Methodist migrants. One day, "the tears began to gush out of my eyes, and my heart to throb within me" (245), and he knew he had just undergone a dramatic conversion. Committed to his renewed faith, he started to travel and preach throughout the peninsula, emphasizing the new birth as well as the striving toward Christian perfection or holiness. He also started corresponding with John Wesley, asking him to send missionaries. As he traveled and spoke to communities, Black tried to walk a middle ground between Calvinism, which many original settlers from New England still adhered to, and the almost mystical tendencies promoted by Alline. In one of his letters, Wesley warned him: "Of Calvinism, Mysticism, and Antinomianism have a care; for they are the bane of true religion" (169). Antinomianism was a trend that led evangelical converts to think of themselves as independent of human law because exclusively reliant on their relationship with God. The more emotional and mystical one's religious experience was, the better chance there was for an antinomian streak. Still, Black and Alline were apparently perceived as very similar charismatic preachers.[67] When he started preaching outdoors to the newly arrived migrants in Shelburne—three thousand people had disembarked just a month before, and few houses had yet been built—Black had an immediate effect.[68] When he came back the next spring, he was happy to see that the work in Shelburne had been kept up, partly thanks to John Mann.[69] Mann, white, born in New York, had converted to Methodism under the influence of Thomas Webb, a Methodist preacher who had been converted by Wesley himself, and of Richard Boardman, who had come from England as part of the Methodist missionary push.[70] Clearly, Shelburne was building a strong Wesleyan Methodist foundation.

This message was confirmed by a towering figure that soon appeared on the scene, Freeborn Garrettson, also white. Born in Maryland of Anglican parents, as a teenager Garrettson became interested in the Methodists, who were preaching in Baltimore, and he went to hear Robert Strawbridge, an Irishman who founded the first Methodist society in Maryland. Hearing Francis Asbury a few years later had a profound effect on him: "I heard him with delight, and bathed in tears could have remained there till the rising of the sun" (41). Finally, after years of searching and doubts, in 1775 he experienced an ecstatic moment of conversion. He soon received his license to preach and became an itinerant preacher, traveling thousands of miles, preaching hundreds of sermons, and making a significant contribution to the spread of Methodism. He attended the 1784 meeting in Baltimore where the Methodist Episcopal Church was founded and, assigned to go to Nova Scotia, he left for Halifax in February 1785. He would stay in Nova Scotia for two years and powerfully revitalize the evangelical movement there.

Judging from Garrettson's actions and beliefs throughout his life, it is clear that his Wesleyan Methodism brought about a commitment to helping blacks achieve equality, or at least freedom. One day shortly after his conversion, as he was leading his family in prayer, a thought came upon him: "It is not right for you to keep your fellow creatures in bondage; you must let the oppressed go free." He then told his slaves that they did not belong to him anymore and that "I did not desire their services without making them a compensation" (48). In the next few years, Garrettson would preach to blacks and let his opinion about slavery be known, and he would suffer persecution for it. One evening, a "gentleman" came to beat him, "affirming I would spoil all his negroes"

(49). While traveling in Virginia and North Carolina, and preaching to blacks, he "endeavoured frequently to inculcate the doctrine of freedom in a private way, and this procured me the ill will of some, who were in that unmerciful practice" (65). When he arrived in Virginia in the early 1780s, "when Cornwallis was ransacking the country," two things caused him great distress: "the spirit of fighting" and "that of slavery which ran among the people" (117). He soon started to preach "against the practice of slave-holding" (118). In 1805, he published a pamphlet entitled *Dialogue between Do-Justice and Professing Christian,* in which an abolitionist convinces Professing Christian of the immorality of slaveholding.[71] His stance was always clear, and he never wavered.

The same cannot be said of the Methodist denomination as a whole, though. It is certainly the case that a number of Methodist preachers were inspired by their faith not only to speak out against slavery but to urge their members to free their slaves.[72] The 1784 conference even ruled that all slaveholding members had to start emancipation procedures. In many ways, these decisions were in keeping with what Nathan O. Hatch has called the "democratization" of American Christianity: as the new, expanding denominations mirrored the democratic and populist rhetoric of the Revolution, they could not ignore one of its building blocks, the notion of individual freedom. But within six months, after an outcry from southern preachers, the rule was suspended. The writing was on the wall: as Donald G. Mathews explains, the choice was between building "an all-embracing evangelical church" and "social ostracism" (18). Slowly but surely, the Methodists retreated from an abolitionist agenda to the idea of equal access to religious instruction. If slaves could not be freed, they should at least be converted. Just as the revolutionary generation could limit the idea of individual freedom to whites, the Methodists could decide to focus their attention on individual salvation at the expense of social change.

Both black and white preachers had difficult choices to make when it came to segregation and slavery. In Jamaica, for example, George Liele decided only to receive slaves who had permission from their owners.[73] White Baptist churches originally accepted slave members, but they were segregated, or services for blacks were relegated to a different time of the day.[74] When Garrettson preached in Shelburne in the summer of 1785, the church became too small, so the solution made perfect sense to him: "Agreeably to my desire, the blacks of Shelburne built themselves a little house at the North end of the town, and I preached to them separately, in order to have more room for the whites" (127). William

Chipman, a Baptist leader who had met David George when he was ten years old, describes his religious fervor with admiration, and then says: "When he was asked to eat at the same table with Mr. Marchington [a wealthy resident] he modestly declined, saying, 'No Massa, God has made a distinction in our colour; give me my food alone'" (Rawlyk, 42). Such an anecdote should of course be taken with a grain of salt. In any case, for black preachers, segregation could be an opportunity to create not just spiritual togetherness but a new racial consciousness.

The people of Birchtown had a chance to make their own choices since, besides the work of Black and Mann, and before Garrettson came in the summer of 1785, they were also exposed to the Methodist message of two black preachers. Both of them are listed in the *Book of Negroes*, and both of them would emigrate to Sierra Leone. Soon after Boston King and his wife, Violet, arrived, Violet started a dramatic process of conversion that took her through "agony" (B. King, 356) all the way to the moment when "her soul" was "at perfect liberty." Interestingly, not unlike George the next year, as she tried to share her enthusiasm with others, "she was not a little opposed by some of our Black brethren" (357). But her husband was intrigued, and soon thereafter, he himself started his own spiritual journey, until in March 1784, "all my doubts and fears vanished away," and "I could truly say, I was now become a new creature" (358). He started exhorting soon afterward. In his narrative, King takes pains to emphasize Garrettson's influence on both himself and his wife. When Violet encountered opposition, "Mr. FREEBORN GARRETTSON . . . encouraged her to hold fast her confidence, and cleave to the Lord with her whole heart" (357). When he experienced doubt, King "heard Mr. GARRETTSON preaching from John ix.25, 'One thing I know, that whereas I was blind, now I see'" (359), and his doubts were removed. The Garrettson connection clearly anchored him in the Wesleyan tradition, a not insignificant detail considering that King wrote the narrative while attending the Kingswood school in England, which had been founded by Wesley in 1748 and was continuing his legacy.

While King would leave Birchtown in search of employment soon after arriving and would later be appointed by Black to lead the Wesleyans in Preston, the other black preacher stayed in Birchtown until the departure for Sierra Leone.[75] Moses Wilkinson, a former slave from Virginia, described in the *Book of Negroes* as "Blind & lame," almost singlehandedly turned Birchtown into a solid Methodist community. He is the one who converted Violet King.[76] When he came to Birchtown in the spring of 1784, Black preached to about two hundred blacks and was struck by their fervor: "Upwards of sixty profess to have found the pearl of great price, within seven or eight months: and what is further remarkable, the chief instrument whom God hath employed in this work is a poor negro, who can neither see, walk, nor stand. He is usually carried to the place of worship, where he sits and speaks, or kneels and prays with the people" (281). By then, the Birchtown blacks formed "the greater part of the Society of 200 members in the Shelbourne circuit" (Findlay and Holdsworth, 290). When Garrettson visited Birchtown in August 1785, about five hundred blacks attended, and by then "they had built themselves a church" (Garrettson, 127). Clearly Wesley's brand of Methodism, with its notions of free grace and striving toward perfection, resonated with the black migrants. We do not know how many of them knew that Wesley was against slavery. They probably did not even know that Wesley thought about them and was planning to send them some books.[77] But they clearly liked the idea of an intimate relationship to God that nevertheless required the constant work and vigilance necessary to build a better self and a better world. Whether or not this world would be racially divided was probably not decided.

•

Aware that he was competing with these various personalities and denominations, Marrant spent the next two years working on spreading his particular brand of Christianity. We know about this work thanks to his *Journal,* the remarkable document he published in London in 1790. Religious journals were quite common, but this one gives us a unique peek into the life of a black preacher on the Canadian frontier in the late eighteenth century. Because he wrote it after his two-year stay in Boston, moreover, it is inevitably shaped by the intellectual growth he went through during that time. The episodic structure and the use of dates indicate that he was relying on notes, but the narrative dimension shows that the composition took place later. So in many ways, the *Journal* expresses the worldview of an older, more experienced man, who can look back on his achievements and try to discern their meaning. And it is a meaning that is informed by his Calvinism, his racial consciousness, and republican cosmopolitanism all at once.

Marrant arrived in Halifax in early December 1785, and for the next two years, he traveled and preached ceaselessly in the southeastern coastal area. When he got to Shelburne by packet from Halifax, two weeks after he arrived in Nova Scotia, he walked into a coffeehouse and felt at first discouraged because he did not know anybody. He even considered returning with the packet, but when he came down for breakfast the next morning, he saw "a gentleman" (103) he knew—they had been to school together. After an emotional reunion, the man took him to see others. The next day, he made his way to Birchtown, and there too, he saw familiar faces. Birchtown became his home base. But all in all, he would end up not spending more than a few months there. Most of his time would be spent traveling in the coastal area to the east of Birchtown, which involved walking through Shelburne, crossing the Jordan River, and making his way to settlements in Green Harbour, Sable River, and Ragged Island. He once went west to Barrington, and he went twice to Halifax, the second time stopping in Liverpool on his way there and back. He left for Boston from Halifax in January 1788.

Marrant's description of events on the ship during the passage from London to Nova Scotia gives the reader a foretaste of his major themes. Early on, he notices that many passengers are swearing and playing cards, and though he sternly reproaches them, they disregard him. During the fourth week, though, there is a violent storm, and suddenly the passengers' behavior changes; they ask him to pray for them, and when he tells them that they must pray for themselves, they comply. He even notices that "the arrows of conviction went to the heart of one of the ladies." When he goes on deck, "the sea seemed to be all on fire"; the captain even declares that "he never saw such a thing in his life." When a mate shouts that the bowsprit is sprung, Marrant actually rejoices, as he can point out that God "warned them of their danger, and if we reject these repeated warnings, we must expect his judgments to fall upon us." After the storm subsides, life on the ship has been transformed, and Marrant even manages to "make a law against swearing" (99). This introductory story foregrounds all the elements of Marrant's ideology—one in which emphases have somewhat changed compared to the *Narrative*. On the one hand, there is attention to the importance of a personal, emotional change in one's relationship to the deity. But it is mostly this deity's omnipotence that is emphasized and the need for humans to decipher its messages and warnings. Once they understand and accept these dictates, they can start transforming or rebuilding their communities.

These "covenants" are clearly not just about an individual new birth; they are about an understanding that men need to create commonwealths that are in harmony with God's laws. On the ship, new behaviors do not just entail giving up swearing. The passengers develop new relationships and activities, and "reading, praying, singing of hymns, and preaching" become the order of the day. "Even the sailors" sing hymns, and come to Marrant for instruction. All in all, "there was a great alteration on the ship for the better" (100). People also notice that the weather remains fair until they reach their destination. With this story, Marrant seems to signal the project he had for his stay in Nova Scotia. Unlike his conversion of the Cherokees back in South Carolina, it is not just a religious but a social project. A bit like the pilgrim fathers on the *Arbella,* he looks to the creation of a covenanted community, or a sort of Calvinist republic, in which deeply held faith will sustain a project of moral and social harmony.[78]

The way he describes his listeners' reactions throughout the *Journal* shows that Marrant's preaching was of course predominantly aimed at eliciting an emotional reaction. He likes to emphasize emotional responses, such as "groaning, and sighing" (102) "tears and groaning" (106), listeners being "pricked to the heart" (104, 111, 117, 129), or him bringing "truth to the hearts of the hearers" (106). He describes a woman spending days and nights in agony before she finally "burst out in tears and fell upon her knees" (115). One day, when he tries to baptize those who are ready, he baptizes five, and since "the rest were fallen to the ground" (109), he baptizes them on the ground. The whole congregation bursts into tears, and their cries are so loud that he can hardly be heard. He also chooses biblical passages that emphasize the power of individual faith, such as Isaiah 40:31: "They will soar on wings like eagles; they will run and not grow weary, they will walk and not be faint." One day, he visits an old woman who feels she has never done anybody any harm, and who regularly goes to prayers, and he asks her if she knows her own heart. Further questioning her, he gives her advice that fairly summarizes his new-birth philosophy. He tells her that "if she had not a better heart than what she was born with, it was a wicked heart, and full of enmity against God." If she does not change, she will forever live "among devils and wicked spirits, where all people go that die without a change of heart" (119). Clearly, a personal relationship with God was still at the core of Marrant's religious vision.

In keeping with this individualistic outlook, one finds in the *Journal* an occasional emphasis on individual suffering that is not dissimilar from what we saw in the *Narrative.* Marrant once gets attacked by a woman he is trying to convert; she hits him hard on the arms and the head with tongs, and he starts to bleed heavily. Still, he returns to her house without any seeming concern for his wounds and starts talking to her, contrasting "the happiness of the saints in heaven" with "the dreadful torment of hell" (112). Most of the suffering throughout the *Journal* comes from his travels in harsh conditions. Several times, he makes river crossings made dangerous by bad weather. Once his boat gets entangled in the ice, but he manages to get it out and row to shore.[79] He gets lost several times, and once, in an episode reminiscent of the *Narrative,* he wanders in a swampy area for two days. Each time he lies down to sleep, he feels pushed; he soon realizes that "it was the Lord" pushing him "because of my slothfulness in going to sleep in the wilderness" (138). During the first months of 1787, he had several bouts of illness, and this was not helped by the rigors of his destitute, itinerant life. In July, while in Birchtown, he was taken by a violent fever, and started spitting blood. He still desired to preach, "seeing a crouded multitude coming from the neighbouring villages round about" (141). He started preaching, but in the end, blood started running out of his nose and mouth, and he had to be carried to his house. Clearly, the *Journal* implies, this is a man who went through extreme physical suffering for his faith.

Some of the emphasis on suffering may be due to the fact that one of Marrant's motivations for publishing the *Journal* was to justify himself against reports that he had squandered some of the Connexion's money. In the preface, he gives a precise account of how much money he had received—"twenty-four pounds seven shillings" (94)—and of how his itinerancy soon consumed the whole amount. He needed money to pay for ferryings, for example, "as that country has so many large rivers and lakes to cross." He even had to pawn his jacket several times. He wrote to England repeatedly asking for support, "so that I might have been able to continue with the people," but never received an answer. (The *Journal* attaches just one short letter from Lady Huntingdon, dated 25 October 1786.) And when he arrived in London and tried to ask for an explanation, he never received one. So the tone in the preface is that of an aggrieved person who has endured considerable physical hardship for the sake of his faith and who now finds himself having to defend his every move. He wants his reader to understand that "there is not a Preacher belonging to the Connection could have suffered more than I have for the Connection, and the glory of God, and for the good of precious souls" (95). So the *Journal* partly functions as a vindication and needs to play up his individual devotion.

Despite this emphasis on individual faith and resilience, though, Marrant's overall Calvinist outlook comes across much more strongly here than in the *Narrative*. One way it does so is that some of the biblical passages he refers to evince a certain fire-and-brimstone tendency, in their emphasis on repentance and the dire consequences of sin or an unconverted state. His very first topics in Birchtown include John 5:28–29, where Jesus promises that "those who have done what is good will rise to live, and those who have done what is evil will rise to be condemned," and 1 Corinthians 1:29–31, which places the wisdom of God far above any earthly or human wisdom. Soon after, he preaches from Mark 16:16, where after his resurrection, Jesus proclaims that "whoever believes and is baptized will be saved, but whoever does not believe will be condemned." He chooses Luke 23:40, in which a criminal crucified together with Jesus is the only one to express fear of God, and Jesus promises him paradise. He quotes from Acts 1:7, which asserts God's authority, and from Acts 2:48, which urges people to "repent and be baptized." To Indians in their wigwam, he preaches from Romans 1, a long tirade about people who practice all kinds of "wickedness," and about how God will severely punish them. Some time later, he preaches to "a great multitude" (114) from Luke 13:5, which admonishes that "unless you repent, you too will all perish," and from Luke 15:7, which promises that "there will be more rejoicing in heaven over one sinner who repents than over ninety-nine righteous persons who do not need to repent." He later preaches from Luke 24:47, Acts 3:19, and Mark 6:12, which are all about repentance.

The funeral sermon he preached in March 1786, and which is appended to the *Journal,* also gives us a good sense of how, in his preaching, he emphasized the omnipotence of God and its workings in everyday life. He asks the question, How are we to gain eternal life? A person who has "the faith of God's elect" will try to follow all the doctrines and duties incumbent upon him. But ultimately, Christ will "do what he will with his own." So "let him dispose of me," and "let him appoint how all my time and talents shall be employed." He is authorized to "effect his own ends by me, with all that I am and have, as he shall direct" (163). It is likely that Marrant worked this idea of complete subjection to the will of God into most of his sermons.

But Marrant's Calvinist theology does not stop at these tenets; the *Narrative* and the biblical references also convey a concern for the establishment of a stable and equal community devoted to the common good, as Marrant projects the republican implications of his Calvinism into the *Journal.* Isaiah 60, which expresses the promise of a heaven-like community or state, looks to a time when "no longer will violence be heard," and "all your people will be righteous." Matthew 6:33–34 concludes a list of recommendations not to worry about the material side of life, whether it be food, drink, or clothing; what matters is practicing virtue here and now. Similarly, Hebrews 13:5 warns against the love of money, after urging toward acts of love and generosity. Indeed, the funeral sermon projects perfection as a state where one is "divested of self" (173). Before returning to Birchtown from Jordan River, he also tells his listeners, following 2 Corinthians 13:11, to "be of one mind," and "live in peace." He seems to want to convey a vision of a future community made perfect by its relationship to the deity. Isaiah 60, which he refers to twice, gives a full description of a future glorious Zion, which will attract the wealth of the nations and the seas, and where God "will be your everlasting light." Here is clearly the idea of a commonwealth energized by covenant. Similarly, his description of heaven in the funeral sermon calls up images of "perfect order," "perfect agreement," "beauty and harmony"—it is a place where God really does "sit at the helm and steer the ship" (171).

Although he does not draw undue attention to it, it seems that Marrant himself was an important participant in the building of community, sometimes even with small gestures. He is once asked to carry a letter from John Lock to his son, an indication that his itinerancy was used as a way to make connections between people in the area.[80] In the spring of 1786, after he had just come back to Birchtown, several people asked him to go to Halifax and deliver three petitions to the governor. The petitions requested "tools, spades, hoes, pickaxes, hammers, saws and files, such as they should want, and blankets" (123). The listing of these items in the *Journal* is more than an attempt at descriptiveness; it is a statement about people in dire need. Later Marrant would bring another petition to the governor, this time from a black community not far from Halifax. In 1787, he and Charles Baley, a former Virginia slave, were issued a warrant for the survey of thirty-eight acres of land in Shelburne Township.[81] This land was probably destined for the building of a chapel, in which Marrant says he "laid out every farthing" he had made in London. "I hope it is standing now," he comments (94).

One question that arises, then, is the racial component in Marrant's communitarian ethos. In an important essay, John Saillant analyzes Marrant's theological tenets as they are stated or implied in the *Journal,* and he highlights Marrant's vision of a providential design, the importance of conversion, and the idea of a covenanted community. He argues more specifically that the *Journal* carries a vision of a "providential restoration to Africa of a holy black community, bound by affection and the covenant of grace" ("Wipe Away," 7). In other words, Marrant developed an "Africanist Calvinism" (9) that offered "instructions for the return to Africa" (11). Saillant points to a number of biblical passages Marrant refers to in the *Journal* that strongly suggest this Africanist vision of Zion. He also describes how, once in Sierra Leone, the Nova Scotians' vision of a covenanted community and desire for land would clash with the commercialism of the company—a classic republican struggle.[82]

It may be the case that Marrant conveys a racial message in the *Journal,* but one can also see the influence of a certain universal republicanism, as Marrant is looking back on his experiences in Nova Scotia through the filter of his time in Boston and trying to reinsert himself into British print culture. He makes it clear, for example, that most of the time, he was addressing white or mixed crowds. He did so from his first days in Halifax, where "God was pleased to manifest his divine power both to black and white" (102). Even in Birchtown a few days later, he preached "to a larger congregation than the morning, of white and black, and Indians" (104), as people "were running from all quarters," including "Barrington, Cape Negro, Shelborn, and Jordan River" (105), and he immediately received requests to travel to those places, which he did ceaselessly in the next two years. (Cape Negro was not a black community; it received its name from Samuel de Champlain in the early seventeenth century because of the appearance of a particular rock.) In early 1786, he crossed the Jordan River and preached to "a great number of Indians and white people" (111). In April 1787, while in Liverpool, he preached at a "New-light meeting house" (135), and after it turned out that they disliked his Calvinist message, he preached "in the large chapel" (136) with great success. Simeon Perkins, the merchant, "heard him & Liked him well" (365). While he clearly presents the black community of Birchtown as his home base, the Christian vision deployed in Marrant's *Journal* usually pertains to the wide multiracial spectrum he encountered during his stay. When he preaches that "you are a chosen people, a royal priesthood, a holy nation, God's special possession" (1 Peter 2:9), it is not in Birchtown, but at Ragged Island, in front of "a large body of people" (131). If anything, Marrant's message was closer to the universal republicanism he would encounter in Boston than to an Africanist fervor.[83]

Indeed, the conflicts he is most adamant about emphasizing are religious, not racial. The first time he arrived in Birchtown, he learned that the people had received a letter from "Mr. Marchenton, in Hallifax . . .

warning them that I was not an Arminian, and did not come from Mr. Westley, and preached, there was no repentance this side the grave; and thus inflamed the minds of the people." Philip Marchinton was a loyalist from Philadelphia, a merchant, a public figure, and a religious zealot who promoted the Wesleyan creed.[84] He had helped Garrettson after his arrival in Halifax earlier that year.[85] Marrant triumphantly reports that "God over-ruled all things for his glory" and that the "letter proved fruitless" (104). Several months later, in the spring of 1786, as he came back to Birchtown from a preaching tour, he learned that "the Arminian had been amongst them, endeavouring to draw them away" (121). The same thing happened shortly after, when he arrived in Barrington, and heard that "Mr. Garrison" (122) had been there. The conflict then came to a head that summer. Marrant describes a dramatic scene in the chapel of Birchtown, where Garrettson, unaware of his presence, openly criticizes him. Some of the elders speak up, and when Marrant makes a move to leave, most of the assembled people go with him. Marrant finally comes back in and forces Garrettson to leave. But Marrant is equally critical of Moses Wilkinson, whom he calls "the old blind man, who preaches for the Arminians." When Wilkinson tries to prevent him from preaching, he goes to prayer, and the old man leaves. "We see here," Marrant comments, "that the devil can never stand against the truth, but will always fly" (124). If there is enmity or competition in the *Journal,* it is about religious dogma.

But in fact, Marrant seems to dislike conflict; he promotes a social vision anchored in peaceful conflict resolution and benevolence, and here also, race seems to matter little. When he realizes that the goods he received from the governor for Shelburne have in fact been sold by an unscrupulous man, he "went and conversed" (124) with the buyers in order to solve the issue. The conflict with Garrettson ends with a public reconciliation in which Garrettson comes down from the pulpit and asks for forgiveness, and Marrant "went up to him, and caught hold of his hand, and he wept, and I sympathized with him, and wept also" (127). The episode, which is supposed to have taken place in July of 1786, is not recorded in Garrettson's journal or letters, but his comments in letters he wrote before and after the summer are very different. In April, he writes Wesley from Shelburne: "A negro man by the name of Morant, lately from England, who says he was sent by lady Huntingdon, has done much hurt in society among the blacks at Burch town. I believe that Satan sent him. Before he came there was a glorious work going on among these poor creatures, now . . . there is much confusion.

The devil's darts are sometimes turned upon his own miserable head" (246). In September, he just writes about Shelburne that "most of the coloured people whom Morant drew off have returned" (249); the absence of further comment is striking. Whether or not the reconciliation happened the way Marrant describes it, the emphasis on an emotional transformation and the establishment of an affectionate new order under God's guidance—the two men "went aside into the wood, and kneeled down to prayer, and then parted in peace and love" (Marrant, *Journal*, 127-28)—suggests Marrant's hope for a commonwealth anchored in interracial, interfaith harmony.

Of course, Marrant inevitably got caught in a web of racial politics. His silence on matters of race does not completely obscure the racial dimension of life in Nova Scotia at that time. His triumphant account of how he brought Garrettson down—literally and figuratively—in front of a large black congregation cannot but have racial overtones. In his journal, Garrettson certainly is racially conscious when he declares that he "applied to their colonel, who was a black, or rather a yellow man, to have him put out of the town, which he consented to" (128). Marrant also sounds bitter when he describes being dragged before the Shelburne court by "false brethren" (141), who accuse him of several illegal acts, including performing a wedding for a woman who was already married.[86] He later finds out that the accusers were "class-leaders of the Methodist society" (143), but the overall acrimony must have had a racial dimension. The fact that Birchtown contributed half of the men and women who left for Sierra Leone shows that there was a strong sense of racial separateness in the community.[87]

Marrant also made a number of connections with black leaders. When he arrived in Halifax, he quickly made contact with fellow Huntingdonian William Furmage, who according to Adam Potkay and Sandra Burr, was black.[88] Furmage had set up a Huntingdonian society there, which consisted of about forty people, and he preached "at the Poor house, and to the Orphans," as well as to "many poor negroes here" (Whytock, 167). In a 3 December 1785 letter to Lady Huntingdon, he wrote that he was happily surprised at the arrival of "my dear Brother Marrant" (168). A year later, he wrote that Marrant had come to Halifax and preached "with much satisfaction" (169), and in a letter to Marrant, a certain Jonathan Allstyne tells him that Furmage gave him "strong recommendations" (157). Marrant mentions Furmage several times in his *Journal*. He says that, after his arrival in Halifax, "the Reverend Mr. Furmage took me from place to place," so that Marrant had a chance to preach to several congregations, some of them "large" or "crowded" or "a large concourse of people" (102). Once he got to Birchtown, Marrant ordained two local men, Cato Perkins and William Ash, as preachers.[89] Both would later move to Sierra Leone. Once there, Perkins would play a role in a carpenters' strike and be elected to go to London and present the settlers' grievances—and strongly protest when the directors of the Sierra Leone company refused to meet with the petitioners. So Marrant certainly had connections with leaders who were particularly concerned about the sufferings and the survival of their black communities.

Marrant also had friendly relations with the family of Stephen Blucke, a black loyalist who played an important role in Nova Scotia but refused to emigrate to Sierra Leone. Described in the *Book of Negroes* as a "stout fellow" who was born free on the island of Barbados, Blucke acquired the title of colonel—he is the same colonel Garrettson applied to—and headed the corps of blacks who were enlisted for the construction of Shelburne and of Birchtown. By April 1786, he had a land grant of two hundred acres, had built a fishing boat, and could afford the high pew fees at the Anglican church in Shelburne. He also efficiently managed a school set up by Anglicans at Birchtown.[90] When the time came to decide whether to emigrate, he headed a petition of fifty-two family heads to Governor Parr, criticizing the Sierra Leone project and requesting that "their share of the royal bounty" (Walker, 128) be expended for the migrants. The *Journal* includes a letter to Marrant from Margaret Blucke, his wife, in which she thanks Marrant for his "very kind and affectionate letter" (159). She is writing from New York, where she had grown up, and had bought her freedom fourteen years before moving to Nova Scotia with her husband.[91] The letter is dated October 1789, and she asks Marrant to try to find her husband because she has not heard from him. Following some suspicion that he had falsified a school record, Blucke disappeared from Shelburne after 1786, and it is possible he found his way to Boston.[92] When he left for Boston, Marrant also knew he would join the sizable community of free blacks who lived there.

But the overall impression left by the *Journal* is that it is marked by both a diverse experience in Nova Scotia and the ideological growth Marrant went through while in Boston. He concludes the *Journal* by mentioning a few people he attended on their death beds, most of whom were probably white. He also gives the names of "those principal gentlemen in Nova Scotia" (155) who knew of his hardships and assisted him, and most of them, such as William Walter, the Anglican preacher, and Isaac Wilkins, a judge, were white. In Boston, Marrant would make contact not only with black Freemasons but also with the city's broader religious and intellectual circles. He stayed there long enough to absorb all these influences before making his way back to London, so when he arrived there and started working on the publication of the *Journal*, his ideological horizons had become more expansive than ever. It was quite a trajectory for a man who had started his religious career in South Carolina, being struck to the ground in a new-birth experience.

Freemason and Cosmopolitan

Late in January 1788, Marrant boarded a ship for Boston; he arrived there five days later. He would spend the next two years preaching and teaching in Boston and in the surrounding area. During this stay, Marrant made connections with a variety of intellectual and ideological circles. A major one was a recently created lodge of black Freemasons. Another one was the circle around Samuel Stillman, a white Baptist minister. The combination of these influences gave Marrant a unique outlook, in which his covenant Calvinism bloomed into a multicultural, multiracial view of history's trajectory. Records show that in August 1788, Marrant went back to Birchtown and married Elizabeth Herries.[93] In an October 1789 letter, Margaret Blucke asks about his children, so it seems that Marrant had a family. We know nothing else of his personal life, but what we know is that Marrant became part of the unique black cosmopolitan generation that inhabited the late-eighteenth-century Atlantic world and left its stamp on it.

•

Marrant arrived in a city of almost twenty thousand people with a black population of about one thousand.[94] There were no slaves. In 1781, Elizabeth Freeman had sued for her freedom and had won the case thanks to the recently ratified Massachusetts constitution, which stated that "all men are born free and equal, and have certain natural, essential, and unalienable rights." There was no legal segregation, but most blacks lived in the West End or the North End, and a few lived on Beacon Hill, in the center of town. They worked predominantly as domestics, skilled tradesmen, or sailors. Some of the men had fought in the Revolutionary War. Some black entrepreneurs had even become rich. Fifteen years earlier, Phillis Wheatley, a slave, had become famous as the first black poet to publish a poetry collection.

The black community had not remained silent or invisible during the eventful past two decades; it had organized and made several interventions in the public sphere. In the 1770s, several petitions to the state legislature had appealed for a lightening, or the abolition, of slavery. In January 1787, a petition signed by seventy-three men had asked for support to emigrate to Africa; in October of that year, another one asked for equal access to education. A 27 February 1788 petition complained about the kidnapping and selling of free blacks; in response, the legislature passed a strict anti-slave-trade law.[95] Since 1775, there had been a lodge of black Freemasons in place, and all the petitions had a number of Freemason signatories. A few years after Marrant's departure, the African Society would be created, a mutual aid organization echoing Newport's African Union Society and Philadelphia's Free African Society. In 1805, the First African Baptist Church was formed, and the next year, it moved into a new building on Beacon Hill. So Marrant arrived at a time when a black communal consciousness was taking official shape, not just in Boston but all over the northern states.

Indeed, Marrant belongs to a generation that Richard S. Newman and Roy E. Finkenbine have called the "black founders" of the republic. Blacks were clearly in the process of shaping their relationship with mainstream society, and the forms this process took ran the gamut from creating separate identities to integrating broader institutions and ideologies. Black churches were created, for example, but blacks never stopped going to white churches, and some attended a white church in the morning and a black one in the afternoon.[96] So on the one hand, blacks created an oppositional discourse that entailed seeing themselves as a separate community. On the other, they started developing "a discourse of civic inclusion" by trying to "reappropriate revolutionary words, symbols, and ideas in the cause of interracial reform" (Newman and Finkenbine, 88). Both of these strands were present in black writings and interventions in the public sphere during the time that Marrant was in Boston.

Besides the presence of an active black community, there were other reasons for Marrant to have found Boston compelling: it had been a major player during the Revolution, and it was in the area of the new republic that had the most solid history of Calvinism. At the time Marrant arrived, a new federal constitution had been drafted in Philadelphia, and it was in the process of being ratified by individual states. In fact, the Massachusetts ratifying convention was in session the day he sailed into Boston harbor. Marrant must also have been aware of Boston's rich Calvinist history. The Old South Church, the Brattle Street Church, the First and the Second Congregational Churches, all but the last one in the heart of the city, were a testament to the enduring strength of Calvinism, even if what was perceived as its rigor was slowly eroding. For someone who had just spent two years in an ongoing preaching war with Arminians, this institutional grounding must have provided some relief. As we will see, this does not mean that Marrant would escape religious conflict. But Boston, with its unique ideological makeup, turned out to be the ideal breeding ground for his Calvinist, cosmopolitan legacy.

•

When he met Prince Hall, Marrant was meeting the most visible black leader in Boston. Hall was a "leather-dresser" and a renowned caterer.[97] A commentator referred to him as "a tall, lean Negro of great dignity" (C. Wesley, 89). Hall had put his name to several of the petitions directed to the Massachusetts legislature in the past decade; the petition about kidnapping was printed that year in the *American Mercury,* a Connecticut newspaper, with his signature only.[98] On 6 March 1775, Hall and fourteen black men had been initiated in Masonry by John Batt, a sergeant in a British infantry regiment stationed in Boston and a member of an Irish Military Lodge. Armed with a permit, they formed the first black lodge in America, which they called "African Lodge. No.1."[99] On 27 December 1782, they celebrated the Feast of St. John, a Masonic ritual in honor of John the Evangelist. According to a report in a Boston newspaper, the event consisted of a procession in which they marched "preceded by a band of music" and "dressed in their aprons and jewels." A few days later, Hall printed a reply to the report, pointing out that their name was not "St. Black's Lodge," as the author of the article had called them, and that the gathering that followed the procession was not "a splendid entertainment" but "an agreeable one in brotherly love" (Upton, 3). In 1784, he petitioned the Grand Lodge of England for a charter; he finally received it in 1787. By the time Marrant arrived, Prince Hall was grand master of an active and publicly acknowledged black lodge and, as Unitarian minister William Bentley put it in his diary, "a person of great influence upon his Colour in Boston" (379).

But Prince Hall's ideals were also interracial. Even as in some petitions blacks asked for permission to create their own schools or bury their own dead, the creation of separate institutions went hand in hand with visions of harmony and equality that were interracial.[100] In a letter to a Virginian, Jeremy Belknap, a Congregational minister and historian who knew Hall, proceeded to answer a question about the state of racial relations in Boston by reporting the answer given him by Hall. "Harmony in a great measure prevails between us as citizens," he wrote. "As to our associating," he continued, "there is here a great number of worthy, good men and good citizens, that are not ashamed to take an African by the hand; but yet there are to be seen, the weeds of pride, envy, tyranny and scorn in this garden of peace, liberty and equality." He then points out that some whites had visited the African lodge, though no blacks had visited the white lodges.[101] In response to an inquiry, Hall provided the grand secretary in London with information about a number of white lodges, where they met, who the current grand master was. The tone of the letter is matter-of-fact, indicating Hall's self-evident view of all the lodges as forming one great contribution to the "flourishing state of the Society" (C. Wesley, 91).

Hall was also eager to participate in the rituals of citizenship. According to Belknap, he voted "constantly for governor and representatives" (C. Wesley, 109). William H. Upton says he was "highly esteemed and trusted by the leaders of the patriotic cause in Boston" (C. Wesley, 83). In a November 1786 letter to governor James Bowdoin, Hall offered the services of the black Freemasons to help in putting down Shays' Rebellion, a series of protests and mob actions that had recently been taking place in western areas of the state. Though their "fraternity" enjoined them "to be peaceable subjects to the Civil power where we reside," Hall says that "we, though unworthy members of this Commonwealth are willing to help and support so far as our weak and feeble abilities may become necessary in this time of trouble and confusion, as you in your wisdom shall direct us." The stance of humility does not detract from the point he wants to make—namely that they have "been protected for many years under this once happy constitution" (42), and that they are ready to defend it as equal citizens. Hall also regularly sent copies of his charges to Bentley, whose political outlook had grown into a full-blown classic republicanism, in defense of "civic virtue" and the "good of the commonwealth" (Ruffin, 110).[102] Hall's notion of citizenship was bound to be republican and all-inclusive.

Even separatist projects necessitated interracial contact and collaboration. In 1805, a number of blacks withdrew from the First and Second Baptist Churches with the intention of founding their own church. Thomas Paul and Scipio Dalton started the process by writing letters to these parent churches, asking for assistance. Samuel Stillman, pastor of the First Baptist Church, attended the organizational meeting. He then put together a subscription list and started a funding campaign. By December 1806, a three-story brick building, the African Meeting House, stood in Smith Court near Belknap Street—currently Joy Street—and its seventy-two pews could accommodate some six hundred persons. Paul immediately became its minister.[103] Two years later, a school for black children moved into the basement of the meeting house. In 1798, Primus Hall, the son of Prince Hall, had received permission from Boston's Board of Selectmen—the town's governing board—to run a school for blacks in his house. Whites, such as Unitarian minister William Ellery Channing and Congregational minister Jedidiah Morse, helped keep the school going until it moved and transform the basement into a schoolroom.[104] This sort of help may sound like run-of-the-mill philanthropy, or even promotion of racial separatism, and in many ways it was, but it did help blacks create institutions from which they could promote an egalitarian civic consciousness. School integration would spread in Massachusetts in the next decades, until the legislature finally made it official in 1855.[105]

Prince Hall was certainly aware of the importance of white allies. Before the January 1788 petition about the kidnapping of three black men was sent to the legislature, he discussed it with Belknap, who had just moved to Boston from New Hampshire. In a letter to Ebenezer Hazard, the postmaster general, Belknap mentions the "share I had in petitioning," during which he had "some conferences with Prince on the subject" (55). He also sent the petition to Hazard, who lived in New York, and the text also appeared in the 24 April 1788 edition of the *Massachusetts Spy* in Worcester.[106] That month, Hazard returned the petition to Belknap and wrote: "It will appear in one of our newspapers on Monday, when a trial will come on between one of our masters of vessels and a member of the society for promoting the manumission of slaves, who accused the former of kidnapping negroes" (28–29). Belknap was then visited by Prince Hall and the three black men who had finally been returned, an event that had "caused a jubilee among blacks." Hall introduced Belknap to them by saying: "There is the gentleman who has been so much your friend" (55), and Belknap was moved by their simple gratitude. These forms of interracial collaboration were integral to the struggle for abolition and civic inclusion. Marrant arrived just as they were taking place.[107]

•

It is possible that the other major influence on Marrant, Boston's strong Calvinist inheritance, fed black separatism. The emphasis on special covenants with God tended to foster the creation of separate communities. Blacks were not blind to the significance of the notion of a suffering chosen people whose protection was assured by an omnipotent deity. Indeed, as Christopher Cameron shows, many blacks in Massachusetts were attracted to Calvinism, and this embrace left an important ideological legacy that is often overlooked. Daniel Rogers, a Congregational itinerant minister, noted that blacks longed for religious instruction, and their testimonies show that blacks were not just attracted to the emotional dimension of religious revivals.[108] They liked the idea of a sovereign god who needed covenants to be respected for the sake of a better world—and of a strong black community.

But some black Calvinist testimony reveals a broader concept of God's covenant. Writing from Newburyport, a town about thirty miles north of Boston, in 1774, a former slave named Caesar Sarter displayed the influence of Calvinism on blacks in the area. In an essay published in the *Essex Journal and Merrimack Packet,* in which he aims to show that slavery is one of the greatest "calamities," he starts by reminding his readers of the struggles of their ancestors, who "came into this country, then a howling wilderness inhabited, only, by savages, rather choosing, under the protection of their GOD, to risk their lives . . . than submit to tyranny at home." This reminder of the goal of a covenanted community under God's guidance colors his subsequent appeals to notions of "*natural rights of mankind*" (168) and to sympathy for people who are torn from their loved ones. Communities under God's guidance that tolerate slavery violate their agreement, and one day, they will be "accountable for all your actions, to that impartial Judge, who hears the groans of the oppressed and who will, sooner or later, avenge them of their oppressors!" (169). In keeping with the form of the jeremiad, Sarter is invoking the prospect of a unified commonwealth even as he is threatening whites with divine judgment. He rallies his Calvinist faith in the service of a just interracial republic.

Sarter may seem to endorse a separatist ideal at the end of his essay, when he asks for "grants in some back parts of the country" (170), but the core of his appeal expresses blacks' religiously inspired desire to become equal members and participants in an interracial society. In that, he may be reflecting the general mood in the black community. Many blacks attended mixed churches. Church records show that black baptisms at Congregational churches increased during the Great Awakening to a total of 175 for the four main churches; between 1745 and 1775, almost eighty blacks were baptized at the Old South and the Brattle Street Churches.[109] Prince Hall was for many years a member of a Congregational church on School Street, in the center of the city.[110] It was a small brick church, built earlier in the century by a group of French Protestants and purchased by a Congregational group a few decades later.[111] The minister, Andrew Croswell, had acquired a reputation as a disputatious New Light who insisted on the primacy of an emotional conversion experience and was not afraid to argue his position vehemently in the Boston press. During his days of itinerant preaching, he had often held lengthy revivals, in which he "pressed children and Negroes into the pulpit to exhort the congregation to frenzy" (Shipton, 390). His mobility in preaching, as he moved from pew to pew, combined with his message, gave an impression of egalitarianism.[112] Other ministers preached at the School Street church; one of them was John Murray, a universalist. It is likely that Prince Hall heard his message of universal salvation in 1773 and 1774, when Murray preached at the church repeatedly.[113] Overall, blacks in Boston had access to various religious messages, some of which encouraged a degree of egalitarian, interracial thought.

Of those, the New Lights were not necessarily the most socially progressive. While they accepted blacks as members and even as exhorters, this tolerance did not automatically translate into racially progressive or even abolitionist language. Croswell never spoke out against slavery. We have seen Whitefield's promotion of slavery in Georgia. James D. Essig points out that no "leading figure of the Great Awakening ever denounced the practice of holding slaves" (14). The New Light Baptists of New England "did not figure prominently in the antislavery activity of the region" (17). Some Baptist and Methodist evangelical preachers expressed sympathy for slaves. The presence of blacks at revival meetings was sometimes pointed out and responded to with even more appeals to emotion.[114] As a consequence, some evangelicals started to criticize slavery. But there was no organized response. The Methodists, as we saw, gradually retreated from the abolitionist stance they had taken at the 1784 Baltimore meeting.

Interestingly, it is at the point of convergence between republicanism and, if not necessarily Calvinism, at least austere Protestantism, that most of the religious antislavery voices were heard. A powerful argument was the idea that America had lost its virtue—a major republican concept—to greed and luxury, and that this state of depravity undermined both its republican aspirations and its sacred covenant with God, as it had been envisioned by the Puritan founders. As Winthrop D. Jordan puts it, "The more explicit denunciations came from men whose intellectual backgrounds were most explicitly Calvinist" (300). In July 1774, for example, Congregationalist Benjamin Colman wrote that the British "were only the rod which God makes use of to correct us" (325), and the main evil that he points to is slavery. God may have allowed slavery in Leviticus, but that was "but a temporary precept" (326), and it is not allowed in the New Testament. Indeed, many things that were allowed "under the Jewish dispensation" are now illegal. Colman then quotes from Isaiah 58, in which the people had fasted and prayed, and yet received no answer from God, and God answers: "Is not this the fast that I have chosen to loose the bands of wickedness, to undo the heavy burdens, and to let the oppressed go free." To Colman, God will remain "offended" (327) until slavery stops vitiating the commonwealth. A number of other preachers yoked together the ideas of a virtuous republic and a city of God, bound for millennial felicity only if slavery is abolished.[115]

Two of the most outspoken voices for abolition in the revolutionary period, Samuel Hopkins and Lemuel Haynes, were Calvinist, and it is probable that Marrant was acquainted with their writings. In many ways, each of them was pushing forth the thought of the great Calvinist theologian Jonathan Edwards.[116] Edwards's views on slavery are not well documented. In the draft of a letter discovered only a few years ago, he rejects the slave trade, in that it does not reflect the new dispensation of the Gospel and negates his millennialist view that the divine kingdom will be universal, but he does not condemn slavery.[117] But it is his major text on ethics, *The Nature of True Virtue,* that was influential. In it, Edwards defines true virtue as "benevolence to Being in general," or "that consent, propensity and union of heart to Being in general, that is immediately exercised in a general good will" (540). He contrasts true virtue with "union of heart to some particular being" or "a private circle or system of beings" (541). Indeed, "the highest good of Being in general" (545) is always the primary goal. He then identifies Being as God, who is thus to be considered the head of the universal moral system, and whose glory is the ultimate end of moral agents. While Hopkins and Haynes would draw different implications from this theory, it was a central inspiration.

The New Divinity movement, which Hopkins was a part of, was a radical extension of Edwards's Calvinism, and it is this radicalization that led him to strict abolitionism. It reemphasized God's absolute sovereignty and asked that adherents commit to "disinterested benevolence," a state of complete self-denial and submission to God "for the glory of God and the good of mankind" (Conforti, 61). In "Inquiry into the Nature of True Holiness," Hopkins pushed the notion of true virtue into the realm of social consciousness and activism. By doing this, he showed that a strict Calvinist theology could have socially progressive implications. It was only one step from this position to his abolitionist stance. In 1776, he published "A Dialogue Concerning the Slavery of the Africans," addressed to the Continental Congress. In it, slavery is presented as a great "public sin" and the reason for the current "calamities" (399) released by God onto the colonies. While he offers specific refutations to various arguments against abolition, including a forceful defense of the blacks' own desire for liberty, it is the Americans' "awful guilt" (424) that he returns to at the end of the essay as the one overwhelming reason to get rid of slavery. And to those who aver that freed slaves will not easily become independent citizens, he responds that, rather than justifying slavery, this argument calls for generalized benevolence and the building of a free, equitable commonwealth.

The republican implications of such a stance were explored more fully by Haynes, an important eighteenth-century black thinker.[118] Haynes was pastor of a Congregational church in Vermont, and his Calvinism inspired his vision of a harmonious, interracial, benevolent society that was to come under the covenant with God. To him, "Liberty must be accompanied by virtue and social harmony" (Saillant, *Black Puritan*, 4), a combination that shows his strong republican grounding. He anchored this vision in a view of the New Testament as the new dispensation that had replaced that of the Old Testament and that was to be spread universally, including to Africa. These "systematic and historicist qualities" (40) of his thought show the extent to which Calvinism could inspire progressive views. Haynes had studied with members of the New Divinity, and he was acquainted with Hopkins's writings. But he pushed New Divinity further, exploiting its "centripetal" instead of its "centrifugal" (92) tendencies, when he envisaged a future interracial republic—unlike the white members of the New Divinity, most of whom embraced the idea of colonization, and even acted on it. In this republic, liberty does not mean "licentiousness"; it means a devotion to the *"common good"* (Haynes, 79); it is only valid as long as "we make no encroachments on the equal rights of our neighbor"; indeed, "the laws of the commonwealth" need to "respect the community." To him, that is "genuine republicanism" (80). It is unclear whether Marrant was familiar with Haynes, but as we will see, the sermon he gave more than a year after his arrival in Boston shows that he had absorbed the New Divinity's peculiar combination of Calvinism and benevolence and that he put it in the service of an interracial vision.

•

One connection that Marrant makes absolutely clear in his *Journal* is the one he had with Samuel Stillman, pastor of the First Baptist Church. By some amazing coincidence, Stillman, who had grown up in Charleston, had undergone conversion through the preaching of the same Oliver Hart who had converted Marrant. Although Stillman had left the southern city before Marrant moved there, this common past experience must have created a bond. Stillman had by now lived in Boston for more than twenty years, and during this time, he had made many contributions not only to the Baptist denomination but to the Revolution. He had helped found the College of Rhode Island—a Baptist institution, and the future Brown University—and was known as a riveting preacher, given to "sudden bursts of impassioned eloquence" (Sprague, 75). He wrote sermons on political questions and was a member of the Ratification Convention that was in session on the day that Marrant arrived.[119] Twenty years Marrant's senior, he clearly made a deep impression on his younger colleague.

Through Stillman, Marrant made a connection with Boston's revolutionary intelligentsia. Stillman in particular saw the Revolution as the expression of a desire not only for liberty but for the establishment of a virtuous republic. Liberty especially entailed religious freedom, a major goal for Baptists eager to break the hold of the Congregational Church in New England. In a 1766 sermon to celebrate the repeal of the Stamp Act, he called it "a royal confirmation of your civil and religious liberties," reminding his listeners that "these stand in immediate connection with each other" (*Good News,* 31). This was the opening salvo in a fight he and other Baptists would lead for disestablishment. When it came to political ideology, according to the *Dictionary of American Biography,* Stillman was "a Federalist of the Washington school" (871). His speech at

Boston's Ratification Convention is said to have swayed many who were wavering.[120] He put his federalism in the service of people's needs. On 4 July 1789, he gave a speech at Faneuil Hall, "at the request of the inhabitants" of Boston, in celebration of independence. Interestingly, after a congratulatory opening, he focuses attention on the common people who have suffered because of the war: soldiers who gave their lives; men who had to "leave their respective occupations" and consequently lost their "means of subsistence" (*Oration*, 12); people who rushed into bad investments after the war ended. He does celebrate the new freedom of trade and manufactures, but with a focus on the benefits for "mechanics," "tradesmen," and "the farmer" (17). He ends with a lofty tribute to George Washington and a celebration of the potential of the new nation, but he reminds his audience that "much depends on the conduct of the great body of the people"; indeed, "knowledge and virtue are the basis and life of a Republic" (25). Ten years earlier, he had said that "we should leave nothing to human virtue, that can be provided for by law or the constitution" ("Duty," 269); in the later speech, he sounds like a civic humanist.

Stillman also seems to have been fascinated with egalitarian and fraternal cultures. He used to start his services by urging his listeners to "remember, with special earnestness and tenderness, the sea-faring portion of the community." As a consequence, "a considerable part of the gallery of his meeting-house was occasionally occupied by this class." An admirer writing thirty years after his death recounts the following anecdote: on a walk with a friend, Stillman passed a black man, who took off his hat and bowed to him; Stillman did the same in return; when asked by his friend why, he answered that "the man made his obeisance to me, and I should be loth to have it said that I had less manners than a negro" (Sprague, 75). While it was hardly a radical gesture, the writer is at pains to present a man who dislikes hierarchy. Stillman was interested in the concept of benevolence, and though he did not push it to the egalitarian conclusions drawn by Hopkins and Haynes, he made it a cornerstone of his sermons and his social commitment. In 1785, he preached a sermon on charity to the Freemasons of Charleston. He starts an 1801 lecture to the members of the Boston female asylum by emphasizing the importance of "benevolent affections," which "unite the great family of man, by interesting them in the joys and sorrows of each other" (*Discourse Delivered,* 3). He then lists institutions that he thinks contribute to this goal: the Boston Marine Society, the Episcopal and Congregational charitable societies, the Masonic societies, the Boston

Humane Society—dedicated to reviving people from suffocation and drowning—the Massachusetts Charitable Fire Society, the Boston Dispensary, the Boston Almshouse. To Stillman, charity was more than a simple gesture; it was a complex network constantly redirecting resources and care.

The fact that Stillman had "strong Calvinistic doctrinal views" (N. Wood, 250) seems to have strengthened this commitment to benevolence. He starts his sermon to Charleston's Freemasons by emphasizing the importance of love to God, who is presented as "the first great cause," the "Alpha and Omega": "By him the worlds are governed, and all events are directed to an end." We are accountable to him, and "therefore we should fear to sin" (*Charity Considered,* 7). Having established God as the supreme law of the cosmos, Stillman then draws connections between love for God, love for others, and personal happiness. "Supreme love to God" (11) is "inseparably connected with love to man" (12), and in a sort of virtuous cycle, man mirrors the benevolence of the universe in his own personal behavior, thus finding "*peace of mind*" and "*tranquility of heart*" (13). There are stoic echoes in this vision, all the more that Stillman urges a charity that "lifts us above national and religious distinctions" and "leads us to consider all men as brethren" (14), imparting a universalist dimension to his message. His universalism is buttressed by his dispensationalism. In another sermon, he emphasizes that God's "glorious plan" is gradually revealed to man, through each "dispensation," for Adam, for the Jewish nation, and at the time of Christ. Here he puts this "universality" (*Discourse Preached,* 10) in the service of the newly created Baptist Missionary society, but it is clear that this historicism underlies his overall social vision.

Despite his universalist, benevolent message, Stillman was not racially progressive. He must have read Hopkins's "Dialogue"; as we saw, he had extended contacts with the black community; his church had "many Black members" (McLoughlin, 765). He did briefly speak out against slavery. In a 1779 speech to the Massachusetts legislature, he declared that "we ought to banish from among us that cruel practice, which has long prevailed, of reducing to a state of slavery for life the freeborn Africans." He states that Africans enjoy "the natural rights of men," but when he points out that "the Deity . . . hath assigned to them a part of the globe for their residence" ("Duty," 285), he seems to subscribe to justifications used at the time for separation of the races. He did not support racial integration. According to a Baptist minister, "When Thomas Paul came to Boston the Dr. [Stillman] told him it was

Boston, and that they did not mix colours; or words of that import. He was not even willing he should preach in the vestry." After Paul created a black church, Stillman tried to dissuade him from admitting white members, "as they may ultimately become the majority & defeat ye intention of their being an *African* church" (McLoughlin, 765). And when he delivered the installation sermon, whites sat in the pews, and blacks in the gallery. In some ways, as we saw, Stillman was helping the black community in its desire to create its own institutions. While he often sounded like a republican, nothing he wrote indicates a universal, interracial vision.

•

It is clear that, in Boston, Marrant maintained his commitment to Calvinism. In the *Journal,* he recounts an incident that happened in late February 1789, when he was pursued by a gang of young men armed with swords and clubs but managed to reach his lodging safely. When interrogated by the authorities the next day, the men said they acted this way "because in the evening when we left our work, we used to go and see our girls, and when we came to their houses, we always found they were gone to meeting" (150). It is not the first time that Marrant emphasizes his sufferings for the sake of fighting sin; in this case, the suspensefully told, action-packed incident implies that he risked his life—the boys confessed they wanted to kill him—in order to keep young women on the straight and narrow path. The beginning of his sermon to the African lodge, which he preached on 24 June 1789, confirms this strict morality, as he condemns "the corruption that is in the world through lust." Indeed, he prefaces his remarks by emphasizing "an entire submission and conformity to the will of God" (78), thereby anchoring the whole sermon in a solid Calvinist vision.

But the main theme of the sermon, brotherly love, and the way he develops it show that he has developed the progressive dimensions of Calvinism, either on his own or through contact with elements of New England's changing culture, as we have seen it in the representatives of the New Divinity, or in Samuel Stillman. Marrant now places the concept of benevolence at the heart of his theological and social vision. He starts by emphasizing "zeal and integrity and benevolence, which is the most important duty, and comprehends all the rest." The themes of "humility, peace and unity," which recall those of order, beauty, and harmony highlighted in the *Journal,* are here put in the service of benevolence, and together, they serve "the glory of God and the good of our own souls and bodies, and the good of all mankind" (78). Marrant's vision entails an overwhelming love for the whole of being, a universal affection that embraces both God and the common good. This all-encompassing, all-embracing feeling is not dissimilar from Jonathan Edwards's definition of virtue and places Marrant squarely in a stoic, Calvinist tradition.

So it should probably not be surprising that Marrant quotes Seneca, a famous Roman stoic. In his description of creation, Marrant first follows the account given in Genesis, showing how "the Grand Architect of the Universe" created heaven, the earth, light, and all the creatures of nature. All these things, he adds, were "in their order prepared" for the coming of man. He may be referring to the order in which they were created, but the formulation also implies that they belong to a grand cosmic order, into which man arrives and needs to fit. At this point, he quotes Seneca, who says that "man is not a work huddled over in haste." Indeed, man "hath not only a body" (79), says Marrant, but he also has a soul, which is "a rational principle to act according to the designs of his creation." Man needs to live in harmony with God and with all the creatures around him because he is "a little world, a world within himself, and containing whatever is found in the Creator" (80). All the elements, and "the virtue" of all these elements, converge and converse in him. By presenting man's soul as rational, and man himself as a microcosm of the universe, Marrant lends a stoic dimension to his story of creation and announces an ethical stance anchored in universality.

In keeping with this ethical stance, one of the most interesting concepts that emerges from the sermon is that of self-love. We already saw that, in his funeral sermon, Marrant projected perfection as a state where one is "divested of self" (173). The suppression of the self makes sense within a Calvinist context, but in his sermon to the Freemasons, Marrant needed to integrate it within a system anchored in universal benevolence. Early in the sermon, he emphasizes "humility" (78), "an humble heart" (79). After his excursus into the history of Freemasonry, he comes back to the notion of benevolence and then warns his listeners to beware of "selfishness": "Such a self-love is the parent of disorder and the source of all those evils that divide the world and destroy the peace of mankind." He pits this self-love against "universal love and friendship" or "benevolent affections and social feelings" (90). The suppression of the self serves not only the glory of God and the order of the universe but the good of mankind. In this system, members are "a living sacrifice," "links of a chain" (79). Clearly, Marrant's ethics now entail a condemnation of self-love for the sake of universal harmony.

The notion of self-love was an important one in Calvinist ethics. Jonathan Edwards devotes a whole chapter to it in *The Nature of True Virtue*. Defining self-love as "a man's love of his own happiness," he gives the phrase two possible meanings: one is a universal happiness or pleasure; the other is "the pleasure a man takes in his own proper, private, and separate good" (575). The latter pleasure can result from an encounter with external beauty or from being the object of love or honor from others. Edwards then proceeds to counter the argument made by some that this kind of self-love emanates from a moral sense. He argues that, instead, it emanates from a sense of "*desert*" (581) or justice, in that others' love appears to deserve our love. He does acknowledge that this could be seen as "a kind of moral sense," but it is "a *secondary* kind, and is entirely different from a sense or relish of the original essential beauty of true virtue." As such, it cannot be equivalent to the true virtue that is inherent in "*public benevolence*" (582). With this discussion, Edwards was laying a strong foundation for a Calvinist ethics that associated true morality with an embrace of the beautiful and the public good.

New Divinity adherents found his theory too abstract, too focused on the personal and the beautiful.[121] To Hopkins, it only encouraged passive contemplation and social quietism. He found Edwards's notion of self-love particularly disappointing because, even if it did not promote the highest kind of virtue, it could still participate in a moral life. In other words, Edwards "created a continuum of virtue with gradations of morality" (Conforti, 115). To Hopkins, "distinguishing self-love from selfishness" meant "developing a moral philosophy that was facilitating the transition from communal to individualistic social ethics," in that it accepted the idea of a moral order resulting from an individual pursuit of happiness. By contrast, Hopkins issued a "radical call for self-denial" (116) that did not fit at all within this theory. To him, self-love was by definition the opposite of disinterested benevolence and could not enter into any moral calculation. There was no middle ground. This view of self-love was at the heart of his ethical system and of his social vision. The new republic he envisioned was not based on self-interest; it harked back to classic republicanism and civic virtue.

In many ways, Marrant's rejection of self-love in the sermon is similarly tied to a vision of universal, republican brotherhood. In its conclusion, he reminds his audience of their obligations to "the whole family of mankind in the world" (88). This is the conclusion to a sermon whose core is devoted to the ancient history of Freemasonry. There has been speculation on the authorship of the sermon, and on the extent of

Prince Hall's contribution to it. My sense is that the sermon was written by Marrant. The way he signals to his listeners that he has reached the end of his introductory remarks, for example, recalls the tactic he used in his funeral sermon. The information on Freemasonry, however, was probably gleaned from papers that Hall put at his disposal. The sermon traces the lineage of Masonry from Adam to Cain, Cain's son's, Noah, Noah's sons, Moses, Solomon, all the while emphasizing skill in geometry and architecture, in a way that seems very much inspired by *Anderson's Constitutions of 1723*. In his own charges, Hall gives his listeners recommendations that mirror the charges in Anderson's book. His statement that a Mason "must be good subject of the laws of the land in which we dwell, giving honour to our lawful Governors and Magistrates" (192), for example, echoes Anderson's second charge, on "the Civil Magistrate," that "a Mason is a peaceable subject to the Civil Powers, wherever he resides or works" (80). When he received the charter from England, Hall also received a book, for which he thanked his correspondent in London, saying he found it "very instructive" (Upton, 6); possibly this book was *Anderson's Constitutions*. Marrant must have found it equally instructive, all the more that it confirmed the message of universal brotherhood.

Marrant's ethical move around the notion of self-love in his sermon reflects the radicalization of virtue developed by the New Divinity in the last decades of the eighteenth century, but at the same time, he leaves some room for self-respect. Early in the sermon, as he is introducing the notion of humility, he stresses the importance "that we may know ourselves," as "we must learn to guide ourselves before we can guide others." It turns out that he is referring to Romans 12.6, which he quotes as follows: "Be not wise in your own conceits" (78). This verse has been translated in different ways; in some translations, it just urges the readers not to be conceited; in others, it urges them not to think they are wiser than they are. But the fact that Marrant introduces it as a verse about self-knowledge implies that he is not urging complete self-negation or self-denial. Toward the end of the sermon, he makes allusions to the fact that his audience is black and marginalized. He urges them not to resent "our enemies" but to make bridges, "to compose their differences and heal up their breaches" (91). He speaks of the advantages of belonging to a society of brothers who can recognize and help each other at any time. When people go to sea, for example, they "know how readily people of this institution can open a passage to the heart of a brother"—a possible reference to how the kidnapped men who had been the subject of a petition managed to make contact with a merchant thanks to their recognition of each other as masons.[122] In the end, benevolence will unite men, and "render them happy in themselves and useful to one another" (90). In so many touches, Marrant conveys the understanding that targeted benevolence can promote the interests of a marginalized group and that disinterested virtue should not undermine a search for survival and self-respect. In these moments, he puts his Calvinist system clearly in the service of racial consciousness.

But overall, the references to Africa and Africans he inserts into his history of Freemasonry expand the themes of brotherhood and universality. After dwelling on the creation of man and emphasizing his rational ability to correspond with the universe, Marrant suddenly launches into a criticism of racism. If men are supposed to live in harmony with God, with each other, and with the whole creation, "then what can these God-provoking wretches think, who despise their fellow men, as tho' they were not of the same species with themselves, and would if in their power deprive them of the blessings and comforts of this life" (80). By inserting his criticism at this point in the sermon, Marrant is not just delivering a social critique; he implies that racism is an existential threat, in that it disturbs the cosmic order and God's design. Interestingly, when he looks back on history at the end of the sermon and wants to highlight the role of "some of the Africans," he praises them as "good, wise, and learned men, and as eloquent as any other nation whatever" (89). In the end, wisdom and rational powers also play a role in Marrant's vision, in this incredible moment that sees a black Calvinist embracing the virtues of cosmopolitanism.

•

Little is known of Marrant's last year in London. He lived on Aldersgate Street and occasionally preached at the Independent Chapel in the borough of Islington. He found time to publish his *Journal,* which obtained forty-one subscribers. It is unlikely he had any contact with the Countess of Huntingdon. He died on 15 April 1791, at the age of thirty-five, and was buried in the graveyard adjoining the chapel.[123] London's reading public had witnessed a man's amazing ideological transformation: in 1785, they had read a narrative that described a dramatic conversion and a search for a self's place in the world; five years later, they read a journal by the same man but one who was now searching for the sources of benevolence and of a devotion to the common good. His experiences in Nova Scotia and in Boston had deepened his Calvinist sense of a virtuous commonwealth, and as a cosmopolitan, he could not but conceive of it as universal, crosscultural, interracial. How could it be otherwise?

Back in Boston, Prince Hall would give two more charges to the black Freemasons before the end of the century, one in 1792 and one in 1797, and the tone strikes me as increasingly bitter. The first one, while still digging into the history of Freemasonry, bemoans the lack of educational opportunities for the black community, pointing out that a school for blacks has recently been set up in Philadelphia. Speaking of the Knights of Malta, Hall asks whether, when an African asked to be admitted, "if they were all whites, they would refuse to accept them as their fellow Christians and brother Masons" or whether "that would make their lodge or army too common or too cheap." And he adds: "Sure this was not our conduct in the late war; for then they marched shoulder to shoulder, brother soldier and brother soldier" (197). One feels an impatience, a disappointment, with the way the republican promises of the Revolution have not been fulfilled. Five years later, Hall starts with the duty of sympathy but immediately attacks the slave trade. The historical excursus is devoted to blacks exclusively, whether it be Moses's father-in-law, Jethro, an Ethiopian, the Ethiopian eunuch, or the queen of Sheba. He discusses the "daily insults you meet with in the streets of Boston," and a recent incident when "helpless old women have their clothes torn off their backs" (203). He sounds downcast, devoid of idealism.

Black Freemasons in the eighteenth century, including Marrant, made a contribution to political thought. Freemasonry was not revolutionary. Indeed, black Freemasonry has been criticized for its focus on what is seen as elitism, social uplift, and a striving toward respectability.[124] But as Stephen Kantrowitz puts it, they fostered "both expansive ideas and extensive networks of leadership" (1003); these ideas were anchored in "a universalist cosmopolitanism that challenged white supremacist rejection" (1004). This cosmopolitanism showed "how tenuous American identity was in the late eighteenth century for a significant cadre of black intelligentsia and activists" (Hinks, 116) and encouraged a fraternal, universalist vision. Possibly Hall saw that, although slavery had disappeared from Massachusetts and was on its way out in New England, the republican promise of equality was actually receding. He saw that race, far from slowly disappearing from social consciousness, was actually becoming entrenched. But he offered an alternative vision, and it is not hard to surmise that, when Marrant left, he was sad to see him go.[125]

NOTES

Introduction

1. For an analysis of the complex moral choices inherent in this kind of cosmopolitanism, see Appiah, *Cosmopolitanism*.
2. For the Atlantic creoles, see Berlin, *Many Thousands Gone*.
3. For an analysis of the ethics of cosmopolitanism in the eighteenth century, see Schlereth, *The Cosmopolitan Ideal*. For a good description of stoic cosmopolitanism, see Nussbaum, "Patriotism and Cosmopolitanism."
4. For the idea of cosmopolitans using the power of the state to bring about change, see Saillant, "Antiguan Methodism."
5. In this sense, they were certainly part of what, in his groundbreaking book, Paul Gilroy referred to as a "counterculture of modernity" (5).
6. Skinner, *Foundations*, 1:152–80.
7. Skinner, *Foundations*, 1:69–112.
8. Skinner argues that Calvinist radicalism was not unique, and not even specifically Calvinist. See *Foundations*, 2:321–23.
9. See *Equiano, the African*, 170.
10. For a detailed analysis of Gronniosaw's Calvinist connections, see Hanley, "Calvinism."
11. For the influence of Jonathan Edwards and his notion of virtue on early black writers, see Saillant, "African American Engagements." For the connections between his millennialism and his stance on slavery, see Minkema, "Jonathan Edwards on Slavery."
12. For an enlightening description of Hopkins's theology, see Conforti, *Samuel Hopkins*.
13. For an analysis of the complexities of race in the eighteenth century, see Barker *The African Link*, and Wheeler, *Complexion of Race*.

1. Jacobus Capitein and the Radical Possibilities of Calvinism

1. The major book-length studies on Capitein are Eekhof, *De negerpredikant;* Kpobi, *Mission in Chains;* Kwesi Kwaa Prah, *Jacobus Eliza Johannes Capitein;* Van der Zee, *'s Heeren slaaf*.
2. I will assume that the first part of the published text was also part of the original lecture, even though it is called "Præfatio ad lectorem," or "preface to the reader" (*Agony*, 81).
3. See introduction.
4. Eekhof, *De negerpredikant*, 6–7.

5. The specific reference to the Latin school is in Capitein, *Uitgewrogte predikatien*, 106.
6. Grant Parker translates from the original Latin text.
7. For the Dutch Enlightenment, see Zwager, *Nederland en de Verlichting*.
8. Zwager, *Nederland en de Verlichting*, 11–12.
9. Mijnhardt, "The Dutch Enlightenment," 202.
10. Eekhof, *De negerpredikant*, 12.
11. Kpobi, *Mission in Chains*, 56; Eekhof, *De negerpredikant*, 9.
12. Kpobi, *Mission in Chains*, 59.
13. Van Bunge et al., *Dictionary*, 611.
14. Bartels, "Jacobus," 4–5.
15. Bartels, "Jacobus," 5. Bartels is translating from the original Latin.
16. "un rationalisme qui fuit les extrêmes" (Buijnsters, 206). All translations from Dutch and French are mine, unless otherwise noted.
17. Buijnsters, "Les Lumières hollandaises," 208–15. Buijnsters refers to critic Ferdinand Sassen, who coined the phrase "Lumières réformatrices."
18. Blom and Lamberts, *History of the Low Countries*, 139.
19. One *stadhouder* could represent several provinces, and most of the time, there were two *stadhouders*.
20. Skinner, *Foundations*, 1:54.
21. Brooke, *Philosophic Pride*, xii.
22. Cicero, *On Duties*, 7.
23. Cicero, *On Duties*, 27, 33, 35, 40.
24. Cicero, *On Duties*, 42–44.
25. Garnsey, *Ideas of Slavery*, 18.
26. See Skinner, *Foundations*, 2:338.
27. Kossmann, *Political Thought in the Dutch Republic*, 60–74.
28. For the idea of a Dutch radical Enlightenment, see Mijnhardt, "The Construction of Silence," and Israel, *Radical Enlightenment*.
29. "de roetzwarte jongen moet in Den Haag een heel aparte verschijning zijn geweest" (32).
30. Eekhof, *De negerpredikant*, 9–10.
31. Mijnhardt, "The Dutch Enlightenment," 206–9.
32. Van der Zee, *'s Heeren slaaf*, 19; Eekhof, *De negerpredikant*, 7.
33. Unger, "Bijdragen," 136. The approximately twenty Africans who were famously brought into Jamestown, Virginia, in 1619 by a Dutch man-of-war had most probably been captured from a Portuguese slave ship. See Sluiter, "New Light," and Thornton, "The African Experience."
34. See Unger, "Bijdragen," 146.
35. Postma, *The Dutch*, 302.
36. Hondius, *Blackness in Western Europe*, 2.
37. See also Van den Boogaart, *Civil and Corrupt Asia*, for an overall sense of the Dutch concept of civility as it applied to other societies as well.
38. See Schmidt, *Innocence Abroad*; de Stoppelaar, *Balthasar de Moucheron*; de Jonge, *De oorsprong*.
39. For an analysis of early Dutch travel accounts about Africa, see Levecq, "Early Dutch."

40. Paasman, "Mens of dier?," 92.
41. Paasman, "Mens of dier?," 95, 98–99.
42. Meijer, *Race and Aesthetics,* 7.
43. See Hondius, "Access," for some of the information included in this paragraph.
44. "heure natuerlicke liberteyt" (Emmer, 34).
45. One can assume that some of them were "accepted" and Christianized but then succumbed very quickly, since between 4 January and 3 March 1597, no fewer than nine "moors" were buried in the Middelburg cemetery. See de Stoppelaar, "Aantekeningen," in *Balthasar de Moucheron,* 61–62.
46. Buve, "Surinaamse slaven," 15.
47. Huussen, "The Dutch Constitution," 105–6.
48. See Hondius, "Access," 382.
49. "was de Zaal . . . nog bovendien met een groot aantal Zwarten en Mooren voorzien, zoo dat het scheen dat alle de Zwarte dienstboden uit geheel Amsterdam aldaar voor dien avond hun beurs hielden" (Fokke Simonsz, 93–94).
50. "de scène van den Zwart" (Fokke Simonsz, 94). The opera, by Jean-François Le Sueur, alters the novel significantly. In act 1, scene 7, Domingo sings about how his emotions are tied to those of his mistress, but the adagio ends on a happy note, when Paul and Virginia promise to help him conquer Babet, who is twenty years younger.
51. "Eene zeer aangename verscheidenheid werd door dit toeval veroorzaakt, wijl men dan eens tegen een aardig meisjen en onmiddelijk daarop tegen een Zwart aangedrongen werd" (Fokke Simonsz, 94).
52. Hondius, "Black Africans," 96–99.
53. Haarnack and Hondius, "'Swart,'" 90.
54. Haarnack and Hondius, "'Swart,'" 94, report on research done by Dirk Tang, indicating that between 1729 and 1775, 456 blacks traveled from Surinam to the Netherlands. Buve speculates that few of the slaves who came to Amsterdam with their masters left them. But we also know that, between 1760 and 1826, about four thousand slaves were manumitted in Surinam and that some of them came to the Netherlands.
55. Oostindie and Maduro, *Antillianen en Surinamers,* 16.
56. Blakely, *Blacks in the Dutch World,* 228.
57. Haarnack and Hondius, "'Swart,'" 103.
58. See Northolt, "Nageslacht."
59. "een zeer braaf man, zijnde een neger uit Congo"; "thans is hij blind, in de 60 jaren oud, en van zijn 6 jaar af in dit land geweest; ook is hij met rhumatieke pijnen gekweld" (Spaans Azn. and Veldhuijzen, 46).
60. Haarnack and Hondius, "'Swart,'" 95–98.
61. Vrij, "Jan Elias van Onna," 139–40.
62. Haarnack and Hondius, "'Swart,'" 101–3.
63. "De vader had het kind van de plantage gekocht, het vrijdom geschonken en het later voor de studie naar Holland gezonden, waar de jongen goed slaagde" (17).
64. "Hij was mij zeer toegenegen, hetgeen ik toeschreef aan het feit dat hij kleurling-kinderen—twee jongens—had, van wien hij zeer veel hield. Hij heeft

ze een goede opvoeding laten geven en zij hebben in de Oost zoowel als in Holland later aanzienlijke plaatsen ingenomen" (35).

65. Vrij, "Jan Elias van Onna," 142.
66. Haarnack and Hondius, "'Swart,'" 103.
67. On Bartelink, see Van Kempen, *Een geschiedenis van de Surinaamse literatuur,* 461-62.
68. Baron's visit to Holland cannot be verified. See Oostindie and Maduro, *Antillianen en Surinamers,* 17-19.
69. "Op de verschillende plantages, waar ik met slaven werkte, heb ik dat verlangen naar vrijheid bij de menschen gezien en met hen naar de verlossing gesmacht" (59).
70. "het volk zou zeker tegen de Regeering in verzet zijn gekomen" (59).
71. "Houd je mij voor den gek?" (75).
72. See Debrunner, *Presence and Prestige,* 35.
73. For the role of Descartes in those theological debates, see Verbeek, *Descartes and the Dutch.*
74. Van der Wall, "The Religious Context"; Van Bunge et al., *Dictionary,* 216-19, 1030-39; Kpobi, *Mission in Chains,* 59.
75. Van Bunge et al., *Dictionary,* 447-49; Kpobi, *Mission in Chains,* 64.
76. "Die dynamische, historiserende benadering moet een impliciete veroordeling van de slavenhandel betekenen voor de nieuwtestamentische bedeling. Maar Coccejus maakt dit met geen woord expliciet" (Schutte, "Bij het schemerlicht," 210).
77. See Paasman, *Reinhart,* 99, quoting *Octroy of privilegie.*
78. Godfried Udemans (1581-1649), *'t Geestelyck roer van 't coopmans schip* (1638). See Paasman, *Reinhart,* 100.
79. That is the case for the argument made by one of the characters in *Beschrijvinge van Guiana* (1676), a dialogue about slavery. See Paasman, *Reinhart,* 102.
80. For Johannes Crucius (1598-1666), see Kpobi, *Mission in Chains,* 102.
81. Huussen, "The Dutch Constitution," 102.
82. "capitulerend voor de aantrekkingskracht van de werkelijkheid en geleid door haar interne theologische logica" (Schutte, "Bij het schemerlich," 194).
83. Schutte, "Bij het schemerlicht," 196-99.
84. Schutte, "Bij het schemerlicht," 203-6.
85. Paasman, *Reinhart,* 99.
86. "sulk een slavigh gemoet" (Schutte, *Indisch Sion,* 200).
87. Schutte, "Bij het schemerlicht," 202.
88. Skinner, *Foundations,* 2:236-38.
89. Kossmann, *Political Thought,* 160-61.
90. "met zeer veel lof en toejuichinge" (1).
91. Bartels, "Jacobus Eliza," 5.
92. The poem was published in *Uitgewrogte predikatien.*
93. "Lofdichten werden op hem gemaakt; beeltenissen in plaatdruk, den neger voorstellende, versierden nog tot in het jaar 1797 den wand der huizen, en in ditzelfde jaar kon men menschen aantreffen, die zich herinnerden hem in de kerken, die den grooten toeloop niet konden bevatten, te hebben hooren prediken" (Eekhof, *De negerpredikant,* 3).

94. Proes, "Asar," 49, mentions that his brother-in-law sent him the portrait from Elmina.
95. Kaplan, "Black Africans," 30; Devisse, *Image of the Black,* 160.
96. See Denucé, *Afrika,* 32, 48.
97. Schreuder, "'Blacks' in Court Culture," 24–25.
98. The question of the race of Moses's wife is still a thorny one. While in Numbers 12:1 she is referred to as an Ethiopian, in Exodus 2:21, Moses marries Zipporah, a Midianite, usually held to mean an Arab. The "black but beautiful" bride in the Song of Solomon has sometimes been interpreted as referring to Moses's wife. It is also possible to interpret the black wife as a common allegory for the church. See McGrath, "Jacob Jordaens."
99. As Kate Lowe puts it, "In every important respect except skin colour, this portrait represents the very essence of a Renaissance gentleman or prince" (46).
100. See Kolfin, "Black Models."
101. Blakely expresses his amazement that generations of art critics have failed to comment on the prominent presence of a black servant in Bartholomeus van der Helst's *Company of Captain Roelof Bicker,* which hangs in Amsterdam's Rijksmuseum directly opposite Rembrandt's *Night Watch,* and in which every other figure has been carefully identified (115).
102. Eekhof, *De negerpredikant,* 28.
103. "was zijn Wel-Eerwaarde, door den toeloop der Menschen, niet vrijwat ontstelt geworden" (1).
104. "Hij zegt ervan in zijn 'Aan den leser' vóór in *Het groote genadeligt Gods,* Leiden, 1744, dat gemelde predikatiën 'op den naam van den Heere Capitein, zonder zijn weten, ja! zonder raad of toestemming van enige zyner vrienden (zijn) uitgekomen, welke deswegens ook voor zijn Eerw. Werk niet behoren gehouden te worden, als merkelijk verschillende van het afschrift der door hem gedane leerredenen, hetwelk tot overtuiging van een ieder nog onder my berust'" (Eekhof, *De negerpredikant,* 29).
105. "Die van hun Evenmensch zijn kopers en verkopers, O! schand'lyke Euveldaen!" (Eekhof, *De negerpredikant,* 23).
106. "sigh wederom na de Kust van Gune sal konnen begeeven, omme aldaar sijn fortuyn verders te soeken" (Eekhof, *De negerpredikant,* 15).
107. Kpobi, who is translating from the Dutch translation by Capitein's fellow student Hieronymus de Wilhelm, says that Capitein refers to "the Board of Governors of Schools in The Hague (de Agtbare Heeren Bezorgers der Haagsche schoolen) and the Council of the Court of Holland (Hof van Holland)." Kpobi's translation might make more sense.
108. See Leiden Regionaal Archief, Archiefblok 19, July 1737: "Op de voorstelling van de heer Cunaus [Petrus Cunaus] so is Jacobus Elisa Johannes Capiteijn, zijnde een [africaanse—word inserted] Moor, geadmitteerd tot een Extraordinaris Beursael alleen op een subsidie van 150 Gl. Jaars." The 1742 lecture was thus part of his duties as a recipient of the Hallet funding. There is uncertainty as to whether it was a doctoral dissertation. There is no record of Capitein ever having received a doctoral degree. But the dissertation was published with eleven *stellingen,* or thesis statements, a practice that is typical for doctoral dissertations.

109. See Leiden Regionaal Archief, Archiefblok 19: "Den Beursaal Jac. Elisa Joh. Capiteijn, nu vier jaren het beneficie van deese Beursse hebbende genoten heeft aan de Heeren Maecenaten gecommuniceert, dat aan hem van weegens de Ed. Heeren Bewindhebberen van de West-Indische Compagnie was gedaan eene offerte, omme als Predikant te gaan na Delmina, dat hij aan deselve Heeren Bewindhebberen hadde versogt uijtstel tot over een jaar, wanneer hij sijne vijfjarige studien soude hebben voltrokken, en des te beeter in staat zijn, om in die qualiteijt den gewensten dienst te doen, dog dat hij geen verder uijtstel hadde kunne obtineren, als tot aanstaande Paasschen, al waaromme hij versogt, dat hem mogte werden gepermitteert die conditie te accepteren, en so wanneer sijn vertrek alsdan voortgang nog te hebben, dat hij echter mochte werden gegratificeert met het subsidie van het geheele jaar, omme daarmede sig te voorsien van boeken en andere noodwendigheden tot die reijs, en tot de waarneming van sijn dienst; 't geen aan hem, mits sig tot sijn vertrek toe na het Reglement in alles gedragende, gratieuselijk is geaccordeert."

110. Eekhof, *De negerpredikant,* 39. The castle usually housed from 100 to 150 people, including soldiers—"Alleen Elmina had een redelijke bezetting van 100 tot 150 man" (Den Heijer, *Goud,* 85).

111. Kpobi, *Mission in Chains,* 35–36.

112. Both the introduction and the letter are dated 21 October 1742.

113. For the whole account, see Feinberg, *Africans and Europeans,* 121–24.

114. Den Heijer, *Goud,* 75.

115. Van Dantzig, *Les Hollandais,* 25.

116. The letter is dated 15 February 1743. For various reasons, a majority of the people employed by the WIC on the African coast were foreigners.

117. See Frijhoff, *Fulfilling God's Mission,* 290.

118. Eekhof, *Jonas Michaëlius,* 46–47.

119. Zijp, "Predikanten," 31–32; Frijhoff, *Fulfilling God's Mission,* 312.

120. Debrunner, *History of Christianity,* 35.

121. "hoererij en dronkenschap" (Zijp, 32).

122. Zijp, "Predikanten," 33.

123. See Quaque, *Life and Letters.*

124. Debrunner, *History of Christianity,* 76–77.

125. See De Jong, *The Dutch Reformed Church,* 147–69, and Noorlander, "Serving God and Mammon."

126. According to Jeroen Dewulf, Dutch slave conversion policy in Brazil and New Netherland showed more flexibility in the first half of the seventeenth century, in the short-lived hope that Calvinism would overtake Catholicism in the New World.

127. Van der Zee, *'s Heeren slaaf,* 87.

128. Today's Elmina was rebuilt on the other side of the river after the town was bombarded by the British in 1873 (Feinberg, 77).

129. The WIC also reprimanded its employees for lending money to Africans, or even for drinking with them: "Every effort was made to maintain social distance between Europeans and Africans" (Postma, 70).

130. Kpobi, *Mission in Chains,* 237. Harvey M. Feinberg has identified 250 mulattoes of Dutch descent for the entire Gold Coast in the eighteenth century,

roughly two-thirds of whom were probably born in Elmina, but he assumes there were probably more (89).

131. Noorlander, "Serving God and Mammon," 210-11.
132. The letter is dated 21 May 1746.
133. Feinberg has uncovered evidence of at least seven marriages following Dutch law performed on the Gold Coast in the eighteenth century, five of which occurred during 1852 and 1853 (97). It is hard to know whether WIC demands had been relaxed or the wives were Christian.
134. Velse's work, *Naauwkeurige berigten nopens de grondvesting van het christendom onder de heidenen op de kust van Choromandel en Malabar door de Deensche missionarissen op Tranquebar,* was published in 1739.
135. After trying to intensify the slave trade for a few years after 1734, the WIC gave up. But they did continue indirectly by selling slaves to private ships (den Heijer, *Geschiedenis van de WIC,* 173-74).
136. The ceremony took place on 7 May 1742 in Amsterdam.
137. See "'Huwelijk naar 's lands wijze'" and "'Cherchez la femme.'"
138. Eekhof, *De negerpredikant,* 95.
139. In his 15 February 1743 letter, Capitein had asked at what point in the children's religious education he was allowed to administer baptism. The WIC had left it to his "good conscience" (Kpobi, 245). This nonchalance is striking considering that baptism in the Asian colonies was a hotly debated issue (see Schutte, *Indisch Sion*). There is a debate among historians about the extent to which the WIC was a fundamentally Calvinist institution. J. G. van Dillen argues that its Calvinist character has been overstated. See Noorlander for a study that argues the contrary.
140. He also occasionally performed as an interpreter for the WIC. According to Proes, he was mentioned as an interpreter for a contract signed by the townspeople, the WIC, and the Fante on 3 September 1744 (49).
141. "Ik heb het niet; verkoop mijn bed, 't is mij geen schande. Laat ongerust wezen diegenen, die geld hebben moeten, maar niet degenen, die geld schuldig zijn" (Proes, 50-51).
142. "Wat meent Van Buren wel, dat ik mijn tafel zal verminderen en mijn buik te kort doen om zijnent wil. Neen, dat niet—dat niet!" (Proes, 51).
143. "advies van het overlijden van de Predicant Capiteyn" (Van der Zee, 151).
144. "De schrijver zoude—zoo luidde het verhaal—kort na het verdedigen zijner dissertatie weder naar *Zuid-Afrika* zijn vertrokken, zich dààr terstond weder bij de Hottentotten begeven, en, met verzaking van hier te lande verkregen beschaving en zoo veel kennis als men in een Theologiae Doctor vooronderstelt, weder onder dat volk geleefd hebben, als of hij nooit onder beschaafde menschen had verkeerd, maar onafgebroken, van zijne geboorte af, onder de Hottentotten verbleven ware" (Curiosus).
145. "Niet zonder leedwezen, is aan ons voorgekomen dat onder de Bediendens van de Compagnie gevonden worden, die met verragtinge spreken van de betamelijke Pogingen, en Godvrugtige arbeijd van den Predikant, om de kinderen der naturellen te onderwijzen, ende te brengen tot de kennis Gods, daar meede spotten, en dus ook door hun ergerlijk gedrag aantonen, dat zij soo

veel hen doenlijk is, den arbeijd van den Predikant tragten vrugteloos te maken, waar omme het aan ons aangenaam zal zijn, dat U ons heijlsaam oogmerk, enden arbeijd van den Predikant, niet alleen zelve, soo veel in denzelven vermogen zal zijn tragten te bevorderen, maar ook de Conduiten van . . . bedienden tegen gaan, en dat U beletten dat de Predikant niet werde bespot en beschimpt, en alsoo moedeloos gemaakt . . . dat hij in zijn Persoon en Caracter gemaintineert, en na behoren gerespecteert werde" (Brieven naar Guinea van Thienen, WIC, 57, Royal Archives, The Hague).

2. JEAN-BAPTISTE BELLEY AND FRENCH REPUBLICANISM

1. "aristocratie cutanée" (Ray, 19:385); "la liberté triomphe, l'égalité est consacrée" (Mavidal and Laurent, 84:256).
2. For the declaration, see CARAN, C352/1837/3/pièce 16.
3. Dubois, *Avengers,* 24–28, 39.
4. King, *Blue Coat or Powdered Wig,* 21–28; McClellan, *Colonialism and Science,* 83–87.
5. Mercier, "La vie au Cap Français," 107.
6. The French usually made a distinction between *noirs* or *nègres,* full-blooded blacks, and *gens de couleur,* people of mixed race, though *gens de couleur* could also refer to a group comprising both mixed-race and full-blooded blacks. Following American usage, I will use the terms "blacks" or "people of color" when referring to both at the same time and will make it clear when I am referring to only one of the two categories. Many historians use the term "free colored," which I have decided to avoid, as it sounds a bit jarring to an American ear.
7. "Les nègres *Sénégalais* . . . sont grands & bienfaits, élancés, d'un noir d'ébène. . . . Dans son moral, le Sénégalais a aussi des marques d'une espèce de supériorité. . . . Il est cultivateur, intelligent, bon, fidèle, même en amour, reconnaissant, excellent domestique" (*Description,* 1:26–27).
8. "Il est partout, au marché, dans les magasins, dans les rues, sur les quais. Il conduit les cabrouets, il emplit les boucauts de sucre et de café et les roule. Il est sur les cales ou wharfs. Les canots sont conduits par lui. Il est cocher, excite l'ardeur des chevaux et dirige à fond de train les carosses en ville et à la campagne. Ses propos bruyants et souvent incompréhensibles aux profanes remplissent Le Cap" (108–9).
9. Moreau de Saint-Méry, *Description,* 1:364–65.
10. For the information that follows in this paragraph, see Fouchard, "Les joies de la lecture."
11. McClellan, *Colonialism and Science,* 97.
12. McClellan, *Colonialism and Science,* 86.
13. "ils s'entretenaient ensemble, riaient et badinaient" (Debien, *Les esclaves aux Antilles,* 268).
14. Debien, *Les esclaves aux Antilles,* 268–76.
15. Debien, *Les esclaves aux Antilles,* 279–87.
16. "par mon pénible travail et mes sueurs" (*Le bout d'oreille,* 5).

17. For the fact that the free black group consisted of one-third full-blooded black and two-thirds mixed-race people, see Moreau de Saint-Méry, *Description* ("Aussi parmi les Affranchis, trouve-t-on deux sixièmes de nègres," 1:89).
18. Debbasch, *Couleur et liberté*, 22–29.
19. "droits, privilèges et immunités" (Chesnais, 38); "un respect singulier" (37).
20. King, *Blue Coat or Powdered Wig*, 84.
21. Debbasch, *Couleur et liberté*, 75.
22. Elisabeth, "The French Antilles," 162, 157; King, *Blue Coat or Powdered Wig*, 168; Rogers, "On the Road," 71–72.
23. Debien, *Les colons de Saint-Domingue*, 170.
24. King, *Blue Coat or Powdered Wig*, xx.
25. Garrigus, "Blue and Brown," 259–61.
26. For Augustin, see King, *Blue Coat or Powdered Wig*, ix. For the list of documents, see Petit et al., "Actes signés."
27. "J'étais possesseur à Saint-Domingue de propriétés pensantes. Par le juste et bienfaisant décret du 16 pluviôse, je n'en possède plus" (CARAN, 353/1838/10/pièce 43).
28. Debbasch, *Couleur et liberté*, 82–91.
29. King, *Blue Coat or Powdered Wig*, 92, 101, 154.
30. King, *Blue Coat or Powdered Wig*, 52–77. Garrigus, "Saint-Domingue's Free People of Color," mentions a source that claims Saint-Domingue had 223 militia companies in 1786 (63).
31. Moreau de Saint-Méry, *Description*, 1:224–25; Marley, *Wars of the Americas*, 212–15.
32. Moreau de Saint-Méry, *Description*, 1:179.
33. Moreau de Saint-Méry, *Loix et constitutions*, 5:166–73.
34. "connaît beaucoup de monde, est sollicité, suscite la confiance"; "un homme d'influence, certainement respecté et écouté" (39). For the documents, see Petit et al., "Actes signés," and King, *Blue Coat and Powdered Wig*, 226–65.
35. According to Joseph Saint-Rémy, a Haitian historian, Belley volunteered in the campaign of Savannah: "comme volontaire, il avait fait la campagne de Savanah" (Price-Mars, 3). In *Haïti et l'indépendance américaine*, Gérard M. Laurent has a list of twenty-eight names, and it includes Belley. His reference is the first volume of Madiou, *Histoire d'Haïti*, but I was unable to find those names in Madiou. Belley is also listed in Nemours, *Haïti et la guerre de l'indépendance américaine*, 72. King, *Blue Coat and Powdered Wig*, though, does not list him as a Chasseur Volontaire (277).
36. The figure is from Lawrence, *Storm over Savannah*, 55, who cites it from French naval records. Charles C. Jones, *Siege of Savannah*, mentions 750 (20).
37. For a reference to the Chasseurs Volontaires during the Seven Years' War, see Moreau de Saint-Méry, *Loix et constitutions*, 4:459.
38. "une entière confiance en l'attachement et fidélité à son service de Ses Sujets libres, Gens de couleur, à Saint-Domingue" (Laurent, 37).
39. *Blue Coat or Powdered Wig*, 68. John D. Garrigus suggests that fatalism, patron-client patronage, and government bullying may have been other motivations ("Catalyst or Catastrophe," 117–18).

40. For the information on d'Estaing, see Calmon-Maison, *L'amiral d'Estaing*.
41. See Garrigus, "Saint-Domingue's Free People of Color," for a distinction between "liberal" patriotism and the Greek and Roman "civic" form of patriotism.
42. *Lettre des députés,* 4, 8.
43. "comme si un Empire, un Gouvernement, une Marine & des Colonies étoient *l'état de pure nature*" (iii).
44. "peu versés dans les grandes questions d'administration, de commerce, de politique & de balance des Empires" (6).
45. "les gens de couleur dont je ne puis pour mon compte faire trop d'éloges" (Weber and McIntosh, 180); "Aussi ne me plaigné-je nullement du décret du 28 mars. Sans doute il sera une des principales causes de notre salut" (181).
46. Lawrence, *Storm over Savannah,* 116.
47. Jones, *Siege of Savannah,* 22, 63; Calmon-Maison, *L'amiral d'Estaing,* 293; Laurent, *Haïti,* 49.
48. Jones, *Siege of Savannah,* gives a description of the layout of the troops. Rouvray's contingent was almost the easternmost troop, while the attack took place on the west side of the city (20–21).
49. The quote is King's, not Rouvray's.
50. Garrigus, "Catalyst or Catastrophe?," 119.
51. King, *Blue Coat or Powdered Wig,* 66–67.
52. See *The Abbé Grégoire,* chapter 4.
53. Debien, *Les colons de Saint-Domingue,* 71–72.
54. For the reduction to six, see Mavidal and Laurent, *Archives parlementaires,* 8:205.
55. Debien, *Les colons de Saint-Domingue,* 58–96, 140–52.
56. Debien, *Les colons de Saint-Domingue,* 153–65.
57. "Le nègre est issu d'un sang pur; le mulâtre, au contraire, est issu d'un sang mélangé; c'est un composé du noir et du blanc"; "il est aussi évident que le nègre est au-dessus du mulâtre qu'il est évident que l'or pur est au-dessus de l'or mélangé"; "protecteurs naturels"; "une exclusion injurieuse à la pureté de leur origine"; "plus généreux que leurs enfants" (Mavidal and Laurent, 10:329).
58. "d'une si parfaite justice aux yeux de la raison, de l'humanité et de tout créole que son intérêt n'aveugle pas tout à fait, qu'elle ne peut pas être un seul instant l'objet d'un doute" (Debien, *Les colons,* 168).
59. "il est temps de se réduire sur les préjugés; le salut des colonies en dépend.... Je crois que les gens de couleur et même les nègres qui ont des propriétés doivent être appelés à voter l'impôt et la loi qui doit les régir" (Debien, *Les colons,* 169).
60. See Mavidal and Laurent, *Archives parlementaires,* 35:481; Raimond, *Véritable origine,* 19.
61. For the lobbying, see a letter sent to the committee by the people of color (Mavidal and Laurent, 10:329–33).
62. "aucunes lois sur l'état des personnes ne seront décrétées pour les colonies, que sur la demande précise et formelle de leurs assemblées coloniales" (Mavidal and Laurent, 19:570).
63. Dubois, *Avengers,* 77–90.
64. Fick, *The Making of Haiti,* 105–6.
65. Dubois, *Avengers,* 79–96.

66. For an overview of these different approaches, see Sepinwall's introduction to *Haitian History*. For an in-depth discussion, see Geggus, *Haitian Revolutionary Studies*.
67. Fick, *The Making of Haiti*, 112.
68. Fick, *The Making of Haiti*, 111–12.
69. Clarkson, *History*, 107–8.
70. See "'Thy Coming Fame.'"
71. "Ne croyez pas qu'un état libre soit celui où l'on goûte les plaisirs du luxe, où l'on s'enivre des jouissances de la volupté" (518).
72. "est parvenue à soutenir parmi les colons l'esprit d'attachement à la mère-patrie" (518).
73. "Quant à la traite et à l'esclavage des nègres, les gouvernemens de l'Europe auront beau résister aux cris de la philosophie, aux principes de liberté universelle qui germent et se propagent parmi les nations. Qu'ils apprennent que ce n'est jamais en vain qu'on montre la vérité au peuple; que l'impulsion une fois donnée, il faudra absolument céder au torrent qui doit entraîner les anciens abus, et que le nouvel ordre de choses s'élèvera malgré toutes les précautions qu'on prend pour en retarder l'établissement. . . . Oui! nous osons le prédire avec confiance, un temps viendra, et le jour n'est pas loin, où l'on verra un Africain, à tête crépue, sans autre recommandation que son bon sens et ses vertus, venir participer à la législation dans le sein de nos assemblées nationales" (523–24).
74. Schama, *Citizens*, 169–74.
75. Stein, *Léger Félicité Sonthonax*, 42–59.
76. "dans un régiment de ligne comme officier" (*Lettre écrite de New-Yorck*, 7).
77. "Dis bien des choses honnêtes à notre ami Sonthonax" (CARAN, T988, 16 Pluviôse an 6).
78. Stein, *Léger Félicité Sonthonax*, 60.
79. Dubois, *Avengers*, 154–59; Garran de Coulon, *Rapport sur les troubles*, 3:443.
80. Dubois, *Avengers*, 161–66; Stein, *Léger Félicité Sonthonax*, 90–94.
81. "d'être fidèle à la République française, d'obéir à toutes les lois de la France, décrétées et à décréter, et de maintenir de tout leur pouvoir la Liberté et l'Egalité" ("Procès-verbal," 266).
82. Belley et al., *Lettre écrite de New-Yorck*, 1–6.
83. "furent de là à Belley, lui saisirent son épée, *le battirent*, le fouillèrent, lui volèrent sa montre, son argent, ses papiers, tous les effets qui étoient correct dans sa chambre, & l'insultèrent" (Belley et al., *Lettre écrite de New-Yorck*, 7).
84. "d'oser servir dans un régiment de ligne comme officier, & commander des blancs" (Belley et al., *Lettre écrite de New-Yorck*, 7).
85. "qu'il ne voyoit dans sa place que des devoirs *envers la France*, qu'il l'avoit servie depuis vingt-cinq ans, & d'ailleurs que quand on savoit sauver des blancs & les défendre, on pouvoit bien les commander" (Belley et al., *Lettre écrite de New-Yorck*, 7).
86. "*qu'il ne l'ôteroit pas; qu'ils n'avoient qu'à frapper*" (Belley et al., *Lettre écrite de New-Yorck*, 7).
87. "*Vous ne pouvez m'ôter celle que je porte dans mon coeur*" (Belley et al., *Lettre écrite de New-Yorck*, 7).

88. "les scélérats de colons émigrés," "je souffrois pour mes frères" (Belley et al., *Lettre de Belley,* 19).

89. "combattre avec eux *tous les ennemis de la République*"; "Songez que la France seule reconnoît la liberté; que les Anglais et les Espagnols, coalisés avec les colons aristocrates ou royalistes, veulent vous replonger dans l'avilissement & dans l'esclavage, & *que vous m'avez promis de mourir tous plutôt que de laisser envahir la partie du Nord*"; "Mes concitoyens, imitez *les Français qui combattent pour leur liberté,* & qui non seulement *savent mourir, mais aussi savent vaincre*" (*Lettre de Belley*, 20).

90. William B. Cohen, *The French Encounter,* mentions Ismeria on page 4. The only verifiable fact is that there is a statue of a black virgin in the Notre-Dame basilica in Liesse, which receives thousands of visitors every year.

91. Cohen, *The French Encounter,* 5.

92. "la manière bienveillante dont ils étaient accueillis en France," "libres et indépendants" (388).

93. "fit merveilles d'un espadon à la main, toujours à la teste des deffendans qu'il encourageoit & par ses paroles & par son exemple"; "la vengeance divine, ayant trop précipitament mis en justice, & par ce moyen livré à la mort, le pauvre nègre" (Daval and Daval, 84).

94. Jules Mathorez, *Les étrangers en France,* quotes a baptismal certificate that refers to a man named Visset, "principal du colliaige affricain vel des Affricins" (390).

95. Hamy, "Les cent quarante nègres," 272.

96. Mathorez, *Les étrangers en France,* 394–95.

97. "un très vaillant champion en la lice de Vénus" (Mathorez, 391).

98. "avec toute la magnificence possible"; "avec honneur" (341); "superbement vêtu"; "personnes de qualité" (346).

99. "*deux Noirs, personnes de qualité... pour leur faire voir les maisons royales et les remplir des grandeurs de cet Etat... pour leur roy et pour eux, et l'assurer de la protection et de l'amitié de Sa Majesté... et pour établir le commerce des François dans son Etat*" (Chouin, *Eguafo*, 123–24).

100. See Diabaté, *Aniaba*. Because of various quarrels, though, he lost the support of the French, and it is not known for certain what became of him after he went back to Issiny.

101. See Grigsby, "Revolutionary Sons."

102. "avec les perroquets et parfois les singes ils font partie de la famille"; "il lui faut des Vénus noires" (400); "chacun voulait posséder son nègre" (401).

103. "négrillon familier, quelque chose comme un chimère humaine, pour apporter les plateaux de rafraîchissements, tenir le parasol et se rouler sur les tapis" (Goncourt and Goncourt, 132).

104. Mathorez, *Les étrangers en France,* 400.

105. For the information in this paragraph and the next, see Boulle, *Race et esclavage,* and Peabody, *"There Are No Slaves in France."*

106. Peabody, *"There Are No Slaves in France,"* 55.

107. "on enlève journellement aux Colonies cette portion d'hommes la plus nécessaire pour la culture des terres" (Boulle, 255).

108. "jusqu'à ce qu'il ait été pourvu, par telle Loi qu'il appartiendra, sur l'état desdits Noirs, Mulâtres, ou autres gens de couleur" (Boulle, 258).

109. "se multiplient dans le Royaume, les couleurs se mêlent, le sang s'altère" (Boulle, 92).
110. "naturellement enclins au vol, au larcin, à la Luxure, à la paresse et à la trahison. . . . En général ils ne sont propres qu'à vivre dans la servitude" (Boulle, 36).
111. "communication avec les Blancs, dont il est résulté un sang mêlé qui augmente tous les jours" (Boulle, 26).
112. See Curran, *The Anatomy of Blackness,* for the information discussed in the following paragraphs.
113. The prize was never given.
114. "Un noir, un jaune, un blanc, vont siéger parmi vous, au nom des citoyens libres de Saint-Domingue" (Mavidal and Laurent, 84:257).
115. "accolade fraternelle" (Mavidal and Laurent, 84:257).
116. "Il est temps de nous élever à la hauteur des principes de la liberté et de l'égalité" (Mavidal and Laurent, 84:283).
117. "Les hommes de couleur ont, comme nous, voulu briser leurs fers; nous avons brisé les nôtres, nous n'avons voulu nous soumettre au joug d'aucun maître; accordons-leur le même bienfait" (Mavidal and Laurent, 84:283).
118. "La Convention nationale décrète que l'esclavage est aboli dans toute l'étendue du territoire de la République; en conséquence, tous les hommes sans distinction de couleur jouiront des droits de citoyens français" (Mavidal and Laurent, 84:283).
119. "C'est avec de l'or que ces monstres avaient rivé vos chaînes, corrompu les moeurs, perverti la morale des nations; c'est avec de la poudre et du fer que nous allons purger la terre de ces brigands, et engraisser l'arbre glorieux de la liberté de leur sang" (Ray, 19:386).
120. The notion of *nations policées* was actually closer to the idea of "civilized nations."
121. Ehrard, *Lumières et esclavage,* 174.
122. "l'établissement d'un droit fondé sur la force, lequel droit rend un homme tellement propre à un autre homme, qu'il est le maître absolu de sa vie, de ses biens, & de sa liberté"; "tous les hommes naissent libres" (Diderot and d'Alembert, 934).
123. Ehrard, *Lumières et esclavage,* 174.
124. "blesse la liberté de l'homme," "est contraire au droit naturel & civil," "est inutile" (Diderot and d'Alembert, 937).
125. "unie si étroitement avec la conservation de l'homme, qu'elle n'en peut être séparée que par ce qui détruit en même tems [*sic*] sa conservation sa vie"; "en état de guerre"; "un attentat manifeste contre sa vie"; "du moment qu'un homme veut me soûmettre malgré moi à son empire, j'ai lieu de présumer que si je tombe entre ses mains, il me traitera selon son caprice, ne fera pas scrupule de me tuer, quand la fantaisie lui en prendra"; "pour ainsi dire, le rempart de ma conservation, le fondement de toutes les autres choses qui m'appartiennent" (Diderot and d'Alembert, 937); "laisser à l'homme la dignité qui lui est naturelle" (938).
126. "l'influence prodigieuse de la liberté sur le développement de la raison humaine, & sur l'établissement de la paix universelle" (6); "de l'humanité, du bien public" (26); "jusqu'à ce qu'elle ait obtenu la liberté de nos frères" (29).

127. "il n'y aurait point à balancer, il faudrait se résoudre à payer le sucre plus cher, ou même à s'en passer, plutôt que de violer si cruellement les droits de l'humanité" (299).

128. The original English speech can be found in *Gentleman's Magazine* 5 (January 1735): 21–23.

129. "dans le luxe et dans la molesse" (342); "leur fade & dégoûtante blancheur," "la couleur noble & majestueuse" (343); "Prenons possession de ce vaste terrain qui sera désormais notre partage, & divisons-le entre nous sans préférence et sans jalousie" (350).

130. "justifier par la politique ce que réprouve la morale" (160); "grandes révolutions"; "s'élever plus haut"; "Je tiens de la nature le droit de me défendre" (161); "Brisons les chaînes de tant de victimes de notre cupidité, dussions-nous renoncer à un commerce qui n'a que l'injustice pour base, & que le luxe pour objet" (165); "Où est-il ce grand homme, que la nature doit peut-être à l'honneur de l'espèce humaine? Où est-il, ce Spartacus nouveau, qui ne trouvera point de Crassus? Alors disparoîtra le *code noir;* & que le *code blanc* sera terrible, si le vainqueur ne consulte que le droit de représailles!" (168).

131. "un nègre, la tête nue, le bras tendu, l'oeil fier, l'attitude noble, imposante"; "*Au vengeur du nouveau monde!*"; "vertueuse vengeance"; "rétablir l'équilibre que l'iniquité de la féroce ambition a su détruire" (127).

132. "qui en ont parlé plus en Marchands ou en Commis qu'en Philosophes ou en Hommes d'Etat" (Diderot and d'Alembert, 2); "intérêt personnel," "intérêt général," "esprit patriotique," "vertus" (12); "à l'esprit de communauté, au bien de la communauté" (28); "le bien général" (54).

133. Saint-Lambert, "Réflexions," 182–83.

134. "un peuple citoyen" (Saint-Lambert, "Réflexions," 184).

135. "si j'ai été pour vous un maître dur, donnez-moi la mort, je l'ai méritée" (50); "des vertus, du grand sens et de l'amitié" (60).

136. "on ne connaît point ce *moi* fatal"; "les plaisirs du luxe n'y sont pas" (9).

137. "ma petite république" (245). Later on, after the good overseer has died, he decides to dissolve his "peaceful republic"—"paisible république" (286)—rather than risk subjecting the workers to someone he does not trust.

138. "humanité" (Mavidal and Laurent, 8:8).

139. "ces hommes semblables à nous par la pensée et surtout par la triste faculté de souffrir"; "un barbare objet de trafic" (Mavidal and Laurent, 8:20).

140. See Clavière, "Lettre."

141. "ces marchés de chair humaine" ("Adresse," 5).

142. See Mavidal and Laurent, *Archives parlementaires,* 41:412.

143. "Jusques à quand, citoyens, permettrez-vous ce commerce infâme? Jusques à quand accorderez-vous des encouragements pour un trafic qui déshonore l'espèce humaine? Montrez-vous dignes de ce que vous avez toujours été, qu'il ne soit plus permis à aucun Français d'aller chercher des hommes, qui sont nos semblables quoique d'une couleur différente, sur leur terre natale, pour les transporter sur un sol étranger, où on les emploie comme des bêtes de somme" (Mavidal and Laurent, 69:580).

144. "sur quel principe on se fonde pour la proportion de la députation des colonies"; "Les colonies prétendent-elles ranger leurs nègres et leurs gens de couleur dans la classe des hommes ou dans celle des bêtes de somme?"; "nous les prierons d'observer qu'en proportionnant le nombre des députés à la population de la France, nous n'avons pas pris en considération la quantité de nos chevaux ni de nos mulets" (Mavidal and Laurent, 8:186).

145. "l'abolition de la servitude et de la traite entraînerait donc la perte de nos colonies"; "des manufactures et du commerce de France" (Mavidal and Laurent, 11:699).

146. Benot, *La révolution,* 118–21. The authors he discusses are Jean Louis de Viefville des Essarts, Mathieu Blanc-Gilli, Benjamin Sigismond Frossard, the Abbé Sibire, Guy-Armand de Kersaint, Jules Solime Milscent, Bernardin de Saint-Pierre, and Marat. To this list, one can add Daniel Lescallier and Lecointe-Marsillac.

147. "Qu'est-ce que cela prouve? Puisque rien n'a été fait, ce ne sont que des mots. Mais ces mots . . . n'en ont pas moins travaillé l'opinion, l'ont préparée à accepter et à soutenir le décret d'abolition de 1794" (*La révolution,* 132).

148. Garrigus, "Opportunist or Patriot?," 5.

149. See Raimond, *Observations adressées,* which reproduces La Luzerne's letters.

150. Raimond describes the pressure from La Luzerne in *Véritable origine,* 16.

151. Debien, *Les colons de Saint-Domingue,* 156–58.

152. Mavidal and Laurent, *Archives parlementaires,* 10:329–33.

153. See Gauthier, "Le rôle de Julien Raimond," 226–27.

154. "au nom des droits sacrés de l'Humanité" (*Réclamations,* 1).

155. "Et que si malheureusement il existe, sous la domination française, un pays où l'on croit l'esclavage nécessaire encore pour un temps" ("Observations," 14); "jusqu'à ce que la Nation ait pris des moyens sûrs pour les ramener à l'état de liberté" (15).

156. "D'abord, on ne rougissait pas de mettre à l'écart et d'abaisser au nombre des bêtes de somme ces milliers d'individus qui sont condamnés à gémir sous le poids honteux de l'esclavage. Ensuite, on faisait une grande différence entre les citoyens de couleur affranchis et leurs descendants, à quelque degré que ce fût, et les colons blancs" (Mavidal and Laurent, 10:330).

157. Raimond, *Véritable origine,* 19.

158. See the debates from 7 to 15 May in Mavidal and Laurent, *Archives parlementaires,* vols. 25–26.

159. "Périssent les colonies" (Mavidal and Laurent, 26:60).

160. "attachement bien reconnu pour les blancs" (Mavidal and Laurent, 26:68).

161. "un sol arrosé du sang de nos frères" (Mavidal and Laurent, 26:80).

162. Duchet, *Anthropologie et histoire,* 177–93.

163. *Les colons de Saint-Domingue,* 155.

164. "délibérer sur les intérêts de leur métropole"; "préparera l'abolition de l'esclavage dans nos colonies" (128).

165. "faire deux demandes à la fois pourrait nuire à l'une et à l'autre et les affaiblir toutes les deux" (Dorigny and Gainot, *La société,* 254).

166. Godechot, "Dejoly et les gens de couleur libres," 55.
167. "La crise de la colonie est . . . une crise nationale" (Mavidal and Laurent, 34:438).
168. "l'indépendance de cinq cent mille hommes noirs" (Benot, *La révolution,* 243); "Il n'y a pas à balancer; les lois de la justice avant celles des convenances commerciales, et nos intérêts après ceux de l'espèce humaine outragée depuis si longtemps" (243–44).
169. "le coeur d'un noir bat aussi pour la liberté" (Mavidal and Laurent, 35:476).
170. "de conserver les colonies, d'y maintenir le calme, d'y contenir les esclaves" (*Véritable origine,* 2).
171. See Gainot, *Les officiers de couleur,* 26.
172. See Courvoisier, "Les soldats noirs," 396.
173. "Si la nature, inépuisable dans ses combinaisons, nous a différenciés des Français par des signes extérieurs, d'un autre côté elle nous a rendus parfaitement semblables, en nous donnant, comme à eux, un coeur brûlant de combattre les ennemis de l'Etat"; "il est impossible que la France ne devienne bientôt la capitale du monde libre et le tombeau de tous les trônes de l'univers" (Mavidal and Laurent, 49:429).
174. Mavidal and Laurent, *Archives parlementaires,* 49:471.
175. Mavidal and Laurent, *Archives parlementaires,* 54:389.
176. *Les officiers de couleur,* 46–48.
177. Reiss, *The Black Count,* 142–43.
178. Garrigus, "Opportunist or Patriot?," 9.
179. "nous voyons la beauté de l'aurore comme eux; nous nous ressentons de la douce haleine des zéphirs . . . nous recueillons, mais pour des hommes qui n'ont pas semé; nous leur amassons des trésors, dont nous ne profitons pas; nous les servons, sans espoir de voir enfin le terme de nos maux" (4); "les droits sacrés de l'homme" (1); "les cris d'un million d'esclaves" (2); "fertiliser une terre aussi riche" (7); "régénèrent les destinées de l'homme"; "entre des hommes égaux?" (9).
180. Piquet, *L'émancipation,* 255–58.
181. See Benot, "Un anti-esclavagiste," 265–66.
182. Gainot, *Les officiers de couleur,* 56.
183. See Gauthier, "Le rôle de la députation," 202.
184. "Notre union sera notre force"; "Il existe encore une aristocratie, celle de la peau"; "J'espère bien que la Convention nationale appliquera les principes d'égalité à nos frères des colonies . . . et qu'incessamment on vous fera un rapport sur lequel vous prononcerez la liberté des noirs" (Mavidal and Laurent, 66:57).
185. "ne s'endort pas"; "Donnez-nous la liberté, ou donnez-nous la mort"; "a tiré le voile de l'oubli sur les plaies que nous leur montrions"; "planter avec nous l'arbre de la liberté" (297).
186. "la liberté de l'Amérique" (Ray, 16:606).
187. Ray, 16:621.
188. "l'orgueil des blancs"; "secouer le joug de la France"; "le peuple, les véritables sans-culottes dans les colonies"; "ils ont défendu vos collègues avec le plus grand courage, ils se sont battus comme des héros" (Mavidal and Laurent, 84:277); "ils ajoutèrent même: *les Droits de l'Homme*" (278).

189. "Elles partagent nos sentiments; pendant que nous nous battrons pour la France, elles les inspireront à nos enfants; elles travailleront pour nourrir les guerriers" (Mavidal and Laurent, 278).

190. "dévoués à la république"; "les germes de la liberté et de l'égalité"; "Je n'ai vu dans la révolution qui s'est opérée à Saint-Domingue que l'accomplissement de mes voeux pour le genre humain" (Mavidal and Laurent, 84:282); "d'y voir tous les hommes égaux et de les embrasser en frèrcs"; "dévouement à la république une et indivisible; Européens, Créoles, Africains, ne connaissent plus aujourd'hui d'autres couleurs, d'autre nom que ceux de Français"; "Créez une seconde fois un nouveau monde" (283).

191. Aulard, *La Société des Jacobins,* 638.

192. "les sentiments les plus ardents pour la liberté"; "Je fus esclave depuis mon enfance"; "Dans le cours de ma vie, je me suis senti digne d'être Français, et mon sang a coulé pour la République française"; "flottera sur nos rivages et sur nos montagnes" ("Séance du 21 Pluviôse," 732).

193. Halpern, "Les fêtes," 189.

194. "L'ESCLAVAGE EST ABOLI" (Chaumette, "Discours," 19).

195. Between February and August, 356 congratulations were sent to the Convention, 285 of which were from popular societies. The whole of France, except for five departments, was represented. See Wanquet, *La France et la première abolition,* 156.

196. See Popkin, *You Are All Free,* 327–75, for a detailed account of the events described in the following paragraphs.

197. Stein, *Léger Félicité Sonthonax,* 108.

198. Page and Brulley, *Développement des causes des troubles,* 1–12.

199. "les agents contre-révolutionnaires d'une faction dont Brissot était le chef" (Ray, 16:343).

200. "liés d'intérêt et d'affection avec la métropole" (Mavidal and Laurent, 69:39).

201. "Ces commissaires sont les créatures et les agents des Brissot, des Clavière" (Mavidal and Laurent, 69:39).

202. "l'assassinat des blancs," "ou d'usurper le pouvoir souverain dans l'île, ou de la livrer aux ennemis" (Ray, 17:559).

203. See Gauthier, "Inédits de Dufay," 517–18, for testimony by a white colon that Page and Brulley misled him into thinking that the deputies were personal emissaries of Sonthonax and Polverel and not democratically elected deputies.

204. "Il y a dans cette horrible affaire la haine de la France, la haine de l'égalité et le préjugé des couleurs, parce qu'il y a deux Députés hommes ci-devant dits de couleur, et que parmi les Députés qui arrivent derrière nous il y en a encore d'autres" (Gauthier, "Inédits de Dufay," 516).

205. "il est bien connu que les Blancs sont les aristocrates dans cette colonie et que les hommes de couleur et les nègres sont les patriotes" (Benot, "Comment," 353).

206. "de nation afriquaine-bambara" (Benot, "Comment," 353).

207. "sans cela l'on prétendroit encore que vous avez voulu dire autre chose" (Mavidal and Laurent, 84:283).

208. Benot, "Comment," 353–57.
209. "en adoptant parmi vous nos frères" (Mavidal and Laurent, 84:470).
210. "*Vos droits vous sont rendus,* car vous n'auriez jamais dû les perdre" (Mavidal and Laurent, 84:470).
211. "Vous n'attendez pas de moi une éloquence brillante. Je parlerai d'après mon coeur; et la vérité naïve sera tout mon talent" (Mavidal and Laurent, 84:471).
212. "La tribune de la Convention est bien actuellement la tribune de l'Egalité, puisqu'un citoyen noir, représentant de Saint-Domingue, vient enfin d'y parler pour la première fois. C'est Jean-Baptiste Belley" (Benot, "Comment," 358).
213. "Ce sont eux qui ont réussi à nous faire mettre au cachot, mes deux collègues et moi, en arrivant ici" (Mavidal and Laurent, 84:471).
214. "Je demande contre ces machinateurs dangereux le décret d'arrestation" (Mavidal and Laurent, 84:471).
215. "*vers le tyran uniquement, avec ordre de ne traiter qu'avec lui, et de se soustraire à toute assemblée nationale*" (Gauthier, "Inédits de Belley" 608).
216. Gauthier, "Inédits de Belley," 610.
217. "Je suis un de ces hommes de la nature que la sagesse et les principes de la nation française ont arrachés au joug du despotisme" (*Belley, de Saint-Domingue,* 1); "avait refusé d'admettre les citoyens de couleur et les noirs qu'à cette époque on ne regardait pas comme des *personnes*" (3); "la liberté et l'égalité parmi tous les hommes indistinctement" (3); "contre les assemblées et convention nationales, les jacobins, les commissaires civils, et tout, enfin, ce qui émanait de la France" (4).
218. "ami intime" (*Belley, de Saint-Domingue,* 4); "fussent mis hors la loi, *et cela sans être entendus*, et sur leur dénonciation spéciale" (5); "attestent le crime et leur trahison" (6); "la haine profonde de la liberté et de l'égalité" (5).
219. Popkin, *You Are All Free,* 116; Stein, *Léger Félicité Sonthonax,* 116.
220. "opprimés, assassinés" (Mavidal and Laurent, 95:375); "Vous devez savoir que les colonies sont perdues. Qui est-ce qui les a perdues? Sont-ce les colons? Sont-ce leurs agents? Oui" (376); "Page et Bruslé sont des scélérats. La justice et la probité sont à l'ordre du jour, mais non l'indulgence pour des hommes couverts de crimes" (376); "BELLEY, *homme de couleur*" (376).
221. "*Garde-t'en bien... Le J...f... n'en a pas pour un mois!*" (Perraud, 12).
222. "les bourreaux des colons, les exterminateurs de leurs familles, les dévastateurs de leurs propriétés" (Verneuil, 6).
223. "inquiéter les gens de couleur sur leurs droits, et les noirs sur leur état et sur leur liberté, afin de les détacher de la France" (Dufaÿ, 2).
224. For a detailed discussion of Gouly's positions, see Wanquet, *La France et la première abolition.*
225. "la Nation n'est point assemblée aujourd'hui pour donner des lois à l'univers; elle ne s'occupera que de la France"; "s'instruiront du caractère des Colons & des étrangers qui habitent les Colonies, de l'influence du climat qu'ils habitent, de la nature des propriétés, des moyens de les conserver" (*Vues générales,* 7); "la constitution & les lois sont relatives aux hommes, aux lieux & aux choses" (14).

226. "facultés individuelles" (*Vues générales,* 31); "dans la couleur de la peau, dans l'habitude du corps, dans la tournure de ses membres, dans la coupe de la tête, dans la forme, dans la disposition des diverses parties du visage" (32); "Tel est l'Africain qu'aujourd'hui vous nommez affectueusement votre frère, votre ami, mais qui ne deviendra jamais votre égal" (34); "le caractère, le génie, les facultés intellectuelles du Français sont les mêmes" (39).

227. "aux droits sacrés de l'homme" (*Le bout d'oreille,* 1); "la morale sublime de notre constitution" (2); "République indivisible" (3); "Qui n'est pas soulevé d'indignation et de pitié en lisant le portrait bizarre que Gouli a fait des noirs"; "Croyez-vous, citoyens collègues, que la nature soit injuste, qu'elle ait, ainsi que l'affirment les colons, formé des hommes pour être les esclaves des autres" (5).

228. "seulement de régler le mode de son exécution, eu égard *aux lieux, aux choses et aux différentes races d'hommes*" (*Réponse au libelle,* 2); "une race d'hommes étrangers, au détriment de la race indigène" (5).

229. "anti-sociales, anti-républicaines, anti-politiques" (Ray, 22:625–26); "contraires à l'unité, à l'indivisibilité de la république" (626).

230. "Membre du Conseil des Cinq-Cents jusqu'au 1er prairial prochain" (Kuscinski, 136–37).

231. *Histoire d'Haïti,* 244.

232. "Je suis persuadé qu'il aura été entendu avec intérêt dans sa justification et qu'il prouvera facilement qu'il n'a été calomnié que par les ennemis de la liberté" (CARAN, T988).

233. "Nous avons trouvé toute la partie du nord dans un état de détresse étonnant"; "Toussaint Louverture était aux Gonaïves lorsque nous sommes arrivés. Il ne s'est point pressé à venir puisque après avoir attendu 15 jours l'agent lui écrivit pour l'inviter à se rendre parce qu'il ne voulait rien faire sans l'avoir consulté"; "Croirais-tu, mon ami, que je n'ai pas su avoir une conférence particulière avec lui?"; "a persuadé à l'agent de ne me donner que le commandement du Département du Nord, de crainte, a-t-il dit, que cela ne me donnât trop d'influence"; "commence à distinguer les amis de la tranquillité d'avec les intrigants et les ambitieux" (CARAN, T988).

234. Dubois, *Avengers,* 222.

235. Ray, *Réimpression,* 29:53.

236. "ne sont point réputés étrangers; ils jouissent des mêmes droits qu'un individu né sur le territoire français" (Ray, 29:119).

237. See Dorigny and Gainot, *La Société,* 311.

238. "C'est le spectacle de 2 millions d'hommes que la plus belle des fêtes invite aujourd'hui à la plus vive allégresse; qui, tantôt les yeux fixés vers le ciel, tantôt vers le rivage où arrivent les vaisseaux de la nation libératrice, confondent, dans leurs transports, et les remerciemens qu'ils adressent à la divinité, et les sentimens de reconnaissance qu'ils expriment à leurs généreux bienfaiteurs" (Thomany, 3).

239. "Toutes créances pour raison de ventes d'esclaves sont éteintes et abolies. Il est interdit aux tribunaux, soit du continent de la République, soit de ses îles et colonies, de prononcer aucune condamnation à cet égard, et tous

jugements rendus et non encore exécutés seront regardés comme non avenus" (Dorigny and Gainot, 354).

240. "sans moyen d'existence avec une femme, un enfant et une soeur, qu'il n'a pas mérité son sort, et que son dévouement pour le gouvernement républicain restera inviolable."

241. The information in this paragraph comes from Mentor's file at the Service Historique de la Défense, GR2YE 2824.

242. "une patrie, des protecteurs, des frères"; "le chaînon des mêmes intérêts, des mêmes sentimens, commence à unir l'Europe à l'Amérique, à l'Afrique et à l'Asie" (*Discours du 12 prairial*, 2); "ceux qui, par des motifs d'ambition personnelle, pourroient se rendre traîtres à la République" (3).

243. "Le temps n'est plus où le Français avoit des esclaves; il ne doit plus avoir que des égaux & des frères"; "qu'ils ne déshonorent point l'humanité, en ressuscitant des souvenirs aussi douloureux qu'humilians pour les infortunés Africains & leurs descendans" (*Discours du 24 Vendémaire*, 2); "doivent s'appliquer à faire oublier leurs torts, au lieu de les rappeler par une demande aussi étrange qu'injuste" (3).

244. *Dictionnaire des jacobins vivans*, 115.

245. Gainot, *Les officiers de couleur*, 60.

246. "du patriotisme, une bonne conduite, du courage" (Gainot, *Les officiers de couleur*, 69).

247. "isolés de leurs compagnons d'armes d'Europe" (*Motion d'ordre*, 2); "reléguant"; "leurs frères d'armes" (3); "un exil qui les dégrade, qui les isole du reste des Français" (4).

248. "un groupe social en pleine ascension" ("La députation," 100).

249. "ainsi qu'à ta chère Adelle à qui je te prie de dire mille choses agréables"; "tu dois te figurer quelle doit être ma douleur"; "nos frères"; "Je suis ton ami, Belley"; "Non, mon ami, je ne m'attends point de ce que tu me regardes comme ton père. Tu peux être certain que je suis ton ami et que je saisirai toutes les occasions pour te le prouver" (CARAN, T988).

250. All this information can be found in the Boisson papers (CARAN, T988).

251. See his declaration in CARAN, C352/1837/3/pièce 16.

252. "ont volé sa montre, son argent, tous ses effets, jusqu'à ceux de son enfant" (Mavidal and Laurent, 84:281).

253. Gainot, *Les officiers de couleur*, 156–66.

254. Benot, *La démence coloniale*, 50.

255. "des propos anti-européens" (Petit et al., "Actes signés par J. B. Belley," 6509).

256. "pour qu'ils soient en partie remis à sa famille à Saint-Domingue" (Petit et al., "Actes signés par J. B. Belley," 6506). Belley's death certificate and testament were found by Jacques Petit in the departmental archives of Morbihan, a department in Brittany.

3. JOHN MARRANT

1. See Carretta, *Unchained Voices,* 128, for the number of printings.
2. Hindmarsh, *The Evangelical Conversion Narrative,* 45–50.
3. On Henry Scougal, see Kidd, *George Whitefield,* 28.
4. Schlenther, *Queen of the Methodists,* 19–39.
5. *Oxford Dictionary of National Biography.*
6. Marrant, *Narrative,* 129. For the connection between Hart and Cook, see Sprague, *Annals of the American Pulpit,* 188.
7. "To pious *Willes* my pious steps I bend,/Who strait admits me as a christian friend" (Whitchurch, 23). For references to Wills and Romaine, see Whitchurch, *A Negro Convert,* 21.
8. Schlenther, *Queen of the Methodists,* 151. In his *Narrative,* Marrant says that he "used to exercise my gifts on a Monday evening in prayer and exhortation, in Spa-fields chapel" (126).
9. Schlenther, "'To Convert,'" 245.
10. Marrant, *Narrative,* 126.
11. For the information in this paragraph, see Morgan, "Black Life in Eighteenth-Century Charleston."
12. Carretta, *Unchained Voices,* 54.
13. I discuss Gronniosaw in chapter 1. For a detailed analysis of his Calvinist connections, see Hanley, "Calvinism."
14. In his *Narrative,* Thomas Brown describes a similar practice: "But the next Night they made a Fire, stripp'd and ty'd him to a Stake, and the Squaws cut Pieces of Pine, like Scures, and thrust them into his Flesh, and set them on Fire" (12).
15. "Pocahontas . . . got his head in her arms and laid her own upon his to save him from death" (64).
16. For an analysis of the evolution of the Pocahontas story, see Tilton, *Pocahontas.*
17. "A Short Account of the British Plantations in America," 312.
18. For a discussion of the captivity narrative's links to that myth, see Derounian-Stodola and Levernier, *The Indian Captivity Narrative,* 40–41.
19. For the information provided in this paragraph, I rely on Hatley, *Dividing Paths.*
20. See Axtell, *The Invasion Within.*
21. Frey and Wood, *Come Shouting to Zion,* 63.
22. Kidd, *George Whitefield,* 110, 199.
23. For the information in this paragraph, see Bolster, *Black Jacks,* 68–101.
24. Ryan, *The World of Thomas Jeremiah,* 27–28.
25. This man is often referred to as David Margate, but I am following Tim Lockley's decision to use the name he signed in the only existing letter from his hand. See "David Margrett," 730.
26. Ryan, *The World of Thomas Jeremiah,* 40–42.
27. Ryan, *The World of Thomas Jeremiah,* 51–52.
28. Laurens, *Papers,* 220.
29. Ryan, *The World of Thomas Jeremiah,* 116–19.

30. This is what he asserts in his narrative. Neither Vincent Carretta nor Ruth Holmes Whitehead found his name in the *Scorpion*'s muster lists.

31. According to Ruth Holmes Whitehead in *Black Loyalists,* once in North Carolina, the *Scorpion* discharged all but five blacks, who were themselves discharged in New York. A number of others accompanied Clinton to South Carolina, where the British were defeated at Charleston, and then on to New York. See pages 78–79. Clinton left New York again for South Carolina in December 1779, and Marrant was on board.

32. Borick, *A Gallant Defense,* 23.
33. Tyson with Schlenther, *In the Midst of Early Methodism,* 273–92.
34. Lockley, "David Margrett," 732–34.
35. Schlenther, *Queen of the Methodists,* 84.
36. Schlenther, *Queen of the Methodists,* 91.
37. Schlenther, *Queen of the Methodists,* 154.
38. *Oxford Dictionary of National Biography.*
39. *Oxford Dictionary of National Biography.*
40. Whitchurch, *A Negro Convert,* 22.
41. Gronniosaw, *Narrative,* 49.
42. Angelo, *Reminiscences,* 347–51.
43. In his *Journal,* he mentions "the little money I saved when I lived in the merchant's employment" (94).
44. Equiano, *Interesting Narrative,* 78.
45. Schama, *Rough Crossings,* 182–83.
46. Bundock, *Fortunes of Francis Barber,* 34.
47. Hoare, *Memoirs of Granville Sharp,* 236.
48. Hoare, *Memoirs of Granville Sharp,* 247.
49. Dixon and Hunter's *Virginia Gazette,* 2 December 1775, 3.
50. See Quarles, *Negro in the American Revolution,* 19–32.
51. Whitehead, *Black Loyalists,* 67.
52. Quarles, *Negro in the American Revolution,* 119.
53. Gilbert, *Black Patriots and Loyalists,* 188. It is possible that some of the blacks listed as in someone's "possession" became free once they reached Canada. Gilbert estimates that a total of about twelve to fifteen thousand free blacks emigrated (205).
54. This book is available as a searchable database at https://novascotia.ca/archives/Africanns/BN.asp.
55. Norton, "The Fate of Some Black Loyalists," 404.
56. Online Institute for Advanced Loyalist Studies, "Claims and Memorials: Petition of Scipio Handley of South Carolina," http://www.royalprovincial.com/military/mems/sc/clmhandley.htm.
57. Gilbert, *Black Patriots and Loyalists,* 205. Possibly Marrant's brother took that alternate route, since his name is not listed in the *Book of Negroes.*
58. Walker, *Black Loyalists,* 67.
59. Walker, *Black Loyalists,* 66–67.
60. See Klein, "Anglicanism."
61. Walker, *Black Loyalists,* 67.
62. Walker, *Black Loyalists,* 67–69; *Dictionary of Canadian Biography.*

63. Walker, *Black Loyalists,* 69, 124.
64. The fact that he says that he "began to sing the first night" is significant, as it points to the essential role of music in reaching out to blacks. See Saillant, "Make a Black Life."
65. Kidd and Hankins, *Baptists in America,* 26–29.
66. Rawlyk, *Canada Fire,* 43.
67. Rawlyk, *Canada Fire,* 25.
68. Wilson, *The Loyal Blacks,* 82.
69. Findlay and Holdsworth, *History of the Wesleyan Methodist,* 290.
70. Wakeley, *Lost Chapters,* 261.
71. Wigger, *Taking Heaven by Storm,* 135.
72. Wigger, *Taking Heaven by Storm,* 137–39.
73. Davis, "George Liele," 123.
74. Brooks, "The Evolution," 13–14.
75. King, *Memoirs,* 362.
76. King, *Memoirs,* 356.
77. Wesley, *Letters,* 225.
78. In her important study, Joanna Brooks highlights how Marrant contributed to a "community regeneration" (88) that was taking place among blacks around the Atlantic.
79. Marrant, *Journal,* 120.
80. Marrant, *Journal,* 116.
81. Hodges, *Black Loyalist Directory,* 107; Wilson, *Loyal Blacks,* 90.
82. Saillant, "'Wipe Away All Tears,'" 18.
83. Joanna Brooks also does not think that Marrant "assumed Africa to be the foreordained destination for American blacks" (104).
84. *Dictionary of Canadian Biography.*
85. Garrettson, *American Methodist,* 8.
86. Joanna Brooks mistakenly reads the passage as referring to Marrant's own marriage (216).
87. Wilson, *Loyal Blacks,* 81.
88. A letter dated May 1785 shows that, contrary to Adam Potkay and Sandra Burr's assertion, he did not travel with Marrant to Nova Scotia but was there before him. See Whytock, "The Huntingdonian Mission," 154; Potkay and Burr, *Black Atlantic Writers,* 68.
89. Walker, *Black Loyalists,* 72.
90. Walker, *Black Loyalists,* 22–23, 47, 70, 83.
91. *Book of Negroes.*
92. Walker, *Black Loyalists,* 387.
93. *Oxford Dictionary of National Biography.* There has been some confusion about when Marrant actually traveled to Boston; some historians indicate January 1789 instead of January 1788. The confusion is due to the fact that Marrant skips a whole year in his *Journal*: he mentions preaching a sermon on Sunday, 3 February, and according to the calendar, that day was in 1788; then a few lines down, he speaks of an event that took place in February 1789. The chronology of events in Nova Scotia as reported in the *Journal* implies that he left in January 1788. But it is true that some letters can lead to confusion. In a November

1788 letter to Lady Huntingdon, he says he is on his way to Liverpool; he also says he is "getting a little better" (158), and we know he was ill while in Nova Scotia in 1788. In a June 1789 letter, Prince Hall reports that he "received into the Lodge since August two members, namely John Bean and John Marrant, a black minister from home but last from Brachtown, Nova Scotia" (Upton, 7). In the face of these inconsistencies, I've decided to follow the chronology of the *Journal*, according to which Marrant left for Boston in January 1788.

94. In the second half of the eighteenth century, Boston's black population varied from 1,541 in 1752 to 811 in 1765. According to the 1790 census, there were 5,369 blacks in Massachusetts and 761 in Boston. See Greene, *The Negro in Colonial New England*, 81, 84–85; Wesley, *Prince Hall*, 82.

95. For a discussion of these petitions, see Cameron, *To Plead Our Own Cause*; Levecq, "'We Beg Your Excellency.'"

96. Cromwell, *The Other Brahmins*, 37.

97. Wesley, *Prince Hall*, 83, 88–89.

98. Wesley, *Prince Hall*, 71.

99. Wesley, *Prince Hall*, 34–35.

100. For petitions to bury their own dead, see Cameron, *To Plead Our Own Cause*, 85.

101. Wesley, *Prince Hall*, 51.

102. "Prince Hall assures me that he has lately published another Charge, which he is to send to me. His first Charge tho' not correct, was useful" (Bentley, 379).

103. Levesque, "Inherent Reformers," 495–96.

104. Cameron, *To Plead Our Own Cause*, 94.

105. Woodson, *Education of the Negro*, 320–25.

106. Cameron, *To Plead Our Own Cause*, 81.

107. For a rebuttal of the idea that black Freemasonry formed an "enclave," see Kantrowitz, "'Intended for the Better Government of Man,'" 1012.

108. Cameron, *To Plead Our Own Cause*, 26–27.

109. Cameron, *To Plead Our Own Cause*, 25.

110. Wesley, *Prince Hall*, 22.

111. Holmes, *Memoir of the French Protestants*, 63.

112. Schmidt, "'A Second and Glorious Reformation,'" 238.

113. Shipton, *Sibley's Harvard Graduates*, 386–407.

114. Essig, *Bonds of Wickedness*, 37–39.

115. Essig, *Bonds of Wickedness*, 73–96.

116. See Minkema and Stout, "The Edwardsian Tradition and the Antislavery Debate."

117. See Minkema, "Jonathan Edwards on Slavery"; Minkema, "Jonathan Edwards's Defense of Slavery."

118. For the information in this paragraph, see Saillant, *Black Puritan, Black Republican*.

119. Sprague, *Annals of the American Pulpit*, 71–79.

120. Moore, *Patriot Preachers*, 260.

121. For the information in this paragraph, see Conforti, *Samuel Hopkins*, 110–24.

122. Belknap says in a letter to Benjamin Rush: "One of them was a sensible fellow and a Freemason. The merchant to whom they were offered was of this fraternity. They soon became acquainted" (C. Wesley, 72).

123. *Oxford Dictionary of Literary Biography.*

124. See Sesay, "Respectability and Representation," for an analysis of this criticism.

125. In an undated letter to Lady Huntingdon, Hall says of Marrant: "We, the members of the African Lodge, have made him a member of that honourable society, and chaplain of the same, which will be a great help to him in his travels, and may do a great deal of good to society" (Upton, 7).

WORKS CITED

Anderson, James. *Anderson's Constitutions of 1723*. Washington, DC: Masonic Service Association of the United States, 1924.
Angelo, Henry. *The Reminiscences of Henry Angelo*. Vol. 1. Edited by H. Lavers Smith. New York: Benjamin Blom, 1969.
Appiah, Kwame Anthony. *Cosmopolitanism: Ethics in a World of Strangers*. London: Allen Lane, 2006.
Aristotle. *The Politics*. Translated by T. A. Sinclair. Edited by Trevor J. Saunders. New York: Penguin, 1992.
Armstrong, Maurice W. *The Great Awakening in Nova Scotia, 1776–1809*. Hartford, CT: American Society of Church History, 1948.
Aulard, François-Alphonse. *La Société des Jacobins*. Vol. 5. Paris: Librairie Jouaust, 1889–97.
Axtell, James. *The Invasion Within: The Contest of Cultures in Colonial North America*. New York: Oxford UP, 1985.
Baker, Keith Michael. "Transformations of Classical Republicanism in Eighteenth-Century France." *Journal of Modern History* 73.1 (2001): 32–53.
Barker, Anthony J. *The African Link: British Attitudes to the Negro in the Era of the Atlantic Slave Trade, 1550-1807*. London: Frank Cass, 1978.
Bartelink, Egbert Jacobus. *Hoe de tijden veranderen: Herinneringen van een ouden planter*. Paramaribo: H. van Ommeren, 1916.
Bartels, F. L. "Jacobus Eliza Johannes Capitein, 1717–1747." *Transactions of the Historical Society of Ghana* 4 (1959): 3–13.
Baym, Nina, et al., eds. *The Norton Anthology of American Literature*. 7th ed. New York: Norton, 2007.
Belknap, Jeremy. *Belknap Papers*. 5th series, vol. 3. Boston: Massachusetts Historical Society, 1877.
Belley, Jean-Baptiste. *Belley, de Saint-Domingue, représentant du peuple, à ses collègues*. Paris: Imprimerie de Pain, 1794.
———. *Le bout d'oreille des colons, ou le système de l'Hôtel Massiac, mis au jour par Gouli*. Paris: Imprimerie de Pain, 1795.
———. *Lettre de Belley, député à la Convention Nationale, à ses frères*. Paris: Imprimerie Nationale, 1794.
Belley, Jean-Baptiste, et al. *Lettre écrite de New-Yorck par les députés de Saint-Domingue à leurs commettans*. Paris: Imprimerie Nationale, 1794.
Benot, Yves. "Un anti-esclavagiste kleptomane? En marge de l'affaire Milscent." *Dix-huitième siècle* 22 (1990): 295–300.

———. "Comment la Convention a-t-elle voté l'abolition de l'esclavage en l'an II?" *Annales historiques de la Révolution française* 65.293 (1993): 349–61.
———. *La démence coloniale sous Napoléon.* Paris: La Découverte, 1992.
———. *La révolution française et la fin des colonies.* Paris: La Découverte, 1988.
Bentley, William. *The Diary of William Bentley, D.D.* Vol. 2. Salem, MA: Essex Institute, 1905–14.
Berlin, Ira. *Many Thousands Gone: The First Two Centuries of Slavery in North America.* Cambridge, MA: Harvard UP, 1998.
Bernardin de Saint-Pierre, Jacques-Henri. *Voeux d'un solitaire: Pour servir de suite aux Etudes de la nature.* Paris: Imprimerie de Monsieur, 1789.
Black, William. "The Life of Mr. William Black. Written by Himself." *The Lives of Early Methodist Preachers, Chiefly Written by Themselves,* vol. 5, edited by Thomas Jackson. London: Wesleyan-Methodist Book-Room, 1865 or 1866. 242–95.
Blakely, Allison. *Blacks in the Dutch World: The Evolution of Racial Imagery in a Modern Society.* Bloomington: Indiana UP, 1993.
Blom, J. C. H., and E. Lamberts. *History of the Low Countries.* New York: Berghahn Books, 1999.
Bolster, W. Jeffrey. *Black Jacks: African American Seamen in the Age of Sail.* Cambridge, MA: Harvard UP, 1997.
Borick, Carl P. *A Gallant Defense: The Siege of Charleston, 1780.* Columbia: U of South Carolina P, 2003.
Boulle, Pierre H. *Race et esclavage dans la France de l'Ancien Régime.* Paris: Perrin, 2007.
Brissot de Warville, Jacques Pierre. "Adresse à l'Assemblée Nationale, pour l'abolition de la traite des noirs." *La révolution française et l'abolition de l'esclavage,* vol. 8. Paris: Editions d'Histoire Sociale, 1968.
———. "Discours sur la nécessité d'établir à Paris une Société pour concourir, avec celle de Londres, à l'abolition de la traite & de l'esclavage des Nègres." *La révolution française et l'abolition de l'esclavage,* vol. 6. Paris: Editions d'Histoire Sociale, 1968.
Broecke, Pieter van den. *Pieter van den Broecke's Journal of Voyages to Cape Verde, Guinea and Angola (1605-1612).* Translated and edited by J. D. La Fleur. London: Hakluyt Society, 2000.
Brooke, Christopher. *Philosophic Pride: Stoicism and Political Thought from Lipsius to Rousseau.* Princeton, NJ: Princeton UP, 2012.
Brooks, Joanna. *American Lazarus: Religion and the Rise of African-American and Native American Literatures.* New York: Oxford UP, 2003.
Brooks, Joanna, and John Saillant, eds. *"Face Zion Forward": First Writers of the Black Atlantic, 1785-1798.* Boston: Northeastern UP, 2002.
Brooks, Walter H. "The Evolution of the Negro Baptist Church." *Journal of Negro History* 71 (1922): 11–22.
Brown, Thomas. *A Plain Narrative of the Uncommon Sufferings and Remarkable Deliverance of Thomas Brown, of Charlestown, in New England.* Boston: Fowle and Draper, 1760.
Bruns, Roger, ed. *Am I Not a Man and a Brother: The Antislavery Crusade of Revolutionary America, 1688-1788.* New York: Chelsea House, 1977.
Buijnsters, P. J. "Les Lumières hollandaises." *Studies on Voltaire and the Eighteenth Century* 87 (1972): 197–215.

Bundock, Michael. *The Fortunes of Francis Barber: The True Story of the Jamaican Slave Who Became Samuel Johnson's Heir*. New Haven, CT: Yale UP, 2015.
Bunyan, John. *Grace Abounding to the Chief of Sinners*. Edited by W. R. Owens. New York: Penguin, 1987.
Buve, Raymond. "Surinaamse slaven en vrije negers in Amsterdam gedurende de achttiende eeuw." *Bijdragen tot de Taal-, Land-, en Volkenkunde* 119.1 (1963): 8–17.
Calmon-Maison, Jean Joseph Robert. *L'amiral d'Estaing, 1729-1794*. Paris: Calmann-Lévy, 1910.
Calvin, John. *Institutes of the Christian Religion*. Vol. 2. Translated by John Allen. Philadelphia: Presbyterian Board of Christian Education, 1936.
Cameron, Christopher. *To Plead Our Own Cause: African Americans in Massachusetts and the Making of the Antislavery Movement*. Kent, OH: Kent State UP, 2014.
Capitein, Jacobus Elisa Johannes. *The Agony of Asar: A Thesis on Slavery by the Former Slave Jacobus Elisa Johannes Capitein, 1717-1747*. Edited and translated by Grant Parker. Princeton, NJ: Markus Wiener, 2001.
———. *Uitgewrogte predikatien*. Amsterdam: Bernardus Mourik and Jacobus Haffman, 1742.
Carretta, Vincent. *Equiano, the African: Biography of a Self-Made Man*. New York: Penguin, 2005.
———, ed. *Unchained Voices: An Anthology of Black Authors in the English-Speaking World of the Eighteenth Century*. Expanded ed. Lexington: UP of Kentucky, 2004.
Charara, Youmna, ed. *Fictions coloniales du XVIIIe siècle*. Paris: L'Harmattan, 2005.
Chaumette, Pierre Gaspard. "Discours prononcé par le citoyen Chaumette, au nom de la commune de Paris." *La révolution française et l'abolition de l'esclavage*, vol. 5. Paris: Editions d'Histoire Sociale, 1968.
Chesnais, Robert, ed. *Le Code noir*. Paris: L'Esprit frappeur, 1998.
Chouin, Gérard. *Eguafo: Un royaume africain "au coeur françois" (1637-1688): Mutations socio-économiques et politique européenne d'un Etat de la Côte de l'Or (Ghana) au XVIIe siècle*. Paris: Karthala, 1998.
Cicero. *On Duties*. Ed. M. T. Griffin and E. M. Atkins. Cambridge: Cambridge UP, 1991.
Clark, William Bell, et al., ed. *Naval Documents of the American Revolution*. Vol. 2. Washington: Naval History Division, 1964–2005.
Clarkson, Thomas. *The History of the Rise, Progress, & Accomplishment of the Abolition of the African Slave-Trade, by the British Parliament*. Vol. 2. Philadelphia: James P. Parke, 1808.
Clavière, Etienne. "Lettre de la Société des amis des noirs à M. Necker, ministre d'état." *La révolution française et l'abolition de l'esclavage*, vol. 7. Paris: Editions d'Histoire Sociale, 1968.
Cohen, William B. *The French Encounter with Africans: White Response to Blacks, 1530-1880*. Bloomington: Indiana UP, 1980.
Colman, Benjamin. "Essay on Slavery." Bruns, 325–27.
Conforti, Joseph A. *Samuel Hopkins and the New Divinity Movement: Calvinism, the Congregational Ministry, and Reform in New England between the Great Awakenings*. Grand Rapids, MI: Christian UP, 1981.

Courvoisier, André. "Les soldats noirs du maréchal de Saxe. Le problème des Antillais et Africains sous les armes en France au XVIIIe siècle." *Revue française d'histoire d'outre-mer* 55.201 (1968): 367–413.

Cromwell, Adelaide M. *The Other Brahmins: Boston's Black Upper Class, 1750–1950.* Fayetteville: U of Arkansas P, 1994.

Curiosus. "Afrikaan in de vorige eeuw in Nederland tot Theologiae Doctor gepromoveerd." *De Navorscher* 4 (1854): 262.

Curran, Andrew S. *The Anatomy of Blackness: Science & Slavery in the Age of Enlightenment.* Baltimore: Johns Hopkins UP, 2011.

Daval, Guillaume, and Jean Daval. *Histoire de la Réformation à Dieppe, 1557–1657.* Vol. 1. Edited by Emile Lesens. Rouen: Espérance Cagnard, 1878.

Davis, John. *Travels of Four Years and a Half in the United States of America during 1798, 1799, 1800, 1801, and 1802.* Ed. A. J. Morrison. New York: Holt, 1909.

Davis, John W. "George Liele and Andrew Bryan, Pioneer Negro Baptist Preachers." *Journal of Negro History* 3.2 (1918): 119–27.

Debbasch, Yvan. *Couleur et liberté: Le jeu du critère ethnique dans un ordre juridique esclavagiste.* Vol. 1, *L'affranchi dans les possessions françaises de la Caraïbe (1635–1833).* Paris: Dalloz, 1967.

Debien, Gabriel. *Les colons de Saint-Domingue et la Révolution: Essai sur le Club Massiac (août 1789–août 1792).* Paris: Armand Colin, 1953.

———. *Les esclaves aux Antilles françaises, XVIIe–XVIIIe siècles.* Gourbeyre: Société d'histoire de la Guadeloupe, 2000.

Debrunner, Hans Werner. *A History of Christianity in Ghana.* Accra: Waterville, 1967.

———. *Presence and Prestige: Africans in Europe.* Basel: Basler Afrika Bibliographien, 1979.

De Jong, Gerald F. *The Dutch Reformed Church in the American Colonies.* Grand Rapids, MI: Eerdmans, 1978.

De Jonge, J. K. J. *De oorsprong van Neerland's bezittingen op de Kust van Guinea.* 's Gravenhage: Martinus Nijhoff, 1871.

De Marees, Pieter. *Description and Historical Account of the Gold Kingdom of Guinea (1602).* Translated and edited by Albert van Dantzig and Adam Jones. Oxford: Oxford UP, 1987.

Den Heijer, Henk. *De geschiedenis van de WIC.* Zutphen: Walburg Pers, 1994.

———. *Goud, ivoor en slaven: Scheepvaart en handel van de Tweede Westindiche Compagnie op Afrika, 1674–1740.* Zutphen: Walburg Pers, 1997.

Denucé, Jan. *Afrika in de XVIde eeuw en de handel van Antwerpen.* Antwerp: De Sikkel, 1937.

Derounian-Stodola, Kathryn Zabelle, and James Arthur Levernier, eds. *The Indian Captivity Narrative, 1550–1900.* New York: Twayne, 1993.

De Stoppelaar, Johannes Hermanus. *Balthasar de Moucheron: Een bladzijde uit de Nederlandsche handelsgeschiedenis tijdens den tachtig-jarigen oorlog.* 's-Gravenhage: Martinus Nijhoff, 1901.

Devisse, Jean. *The Image of the Black in Western Art.* Vol. 2, *From the Early Christian Era to the Age of Discovery,* part 1, *From the Demonic Threat to the Incarnation of Sainthood.* New York: W. Morrow, 1976.

Dewulf, Jeroen. "Emulating a Portuguese Model: The Slave Policy of the West India Company and the Dutch Reformed Church in Dutch Brazil

(1630–1654) and New Netherland (1614–1664) in Comparative Perspective." *Journal of Early American History* 4.1 (2014): 3–36.

Diabaté, Henriette. *Aniaba: Un Assinien à la cour de Louis XIV.* Paris: ABC, 1975.

Dictionnaire des jacobins vivans. Par QUELQU'UN, citoyen français. Hamburg: 1799.

Dickinson, Jonathan. *Jonathan Dickinson's Journal or, God's Protecting Providence. Being the Narrative of a Journey from Port Royal in Jamaica to Philadelphia between August 23, 1696 and April 1, 1697.* Edited by Evangeline Walker Andrews and Charles McLean Andrews. New Haven, CT: Yale UP, 1945.

Diderot, Denis, and Jean-Baptiste le Rond d'Alembert. *Encyclopédie ou Dictionnaire raisonné des sciences, des arts et des métiers.* Paris, 1751–72.

Dobie, Madeleine. *Trading Places: Colonization and Slavery in Eighteenth-Century French Culture.* Ithaca, NY: Cornell UP, 2010.

Donnadieu, Jean-Louis. "Derrière le portrait, l'homme: Jean-Baptiste Belley." *Bulletin de la Société d'Histoire de la Guadeloupe* 170 (2015): 29–54.

Dorigny, Marcel. *Les abolitions de l'esclavage: De L. F. Sonthonax à V. Schoelcher, 1793, 1794, 1848.* Paris: Presses Universitaires de Vincennes et Editions UNESCO, 1995.

Dorigny, Marcel, and Bernard Gainot. *La Société des Amis des Noirs 1788–1799: Contribution à l'histoire de l'abolition de l'esclavage.* Paris: Editions UNESCO, 1998.

Dubois, Laurent. *Avengers of the New World: The Story of the Haitian Revolution.* Cambridge, MA: Harvard UP, 2004.

Dubois, Laurent, and John D. Garrigus. *Slave Revolution in the Caribbean, 1789–1804: A Brief History with Documents.* Boston: Bedford / St. Martin's, 2006.

Duchet, Michèle. *Anthropologie et histoire au siècle des Lumières.* Paris: François Maspero, 1971.

Dufaÿ, Louis-Pierre, et al. *Copie d'une note remise au Comité de Salut Public par la députation de Saint-Domingue.* 1795.

Du Pont de Nemours, Pierre Samuel. "From *Ephémérides du citoyen.*" Charara, 299–310.

Eaton, Arthur Wentworth Hamilton. *The Church of England in Nova Scotia and the Tory Clergy of the Revolution.* New York: Thomas Whittaker, 1891.

Edwards, Jonathan. *The Nature of True Virtue. The Works of Jonathan Edwards,* vol. 8, *Ethical Writings,.* edited by Paul Ramsey. New Haven, CT: Yale UP, 1989. 537–627.

Eekhof, Albert. *Jonas Michaëlius: Founder of the Church in New Netherland.* Leiden: A. W. Sijthoff, 1926.

———. *De negerpredikant Jacobus Elisa Joannes Capitein.* 's Gravenhage: Nijhoff, 1917.

Ehrard, Jean. *Lumières et esclavage: L'esclavage colonial et l'opinion publique en France au XVIIIe siècle.* Waterloo: André Versaille éditeur, 2008.

Elisabeth, Léo. "The French Antilles." *Neither Slave nor Free: The Freedman of African Descent in the Slave Societies of the New World,* edited by David W. Cohen and Jack P. Greene. Baltimore: Johns Hopkins UP, 1972. 134–71.

Emmer, P. C. *De Nederlandse slavenhandel, 1500–1850.* Amsterdam: De Arbeiderspers, 2000.

Equiano, Olaudah. *The Interesting Narrative and Other Writings.* Edited by Vincent Carretta. New York: Penguin, 1995.

Essig, James D. *The Bonds of Wickedness: American Evangelicals against Slavery, 1770-1808.* Philadelphia: Temple UP, 192.

Everts, Natalie. "'Cherchez la femme': Gender-Related Issues in Eighteenth-Century Elmina." *Itinerario* 20.1 (1996): 45–57.

———. "'Huwelijk naar 's lands wijze': Relaties tussen Afrikaanse vrouwen en Europeanen aan de Goudkust (West-Afrika) 1700–1817: Een aanpassing van de beeldvorming." *Tijdschrift voor Geschiedenis* 111 (1998): 598–616.

Ewald, Johann. *Diary of the American War: A Hessian Journal.* Translated by Joseph P. Tustin. New Haven, CT: Yale UP, 1979.

Feinberg, Harvey M. *Africans and Europeans in West Africa: Elminans and Dutchmen on the Gold Coast during the Eighteenth Century.* Philadelphia: American Philosophical Society, 1989.

Fick, Carolyn E. *The Making of Haiti: The Saint Domingue Revolution from Below.* Knoxville: U of Tennessee P, 1990.

Fielding, John. *Extracts from Such of the Penal Laws, as Particularly Relate to the Peace and Good Order of This Metropolis.* London: H. Woodfall and W. Strahan, 1762.

Filson, John. *The Discovery, Settlement and Present State of Kentucke.* Wilmington, DE, 1784.

Findlay, George G., and W. W. Holdsworth. *The History of the Wesleyan Methodist Missionary Society.* Vol. 1. London: Epworth, 1920–24.

Fleming, William, and Elizabeth Fleming. *A Narrative of the Sufferings and Surprizing Deliverances of William and Elizabeth Fleming.* Boston: Green and Russell, 1756.

Fokke Simonsz, Arend. *Amsterdamsche burgers—winteravond-uitspattingen.* Amsterdam: Timmer, 1808.

Fouchard, Jean. "Les joies de la lecture à Saint-Domingue." *Revue d'histoire des colonies* 41.142 (1954): 103–11.

Frey, Sylvia R., and Betty Wood. *Come Shouting to Zion: African American Protestantism in the American South and British Caribbean to 1830.* Chapel Hill: U of North Carolina P, 1998.

Frijhoff, Willem. *Fulfilling God's Mission: The Two Worlds of Dominie Everardus Bogardus, 1607–1647.* Leiden: Brill, 2007.

Fryer, Peter. *Staying Power: The History of Black People in Britain.* London: Pluto, 1984.

Gainot, Bernard. "La députation de Saint-Domingue au corps législatif du Directoire." *Revue française d'histoire d'outre-mer* 84.316 (1997): 95–110.

———. *Les officiers de couleur dans les armées de la République et de l'Empire (1792–1815).* Paris: Karthala, 2007.

Garnsey, Peter. *Ideas of Slavery from Aristotle to Augustine.* Cambridge: Cambridge UP, 1996.

Garran de Coulon, Jean-Philippe. *Rapport sur les troubles de Saint-Domingue.* Paris: Imprimerie Nationale, 1797–99.

Garrettson, Freeborn. *American Methodist Pioneer: The Life and Journals of the Rev. Freeborn Garrettson, 1752–1827.* Edited by Robert Drew Simpson. Rutland, VT, 1984.

Garrigus, John D. "Blue and Brown: Contraband Indigo and the Rise of a Free Colored Planter Class in French Saint-Domingue." *Americas* 50.2 (1993): 233–63.

———. "Catalyst or Catastrophe? Saint-Domingue's Free Men of Color and the Battle of Savannah, 1779–1782." *Revista/review interamericana* 22.1–2 (1992): 109–24.

———. "Opportunist or Patriot? Julien Raimond (1744–1801) and the Haitian Revolution." *Slavery and Abolition* 28.1 (2007): 1–21.
———. "Saint-Domingue's Free People of Color and the Tools of Revolution." Geggus and Fiering, 49–64.
———. "'Thy Coming Fame, Ogé! Is Sure': New Evidence on Ogé's 1790 Revolt and the Beginnings of the Haitian Revolution." *Assumed Identities: The Meanings of Race in the Atlantic World*, edited by John D. Garrigus and Christopher Morris. College Station: Texas A&M UP, 2010. 19–45.
Gates, Henry Louis, Jr. *The Signifying Monkey: A Theory of Afro-American Criticism*. New York: Oxford UP, 1988.
Gauthier, Florence. "Inédits de Belley, Mills et Dufay, députés de Saint-Domingue, de Roume et du Comité de Salut Public." *Annales historiques de la Révolution française* 67.302 (1995): 607–11.
———. "Inédits de Dufay, Santerre et Léonard Leblois, au sujet de l'arrivée de la députation de Saint-Domingue à Paris janvier-février 1794." *Annales historiques de la Révolution française* 65.293 (1993): 514–18.
———. "Le rôle de Julien Raimond dans la formation du nouveau peuple de Saint-Domingue, 1789–1793." *Esclavage, résistances et abolitions*, edited by Marcel Dorigny. Paris: Editions du comité des travaux historiques et scientifiques, 1999. 223–33.
———. "Le rôle de la députation de Saint-Domingue dans l'abolition de l'esclavage." Dorigny, 199–211.
Geggus, David Patrick. *Haitian Revolutionary Studies*. Bloomington: Indiana UP, 2002.
Geggus, David Patrick, and Norman Fiering, eds. *The World of the Haitian Revolution*. Bloomington: Indiana UP, 2009.
George, David. *An Account of the Life of Mr. David George, from Sierra Leone in Africa*. Carretta, *Unchained Voices*, 333–50.
Gerzina, Gretchen. *Black London: Life before Emancipation*. New Brunswick, NJ: Rutgers UP, 1995.
———. "Black Loyalists in London after the American Revolution." *Moving On: Black Loyalists in the Afro-Atlantic World*, edited by John W. Pulis. New York: Garland. 85–102.
Gilbert, Alan. *Black Patriots and Loyalists: Fighting for Emancipation in the War for Independence*. Chicago: U of Chicago P, 2012.
Gilroy, Paul. *The Black Atlantic: Modernity and Double Consciousness*. Cambridge, MA: Harvard UP, 1993.
Godechot, Jacques. "Dejoly et les gens de couleur libres." *Annales historiques de la révolution française* 23 (1951): 48–61.
Goncourt, Edmond de, and Jules de Goncourt. *La Du Barry*. Paris: Charpentier, 1878.
Gouly, Benoît. *Réponse au libelle distribué par l'Affricain Belley*.
———. *Vues générales sur l'importance du commerce des colonies, sur l'origine et le caractère du peuple qui les cultive, ainsi que sur les moyens de faire la constitution qui leur convient*. Paris: Imprimerie Nationale, 1794.
Greene, Lorenzo. *The Negro in Colonial New England, 1620–1776*. New York: Columbia UP, 1942.

Grigsby, Darcy Grimaldo. *Extremities: Painting Empire in Post-Revolutionary France.* New Haven, CT: Yale UP, 2002.

———. "Revolutionary Sons, White Fathers, and Creole Difference: Guillaume Guillon Lethière's *Oath of the Ancestors* of 1822." *Yale French Studies* 101 (2002): 201–26.

Gronniosaw, James Albert Ukawsaw. *A Narrative of the Most Remarkable Particulars in the Life of James Albert Ukawsaw Gronniosaw, an African Prince, as Related by Himself.* Carretta, *Unchained Voices*, 32–58.

Gyles, John. *Memoirs of Odd Adventures, Strange Deliverances, etc., in the Captivity of John Giles, Esq.: Commander of the Garrison on Saint George River, in the District of Maine. Written by Himself.* 1736. Cincinnati: Spiller and Gates, 1869.

Haarnack, Carl, and Dienke Hondius. "'Swart' (Black) in the Netherlands: Africans and Creoles in the Northern Netherlands from the Middle Ages to the Twentieth Century." Schreuder and Kolfin, 88–107.

Hall, Prince. "A Charge Delivered to the Brethren of the African Lodge on the 25th of June, 1792. At the Hall of Brother William Smith, in Charlestown. By the Right Worshipful Master Prince Hall." Brooks and Saillant, 191–98.

———. "A Charge, Delivered to the African Lodge, June 24, 1797, at Menotomy." Brooks and Saillant, 199–208.

Halpern, Jean-Claude. "Les fêtes révolutionnaires et l'abolition de l'esclavage en l'An II." Dorigny, 187–98.

Hamy, M. E. T. "Les cent quarante nègres de M. d'Avaux à Münster (1644): Anecdote ethnologique racontée." *Bulletins et mémoires de la Société d'anthropologie de Paris* 7.7 (1906): 271–89.

Hanley, Ryan. "Calvinism, Proslavery and James Albert Ukawsaw Gronniosaw." *Slavery & Abolition* 36.2 (2015): 360–81.

Hanson, Elizabeth. *An Account of the Captivity of Elizabeth Hanson, Now or Late of Kachecky, in New-England: Who, with Four of Her Children and Servant-Maid, Was Taken Captive by the Indians, and Carried into Canada. Setting Forth the Various Remarkable Occurrences, Sore Trials, and Wonderful Deliverances Which Befel Them after Their Departure, to the Time of Their Redemption. Taken in Substance from Her Own Mouth, by Samuel Bownas. Held Captive by Indians: Selected Narratives, 1642–1836,* edited by Richard VanDerBeets. Knoxville: U of Tennessee P, 1973. 130–50.

Hatch, Nathan O. *The Democratization of American Christianity.* New Haven, CT: Yale UP, 1989.

Hatley, Tom. *The Dividing Paths: Cherokees and South Carolinians through the Era of Revolution.* New York: Oxford UP, 1993.

Haynes, Lemuel. "The Nature and Importance of True Republicanism." *Black Preacher to White America: The Collected Writings of Lemuel Haynes, 1774–1833,* edited by Richard Newman. Brooklyn: Carlson, 1990. 77–88.

Hecht, J. Jean. *Continental and Colonial Servants in Eighteenth Century England.* Northampton, MA: Department of History of Smith College, 1954.

Hindmarsh, D. Bruce. *The Evangelical Conversion Narrative: Spiritual Autobiography in Early Modern England.* New York: Oxford UP, 2005.

Hinks, Peter P. "John Marrant and the Meaning of Early Free Black Freemasonry." *William and Mary Quarterly* 64.1 (2007): 105–16.

Hoare, Prince. *Memoirs of Granville Sharp.* London: Henry Colburn, 1820.

Hodges, Graham Russell, ed. *The Black Loyalist Directory: African Americans in Exile after the American Revolution.* New York: Garland, 1996.

Holmes, Abiel. *A Memoir of the French Protestants Who Settled at Oxford in Massachusetts, A.D. MDCLXXXVI.* Cambridge, MA: Hilliard and Metcalf, 1826.

Hondius, Dienke. "Access to the Netherlands of Enslaved and Free Black Africans: Exploring Legal and Social Historical Practices in the Sixteenth-Nineteenth Centuries." *Slavery & Abolition* 32.3 (2011): 377–95.

———. "Afrikanen in Zeeland, Moren in Middelburg." *Zeeland: Tijdschrift van het Koninklijk Zeeuws Genootschap der Wetenschappen* 14.1 (2005): 13–24.

———. "Black Africans in Seventeenth-Century Amsterdam." *Renaissance and Reformation / Renaissance et Réforme* 31.2 (2008): 89–108.

———. *Blackness in Western Europe: Racial Patterns of Paternalism and Exclusion.* New Brunswick, NJ: Transaction, 2014.

Hopkins, Samuel. "A Dialogue on Slavery, 1776." Bruns, 397–426.

Huussen, Arend H., Jr. "The Dutch Constitution of 1798 and the Problem of Slavery." *Tijdschrift voor rechtsgeschiedenis* 67 (1999): 99–114.

Israel, Jonathan. "The Intellectual Origins of Modern Democratic Republicanism." *European Journal of Political Theory* 3.1 (2004): 7–36.

———. *Radical Enlightenment: Philosophy and the Making of Modernity, 1650-1750.* New York: Oxford UP, 2001.

Jacob, Margaret C., and Wijnand W. Mijnhardt, eds. *The Dutch Republic in the Eighteenth Century: Decline, Enlightenment, and Revolution.* Ithaca, NY: Cornell UP, 1992.

Jones, Charles C., ed. *The Siege of Savannah, in 1779, as Described in Two Contemporaneous Journals of French Officers in the Fleet of Count d'Estaing.* Albany, NY: J. Munsel, 1874.

Jordan, Winthrop D. *White over Black: American Attitudes toward the Negro, 1550-1812.* Chapel Hill: U of North Carolina P, 1968.

Jurriaanse, Maria Wilhelmina. *The Founding of Leyden University.* Leiden: Brill, 1965.

Kantrowitz, Stephen. "'Intended for the Better Government of Man': The Political History of African American Freemasonry in the Era of Emancipation." *Journal of American History* 96.4 (2010): 1001–26.

Kaplan, Paul Henry Daniel. "Black Africans in Hohenstaufen Iconography." *Gesta* 26.1 (1987): 29–36.

Kidd, Thomas S. *George Whitefield: America's Spiritual Founding Father.* New Haven, CT: Yale UP, 2014.

Kidd, Thomas S., and Barry Hankins. *Baptists in America: A History.* New York: Oxford UP, 2015.

King, Boston. *Memoirs of the Life of Boston King, a Black Preacher. Written by Himself, during His Residence at Kingswood School.* Carretta, *Unchained Voices,* 351–68.

King, Stewart R. *Blue Coat or Powdered Wig: Free People of Color in Pre-Revolutionary Saint Domingue.* Athens: U of Georgia P, 2001.

Klein, Herbert S. "Anglicanism, Catholicism and the Negro Slave." *Comparative Studies in Society and History* 8.3 (1966): 295–327.

Kolfin, Elmer. "Black Models in Dutch Art between 1580 and 1800: Fact and Fiction." Schreuder and Kolfin, 70–87.

Kossmann, E. H. *Political Thought in the Dutch Republic.* Amsterdam: Koninklijke Nederlandse Akademie van Wetenschappen, 2000.

Kpobi, David Nii Anum. *Mission in Chains: The Life, Theology and Ministry of the Ex-Slave Jacobus E. J. Capitein (1717-1747) with a Translation of His Major Publications.* Zoetermeer: Uitgeverij Boekencentrum, 1993.

Kuscinski, Auguste. *Les députés au Corps législatif: Conseil des cinq-cents, Conseil des anciens, de l'an IV à l'an VII.* Paris: Au Siège de la Société, 1905.

Kwamena Ekem, John D. "Jacobus Capitein's Translation of 'The Lord's Prayer' into Mfantse: An Example of Creative Mother Tongue Hermeneutics." *Ghana Bulletin of Theology* 2 (2007): 66-79.

Labat, Jean-Baptiste. *Voyage du chevalier Des Marchais en Guinée, isles voisines, et à Cayenne, fait en 1725, 1727 & 1728.* Vol. 2. Paris: Saugrain, 1730.

Labuissonnière, Julien, et al. "Adresse à la Convention Nationale, à tous les clubs et sociétés patriotiques, pour les nègres détenus en esclavage dans les colonies françaises de l'Amérique, sous le régime de la République." *La révolution française et l'abolition de l'esclavage,* vol. 5. Paris: Editions d'Histoire Sociale, 1968.

Laurens, Henry. *The Papers of Henry Laurens.* Vol. 10. Edited by David R. Chesnutt et al. Columbia: U of South Carolina P, 1985.

Laurent, Gérard M. *Haïti et l'indépendance américaine.* Port-au-Prince: Imprimerie du Séminaire Adventiste, 1976.

Lavallée, Joseph. *Le nègre comme il y a peu de blancs.* Edited by Carminella Biondi. Paris: L'Harmattan, 2014.

Lawrence, Alexander A. *Storm over Savannah: The Story of Count d'Estaing and the Siege of the Town in 1776.* Athens: U of Georgia P, 1951.

Lecointe-Marsillac, Jean-Louis. "Le More-Lack." *La révolution française et l'abolition de l'esclavage,* vol. 3. Paris: Editions d'Histoire Sociale, 1968.

Lescallier, Daniel. "Réflexions sur le sort des noirs dans nos colonies." *La révolution française et l'abolition de l'esclavage,* vol. 1. Paris: Editions d'Histoire Sociale, 1968.

Lettre des députés de Saint-Domingue à leurs commettans, en date du 12 août 1789. Paris, 1790.

Levecq, Christine. "Early Dutch Travel Writing on Africa." *Dutch Crossing* 37.3 (November 2013): 220-39.

———. "'We Beg Your Excellency': The Sentimental Politics of Abolitionist Petitions in the Late Eighteenth Century." *Affect and Abolition in the Anglo-Atlantic, 1770-1830,* edited by Stephen Ahern. Burlington, VT: Ashgate, 2013. 151-67.

Levesque, George A. "Inherent Reformers-Inherited Orthodoxy: Black Baptists in London, 1800-1873." *Journal of Negro History* 60.4 (1975): 491-525.

Lewis, Michael. *A Social History of the Navy, 1793-1815.* London: George Allen and Unwin, 1960.

Locke, John. *The Second Treatise on Civil Government.* 1689. Amherst, NY: Prometheus Books, 1986.

Lockley, Tim. "David Margrett: A Black Missionary in the Revolutionary Atlantic." *Journal of American Studies* 46.3 (2012): 729-45.

Lowe, Kate. "The Stereotyping of Black Africans in Renaissance Europe." *Black Africans in Renaissance Europe,* edited by T. F. Earle and K. J. P. Lowe. Cambridge: Cambridge UP, 2005. 17-47.

Lunsingh Scheurleer, T. H., and G. H. M. Posthumus Meyjes, eds. *Leiden University in the Seventeenth Century: An Exchange of Learning.* Leiden: Brill, 1975.

Madiou, Thomas. *Histoire d'Haïti.* Vol. 1. Port-au-Prince: Courtois, 1847.
Marley, David F. *Wars of the Americas: A Chronology of Armed Conflict in the New World, 1492 to the Present.* Santa Barbara, CA: ABC-CLIO, 1998.
Marrant, John. "A Funeral Sermon Preached by the Desire of the Deceased, John Lock; the Text Chosen by Himself, from the Epistle of St. Paul to the Philippians, Chap. 1, ver. 21, and Was Preached according to Promise, before His Father and Mother, Brothers and Sisters, and All the Inhabitants round the Neighbouring Village, by the Rev. John Marrant." Brooks and Saillant, 161–76.

———. *A Journal of the Rev. John Marrant, from August the 18th, 1785, to the 16th of March, 1790.* Brooks and Saillant, 93–160.

———. *A Narrative of the Lord's Wonderful Dealings with John Marrant, a Black, (Now Going to Preach the Gospel in Nova-Scotia) Born in New-York, in North-America. Taken Down from His Own Relation, Arranged, Corrected, and Published by the Rev. Mr. Aldridge. The Fourth Edition, Enlarged by Mr. Marrant, and Printed (with Permission) for His Sole Benefit, with Notes Explanatory.* Carretta, *Unchained Voices,* 110–33.

———. "A Sermon Preached on the 24th Day of June 1789, Being the Festival of St. John the Baptist, at the Request of the Right Worshipful the Grand Master Prince Hall, and the Rest of the Brethren of the African Lodge of the Honorable Society of Free and Accepted Masons in Boston. By the Reverend Brother John Marrant, Chaplain." Brooks and Saillant, 77–92.

Mathews, Donald G. *Slavery and Methodism: A Chapter in American Morality, 1780–1845.* Princeton, NJ: Princeton UP, 1965.
Mathorez, Jules. *Les étrangers en France sous l'Ancien Régime: Histoire de la formation de la population française.* Vol. 1. Paris: Edouard Champion, 1919.
Mavidal, Jérôme, and Emile Laurent, eds. *Archives parlementaires de 1787 à 1860.* First series (1787–1799). Nendeln, Liechtenstein: Kraus-Thomson, 1969.
McClellan, James. *Colonialism and Science: Saint-Domingue in the Old Regime.* Chicago: University of Chicago Press, 2010
McCloy, Shelby T. *The Negro in France.* Lexington: UP of Kentucky, 1961.
McGrath, Elizabeth. "Jacob Jordaens and Moses' Ethiopian Wife." *Journal of the Warburg and Courtauld Institutes* 70 (2007): 247–85.
McLoughlin, William G. *New England Dissent, 1630–1883: The Baptists and the Separation of Church and State.* Vol. 2. Cambridge, MA: Harvard UP, 1971.
Meijer, Miriam Claude. *Race and Aesthetics: On the Anthropology of Petrus Camper (1722–1789).* Amsterdam: Rodopi, 1999.
Mentor, Etienne. *Discours prononcé par Mentor, représentant du peuple, député par la colonie de Saint-Domingue, dans la séance du 12 prairial an 6.* Paris: Imprimerie nationale, 1798.

———. *Discours prononcé par Mentor, sur le projet de résolution tendant à faire annuler les dettes contractées par achat de Noirs. Séance du 24 Vendémiaire an 7.* Paris: Imprimerie Nationale, 1798.

———. *Motion d'ordre faite par Mentor, sur l'arrêté du Directoire exécutif du 3 prairial an 6, relatif aux militaires noirs et de couleur exilés à l'Isle d'Aix.* Paris: Imprimerie Nationale, 1799.

Mercier, Louis. "La vie au Cap Français en 1789." *Revue d'histoire des colonies* 26 (1933): 101–30.

Mercier, Louis-Sébastien. *L'an 2440: Rêve s'il en fut jamais.* Paris: Editions France Adel, 1977.
Mijnhardt, Wijnand. "The Construction of Silence: Religious and Political Radicalism in Dutch History." Van Bunge, 231–62.
———. "The Dutch Enlightenment: Humanism, Nationalism, and Decline." Jacob and Mijnhardt, 197–223.
Miles, Tiya. "'His Kingdom for a Kiss': Indians and Intimacy in the Narrative of John Marrant." *Haunted by Empire: Geographies of Intimacy in North American History,* edited by Ann Laura Stoler. Durham, NC: Duke UP, 2006. 153–88.
Minkema, Kenneth P. "Jonathan Edwards on Slavery and the Slave Trade." *William and Mary Quarterly* 54.4 (1997): 23–34.
———. "Jonathan Edwards's Defense of Slavery." *Massachusetts Historical Review* 4 (2002): 23–59.
Minkema, Kenneth P., and Harry S. Stout. "The Edwardsian Tradition and the Antislavery Debate, 1740–1865." *Journal of American History* 92.1 (2005): 47–74.
Montesquieu, Charles de Secondat. *The Spirit of the Laws.* Translated by Anne M. Cohler, Basia Carolyn Miller, and Harold Samuel Stone. Cambridge: Cambridge UP, 1989.
Moreau de Saint-Méry, Médéric Louis Elie. *Description topographique, physique, civile, politique et historique de la partie française de l'Isle Saint-Domingue.* 3 vols. Philadelphia, 1797.
———. *Loix et constitutions des colonies françoises de l'Amérique Sous le Vent.* 6 vols. Paris, 1784.
Morgan, Philip D. "Black Life in Eighteenth-Century Charleston." *Perspectives in American History,* new series, 1 (1984): 187–232.
Necheles, Ruth. *The Abbé Grégoire, 1787–1831: The Odyssey of an Egalitarian.* Westport, CT: Greenwood, 1971.
Nemours, Alfred. *Haïti et la guerre de l'indépendance américaine.* Port-au-Prince: Henri Deschamps, 1952.
Newman, Richard S., and Roy E. Finkenbine. "Black Founders in the New Republic." *William and Mary Quarterly* 64.1 (2007): 83–94.
Noorlander, Danny L. "Serving God and Mammon: The Reformed Church and the Dutch West India Company in the Atlantic World, 1621–1674." Ph.D. diss., Georgetown University, 2011.
Northolt, Maurits. "Nageslacht van Carolina van Emicke en Hans Joachim Emicke." *Wi Rutu: Tijdschrift voor Surinaamse genealogie* 5.2 (2005): 30–41.
Norton, Mary Beth. "The Fate of Some Black Loyalists of the American Revolution." *Journal of Negro History* 58.4 (Oct 1973): 402–26.
Nussbaum, Martha. "Patriotism and Cosmopolitanism." *Boston Review* 19.5 (1994): 3–16.
Ogé, Vincent. "Motion Faite par M. Vincent Ogé, jeune à l'Assemblée des Colons, Habitans de Saint-Domingue, à l'Hôtel de Massiac, Place des Victoires." *La révolution française et l'abolition de l'esclavage,* vol. 11. Paris: Editions d'Histoire Sociale, 1968.
Oostindie, Gert, and Emy Maduro. *In het land van de overheerser: Antillianen en Surinamers in Nederland, 1634/1667–1954.* Dordrecht: Forlis, 1986.

Owens, Loulie Latimer. *Oliver Hart, 1723-1795: A Biography.* Greenville: South Carolina Baptist Historical Society, 1966.
Paasman, Bert. "Mens of dier? Beeldvorming over negers in de tijd voor de rassentheorieën." *Vreemd gespuis,* edited by Jan Erik Dubbelman and Jaap Tanja. Amsterdam: Anne Frank Stichting, 1987. 92-107.
———. *Reinhart: Nederlandse literatuur en slavernij ten tijde van de Verlichting.* Leiden: Nijhoff, 1984.
Page, Pierre-François, and Augustin-Jean Brulley. *Développement des causes des troubles et désastres des colonies françaises.* N.p., n.d.
Peabody, Sue. *"There Are No Slaves in France": The Political Culture of Race and Slavery in the Ancien Régime.* New York: Oxford UP, 1996.
Perkins, Simeon. *The Diary of Simeon Perkins, 1780-1789.* Toronto: Champlain Society, 1958.
Perraud, Léonie. *Notice biographique sur M. Garnot.* Paris: Bureau du Panthéon Biographique Universel, 1851.
Petit, Jacques, Pierre Bardin, Bernadette Rossignol, and Philippe Rossignol. "Actes signés par J. B. Belley dans les registres conservés du Cap Français (1777-1788)." Complement to *Généalogie et Histoire de la Caraïbe* 241 (2010): 6506-11. https://www.ghcaraibe.org/bul/ghc241/actes-belley.html.
———. "Le décès de Jean-Baptiste BELLEY (ex-député de Saint-Domingue à la Convention) et de son demi-frère Joseph DOMINGUE."
Piquet, Jean-Daniel. *L'émancipation des Noirs dans la Révolution française (1789-1795).* Paris: Karthala, 2002.
Pocock, J. G. A. *The Machiavellian Moment: Florentine Political Thought and the Atlantic Republican Tradition.* Princeton, NJ: Princeton UP, 1975.
Popkin, Jeremy D. *You Are All Free: The Haitian Revolution and the Abolition of Slavery.* New York: Cambridge UP, 2010.
Postma, Johannes Menne. *The Dutch in the Atlantic Slave Trade, 1600-1815.* Cambridge: Cambridge UP, 1990.
Potkay, Adam, and Sandra Burr, eds. *Black Atlantic Writers of the Eighteenth Century.* Houndmills: Macmillan, 1995.
Prah, Kwesi Kwaa. *Jacobus Eliza Johannes Capitein, 1717-1747: A Critical Study of an Eighteenth-Century African.* Braamfontein: Skotaville, 1989.
Prévost, Antoine François. "Speech de Moses Sam Boom." *Le pour et contre* 6 (1735): 340-53.
Price-Mars, Jean. "Les origines et le destin d'un nom: Jean-Baptiste Belley Mars, l'ancêtre." *Revue de la société haïtienne d'histoire et de géographie* 12.36 (1940): 1-24.
"Procès-verbal d'élection des députés de Saint Domingue. Séance du 23 sept. 1793." Mavidal and Laurent, 84:265-66.
Proes, L. "Asar." *De Navorscher* 27 (1877): 49-52.
Quaque, Philip. *The Life and Letters of Philip Quaque.* Edited by Vincent Carretta and Ty M. Reese. Athens: U of Georgia P, 2010.
Quarles, Benjamin. *The Negro in the American Revolution.* New York: Norton, 1961.
Raimond, Julien. *Observations adressées à l'Assemblée Nationale, par un député des colons amériquains.* 1789.
———. *Réclamations adressées à l'Assemblée Nationale, par les personnes de couleur, propriétaires & cultivateurs de la colonie françoise de Saint-Domingue.* 1789.

———. *Véritable origine des troubles de Saint-Domingue, et des différentes causes qui les ont produits.* Paris, 1792.
Rawlyk, G. A. *The Canada Fire: Radical Evangelicalism in British North America, 1775-1812.* Kingston, ON: McGill-Queen's University Press, 1994.
Ray, Alexandre. *Réimpression de l'ancien Moniteur.* 32 vols. Paris: Plon, 1854.
Raynal, Guillaume Thomas François, ed. *Histoire philosophique et politique des établissements & du commerce des Européens dans les deux Indes.* Vol. 4, book 11. The Hague, 1774.
Reiss, Tom. *The Black Count: Glory, Revolution, Betrayal, and the Real Count of Monte Cristo.* New York: Broadway Books, 2012.
Robertson, William. *The History of America.* Vol. 2. London: 1821.
Rodger, N. A. M. *The Wooden World: An Anatomy of the Georgian Navy.* London: Collins, 1986.
Rodgers, Daniel T. "Republicanism: The Career of a Concept." *Journal of American History* 79.1 (1992): 11–38.
Rogers, Dominique. "On the Road to Citizenship: The Complex Route to Integration of the Free People of Color in the Two Capitals of Saint-Domingue." Geggus and Fiering, 65–78.
Rosen, Robert N. *A Short History of Charleston.* Columbia: U of South Carolina P, 1992.
Rouvray, Laurent-François Le Noir. *De l'état des nègres relativement à la prospérité des colonies françaises et de leur métropole.* Paris, 1789.
Rowlandson, Mary. *A Narrative of the Captivity and Restoration of Mrs. Mary Rowlandson.* Baym, 236–67.
Ruffin, J. Rixey. *A Paradise of Reason: William Bentley and Enlightenment Christianity in the Early Republic.* New York: Oxford UP, 2008.
Ruttenburg, Nancy. "George Whitefield, Spectacular Conversion, and the Rise of Democratic Personality." *American Literary History* 5.3 (1993): 429–58.
Ryan, William R. *The World of Thomas Jeremiah: Charles Town on the Eve of the American Revolution.* New York: Oxford UP, 2010.
Saillant, John. "African American Engagements with Edwards in the Era of the Slave Trade." *Jonathan Edwards at 300: Essays on the Tercentenary of His Birth*, edited by Harry S. Stout et al. UP of America, 2005. 141–51.
———. "Antiguan Methodism and Antislavery Activity: Anne and Elizabeth Hart in the Eighteenth-Century Black Atlantic." *Church History* 69.1 (2000): 86–115.
———. *Black Puritan, Black Republican: The Life and Thought of Lemuel Haynes, 1753-1833.* New York: Oxford UP, 2003.
———. "Make a Black Life, and Bid It Sing: Sacred Song in *The Life, History, and Unparalleled Sufferings of John Jea*." *a/b: Auto/Biography Studies* 31.1 (2016): 147–73.
———. "'Remarkably Emancipated from Bondage, Slavery, and Death': An African American Retelling of the Puritan Captivity Narrative, 1820." *Early American Literature* 29.2 (1994): 122–40.
———. "'Wipe Away All Tears from Their Eyes': John Marrant's Theology in the Black Atlantic, 1785–1808." *Journal of Millennial Studies* 1.2 (1999). http://www.mille.org/publications/winter98/saillant.PDF.
Saint-Lambert, Jean-François de. "Essai sur le luxe." 1764.

———. "Réflexions sur les moyens de rendre meilleur l'état des nègres ou des affranchis de nos colonies." Duchet, 181–93.
———. *Ziméo*. Charara, 49–78.
Sarter, Caesar. "Essay on Slavery." *Race and Revolution*, edited by Gary B. Nash. Madison, WI: Madison House, 1990. 167–70.
Schama, Simon. *Citizens*. New York: Random House, 1989.
———. *The Embarrassment of Riches: An Interpretation of Dutch Culture in the Golden Age*. New York: Vintage, 1997.
———. *Rough Crossings: Britain, the Slaves, and the American Revolution*. New York: Ecco, 2006.
Schlenther, Boyd Stanley. *Queen of the Methodists: The Countess of Huntingdon and the Eighteenth-Century Crisis of Faith and Society*. Durham, UK: Durham Academic, 1997.
———. "'To Convert the Poor People in America': The Bethesda Orphanage and the Thwarted Zeal of the Countess of Huntingdon." *Georgia Historical Quarterly* 78.2 (1994): 225–56.
Schlereth, Thomas J. *The Cosmopolitan Ideal in Enlightenment Thought: Its Form and Function in the Ideas of Franklin, Hume, and Voltaire, 1694–1790*. Notre Dame, IN: U of Notre Dame P, 1977.
Schmidt, Benjamin. *Innocence Abroad: The Dutch Imagination and the New World, 1570–1670*. New York: Cambridge UP, 2001.
Schmidt, Leigh Eric. "'A Second and Glorious Reformation': The New Light Extremism of Andrew Croswell." *William and Mary Quarterly* 43.2 (1986): 214–44.
Schreuder, Esther. "'Blacks' in Court Culture in the Period 1300–1900: Propaganda and Consolation." Schreuder and Kolfin, 20–31.
Schreuder, Esther, and Elmer Kolfin, eds. *Black Is Beautiful: Rubens to Dumas*. Zwolle: Waanders, 2008.
Schutte, G. J. "Bij het schemerlicht van hun tijd: Zeventiende-eeuwse gereformeerden en de slavenhandel." *Mensen van de Nieuwe Tijd*, edited by M. Bruggeman et al. Amsterdam: Bert Bakker, 1996. 193–217.
———. *Het Indisch Sion: De Gereformeerde kerk onder de Verenigde Oost-Indische Compagnie*. Hilversum: Verloren, 2002.
"Séance du 21 Pluviôse." *Journal de la Montagne* 92 (13 February 1794): 732–33.
Sekora, John. "Red, White, and Black: Indian Captivities, Colonial Printers, and the Early African-American Narrative." *A Mixed Race: Ethnicity in Early America*, edited by Frank Shuffelton. New York: Oxford UP, 1993. 92–104.
Sensbach, Jon F. *Rebecca's Revival: Creating Black Christianity in the Atlantic World*. Cambridge, MA: Harvard UP, 2005.
Sepinwall, Alyssa Goldstein. *The Abbé Grégoire and the French Revolution: The Making of Modern Universalism*. Berkeley: U of California P, 2005.
———, ed. *Haitian History: New Perspectives*. New York: Routledge, 2013.
Sesay, Chernoh M., Jr. "Respectability and Representation: Black Freemasonry, Race, and Early Free Black Leadership." *Black Knowledges / Black Struggles: Essays in Critical Epistemology*, edited by Jason R. Ambroise and Sabine Broeck. Liverpool: Liverpool UP, 2015. 44–67.

Shipton, Clifford K. *Sibley's Harvard Graduates: Biographical Sketches of Those Who Attended Harvard College in the Classes 1726-1730*. Vol. 3. Boston: Massachusetts Historical Society, 1951.

"A Short Account of the British Plantations in America." *London Magazine. Or, Gentleman's Monthly Intelligencer,* July 1755, 307-12.

Skinner, Quentin. *The Foundations of Modern Political Thought*. 2 vols. New York: Cambridge UP, 1978.

Slotkin, Richard. *Regeneration through Violence: The Mythology of the American Frontier, 1600-1860*. Middletown, CT: Wesleyan UP, 1973.

Sluiter, Engel. "Dutch Maritime Power and the Colonial Status Quo, 1585-1641." *Pacific Historical Review* 11.1 (1942): 29-41.

———. "New Light on the '20. And Odd Negroes' Arriving in Virginia, August 1619." *William and Mary Quarterly* 54.2 (1997): 395-98.

Smith, John. "From *The General History of Virginia, New England, and the Summer Isles*." Baym, 57-66.

Sonthonax, Léger Félicité. "Colonies françaises." *Révolutions de Paris* 63 (18-25 September 1790): 517-24.

Spaans Azn., Martin, and Sv. E. Veldhuijzen. "Congo Loango / Congo Lowango." *Wi Rutu: Tijdschrift voor Surinaamse genealogie* 3 (2003): 36-47.

Sprague, William Buell. *Annals of the American Pulpit; Or Commemorative Notices of Distinguished American Clergymen of Various Denominations, from the Early Settlement of the Country to the Close of the Year Eighteen Hundred and Fifty-Five*. Vol. 6. New York: Robert Carter and Brothers, 1860.

Stein, Robert Louis. *Léger Félicité Sonthonax: The Lost Sentinel of the Republic*. Cranbury, NJ: Associated UPs, 1985.

Stillman, Samuel. *Charity Considered in a Sermon Preached at Charles-Town, June 24, 1785, before the Most Ancient and Honorable Society of Free and Accepted Masons*. Boston: T. and J. Fleet, 1785.

———. *A Discourse Delivered before the Members of the Boston Female Asylum*. Boston: Russell and Cutler, 1801.

———. *A Discourse Preached in Boston, before the Massachusetts Baptist Missionary Society*. Boston: Manning and Loring, 1803.

———. "The Duty of Magistrates." *The Patriot Preachers of the American Revolution,* edited by Frank Moore. New York: C. T. Evans, 1862. 261-88.

———. *Good News from a Far Country: A Sermon Preached at Boston, May 17, 1766, upon the Arrival of the Important News of the Repeal of the Stamp-Act*. Boston: Kneeland and Adams, 1766.

———. *An Oration, Delivered July 4th, 1789, at the Request of the Inhabitants of the Town of Boston, in Celebration of the Anniversary of American Independence*. Boston: B. Edes and Son, 1789.

Tanis, James. *Dutch Calvinistic Pietism in the Middle Colonies: A Study in the Life and Theology of Theodorus Jacobus Frelinghuysen*. The Hague: Martinus Nijhoff, 1967.

Thomany, Pierre. *Motion d'ordre faite par P. Thomany, député du Département du Nord de Saint-Domingue, sur l'anniversaire de la liberté des noirs dans les colonies françaises*. Séance du 16 Pluviôse an VII. Paris: Imprimerie Nationale, 1799.

Thornton, John. "The African Experience of the '20. And Odd Negroes' Arriving in Virginia in 1619." *William and Mary Quarterly* 55.3 (1998): 421-34.

Tilton, Robert S. *Pocahontas: The Evolution of an American Narrative*. New York: Cambridge UP, 1994.
Tyson, John R., with Boyd S. Schlenther, eds. *In the Midst of Early Methodism: Lady Huntingdon and Her Correspondence*. Lanham, MD: Scarecrow, 2006.
Unger, W. S. "Bijdragen tot de geschiedenis van de Nederlandse slavenhandel." *Economisch-historisch jaarboek: Bijdragen tot de economische geschiedenis van Nederland* 26 (1954): 133–74.
Upton, William H. *Prince Hall's Letter Book*. Margats: H. Keble.
Van Bunge, Wiep, ed. *The Early Enlightenment in the Dutch Republic, 1650–1750*. Leiden: Brill, 2003.
Van Bunge, Wiep, et al., eds. *The Dictionary of Seventeenth and Eighteenth-Century Philosophers*. Bristol: Thoemmes Press, 2003. 2 vols.
Van Dantzig, Albert. *Les Hollandais sur la côte de Guinée à l'époque de l'essor de l'Ashanti et du Dahomey, 1680–1740*. Paris: Société Française d'Histoire d'Outre-Mer, 1980.
Van den Berg, Johannes. *Religious Currents and Cross-Currents: Essays on Early Modern Protestantism and the Protestant Enlightenment*. Leiden: Brill, 1999.
Van den Boogaart, Ernst. *Civil and Corrupt Asia: Image and Text in the "Itinerario" and the "Icones" of Jan Huygen van Linschoten*. Chicago: U of Chicago P, 2003.
Van der Wall, Ernestine. "The Religious Context of the Early Dutch Enlightenment: Moral Religion and Society." Van Bunge, 39–57.
Van der Zee, Henri. *'s Heeren slaaf: Het dramatische leven van Jacobus Capitein*. Amsterdam: Balans, 2000.
Van Dillen, Johannes Gerard. "The West India Company, Calvinism and Politics." *Dutch Authors on West Indian History: A Historiographical Selection,* edited by M. A. P. Meilink-Roelofsz. The Hague: Martinus Nijhoff, 1982. 146–80.
Van Kempen, Michiel. *Een geschiedenis van de Surinaamse literatuur*. Breda: De Geus, 2003.
Verbeek, Theo. *Descartes and the Dutch: Early Reactions to Cartesian Philosophy, 1637–1650*. Carbondale: Southern Illinois UP, 1992.
Verneuil, Louis François René, et al. *Au Comité de Salut Public, Observations sur une note remise par Dufaÿ, Garnot, Mills, Belley et Boisson*. Paris: Imprimerie de Laurens aîné, 1795.
Voltaire. *"Candide," "Zadig," and Selected Stories*. Translated by Daniel M. Frame. New York: New American Library, 1961.
Vrij, Jean Jacques. "Jan Elias van Onna en het 'politiek systhema' van de Surinaamse slaventijd, circa 1770–1820." *Oso: Tijdschrift voor Surinaamse taalkunde, letterkunde en geschiedenis* 17 (1998): 130–47.
Wakeley, J. B. *Lost Chapters Recovered from the Early History of American Methodism*. New York: Carlton and Porter, 1858.
Walker, James W. St. G. *The Black Loyalists: The Search for a Promised Land in Nova Scotia and Sierra Leone, 1783–1870*. New York: Dalhousie UP, 1976.
Walzer, Michael. *The Revolution of the Saints: A Study in the Origins of Radical Politics*. New York: Atheneum, 1970.
Wanquet, Claude. *La France et la première abolition de l'esclavage, 1794–1802: Le cas des colonies orientales Ile de France (Maurice) et La Réunion*. Paris: Karthala, 1998.
Weber, B. C., and M. E. McIntosh. "Une correspondance familiale au temps des troubles de Saint-Domingue (1791–1796). Lettres du marquis et de la

marquise de Rouvray à leur fille." *Revue d'histoire des colonies* 45.159–60 (1958): 119–279.
Wesley, Charles H. *Prince Hall: Life and Legacy.* 2nd ed. Washington, DC: United Supreme Council, 1983.
Wesley, John. *The Letters of the Rev. John Wesley, A.M.* Vol. 7. Edited by John Telford. London: Epworth, 1931.
Wheatley, Phillis. *Complete Writings.* Edited by Vincent Carretta. New York: Penguin, 2001.
Wheeler, Roxann. *The Complexion of Race: Categories of Difference in Eighteenth-Century British Culture.* Philadelphia: U of Pennsylvania P, 2000.
Whitchurch, Samuel. *A Negro Convert, a Poem; Being the Substance of the Experience of Mr. John Marrant, a Negro, as Related by Himself, Previous to His Ordination, at the Countess of Huntingdon's Chapel in Bath, on Sunday the 15th of May, 1785, Together with a Concise Account of the Most Remarkable Events in His Very Singular Life.* Bath, n.d.
Whitefield, George. *George Whitefield's Journals.* Edited by William V. Davis. Gainesville, FL: Scholars' Facsimiles and Reprints, 1969.
———. *Memoirs of Rev. George Whitefield.* Middletown, CT: Hunt and Noyes, 1841.
———. *A Short Account of God's Dealings with the Reverend Mr. George Whitefield.* Whitefield, *Journals*, 23–64.
———. *Three Letters from the Reverend Mr. G. Whitefield.* Philadelphia, 1740.
Whitehead, Ruth Holmes. *Black Loyalists: Southern Settlers of Nova Scotia's First Free Black Communities.* Halifax: Nimbus, 2013.
Whytock, Jack C. "The Huntingdonian Mission to Nova Scotia, 1782–1791: A Study in Calvinistic Methodism." *Canadian Society of Church History Historical Papers 2003,* edited by Bruce L. Guenther. Canadian Society of Church History, 2003. 149–70.
Wigger, John H. *Taking Heaven by Storm: Methodism and the Rise of Popular Christianity in America.* New York: Oxford UP, 1998.
Williams, John. *The Redeemed Captive Returning to Zion or the Captivity and Deliverance of Rev. John Williams of Deerfield.* Springfield, MA: H. R. Huntting, 1908.
Williamson, Peter. *French and Indian Cruelty; Exemplified in the Life and Various Vicissitudes of Fortune of Peter Williamson.* 1757. Bristol: Thoemmes, 1996.
Wilson, Ellen Gibson. *The Loyal Blacks.* New York: Putnam's, 1976.
Wood, Nathan E. *The History of the First Baptist Church of Boston (1665–1899).* Philadelphia: American Baptist Publication Society, 1899.
Wood, Peter. "'Jesus Has Got Thee at Last': Afro-American Conversion as a Forgotten Chapter in Eighteenth-Century Southern Intellectual History." *Bulletin of the Center for the Study of Southern Culture and Religion* 3.3 (1979): 1–7.
Woodson, Carter G. *The Education of the Negro prior to 1861: A History of the Education of the Colored People of the United States from the Beginning of Slavery to the Civil War.* 2nd ed. Washington, DC: Associated Publishers, 1919.
Zarate, Augustin de. *A History of the Discovery and Conquest of Peru.* Translated by Thomas Nicholas. London: Penguin, 1933.
Zijp, R. P. "Predikanten in Guinea, 1600–1800." *De heiden moest eraan geloven: Geschiedenis van zending, missie en ontwikkelingssamenwerking.* Utrecht: Stichting Het Catharijneconvent, 1983. 30–37.
Zwager, H. H. *Nederland en de Verlichting.* Bussum: Fibula-Van Dishoeck, 1972.

INDEX

abolition: and Calvinism, 8, 10–12, 49–50, 225–26; French abolitionism, 16, 89, 97, 99–100, 117–41, 143–44, 146, 151–52, 154–55; and the Haitian Revolution, 97–101, 104–5, 139; and Methodism, 206, 224; US abolitionism, 181, 195, 206, 219
Act of Abjuration (Plakkaat van Verlatinghe, 1851), 25
Ailhaud, Jean Antoine, 100, 103
Alberti, Johannes, 46
Aldridge, William, 165–66, 180, 191
Alline, Henry, 200–201, 203–5
Allstyne, Jonathan, 216
Althusius, Johannes, 51
Amar, Jean-Pierre-André, 143
American Revolution: black loyalists, 197–98; influence on French Revolution, 85, 87; and Marrant's *Narrative*, 160, 165, 167, 184; and republicanism, 4–5, 14
Anderson's Constitutions of 1723, 233
Aniaba, 111
Annecy, Jean-Louis, 151
Antinomianism, 204–5
Arbuthnot, Marriot, 188
Aristophanes, 27
Aristotle, 5, 29, 46, 48, 50
Arminius, Jacobus, 44
Articles of Capitulation, 198
Asbury, Francis, 204–5
Ash, William, 217
Atahualpa, 176
Auba, Etienne, 86
Augustin, Pierre, 84–85, 87

Backer, Willem, 55
Baker, John, 193
Baker, Keith Michael, 120
Bakkers, Wolmetje, 40
Baley, Charles, 213
Barber, Francis, 193
Barère, Bertrand, 119, 143
Barrère, Pierre, 116
Bartelink, Egbert Jacobus, 41–42
Batt, John, 220
Baudière, Ferrand de, 132
Bazonga, Isaac, 156–57
Bean, John, 259n93
Beaufort, Lieven de, 26
Beaumarchais, Pierre, 79
Beef, Jack, 193
Behn, Aphra, 126
Bekker, Balthasar, 23
Belknap, Jeremy, 221–22, 261n122
Belley, Jean-Baptiste: and the French Revolution, 91–92, 97, 99; life, 1–3, 6, 12, 14–16, 188, 245n35; life in Saint-Domingue, 76–81, 83–91, 152–53, 157–58; and the National Convention in Paris, 75–76, 106, 143–48, 151; and racial identity in France, 108, 112, 117, 141; and republicanism, 4, 100, 103–5, 107–8, 119, 128, 140–41, 145–50, 154, 156, 161
Belley, Joseph Domingue, 159
Benderius, Laurentius, 64
Benezet, Anthony, 11
Benot, Yves, 130, 137, 144
Bentley, William, 220–21
Berlin, Ira, 3
Beunje, Jacobus de, 71

Billaud-Varenne, Jacques Nicolas, 142
Bisetus, 27
Black, William, 204–5, 207
Blakely, Allison, 55, 241n101
Blanchelande, Vicomte de, 98
Blucke, Margaret, 217–18
Blucke, Stephen, 217
Boardman, Richard, 205
Bodin, Jean, 30
Boeckhorst, Jan, 54
Boerhaave, Herman, 24
Boileau, 79
Boisrond, Louis François, 151
Boisson, Joseph Georges, 103, 106–7, 148, 151–53, 157
Bolster, W. Jeffrey, 185
Bonaparte, Napoleon, 158–59
Boni Rebellion, 42
Boogaart, Ernst van den, 36
Book of Negroes, 198–99, 202, 207, 217
Boone, Daniel, 178–79
Bossuet, Jacques-Bénigne, 111
Boufflers, Knight de, 113
Boulle, Pierre H., 115
Boutin, Father, 80
Bowdoin, James, 221
Breynton, John, 201
Brissot de Warville, Jacques Pierre, 101, 128–29, 133–34, 142, 145
Brooks, Joanna, 259n78, 259n83
Brothier, Martin Noël, 151
Brown, Thomas, 179, 257n14
Brulley, Augustin-Jean, 142–48, 253n203
Bruni, Leonardo, 6
Buffon, Georges-Louis Leclerc, Count de, 37, 116–17
Bundock, Michael, 194
Bunyan, John, 163–64
Burr, Sandra, 259n88
Busbecq, Augier Ghislain de, 50
Buve, Raymond, 239n54

Calvin, John, 7, 47–48
Calvinism: and abolitionism, 10–12, 50–51; and antinomianism, 204; and Jacobus Capitein, 1, 7, 15–16, 21, 24, 30, 44–49, 72; and the Dutch Enlightenment, 1, 15–16, 21; and John Marrant, 160, 168, 174, 208, 212, 214, 218–20, 223, 230; and republicanism, 7–8; and slavery, 30, 44–51, 208, 212, 225–27
Camboulas, Simon, 117
Cameron, Christopher, 223
Campbell, Joseph, 178
Campbell, Lord, 186–87
Camper, Petrus, 37, 116
Cap, Jean-Baptiste, 98
Capitein, Jacobus: and Calvinism, 1, 4, 7, 12, 15–16, 21, 24, 30, 44–49, 72, 160, 241nn107–8, 243n139; and civic humanism, 26–27, 29; death, 74; defense of slavery, 19–20, 30, 38, 44–51, 57–58, 183; life, 1–4, 6–7, 12, 14–16, 21–26; life in Elmina, 59–73; race and identity, 14, 33–34, 37, 41, 44, 161; republicanism, 24–27, 29–32, 112; self-image, 51–59; stoicism, 28
Carleton, Sir Guy, 198
Carretta, Vincent, 9, 258n30
Cezar, Joseph dit, 87, 99
Champlain, Samuel de, 214
Channing, William Ellery, 222
Charles (king of England), 176
Chaumette, Pierre Gaspard, 140
Chauncy, Charles, 174
Chipman, William, 207
Choiseul, Duke de, 115
Choiseul-Praslin, Count de, 113
Cicero, 5–6, 27–28, 46
civic humanism, 4, 6, 26–27. *See also* republicanism
Clarkson, Thomas, 99
Clavière, Brissot, 122
Clavière, Etienne, 122, 142
Clinton, Henry, 181, 188, 258n31
Cocceius, Johannes, 45–46, 48, 52
Cohen, William B., 248n90
Colbert, Sampson, 202
Colman, Benjamin, 225

Conny, John, 61
Constantine the Great, 48
constitutionalism, 8, 29–30
conversion narratives, 163–65, 170; *Narrative of the Lord's Wonderful Dealings with John Marrant,* 160–65, 167–80, 183–84
Cook, Joseph, 165–66
Corday, Charlotte, 119
Cornwallis, Charles, 197, 206
cosmopolitanism: and Jean-Baptiste Belley, 6, 16, 76, 78, 91, 141–42, 154; and Jacobus Capitein, 6, 16, 20–21, 30, 41–42, 60, 68, 73–74; definition of, 1–4; and freemasonry, 235; and John Marrant, 6, 17, 160–61, 167, 185, 188, 192, 208, 218, 220, 234–35; and military service, 156. *See also* republicanism
Countess of Roosendaal, 40
Coymans, Balthasar, 35
Croswell, Andrew, 224
Crucius, Johannes, 49
Cugoano, Quobna Ottobah, 193, 195
Cuming, Alexander, 181
Cunaeus, Peter, 58
Curran, Andrew S., 116

Dalton, Scipio, 222
Danton, Georges, 75, 117, 119
Dapper, Olfert, 43
d'Arcy, Louis-Marthe Gouy, 131
Daval, Jean, 109
Daval, Guillaume, 109
d'Avaux, Count, 109
David, Jacques-Louis, 102, 112
Davis, John, 175
Debien, Gabriel, 133
De Bordes, Martinus, 62, 64
Declaration of the Rights of Man and of the Citizen, 93, 105, 130
Dejoly, Etienne Louis Hector, 94, 130, 133–34
De La Court, Johan, 29
Delacroix, Jean-François, 118, 144

De Marees, Pieter, 36
Denucé, Jan, 54
De Petersen, Jacob, 60, 62, 73
d'Eppes, Robert, 109
De Sales, Jean-Baptiste-Claude Delisle, 116
Descartes, René, 23, 45
Desjean, Bernard, 86
Dessalines, Jean-Jacques, 159
d'Estaing, Count, 88–90
De Touchelongue, Fleuriau, 95
De Vogel, Pieter, 23
De Witt, Johan, 25
Dewulf, Jeroen, 242n126
d'Holbach, Paul-Henri Thiry, 23
Dickinson, Jonathan, 172
Diderot, Denis, 117, 124–25
Dobie, Madeleine, 123
Donnadieu, Jean-Louis, 87
Du Barry, Countess, 113
Dufaÿ, Louis-Pierre, 75, 106–7, 118, 138–39, 143–44, 150–51, 154, 158
Dumas, Alexandre (author), 112
Dumas, Alexandre (general), 112, 136, 148
Dunmore, Lord, 187, 197
Du Pont de Nemours, Pierre Samuel, 123
Dürer, Albrecht, 54
Dutch Enlightenment, 15–16, 24. *See also* Calvinism; republicanism
Dutch Reformed Church, 21–22, 44, 48, 65, 69. *See also* Calvinism
Duverne, Isaac, 34

Edwards, Jonathan, 11, 225–26, 231–32
Eekhof, Albert, 56
Ehrard, Jean, 121
Emicke, Johanna, 40
English Civil War, 5, 8, 189
Equiano, Olaudah, 9–11, 194–95
Erasmus of Rotterdam, 22
Essig, James D., 224
evangelism, 7, 9, 16, 65, 68, 161–67, 177, 189, 191, 203, 204–6, 224.

evangelism (*continued*)
See also antinomianism; Capitein, Jacobus; Great Awakening; Marrant, John; Methodism; Whitefield, George
Everts, Natalie, 69

Feinberg, Harvey M., 242n130, 243n133
Fielding, Sir John, 194
Filson, John, 179
Finkenbine, Roy E., 219
Fleming, Elizabeth, 179
Fouquier-Thinville, Antoine, 147
François I, 109
Franklin, Benjamin, 182
Frederick II, Holy Roman Emperor, 53
freemasonry, 1, 4, 15, 17, 160–61, 218–19, 221, 228–29, 231–35
Frelinghuysen, Theodorus Jacobus, 10, 46
French and Indian War, 179–80
French Revolution, 1–2, 15–16, 76, 91–97, 100, 108, 117–19, 147. *See also* Haitian Revolution
Frey, Sylvia R., 204
Fryer, Peter, 194
Furmage, William, 216

Gainot, Bernard, 136, 157–58
Galbaud, Thomas François, 103, 138
Garat, Dominique Joseph, 129
Garcia, Antonio, 35
Garnot, Pierre-Nicolas, 106–7, 148, 151
Garrettson, Freeborn, 205–8, 215–17
Garrigus, John D., 100, 245n39
Gates, Henry Louis, Jr., 175–76
George, David, 201–4, 207
Gerzina, Gretchen, 192
Gilbert, Alan, 258n53
Gilroy, Paul, 237n5
Girodet de Roussy-Trioson, Anne-Louis, 140
Gomarus, Franciscus, 44

Gouly, Benoît-Louis, 149–51
Gradis, Abraham, 113
Graham, Billy, 164
Gravesande, Willem 's, 24
Great Awakening, 163, 174, 181, 200, 203–4, 224
Grégoire, Abbé, 95–96, 101, 129, 131, 133, 137, 144
Grigsby, Darcy Grimaldo, 141
Grillo, Domingo, 35
Gronniosaw, James Albert Ukawsaw, 9–10, 46, 168–69, 176, 193–94
Grotius, Hugo, 49–50
Gyles, John, 179

Habersham, James, 190
Haitian Revolution, 16, 91, 97–100, 144
Hall, Primus, 222
Hall, Prince, 220–22, 224, 233, 235, 259n88, 260n102
Handley, Scipio, 198
Hanson, Elizabeth, 173, 179
Hanssen, Philip Samuel, 41
Hanssen, Susanna, 41
Harding, Harris, 203
Harmenopoulos, 27
Hart, Oliver, 166, 186, 203, 227
Hatch, Nathan O., 206
Haynes, Lemuel, 11–12, 16, 225–28
Hazard, Ebenezer, 222
Hébert, Jacques, 156
Hector, Charles, 88
Hédouville, Gabriel, 152–53
Heinsius, Daniel, 24
Heinsius, Nicolaas, 24
Hendricksen, Meynaert, 64
Henri III (king of France), 109
Hérault de Séchelles, Marie-Jean, 135
Hermansz, Jan, 63
Herries, Elizabeth, 218
Heurnius, Pastor, 50
Hobbes, Thomas, 29
Hondius, Dienke, 39
Hondius, Jacobus, 49

Hopkins, Samuel, 12, 225–26, 228–29, 232
Horace, 27
Houtman, Abraham, 63
Howe, Sir William, 198
Huntingdon, Lady (Selina Hastings), 9, 165–66, 168, 189–90, 195, 211, 215–16, 234, 259n93

Indian War of 1776, 181
Isabella of Portugal, 53
Ismeria, 108–9
Italian Renaissance, 6

Jacob, Margaret C., 24
Jacobin club, 100, 102, 104, 117–19, 137, 139, 142, 146
Jansz, Tabo, 40
Jaucourt, Chevalier Louis de, 121–22
Jeremiah, Thomas, 186–87
Johnson, Samuel, 193
Jones, Charles C., 246n48
Jordaens, Jacob, 54
Jordan, Winthrop D., 225

Kantrowitz, Stephen, 235
Ketelanus, Isaacus, 70
Kidd, Thomas, 182
King, Boston, 207
King, Stewart R., 84–85, 87–88
King, Violet, 207
King William's War, 179
Koerbagh, Adriaan, 22
Kossmann, E. H., 51
Kpobi, David Nii Anum, 241n107
Kwamena Ekem, John D., 71

Labat, Jean-Baptiste, 80, 110
Labuissonnière, Julien, 136–38
La Fontaine, Jean de, 79
Laforest, Etienne Bussière, 106, 151
La Luzerne, Anne-César de, 130
La Mettrie, Julien Offray de, 23

La Rondière, Louis, 87
Laurent, Gérard M., 245n35
Laurens, Henry, 187
Lavallée, Joseph, 127–28
Laveaux, Etienne, 151
Le Bon, Philippe, 43, 53–54
Le Cat, Claude-Nicolas, 116
Leclerc, Charles Victor Emmanuel, 158–59
Légion des Américains (Légion de Saint-George), 136–37, 156
Le Sueur, Jean-François, 239n50
Lethière, Guillaume Guillon, 112
Lewis, Michael, 185
Liedet, Loyset, 54
Liele, George, 201, 206
Limbourg, Herman, Paul, and Johan, 53
Limerick, Isaac, 201
Linnaeus, Carl, 116
Lipsius, Justus, 28, 44
Loango, Christiaan Congo, 40
Lock, John, 213
Locke, John, 4–5, 23, 29
Lomelino, Ambrosio, 35
Lopez, Matteo, 110
Louis the Moor, 41
Louis-Hector, Marquis de Villars, 86
Louis X (king of France), 121
Louis XIII (king of France), 109
Louis XIV (king of France), 77, 86, 109, 111
Louis XV (king of France), 113
Louis XVI (king of France), 79, 146
Lowe, Kate, 249n99

Machiavelli, 6
Madiou, Thomas, 152, 245n35
Maitland, John, 90
Malic, Jean-Baptiste Magny *dit*, 87
Manger, Johann Philipp, 22–23, 31–32, 52
Mann, John, 205, 207
Mansfield, Lord, 193
Marat, Jean-Paul, 119, 142
Marc, Jean-Baptiste, 99

Marchinton, Philip, 215
Margrett, David, 186, 190, 192
Marie Antoinette, 79, 113
Marrant, John: "Africanist Calvinism," 214; life, 1–4, 14–16, 160–61, 184, 193–95, 198, 208, 211, 213, 217–20, 223, 258n31, 259n88, 259n93; military service, 185–88; *Narrative of the Lord's Wonderful Dealings with John Marrant,* 160–65, 167–80, 183–84; Nova Scotia, 191–92, 196, 199, 208, 213; religious thought, 9, 12, 15, 160–71, 173–78, 180–81, 183–84, 189–92, 203–4, 209–10, 212, 214–16, 220, 225, 227, 230–35, 257n8; and republicanism, 6, 17, 214, 216, 218–20, 232–35
Marsden, John, 165–66
Mary (queen of England), 8
Mathews, Donald G., 206
Mathorez, Jules, 109, 113, 248n94
Maurus, Johannes, 53
Maury, Abbé, 132
McCloy, Shelby T., 112, 115
McGrath, Elizabeth, 54
Meckel, Johann Friedrich, 37, 116
Meinertzhagen, Sara Elizabeth, 23
Mentor, Etienne, 16, 151, 154–57
Mercier, Louis, 79
Mercier, Louis-Sébastien, 124
Mercure, 113
Mesnier, Jacques, 91
Methodism: and abolition, 205–8, 224; influence on John Marrant, 1, 15, 160, 164–65, 184, 189, 195, 204, 216; theological tenets, 9, 15, 182, 204–8
Michaëlius, Jonas, 63–64
Mijnhardt, Wijnand W., 24
Miles, Tiya, 177
Mills, Jean-Baptiste, 75, 106, 140, 143
Mirabeau, Comte de, 95, 129
Molière (Jean-Baptiste Poquelin), 79
Montesquieu, Charles de Secondat, Baron de, 116–17, 120–21
More, Henry, 28

Moreau de Saint-Méry, Médéric Louis Elie, 78–79, 86, 131
Morse, Jedidiah, 222
Mostaert, Jan, 54
Murray, John, 224

Necker, Jacques, 93, 128
Nesker, Peter, 23, 73
New Light Baptists, 200, 203, 214, 224
Newman, Richard S., 219
Nicholas, Thomas, 176

Occom, Samson, 10
Odo, Jeanne, 137–38
Ogé, Vincent, 96, 98–100, 133, 135
Oglethorpe, James, 181
Ollivier, Vincent, 86–87
Oroonoko (Behn), 126–27

Page, Pierre-François, 142–48, 253n203
Palmer, Wait, 201, 203
Panaetius, 27
Panton, George, 201
Parr, Governor, 217
Paul, Thomas, 222, 229–30
Peabody, Sue, 114
Peckwell, Henry, 195
Perkins, Cato, 217
Perkins, Simeon, 203, 214
Peters, George, 198
Peters, Hector, 202
Pétiniaud, François, 151
Pétion de Villeneuve, Jérôme, 101, 131
Philip II (king of Spain), 25
Piercy, William, 190–91
Pizarro, Francisco, 176
Planche, Captain, 106
Pocahontas, 175
Pocock, J. G. A., 4–5
Poivre, Pierre, 122
Poix-Blanc, 109

Polverel, Etienne, 100, 102–5, 138, 141–43, 145, 147–48, 253n203
Polybius, 5
Poncet de la Grave, Guillaume, 115
Potkay, Adam, 216, 259n88
Poudroyen, Cornelius, 50
Prah, Kwesi Kwaa, 67
Pranger, Jan, 62
Prévost, Abbé, 123–24
Protten, Christian Jacob, 64
Protten, Rebecca, 64
Pufendorf, Samuel von, 29

Quaco, 40
Quaque, Philip, 64, 190

Raimond, Julien, 130–36, 138, 143
Ramsay, James, 195
Raynal, Guillaume Thomas François Raynal, 124–25, 141
Réchin, 106
Rembrandt van Rijn, 54, 241n101
republicanism: and abolitionism, 16, 118, 123, 124, 125–28, 225–27, 235; and Jean-Baptiste Belley, 76, 80, 100–101, 103, 107–8, 120, 141–42, 145, 150, 153–54, 156–58; and Jacobus Capitein, 30, 50, 59, 68, 72, 74; definition of, 3–7, 29; and Dutch republicanism, 25–27, 29–30, 38; and the French Revolution, 16, 102, 105, 108, 118–19, 138–40, 145; and John Marrant, 161, 208, 212, 214, 232; and *Ziméo*, 125–28. *See also* civic humanism; cosmopolitanism
Richards, Peter, 202
Richelieu, Cardinal de, 110
Robespierre, Maximilien, 101–2, 119, 131–33, 147–48, 156
Rochambeau, Viscount de, 159
Rochefort, Marquess de, 111
Rodger, N. A. M., 185
Rodgers, Daniel T., 5
Rodrigues, Antoon, 39

Rogers, Daniel, 223
Rogers, Dominique, 82
Rolfe, John, 175
Romaine, William, 166, 191, 195
Roscam, F. C., 58
Rosen, Robert N., 167
Rousseau, Jean-Jacques, 79–80, 101
Rouvray, Laurent-François Le Noir, 88–91, 246n48
Rowlandson, Mary, 172–74
Rubens, Pieter Paul, 54
Rühle, Jacob, 40
Rush, Benjamin, 261n122
Ruttenburg, Nancy, 174
Ryser, Brandijn, 55–56

Saam, Moses Bom, 123–24
Sabran, Madame de, 113
Saillant, John, 11, 174, 213–14
Saint-André, Jean Bon, 142
Saint-Georges, Chevalier de, 112
Saint-Lambert, Jean-François de, 125–26, 133
Saint-Pierre, Bernardin de, 133
Saint-Pierre, Jacques Bernardin-Henri de, 39
Saint-Rémy, Joseph, 245n35
Saint-Venant, Jean Barré de, 95
Samson, Elisabeth, 42
Sancho, Ignatius, 193
Sarter, Caesar, 223
Sartine, Antoine de, 114
Saumaise, Claude, 24
Scalinger, Joseph, 24
Schama, Simon, 119
Schies, J. C., 64
Schlenther, Boyd Stanley, 190
Schouten, Gerrit, 41
Scougal, Henry, 164
Sekora, John, 178
Seneca, 28, 231
Sepinwall, Alyssa Goldstein, 91
Seven Years' War, 82, 85–86, 88
Sharp, Granville, 195
Shays' Rebellion, 221

Shirley, Walter, 168
Sigongne, 109
Skinner, Quentin, 237n8
Slotkin, Richard, 178
Smets, Marten, 52
Smith, John, 175–76
Smytegelt, Bernardus, 49
Société des Amis des Noirs, 97, 101, 104, 122–23, 128, 133, 154
Society for Effecting the Abolition of the Slave Trade, 122
Society for the Propagation of the Gospel, 64, 181, 190, 200
Sonthonax, Léger Félicité, 100–5, 120, 130, 138, 141–43, 145, 147–48, 151–53, 155, 158, 253n203
Soubise, Charles, 156–57, 193
Spinoza, Baruch, 22, 29
Stearns, Shubal, 203
Stedman, John Gabriel, 40
Steenhart, Aarnout, 22, 33–34
Stillman, Samuel, 218, 222, 227–30
stoicism, 27–29, 102, 229, 231
Strawbridge, Robert, 205
Suurdeeg, Abraham, 65

Tang, Dirk, 239n54
Taylor, William, 189
Tekki, 62
Télémaque, César, 144
Thomany, Pierre, 16, 151, 154–55, 157–58
Thomasius, Christian, 28
Thompson, Thomas, 64
Thuriot de la Rosière, Jacques-Alexis, 148
Timberlake, Henry, 181
Tollemache, John, 187
Toussaint Louverture, François-Dominique (Toussaint Bréda), 99, 151–53, 155–56, 158
Treaty of Münster (1648), 34, 53
Treaty of Paris (1783), 198
Treaty of Rijswijk (1697), 77
Treaty of Westphalia (1648), 109

Udemans, Godfried, 49
Upton, William H., 221
Usselincx, Willem, 49–50

Valkenaar, Isaac, 23, 32
Valverde, Vincent, 176
Van Bredehoff, Adriaan (Adriaan de Bruijn), 40
Van Condet, Casper, 23
Van den Broecke, Pieter, 36
Van den Enden, Franciscus, 23, 29
Van den Honert, Johannes, 45
Van den Honert, Taco Hajo, 45–46, 52
van der Helst, Bartholomeus, 241n101
Van der Zee, Henri, 31
Van Dillen, Johannes Gerard, 243n139
Van Goch, Catharina, 57
Van Goch, Elisabeth, 23, 57
Van Goch, Jacob, 22–23, 31–34, 51, 57–58, 60, 73
Van Musschenbroek, Pieter, 24
Van Oldenbarnevelt, Johan, 25
Van Onna, Jan Elias, 41–42
Van Slingelandt, Simon, 30
Velse, Hendrik, 31, 58, 68, 70
Verneuil, Louis François René, 147
Voltaire, 79–80, 117, 121, 125
Voet, Paul, 38
Voetius, Gisbertus, 45, 50
Vossius, Isaac, 24

Wadtsröm, Carl Bernhard, 154
Walker, James W. St. G., 199–200
Walter, William, 201, 218
War of Spanish Succession, 86
Ware, Opoku, 66
Washington, George, 190–91, 198, 228
Webb, Thomas, 205
Wesley, Charles, 164
Wesley, John, 9, 164–65, 204–5, 208, 214

Weyne, Jan, 41
Wheatley, Phillis, 9–10, 219
Whitchurch, Samuel, 166, 192
Whitefield, George, 9–10, 12, 46, 162–66, 168–70, 174, 177, 181–83, 189–90, 200, 204, 224
Whitehead, Ruth Holmes, 258nn30–31
WIC (West India Company), 22, 34–35, 40, 55, 57–68, 70–74, 242n116, 242n129, 243n133, 243nn139–40
Wilhelm, Hieronymus de, 56, 71, 241n107
Wilkins, Isaac, 218
Wilkinson, Moses, 207, 215
Willem II (Dutch *stadhouder*), 25
Willem III (Dutch *stadhouder*), 25
Willem IV (Dutch *stadhouder*), 25
William of Orange, 29
Williams, John, 172–74
Williamson, Peter, 179
Wills, Thomas, 166, 189, 191–92
Wood, Betty, 204
Wood, Peter, 181
Woods, Joseph, 195

Yamassee War of 1715, 180
Ysebout, Bartholomeus, 64

Zaga-Christ, 110
Zamor, 113
Zarate, Augustin de, 176
Ziméo (Saint-Lambert), 125–27, 133